Powell's Private Libraries: V. 6 (NoDJ)

OP/4.98   **NDJ**

Medieval & Renaissance   97851

McClurg's Library Reprints of Americana

HISTORY OF THE EXPEDITION OF CAPTAINS LEWIS AND CLARK
1804-5-6

Reprinted from the Edition of 1814. With an Introduction by JAMES K. HOSMER, LL.D., an analytical Index, photogravure portraits, and maps.

This edition of the famous Journal has been prepared to meet the urgent need for a standard, popular edition, something that has not been available for years.

"The republication of the complete narrative is both timely and invaluable. . . . Dr. Hosmer is well known as an authority on Western history; hence to see his name on the title-page is to know that the work has been well done."—*Portland Oregonian.*

"The celebrated story of the expedition of Lewis and Clark has now been put in an easily accessible form."—*N. Y. Times Saturday Review.*

"Of the several new editions of this valuable narrative, this is by far the best and most complete."—*Minneapolis Journal.*

"The most complete and satisfactory edition of this classic that has come to our notice."—*San Francisco Chronicle.*

"We have nothing but praise for this clear and handsome reprint."—*The Nation.*

In two octavo volumes, boxed, $5.00 net
Large-paper edition (limited) on Brown's hand-made paper, illustrations on Japan paper, $15.00 net

A. C. McCLURG & CO., *Publishers*, CHICAGO

OTHER VOLUMES IN
McCLURG'S LIBRARY
REPRINTS OF AMERICANA

UNIFORM IN STYLE AND BINDING

McClurg's Library Reprints of Americana

FATHER HENNEPIN'S "A NEW DISCOVERY"

(*NOUVELLE DÉCOUVERTE*)

Exact Reprint of the Second Issue of 1698. With Introduction, Notes, and analytical Index by REUBEN GOLD THWAITES, LL.D., a new Bibliography by VICTOR HUGO PALTSITS, fac-similes of the seven full-page illustrations, and two large folding maps.

This particular book by Father Hennepin is generally considered the most representative product of his pen, and as a human document it has few rivals in our literature. Moreover, it is the only one of the Hennepin books now upon the market.

" None of the many recent reprints of Americana is of greater importance to collectors and students than the re-issue of Father Louis Hennepin's ' A New Discovery of a Vast Country in America.'. . . Mechanically, the book is superbly produced, and it seems to us to be the best made book, in every particular, that has been offered the trade during the current season." — *Chicago Evening Post.*

" It should be a subject of rejoicing among those of our citizens who cherish the past, that Dr. Thwaites and his publishers have given us these two beautiful and scholarly volumes — a presentment which leaves nothing more to be desired." — *Minneapolis Times.*

In two octavo volumes, boxed, $6.00 net
Large-paper edition (limited) on Brown's hand-made paper, illustrations on Japan paper, $18.00 net

---

A. C. McCLURG & CO., *Publishers*, CHICAGO

McClurg's Library Reprints of Americana

LAHONTAN'S NEW VOYAGES TO NORTH AMERICA

Reprinted from the English Edition of 1703. With Introduction, Notes, and analytical Index by REUBEN GOLD THWAITES, LL.D., a Bibliography by VICTOR HUGO PALTSITS, fac-similes of original title-pages, and twenty-four maps and illustrations.

The selection of the famous writings of Baron Lahontan for republication is a natural one after the success of the reprint of Hennepin issued in 1903. It is a logical step in the preparation of the Americana series planned by Messrs. McClurg & Co., and the appearance of Lahontan's Voyages in a standard library edition will be as welcome as that of the preceding volumes. Like the Hennepin, it is a word-for-word reprint.

In two 8vo volumes, boxed, $6.00 net
Large-paper edition (limited) on Brown's hand-made paper, illustrations on Japan paper, $18.00 net

A. C. McCLURG & CO., *Publishers*, CHICAGO

PRIVATE LIBRARIES IN RENAISSANCE ENGLAND

*A Collection and Catalogue of
Tudor and Early Stuart Book-Lists*

Volume VI
PLRE 138–150

Medieval and Renaissance Texts and Studies

Volume 271

PRIVATE LIBRARIES IN RENAISSANCE ENGLAND

A Collection and Catalogue of Tudor and Early Stuart Book-Lists

Volume VI
PLRE 138–150

R. J. FEHRENBACH
General Editor

E. S. LEEDHAM-GREEN
Editor in the United Kingdom

Arizona Center for Medieval and Renaissance Studies
Tempe, Arizona
2004

> *The publication of this volume has been supported
> by a grant from the National Endowment for the Humanities,
> an independent federal agency.*

© Copyright 2004
Arizona Board of Regents for Arizona State University

Library of Congress Cataloging-in-Publication Data

Private libraries in Renaissance England : a collection and catalogue of Tudor and early Stuart
  book-lists / R. J. Fehrenbach, general editor, E. S. Leedham-Green, editor in the United
  Kingdom.
    v. 1 — (Medieval & renaissance texts & studies : v. 87, 105, 117, 148, 189, 271)
    Includes bibliographical references and index.
    Contents: v. 1. PLRE 1–4. — v. 2. PLRE 5–66. — v. 3. PLRE 67–86. — v. 4. PLRE 87–112.
— v. 5. PLRE 113–137. — v. 6. PLRE 138–150.
    ISBN 0–86698–099–7, v. 1; ISBN 0–86698–151–9, v. 2; ISBN 0–86698–170–5, v. 3; ISBN
0–86698–188–8, v. 4; ISBN 0–86698–231–0, v. 5; ISBN 0–86698–314–7, v. 6.
    1. Private libraries—England—History—1400–1600— Sources. 2. Private libraries—
England—History—17th–18th centuries—Sources. 3. Books and reading—England—History—16th century—Sources. 4. Books and reading—England—History—17th century—
Sources. 5. Private libraries—England—Catalogs—Bibliography. 6. Book collecting—England—History—Sources. 7. Library catalogs—England—Bibliography. I. Series.
Z997.2.G7P75 2004
017'.1'0942—dc20   91-18418
                                                                                         CIP

This book is made to last.
It is set in Baskerton, smythe-sewn,
and printed on acid-free paper
to library specifications

Printed in the United States of America

Table of Contents

Table of Annotated Book-lists by PLRE Number	vii
Table of Annotated Book-lists by Owner	ix
Contributing Editors	x
Advisory Editors	xii
Acknowledgments	xiii
Common Abbreviations	
Sources	xv
Degrees	xxi
Introduction	xxiii
Annotated Book-lists	1
Appendices	
PLRE Cumulative Catalogue	257
Additions and Corrections, PLRE Addresses	279
Indices	
Authors and Works	283
Editors and Compilers	308
Translators	310
Stationers	312
Places of Publication	316
Dates of Publication	322

Table of Annotated Book-lists by PLRE Number

PLRE 138: Henry Cheyne (inventory 1581) *Scholar (M.A.)*
R. J. FEHRENBACH & RIVES NICHOLSON
PLRE 139: Thomas Ruckwood (d.1581) *Scholar (student)*
GRADY A. SMITH
PLRE 140: John Heath (inventory 1582) *Scholar (M.A.)*
RIVES NICHOLSON
PLRE 141: John Forster (d.1584) *Scholar (B.C.L.)*
RIVES NICHOLSON
PLRE 142: Thomas Morrey (d.1584) *Scholar (M.A.)*
D. V. N. BAGCHI
PLRE 143: Anthony Tye (d.1584) *Scholar (M.A.)*
LEE PIEPHO
PLRE 144: John Haynes (d.1585) *Scholar (M.A.)*
RUDOLPH P. ALMASY
PLRE 145: Thomas Hill (d.1585) *Probably Scholar*
JOCELYN SHEPPARD
PLRE 146: Thomas Tatham (d.1586) *Scholar (M.A.)*
JULIETTE M. CUNICO & DAVID C. MCPHERSON
PLRE 147: Thomas Newby (d.1587) *Scholar (M.A.)*
DAVID GALBRAITH
PLRE 148: Robert Dowe (d.1588) *Scholar (B.C.L.)*
RICHARD OVENDEN

PLRE 149: Edward Higgins (d.1588) *Scholar (M.A.)*
R. J. FEHRENBACH & RIVES NICHOLSON
PLRE 150: Matthew Parkin (d.1589) *Scholar (B.A.)*
R. J. FEHRENBACH

Table of Annotated Book-lists by Owner

Henry Cheyne (inventory 1581)   PLRE 138
Robert Dowe (d.1588)   PLRE 148
John Forster (d.1584)   PLRE 141
John Haynes (d.1585)   PLRE 144
John Heath (inventory 1582)   PLRE 140
Edward Higgins (d.1588)   PLRE 149
Thomas Hill (d.1585)   PLRE 145
Thomas Morrey (d.1584)   PLRE 142
Thomas Newby (d.1587)   PLRE 147
Matthew Parkin (d.1589)   PLRE 150
Thomas Ruckwood (d.1581)   PLRE 139
Thomas Tatham (d.1586)   PLRE 146
Anthony Tye (d.1584)   PLRE 143

Contributing Editors

RUDOLPH P. ALMASY
Professor of English and
Associate Dean of Academic Affairs, Eberly College of Arts and Sciences
West Virginia University

D. V. N. BAGCHI
Lecturer in Theology, University of Hull

JULIETTE M. CUNICO
Adjunct Faculty, Department of English and University
Honors Program, University of New Mexico

R. J. FEHRENBACH
Professor of English, Emeritus, College of William and Mary

DAVID GALBRAITH
Associate Professor of English, University of Toronto

DAVID C. MCPHERSON
Professor of English, Emeritus, University of New Mexico

RIVES NICHOLSON
Assistant Editor, *Private Libraries in Renaissance England*

RICHARD OVENDEN
Director of Collections, Edinburgh University Library

LEE PIEPHO
Schallenberger Brown Professor of English Language and Literature
Sweet Briar College

JOCELYN SHEPPARD
Principal Consultant, Red House Consulting

GRADY A. SMITH
Adjunct Professor, George Mason University

Advisory Editors

Peter W. M. Blayney
Mark H. Curtis † 1994
W. Speed Hill
Arthur F. Kinney
Nati H. Krivatsy
F. J. Levy
James K. McConica
David McKitterick
W. B. Stephens
Laetitia Yeandle
Georgianna Ziegler

Assistant Editors

Sandra Burr
Rives Nicholson

Consulting Editor for the Oxford Project

Simon Bailey

Acknowledgments

I remain greatly indebted to the following for financial support: the National Endowment for the Humanitites, an independent federal agency; the Gladys Krieble Delmas Foundation; Katherine K. Curtis for her gift from the estate of her husband, Mark H. Curtis, one of PLRE's original Advisory Editors; Gillian T. Cell, Provost of the College of William and Mary; and P. Geoffrey Feiss, Dean of the Faculty of Arts and Sciences at the College of William and Mary.

Simon Bailey, Archivist of Oxford University and Editorial Consultant to PLRE, always available to answer questions about the Oxford inventories, was particularly helpful in untangling matters related to the date of the Matthew Parkin book-list. I am grateful to Alan H. Nelson of the University of California at Berkeley for providing new material on the books of Richard Stonely from Stonely's diaries that correct two identifications and add information to other records in Stonely's book-list (PLRE Ad4). The contribution of the late Walter Mitchell is noted in the general introduction, but these acknowledgments would be woefully incomplete without giving special notice of his generosity in making available his transcriptions of the Oxford inventories. My continuing thanks to Lance Richardson and Pete Hoyle; they know what they do, and they do it well. And, as she has for the fifteen years of this project's life, my colleague, Elisabeth Leedham-Green, remains indispensable.

Williamsburg, Virginia   R.J.F.
2002

Common Abbreviations

SOURCES

A&R A. F. Allison and D. M. Rogers. *A Catalogue of Catholic Books in English Printed Abroad or Secretly in England 1558–1640*. Bognor Regis, 1956 [Reprints 1964 and 1968].

ARCR A. F. Allison and D. M. Rogers. *The Contemporary Printed Literature of the English Counter-Reformation between 1558 and 1640*. 2 volumes. Aldershot, 1989–1994.

Adams H. M. Adams. *Catalogue of Books Printed on the Continent of Europe, 1501–1600, in Cambridge Libraries*. 2 volumes. Cambridge, 1967.

Alumni Cantabrigienses — John Venn and John Archibald Venn. *Alumni Cantabrigienses: A Biographical List of All Known Students, Graduates and Holders of Office at the University of Cambridge from the Earliest Times to 1751, Part I*. 4 volumes. Cambridge, 1922–1927 [Reprint 1974].

Alumni Oxonienses — Joseph Foster, compiler. *Alumni Oxonienses: The Members of the University of Oxford, 1500–1714, Their Parentage, Birthplace, and Year of Birth* . . . 4 volumes. Oxford, 1891–1892.

Arber *A Transcript of the Registers of the Company of Stationers of London*, edited by Edward Arber. 5 volumes. London/Birmingham, 1875–1894 [Reprint 1967].

Athenae Cantabrigienses — C. H. Cooper and T. Cooper. *Athenae Cantabrigienses.* 3 volumes. Cambridge and London, 1858–1913 [Reprint 1967].

Athenae Oxonienses — Anthony à Wood, with additions by Philip Bliss. *Athenae Oxonienses: An Exact History of All the Writers and Bishops Who Have Had Their Education in the University of Oxford. To Which Are Added the Fasti, or Annals of the Said University.* 5 volumes. London, 1813–1820.

Aureliensis — *Index Aureliensis: Catalogus librorum sedecimo saeculo impressorum.* Volumes 1–11. Baden-Baden, 1965–1996 [incomplete].

Benzing   Josef Benzing. *Lutherbibliographie. Verzeichnis der gedruckten Schriften Martin Luthers bis zu dessen Tod.* Baden-Baden, 1966.

Bezzel   Irmgard Bezzel. *Erasmusdrucke des 16. Jahrhunderts in Bayerischen Bibliotheken.* Stuttgart, 1979.

BCI   E. S. Leedham-Green. *Books in Cambridge Inventories: Book-lists from Vice-Chancellor's Court Probate Inventories in the Tudor and Stuart Periods.* 2 volumes. Cambridge, 1986.

BL   *General Catalogue of Books Printed to 1955* [in the British Library].

BN   *Catalogue Général des Livres Imprimés de la Bibliothèque Nationale* [Paris].

Boase   C. W. Boase, ed. *Register of the University of Oxford.* Volume 1 (1449–1463; 1505–1571). Oxford, 1885.

Bodleian   *Catalogus librorum impressorum Bibliothecae Bodleianae in Academia Oxoniensi.* 4 volumes. Oxford, 1843–1851.

BRUC   A. B. Emden. *A Biographical Register of the University of Cambridge to 1500.* Cambridge, 1963.

Brunet   Jacques-Charles Brunet. *Manuel du libraire et de l'amateur de livres.* 6 volumes. Paris, 1860–1865 [Reprint 1922] (Supplements, 2 volumes, 1878–1880).

BRUO   A. B. Emden. *A Biographical Register of the University of Oxford to AD 1500.* 3 volumes. Oxford, 1957–1959.

BRUO2   A. B. Emden. *A Biographical Register of the University of Oxford AD 1501 to 1540.* Oxford, 1974.

BSB   *Bayerische Staatsbibliothek alphabetische Katalog 1501–1840.* 60 volumes. Munich, New York, London, Paris, 1987–1990.

BT   Elly Cockx-Indestege and Geneviève Glorieux. *Belgica Typographica 1541–1600. Catalogus librorum impressorum ab anno MDXLI ad annum MDC in regionibus quae nunc Regni Belgarum partes sunt.* Nieuwkoop, 1968.

CBEL   George Watson, editor. *The New Cambridge Bibliography of English Literature [600–1660].* Volume 1. Cambridge, 1974.

CLC	David J. Shaw, *The Cathedral Libraries Catalogue: Books Printed on the Continent of Europe before 1701 in the Libraries of the Anglican Cathedrals of England and Wales*. Volume 2. 2 parts. London, 1998.
Clark	Andrew Clark, ed. *Register of the University of Oxford*. Volume 2. 4 parts (1571–1622). Oxford, 1887–1889.
Clessius	Joannes Clessius. *Unius seculi eiusque virorum literatorum monumentis tum florentissimi, tum fertilissimi, ab anno Dom. 1500 ad 1602. Nundinarum autumnalium inclusive elenchus consummatissimus librorum*. Frankfurt am Main, 1602.
Cockle	Maurice J. D. Cockle. *A Bibliography of Military Books up to 1642*. Second edition. London, 1957 [Reprint 1978].
Copinger	W. A. Copinger. *Supplement to Hain's Repertorium Bibliographicum* [with supplements]. London, 1895 [–1914] [Reprints 1926 and 1950].
Cranz	F. Edward Cranz. *A Bibliography of Aristotle Editions, 1501–1600*. Second edition, with addenda and revisions by Charles B. Schmitt. Baden-Baden, 1984.
CSPD	*Calendar of State Papers: Domestic Series.*
CSPD, Addenda	*— Calendar of State Papers: Domestic Series, Addenda, 1580–1625.*
CTC	*Catalogus Translationum et Commentariorum: Medieval and Renaissance Latin Translations and Commentaries*. Eds. Paul Oskar Kristeller, F. Edward Cranz, and Virginia Brown. Volumes 1–8. Washington, D.C., 1960–2003 [incomplete].
DM	T. H. Darlow and H. F. Moule. *Historical Catalogue of the Printed Editions of the Holy Scripture in the Library of the British and Foreign Bible Society*. [English and Non-English] 2 volumes. London, 1903–1911. [See DMH following.]
DMH	T. H. Darlow and H. F. Moule (with revisions by A. S. Herbert). *Historical Catalogue of the Printed Editions of the Holy Scripture in the Library of the British and Foreign Bible Society*. [English; Volume 1 of DM revised] London, 1968.
DNB	*Dictionary of National Biography.*
Durling	Richard J. Durling. "A Chronological Census of Renaissance Editions and Translations of Galen." *Journal of the Warburg and Courtauld Institutes* (1961), 24:230–305.
EUL	*Catalogue of the Printed Books in the Library of the University of Edinburgh*. 3 volumes. Edinburgh, 1918–1923.
Erichson	Alfredus Erichson, ed. *Bibliographia Calviniana*. Berlin, 1900 [Reprints Nieuwkoop, 1960, 1965, and 1979].
Gardy	Frédéric Gardy. *Bibliographie des oeuvres théologiques, littéraires, historiques et juridiques de Théodore de Bèze*. Geneva, 1960.

Goff	F. R. Goff. *Incunabula in American Libraries: A Third Census* [with supplements]. New York, 1973 [Revised 1964 edition].
Greg	W. W. Greg. *A Bibliography of the English Printed Drama to the Restoration*. 4 volumes. London, 1939–1959 [Reprint 1970].
GW	*Gesamtkatalog der Wiegendrucke*. 9 volumes. Leipzig/Stuttgart, 1925–1938, 1968–1991 [incomplete].
Hain	L. Hain. *Repertorium Bibliographicum*. 2 volumes. Stuttgart, 1826–1838, 1891 [Reprints 1948 and 1966].
HC *1509–1558*	S. T. Bindoff, editor. *The House of Commons 1509–1558 (The History of Parliament)*. 3 volumes. London, 1982.
HC *1558–1603*	P. W. Hasler, editor. *The House of Commons 1558–1603 (The History of Parliament)*. 3 volumes. London, 1981.
HMC	*Historical Manuscripts Commission*.
Harris	C. R. S. Harris. *Duns Scotus*. Volume 1. Oxford, 1927.
IGI	*Indice generale degli incunaboli delle biblioteche d'Italia*. 6 volumes. Rome, 1943–1981 [incomplete].
Jayne	Sears Jayne. *Library Catalogues of the English Renaissance*. Reissue with new preface and notes. Godalming, 1983.
Keen	Ralph Keen. *A Checklist of Melanchthon Imprints Through 1560*. Sixteenth Century Bibliography 27. St. Louis, 1988.
Ker	N. R. Ker. "The Provision of Books," in *The Collegiate University*, edited by James McConica. Volume 3 of *The History of the University of Oxford*, General Editor, T. H. Aston. Oxford, 1986.
Klaiber	Wilbirgis Klaiber. *Katholische Kontroverstheologen und Reformer des 16. Jahrhunderts*. Münster, 1978.
Köhler	W. Köhler. *Bibliographia Brentiana*. Berlin, 1904 [Reprint 1963].
Labarre	Albert Labarre. *Bibliographie du Dictionarium d'Ambrogio Calepino (1502–1779)*. Baden-Baden, 1975.
LohrII	Charles H. Lohr. *Latin Aristotle Commentaries*, II. *Renaissance Authors*. Florence: Leo S. Olschki Editore, 1988.
Madan	Falconer Madan. *Oxford Books: A Bibliography of Printed Works Relating to the University and City of Oxford or Printed or Published There*. 3 volumes. Oxford, 1895–1931 [Reprint 1964].
McConica	James McConica. "Elizabethan Oxford: The Collegiate Society," in *The Collegiate University*, edited by James McConica. Volume 3 of *The History of the University of Oxford*, General Editor, T. H. Aston. Oxford, 1986.
NK	Wouter Nijhoff and M. E. Kronenberg. *Nederlandsche Bibliographie van 1500 tot 1540*. The Hague, 1923–1966.
NLM6	Richard J. Durling. *A Catalogue of Sixteenth Century Printed*

	Books in the National Library of Medicine. Bethesda, Maryland, 1967.
NUC	*National Union Catalogue. Pre-1956 Imprints.*
OED	*The Oxford English Dictionary.* 20 volumes. Second edition. Prepared by J. A. Simpson and E. S. C. Weiner. Oxford, 1989.
Oates	J. C. T. Oates. *A Catalogue of the Fifteenth-Century Printed Books in the University Library, Cambridge.* Cambridge, 1954.
Ong	Walter J. Ong, S. J. *Ramus and Talon Inventory. A Short-Title Inventory of the Published Works of Peter Ramus (1515–1572) and of Omer Talon (ca. 1510–1562) in Their Original and in Their Variously Altered Forms.* Cambridge, Massachusetts, 1958.
PCC	*Prerogative Court of Canterbury.*
Pell	M. Pellechet and M. L. Polain. *Catalogue général des incunables des bibliothèques publiques de France.* 26 volumes. Liechtenstein, 1970 [Reprint].
Polain	Marie Louis Polain. *Catalogue de livres imprimés au XVe siècle des bibliothèques de Belgique.* 4 volumes [and supplements]. Brussels, 1931–1978.
Proctor	Robert Proctor. *An Index to the Early Printed Books in the British Museum: From the Invention of Printing to the Year MD.* 2 volumes [and supplements]. London, 1898–1906 [several reprints in the 1920s].
RRstc	James J. Murphy. *Renaissance Rhetoric: A Short-Title Catalogue of Works on Rhetorical Theory from the Beginning of Printing to A.D. 1700, with Special Attention to the Holdings of the Bodleian Library, Oxford.* New York and London, 1981.
Shaaber	M. A. Shaaber. *Check-list of Works of British Authors Printed Abroad, in Languages Other Than English, to 1641.* New York, 1975.
Staedtke	Joachim Staedtke. *Heinrich Bullinger Bibliographie.* Volume 1. Zürich, 1972.
STC	A. W. Pollard, G. R. Redgrave, W. A. Jackson, F. S. Ferguson, and Katherine F. Pantzer. *A Short-title Catalogue of Books Printed in England, Scotland, and Ireland and of English Books Printed Abroad, 1475–1640.* Second edition. 3 volumes. London, 1976–1991.
Stübler	Eberhard Stübler. *Leonhart Fuchs: Leben und Werk.* München, 1928.
VD16	*Verzeichnis der im deutschen Sprachbereich erschienenen Drucke des XVI. Jahrhunderts.* 22 volumes. Stuttgart, 1983–1995.
VHc	Ferdinand Vander Haeghen. *Bibliographie des oeuvres de Josse Clicthove.* Ghent, 1888.

VHe	Ferdinand Vander Haeghen. *Bibliotheca Erasmiana*. Ghent, 1893 [Reprints in 1961, 1972, and 1990].
Wellcome	*A Catalogue of Printed Books in the Wellcome Historical Medical Library*. Volumes 1–2. London, 1962.
Wing	Donald Wing. *Short-title Catalogue of Books Printed in England, Scotland, Ireland, Wales, and British America and of English Books Printed in Other Countries: 1641–1700*. Revised edition. 3 volumes. New York, 1972–1988.

DEGREES

B.A.	Bachelor of Arts
M.A.	Master of Arts
B.C.L.	Bachelor of Civil Law
B.Cn.L.	Bachelor of Canon Law
B.Gram.	Bachelor of Grammar
B.M.	Bachelor of Medicine
B.Th.	Bachelor of Theology
D.C.L.	Doctor of Civil Law
D.Cn.L.	Doctor of Canon Law
D.U.L.	Doctor of Civil and Canon Law (LL.D.)
D.M.	Doctor of Medicine
D.Th.	Doctor of Theology
O.P.	Ordinis Praedicatorum

Introduction

With this volume, PLRE continues publication of 162 book-lists[1] contained in the inventories taken between 1507 and 1653 under the jurisdiction of the Chancellor of Oxford University (exercised by the Vice-Chancellor), mostly for the purposes of probate. The lists are published in chronological order (see **Order** under *Methodology and Format* below); thirteen lists, dating from 1581 to 1589, appear in the present volume to bring the total of Oxford lists edited in PLRE to 146 (Volume 2 of PLRE [1993] contains sixty-two lists, Volume 3 [1994] contains twenty, Volume 4 [1995] contains twenty-six), and Volume 5 [1998] contains twenty-five. The remaining sixteen Oxford lists will be published in Volume 7. Like all book-lists in this Oxford series, the lists appearing in this volume are found in manuscripts in the Oxford University Archives housed in the Bodleian, specifically in the probate records and the Chancellors' Registers. These records have been made available on microfilm by Research Publications under the title *The Social History of Property and Possessions: Part I: Inventories and Wills, Including Renaissance Library Catalogues, from the Bodleian Library, Oxford, 1436–1814* (Reading, England, 1990).

Contributing Editors work from transcriptions of the manuscripts

---

[1] This number differs from the total given in Volume 1; in editing, several lists were identified as printer's stock or as books borrowed from colleges, not personally owned books.

made by the late Walter Mitchell, M.A. (sometime Assistant to the Keeper of the University Archives). By granting PLRE permission to use his transcriptions, a labor of many years, Mr. Mitchell immeasurably reduced the time required to make this information available to the scholarly community. Mr. Mitchell's professional generosity placed the PLRE project and scholars working in the Tudor and early Stuart periods greatly in his debt.

The purpose and three-part design of PLRE has been described in its first volume, to which the reader is referred for details (PLRE, Volume 1, pp. xvi–xviii). In brief, however, Part 1 of PLRE is the published form of annotated book-lists associated with Tudor and early Stuart men and women; PLRE 138–150 are contained in this volume. Part 2 is in electronic form and is a cumulative and more detailed catalogue of those lists and others (Appended, or APND lists) previously published elsewhere. This electronic form of the entire PLRE database, Volumes 1–5 and all the APND lists (as found under 2, APND LISTS in the Cumulative Catalogue at the end of PLRE volumes), appears as *exPLoRE* on CD-ROM and is available from Pegasus Press (P.O. Box 15806, Asheville, North Carolina 28813) and Adam Matthew Publications, Ltd., Pelham House, London Road, Marlborough, Wiltshire SN8 2AA, England. As it is made clear in the detailed descriptions of the published and electronic forms (PLRE, Volume 1, pp. xvi–xvii), *exPLoRE* and the PLRE volumes are different and complementary presentations of the PLRE database. They are not substitutes one for the other. Part 3, the PLRE Cumulative Catalogue, is a series of indices and concordances to the complete PLRE database. This Cumulative Catalogue, which appears near the end of each volume of PLRE, is regularly enlarged and revised to incorporate newly edited book-lists. The lists in this volume will be added to *exPLoRE* in due course. In the meantime, scholars are invited to inquire of the General Editor for information in the Volume 6 database that does not appear in this printed form.

Errors and Corrections

Anyone with even a passing acquaintance with early book-lists knows that their fragmentary and too often simply illegible entries make identifying books an extremely difficult task. Further, details of these early books resist uniformity, even when the works are identifiable; yet this information must be uniformly entered into a database to meet the categorical requirements of PLRE's design and purpose. However methodical and careful the labor, providing error-free information under such conditions is more to be wished than realized. Happily, however, the ease with which a database can be corrected promises that any misdirection PLRE may inadvertently provide will be temporary, and will encourage PLRE's users to become part of the scholarly collaboration that has always been central to the project. The editors of PLRE ask, therefore, that errors noted and corrections proposed be forwarded (with supporting evidence for the corrections) to either address found in the Appendix.

Methodology and Format

Identification and Annotation. Identification of items, the annotations, and the bio-bibliographical introductions preceding the book-lists are the work of diverse scholars and reflect their individual research and study. But collaboration, intending to provide a reasonable uniformity, is routine at all editorial stages of the PLRE project. Consistency is necessary to avoid offering confusing information when the results of research conducted by individual scholars are combined; it is also required to meet the practical demands of a searchable database. For example, editorial consultation would discourage identifying a late sixteenth-century manuscript entry of *Elucidarius poeticus* as the school text written by Johann Gast and issued, apparently, in a single edition (1544) to the disregard of the widely published encyclopedic work of the same name by Hermann Torrentinus, appearing as it did in at least a dozen editions before 1600. If, however, a Contributing Editor has good reason to question whether such an entry represents the Torrentinus title, the Gast work, or Robert Estienne's book, another popular work of that same name, the Torrentinus identification would carry one of the standard PLRE qualifying terms, *probable* or *perhaps*. Understandably, annotations to such an item may also vary from one Contributing Editor to another.

Among the most troublesome entries to identify with consistency and uniformity are the appearances, by name only, of various widely published authors such as Virgil, Quintilian, Horace, Terence, Sallust, Lucian, and Homer. On occasion, context and supplementary information (e.g., *cum commento*) will help to identify these entries as *Works*, but generally editors choose to qualify such items with *probable* or *perhaps* if they do not list them as *Unidentified*. Similarly, when an entry consists of the name of an author popularly associated with one particular title, that work is assumed in the absence of a clear connection to one of his less well-known works, with a qualification often attached. Thus, an entry of "Agostino Dati" will usually result in an identification of *Elegantiolae*, and an entry of "Theodorus, *Gaza*" will normally result in an identification of *Institutiones grammaticae*, both usually qualified. Such differences as may appear in identifications and commentary, then, reflect the regard that

PLRE has for reasonable disagreement among scholars, particularly in an area of research where the primary material is so often fragmentary and imprecise.

Order. Within each volume, the book-lists are presented in chronological order by year of the owner's death, or, if the date of death is unknown, by year of an owner's will if extant, and then alphabetically within each year. In some cases, however, the dates of death and a will are unknown; in others, documents and biographical sources disagree about the dates; and in still others, such dates are irrelevant (e.g., an inventory of books may have been compiled for purposes other than evaluating an owner's estate, with the owner dying years later). In these cases, other information, such as the date of the inventory, is used to determine the place of a book-list in PLRE order. An explanation of the determining date is parenthetically appended to each owner's name in the Table of Contents. For more complete information about the owners' dates of deaths, wills, and inventories, readers are directed to the individual introductions and to the PLRE database.

Introduction. Each book-list is preceded by an introductory essay treating biographical and bibliographical matters relating to the owner and the collection. The introduction is not intended to provide a complete analysis of the book-list, and even less a full study of the owner's life. Except where two dates are provided (e.g., 25 February 1587/88), all dates are given in new style.

Names of owners have been regularized according to modern forms with, in many cases, variant spellings provided. Such alternate forms are derived from published sources such as BRUO, BRUO2, and *Alumni Oxonienses*; whenever the form given in BRUO or BRUO2 (the standard authorities on members of Oxford University to 1540) differs from the adopted PLRE form, it is listed first among the variants and identified. The name of the owner at the head of the introduction is followed by: the owner's profession and appropriate academic degrees (if any), the kind of source the list of books is taken from (inventory, receipt, will, etc.), and the date of that book-list.

For nearly all of these Oxford men happening to die in residence at whatever stage of their academic career, PLRE has chosen to use the generic term "scholar" to indicate their presumed avocations at the time of death and to distinguish graduates still at the University from those who had gone out into the world. Most of them would have been at least in minor orders, and a good many of them supported in their studies by the revenue of one or more benefices, but they are not here designated "clerics" except where there is some evidence that they were actively serving a cure. (Similarly, medical graduates are not designated "physician" in the absence of evidence for their actually having practiced as such.) Instead their status is indicated either by the term "student," for those who had not yet graduated, or by their degree or degrees. A Doctor of Theology who had pursued the conventional course would previously have graduated B.A., M.A., and B.Th. The dates, and any other details, of these earlier degrees will, when documented, be found in the introductions to each list, but in the headings the senior degree alone will usually be found. Two degrees are given where neither is significantly senior to the other (as in the case of a Doctor of both Civil and Canon Law), where more than one senior faculty is involved (as in the case of a theologian having also qualified in canon law), or when holding certain degrees together indicates the exercise of an option (it was, for example, possible to proceed to medical degrees either via the arts course or not: where a Bachelor of Medicine had previously graduated M.A., both degrees are shown).

Classmarks and Transcriptions. The Oxford University Archives classmark of the document containing the book-list and the source of any previously published transcriptions of the list are appended to the introduction.

Reference List. Placed between the introduction and the annotated entries and serving both, a reference list provides a bibliography of works cited in each (except for the sources found in the Common Abbreviations). The form used in the reference list is the Author-Date System of the *Chicago Manual of Style*, 13th ed., 1982, 399–435.

The List of Books. The book-list is presented, with clarifying emendations, as it appears in the manuscript. Each entry is preceded by its assigned PLRE Number.

Entries. Each entry is composed of some or all of the following:[2]

> **PLRE Number Book-list entry**
> Name of author (alternative name of author). *Title of work*. Other contributors. Place of publication: stationer(s), date or range of dates.
> STC status. Annotations. Language(s) of book. Cost or appraised value and date of same. Current location of the book.[2]

---

[2] PLRE has attempted to avoid the use of signs and symbols; this design is most prominently seen in the use of *perhaps* and *probable* (or *probably*) to convey degrees of doubt, and of commonly employed abbreviations, such as *c.* and *et seq.*

PLRE Number. A PLRE Number is always composed of at least two numbers separated by a period. The number preceding the period identifies the place of the book-list within the PLRE catalogue, and the number following the period identifies the individual entries within that book-list. Thus, the forty-seventh item in the third book-list published in PLRE is assigned *3.47*. A PLRE Number that carries an extension (beginning with a colon) identifies an entry in the book-list that represents two or more works. If published separately, the works are assigned numeric extensions (e.g., *3.48:1* and *3.48:2*); if published together in one volume, they are assigned letters (e.g., *3.49:A* and *3.49:B*). Entries that contain unidentified multiple works are assigned an appropriate range extension (e.g., *3.50:1– 4* would be used to identify "four bookes of verse"). If the number of works listed is unknown, the extension given is "multiple" (e.g., *3.51 multiple* would be used to identify "divers small bookes"). PLRE numbers in APND lists (see p. xxiv above) are preceded by *Ad*, as in *Ad4.36*.

Book-list entry. Within certain limits, book-lists are transcribed to reproduce as faithfully as possible the entries as they appear in the manuscript. The letters *u/v* and *i/j* are regularized and modernized, and thorn is transcribed *th*. Readily identifiable contractions and abbreviations are not altered (e.g., *agt*, *Mr*, and *wch*), but the less common ones, along with unusual or ambiguous spellings, are followed by an emendation placed in square brackets (e.g., *The trades inclease* is transcribed as *The trades inclease* [*increase*]). Damaged or otherwise illegible portions of the manuscript are treated similarly (e.g., *fil us* [to represent a hole between the *l* and the *u* in the manuscript] is transcribed as *fil*us* [*filius*]). Where an item is recorded as an object of bequest in a Latin will, its accusative form is retained.

Name of author (alternative name of author). Names are STC forms; for names not appearing in the STC, forms are taken from a list of Uniform Names developed by PLRE. Uniformity, as well as ease of recognition, is the goal of PLRE in establishing names. But 1) in cases where the established name differs from the form in the entry and may cause confusion for the user, and 2) in cases where two different forms make virtually equal claims for recognition among scholars, parenthetical alternative forms are given. Examples: *Nicolas Des Gallars* is followed by *(Nicolaus Salicetus)*, *John Holywood* by *(Joannes Sacrobosco)*, and *Nicolaus Tudeschis* by *(Panormitanus)*.

On occasion, the name of an editor will appear in this place, his role appropriately identified. *Unidentified* is used when the author cannot be identified from the entry (which is different from an identified work having been published anonymously).

Title of work. The title of a work (short title, usually terminating with the first full stop) is entered when known. Often, however, the precise title is impossible to determine from the truncated and abbreviated entries commonly found in early book-lists. Further, the standard bibliographical sources (e.g., BL, Goff, Adams), on which Contributing Editors usually depend for determining titles, frequently modify the actual titles. The main principle here, then, must be to identify the *work* rather than a particular title, especially when a work has gone through several editions with varied titles. As with names, uniformity is essential if titles in the PLRE database are to be selected for analysis. Accordingly, a Uniform Titles list has been developed by PLRE along the following principles: 1) a work that exists in a single edition is identified by its short title; 2) a work that exists in two or more editions that bear only slightly varying titles is identified by one of these titles; 3) a work that exists in several editions with widely varied titles is identified by an artificial title, a) in a construction to reflect one or more of the existing titles, but b) often in a construction designed to describe the work without any attempt to simulate a title. Artificial titles are always enclosed in square brackets. Livy's [*Historiae Romanae decades*] is an example of the first kind of artificial title mentioned above (3a), and [*Aristotle—Ethica: commentary*] by Walter Burley is an example of the latter (3b). *Unidentified* is provided when the precise work represented by the entry cannot be determined.

Other contributors. The names of translators, editors, compilers, and illustrators (their contributions appropriately described) are found here. The forms used follow the same principles described in the section *Name of author* above.

Place of publication. If an entry is identified as a single edition of a single work, the city of publication is provided, regularized and modernized. If the entry represents a work of more than one edition printed in more than one city, one of three general locations is provided: *Britain* (if the identified printing houses were all in the British Isles), *Continent* (if the identified printing houses were all located on the Continent), and *Britain or Continent* (if editions were known to have been issued from different presses located in the British Isles and on the Continent). If a work is completely unidentified, the phrase *Place unknown* is used; where the place of publication of an identified book is unknown, the phrase *Place not given* is used. For non-extant manuscripts, the phrase used is *Provenance unknown* in accordance with the generally less precise geographical origins of most surviving manuscripts. The phrase should not be interpreted as relating to previous ownership.

Stationer(s). When an entry represents a specific, identifiable edition, every stationer involved in the publication of the book (printer, publisher, bookseller) is supplied. But since Contributing Editors generally rely upon bibliographical sources rather than a copy of the identified book for this information, the forms of presentation differ. Accordingly, varied forms will be found, such as: "G. Eld for L. Lisle'" and "per Johannem Barbier, expensis Dionisii Roce," but also the non-distinguishing "George Bishop, Ralph Newberie, and Robert Barker"; the same stationer will appear in various constructions: "ap. J. Dayum," but elsewhere "John Day" and "J. Daye." All stationers, however, are accessible by uniform names in the database and in the index to stationers at the end of each volume.

When a work is identified as having been published in a single city, but the precise edition of several possibilities issued by different printing houses cannot be determined, the phrase *different houses* is given. If the place of publication is identified as *Britain, Continent,* or *Britain or Continent*—signifying the impossibility of determining a precise place of publication—the impossibility of determining the stationer obviously follows and this section is left blank. *Stationer unknown* is used when a work is completely unidentified or when the printer, publisher, or bookseller for a known book has not been identified by bibliographers.

Date or range of dates. If a precise date of publication is known, it is provided. If two or more editions of different dates are possibilities, either a range of dates (given as, for example, *1562–1573*) or the phrase *date indeterminable* is provided. NOTE: except for works listed in the STC and in Shaaber (which together offer for English authors a practical comprehensiveness if not absolute inclusiveness) date ranges must be understood to be at best a guide. The range represents the limit known to the Contributing Editor who has consulted a number of bibliographical sources, but the chance that at least one earlier or later edition exists unknown to the Contributing Editor remains a possibility. The same reservation also applies to works presented as a sole edition, and doubts, therefore, must be harbored even when a single date is given. A work, however, that is known to have gone through several editions over several years understandably invites questions about any attempt to assign a date range with certainty (excepting the few authors for whom comprehensive censuses exist). Such uncertainty is particularly a problem with authors who were widely published during this period (Aristotle, Saint Augustine, Cicero, Duns, *Scotus*, Peter Lombard, and Virgil, to name but a few).

STC status. A variety of self-explanatory phrases appear in this section, but the primary purpose of this information is to identify the work represented as an STC (or Wing) book. When a work is *known* to have been published both in England and on the Continent, and the edition cannot be identified, its STC (or Wing) number and its non-STC status are both cited. If, however, an entry is unidentified, nothing can be determined about its place of publication; therefore, the phrase *STC/non-STC status unknown* is used. When a work issued in more than one edition is identified as an STC (or Wing) book, but the precise edition cannot be determined, only the first possible STC (or Wing) number is given, and *et seq.* is appended.

Here also is indicated whether an entry is considered to be something other than a printed book, e.g., a manuscript or a book of blank leaves intended for use as a notebook. An entry is assumed to be a printed book unless clear evidence is provided to the contrary (the use of terms and phrases such as *scriptus, books of parchment, written sermons,* or *a book of clean paper*).

Annotations. Here Contributing Editors furnish whatever information they believe will be useful and instructive in connection with the entry. All citations are abbreviated according to the *Chicago Manual of Style*'s Author-Date System (Chapter 15); full bibliographical sources are found in the Common Abbreviations and in the Reference Lists appended to the individual introductions to book-lists.

Language(s). The language (or languages) of the book is given here. If multiple, the languages are listed, without punctuation, in alphabetical order and in the order of probability. Thus, *English Greek Latin* will be found if all are known to have been employed, but *Latin Greek (probable) English (perhaps)* when doubts of varying degrees exist. When two or more languages are of equal probability, even if the book is not likely to be in multiple languages, they are entered alphabetically with the same qualifying term as in *English (probable) Latin (probable)*, not *English or Latin*.

Cost or appraised value and date of same. Either 1) the amount the owner paid for the book represented or 2) its appraised value as estimated by the compiler of the book-list is furnished here; the date when the amount was paid or when the appraisal was made is usually limited to a year, which always precedes the day and month when they are given.

Current location of the book. This information is restricted to the physical book cited in the book-list and should not be misunderstood to identify locations of other copies of the book. Whenever possible, the repositories are cited as they appear in the STC (1:xlix–liii), identified by name, not by symbol.

PRIVATE LIBRARIES IN RENAISSANCE ENGLAND

A Collection and Catalogue of Tudor and Early Stuart Book-Lists

Volume VI
PLRE 138–150

Henry Cheyne. Scholar (M.A.): Inventory against debt. 1581

R. J. FEHRENBACH and RIVES NICHOLSON

Henry Cheyne (Chayney, Chaney, Chevnye, Cheyney), though identified in the inventory as "m[aste]r of arte, late commoner of... Brodeyates," is not found in the standard registers of Oxford scholars. The inventory was compiled at the decree of the Vice-Chancellor as a result of a "sute of William Coles," manciple of Broadgates, against a debt of £5 8s 3d that Cheyne owed Coles. Participating in the appraisal were an unusual number of persons, seven, including the principal and registrar of Broadgates.

Cheyne's collection is particularly specialized, overwhelmingly medical. Probably only a portion of his books was selected to meet the demands of the debt since the value of the books appraised totals exactly the amount of the debt (£5 8s 3d), and no property other than books is inventoried and appraised. Complementing the medical works are books of science, including mathematics and astronomy; a few exceptions to these two categories are works of grammar, geography, military science, and numismatics. One notable work in philosophy appears: Plato's *opera* in Greek, rather surprisingly the only such appearance in all the Oxford booklists for this period. The manuscript entry, "Bacon's Philosophie in french," at the date of this inventory necessarily refers to Roger Bacon, the medieval natural philosopher, not Francis Bacon. In addition to Latin and Greek, Cheyne apparently read both French and Italian; one assumes that the Italian, represented by an unidentified work of Petrarch's, was employed by Cheyne to study the poet's medical treatises, not his sonnets.

Oxford University Archives, Bodleian Library: Hyp.B.17.

§

138.1	Plinii Historiae, one volume in folio
138.2	Mesuae Graecorum ac Arabum Clarissimi Medici Opera in uno volumine in folio
138.3	Valerii Cordi Annotationes in Pedacii Dioscoridis Anazarbei De Medica Materia Libros V
138.4:1	Vivae Imagines Partium Corporis Humani AEreis Formis Expressae una cum Pedacii Dioscoridae De Materia Medica Libri V
138.4:2	[See 138.4:1]
138.5:1	Tacvini Sex Rerum Non Naturalium cum earum naturis operationibus et rectificationibus cum Petro Crescentinense
138.5:2	[See 138.5:1]
138.6:1	compositione medicamentorum fuchsius fibri 4 and bounde with him Bernardus dissenius de compositione medicamentoruum
138.6:2	[See 138.6:1]
138.7	Gemma Phrysius De principiis Astronomiae et Cosmographiae deque usu Globi ab eodem editi Item de orbis divisione et Insulis rebusque nuper inventis
138.8	Petrarca, Italian
138.9	Lucii Annei Senecae naturalium quaestionum libri vii
138.10	Hieronymi Cardani Mediolanensis medici et philosophi praestantissimi in Ptolemei libros Commentaria
138.11	Budae Commentaria
138.12	divers questions in Frenche
138.13	Fuchsius in Galene
138.14	Bacchanellus
138.15	Petri Bayii
138.16	Flavii Vegetii
138.17	Cosmographi Appiani
138.18:1	Medici Antiqui, Famanellus et Cetera
138.18:2	[See 138.18:1]
138.19	Johannes Serapion De Simplicium Medicamentorum Historia
138.20	Opera Platonis graece
138.21	Sextus Placitus
138.22	Constantinus Africanus
138.23	Santers Ardoinus De Venenis
138.24	Antonius Musa in folio
138.25	Galenus De simplicium medicamentorum facultatibus in octavo
138.26	Hippocratis opera
138.27	chirurgia Guidonis
138.28	Georgii Agricola
138.29	Budeus De asse
138.30	Cordanus De varietate
138.31	Stephanus Atheniensis in Galenum
138.32	Guido in frenche
138.33	Ruellus De natura stirpium

138.34   Hippocrates de vulneribus
138.35   Phallopius de morbo gallico
138.36   Dictionarium medicum octavo
138.37   Bacon's Philosophie in frenche
138.38   Callendarium Historicum
138.39   Opera nova de Achille

§

138.1   Plinii Historiae, one volume in folio
Pliny, *the Elder*. *Historia naturalis*. Continent: date indeterminable.
Language(s): Latin. Appraised at 4s in 1581.

138.2   Mesuae Graecorum ac Arabum Clarissimi Medici Opera in uno volumine in folio
Joannes Mesue (Yahya Ibn Masawaih). *Mesuae qui Graecorum ac Arabum postremus medicinam practicam illustravit*. Venice: in officina haeredum Lucae Antonii Juntae, 1558.
This edition of his *opera* contains many works by others; see NLM6 no. 3127.
Language(s): Latin. Appraised at 10s in 1581.

138.3   Valerii Cordi Annotationes in Pedacii Dioscoridis Anazarbei De Medica Materia Libros V
Valerius Cordus. *Annotationes in Pedacii Dioscoridis Anazarbei De medica materia libros V* [and other works]. Strassburg: excud. Josias Rihelius, 1561.
Language(s): Latin. Appraised at 5s in 1581.

138.4:1   Vivae Imagines Partium Corporis Humani AEreis Formis Expressae una cum Pedacii Dioscoridae De Materia Medica Libri V
Juan Valverde de Amusco. *Vivae imagines partium corporis humani*. Antwerp: ex off. Christophori Plantini, 1566–1579.
Language(s): Latin. Appraised at 8s in 1581.

138.4:2   [See 138.4:1]
Dioscorides. *De medica materia*. Continent: date indeterminable.
Language(s): Latin. Appraised at 8s in 1581.

138.5:1   Tacvini Sex Rerum Non Naturalium cum earum naturis operationibus et rectificationibus cum Petro Crescentinense
Ibn Butlan. *Tacuini sanitatis*. Strassburg: apud Joannem Schottem, 1531–1533.
Language(s): Latin. Appraised at 5s in 1581.

138.5:2   [See 138.5:1]
Petrus de Crescentiis. Unidentified. Continent: date indeterminable.
Language(s): Latin. Appraised at 5s in 1581.

138.6:1 compositione medicamentorum fuchsius fibri 4 and bounde with him Bernardus dissenius de compositione medicamentoruum

Leonard Fuchs. *De componendorum medicamentorum ratione*. Continent: 1555–1563.

If this item is a folio edition, which at the valuation is likely, then the 1555 date alone is possible. *Language(s)*: Latin. Appraised with one other at 5s in 1581.

138.6:2 [See 138.6:1]

Bernardus Dessenius. *De compositione medicamentorum*. Continent: 1555–1556.

Like the preceding, if a folio edition, the 1555 edition is the only possibility. *Language(s)*: Latin. Appraised with one other at 5s in 1581.

138.7 Gemma Phrysius De principiis Astronomiae et Cosmographiae deque usu Globi ab eodem editi Item de orbis divisione et Insulis rebusque nuper inventis

Reiner Gemma, *Frisius*. *De principiis astronomiae et cosmographiae, deque usu globi. De orbis divisione et insulis*. Continent: date indeterminable.

The two titles were published together several times. *Language(s)*: Latin. Appraised at 2s in 1581.

138.8 Petrarca, Italian

Francesco Petrarca. Unidentified. Continent: date indeterminable.

Given the character of the collection, likely one of Petrarch's medical works, perhaps *Opera de rimedi de l'una et l'attra fortuna*, the Italian translation of his widely published *De remedis*. *Language(s)*: Italian. Appraised at 16d in 1581.

138.9 Lucii Annei Senecae naturalium quaestionum libri vii

Lucius Annaeus Seneca. *Naturales quaestiones*. Continent: date indeterminable. *Language(s)*: Latin. Appraised at 20d in 1581.

138.10 Hieronymi Cardani Mediolanensis medici et philosophi praestantissimi in Ptolemei libros Commentaria

Girolamo Cardano. *In Cl. Ptolemaei de astrorum judiciis*. Continent: 1554–1578. *Language(s)*: Latin. Appraised at 18d in 1581.

138.11 Budae Commentaria

Gulielmus Budaeus. *Commentarii linguae graecae*. Continent: 1529–1556. *Language(s)*: Greek Latin. Appraised at 4s in 1581.

138.12 divers questions in Frenche

Unidentified. Continent (probable): date indeterminable.

Probably not an STC book. *Language(s)*: French. Appraised at 12d in 1581.

138.13 Fuchsius in Galene

Leonard Fuchs. Unidentified. Continent: date indeterminable.

Fuchs edited and translated many of Galen's works. Fuchs's widely published *Institutiones medicinae, sive methodi ad Hippocrates, Galeni* ... might have been referred to in this manner by the compiler. *Language(s)*: Latin. Appraised at 4s in 1581.

138.14 Bacchanellus
Giovanni Battista Baccanelli. Probably *De consensu medicorum in curandis morbis. De consensu medicorum in cognoscendis simplicibus*. Continent: 1553–1572.

The second work, *De consensu medicorum in cognoscendis simplicibus*, was published solo in 1554, which may have been intended here. *Language(s)*: Latin. Appraised at 12d in 1581.

138.15 Petri Bayii
Pietro Bairo. Unidentified. Continent: date indeterminable.
Language(s): Latin. Appraised at 12d in 1581.

138.16 Flavii Vegetii
Flavius Vegetius Renatus. Probably *De re militari libri quatuor*. Continent: 1515–1535.
Language(s): Latin. Appraised at 8d in 1581.

138.17 Cosmographi Appiani
Peter Apian. *Cosmographia*. Continent: date indeterminable.
Language(s): Latin. Appraised at 14d in 1581.

138.18:1 Medici Antiqui, Famanellus et Cetera
Medici antiqui omnes, qui latinis literis diversorum morborum genera et remedia persecuti sunt. Venice: apud Aldus filios, 1547.

This inventory, compiled on 3 January 1581, would hardly contain the *Medici antiqui graeci* which was published in 1581. Conceivably the terminal *et Cetera* in the manuscript entry refers to a work or works in addition to the unidentified Fumanelli at 138.18:2. *Language(s)*: Latin. Appraised with one other at 8s in 1581.

138.18:2 [See 138.18:1]
Probably Antonio Fumanelli. Unidentified. Continent: date indeterminable.
Language(s): Latin. Appraised with one other at 8s in 1581.

138.19 Johannes Serapion De Simplicium Medicamentorum Historia
Serapion, *the Elder* (Ibn Sarafyun). [*De simplicium medicamentorum historia libri septem*]. Translated by Niccolo Mutoni. Venice: apud Andream Arrivabenum, 1552.

Sometimes assigned to Serapion, *the Younger*. *Language(s)*: Latin. Appraised at 3s 4d in 1581.

138.20 Opera Platonis graece
Plato. [*Works*]. Continent: date indeterminable.

James McConica cites this appearance of Plato's opera in Greek as "an almost singular occurrence" of Plato's works among Oxford scholars at this time (McConica, 706). *Language(s)*: Greek. Appraised at 4s 6d in 1581.

138.21 Sextus Placitus
Sextus Placitus (Papyriensis). Unidentified. Continent: date indeterminable. *Language(s)*: Latin. Appraised at 2s in 1581.

138.22 Constantinus Africanus
Constantinus, *Africanus*. Probably [*Works*]. Basle: apud Henricum Petrum, 1536–1539.

May include the *Opera relique*, an appendix to the 1536 *Opera* of additional works, or, as it were, part two of the *Opera*. *Language(s)*: Latin. Appraised at 3s 4d in 1581.

138.23 Santers Ardoinus De Venenis
Santes de Ardoynis. *Opus de venenis*. Continent: date indeterminable.

A 1562 edition is much more likely than the 1492 edition, the only other edition of this work, but the earlier must remain a possibility. *Language(s)*: Latin. Appraised at 5s in 1581.

138.24 Antonius Musa in folio
Antonio Musa Brasavola. Unidentified. Continent: date indeterminable. *Language(s)*: Latin. Appraised at 6s in 1581.

138.25 Galenus De simplicium medicamentorum facultatibus in octavo
Galen. *De simplicium medicamentorum facultatibus*. Paris: apud Joannem Roigny, 1543.

This is the only octavo edition given by the standard sources. *Language(s)*: Latin. Appraised at 16d in 1581.

138.26 Hippocratis opera
Hippocrates. [*Works*]. Continent: date indeterminable.
Language(s): Latin (probable) Greek (perhaps). Appraised at 2s 6d in 1581.

138.27 chirurgia Guidonis
Guido, *de Cauliaco*. *Chirurgia*. Continent: date indeterminable.
See 138.32. *Language(s)*: Latin. Appraised at 20d in 1581.

138.28 Georgii Agricola
Georgius Agricola. Unidentified. Continent: date indeterminable.
Language(s): Latin. Appraised at 3s 6d in 1581.

138.29 Budeus De asse
Gulielmus Budaeus. *De asse et partibus eius*. Continent: date indeterminable.
Language(s): Latin. Appraised at 18d in 1581.

138.30 Cordanus De varietate
Girolamo Cardano. *De rerum varietate*. Continent: 1556–1581.
Language(s): Latin. Appraised at 16d in 1581.

138.31 Stephanus Atheniensis in Galenum
Stephanus, *Atheniensis*. [*Galen–De methodo medendi ad Glauconem: commentary*]. Translated by Agostino Gadaldini. Continent: date indeterminable.
Language(s): Latin. Appraised at 18d in 1581.

138.32 Guido in frenche
Probably Guido, *de Cauliaco*. Unidentified. Continent: date indeterminable.
Several of his works were published in French, particularly his *Chirurgia*, which is found elsewhere in this collection. See 138.27. *Language(s)*: French. Appraised at 16d in 1581.

138.33 Ruellus De natura stirpium
Joannes Ruellius. *De natura stirpium*. Continent: 1536–1543.
Most editions are in folio, one of which, at the valuation, is probably represented here. *Language(s)*: Latin. Appraised at 4s in 1581.

138.34 Hippocrates de vulneribus
Hippocrates. [*De capitis vulneribus liber*]. Continent: date indeterminable.
Not appraised. Struck out. *Language(s)*: Latin Greek (perhaps).

138.35 Phallopius de morbo gallico
Gabriel Fallopius. *De morbo gallico*. Edited by Giovanni Bonacci. Continent: date indeterminable.
Language(s): Latin. Appraised at 5s in 1581.

138.36 Dictionarium medicum octavo
Henri Estienne. *Dictionarium medicum*. Geneva: excud. Henricus Stephanus, 1564.
Language(s): Greek Latin. Appraised at 2s in 1581.

138.37 Bacon's Philosophie in frenche
Roger Bacon. *De l'admirable pouvoir et puissance de l'art et nature, ou est traicté de la pierre philosophale*. Translated by Jacques Girard de Tournus. Lyon: par Macé Bonhomme, 1557.
This work was issued as the third part of a collection, *Le miroir d'alchemie*, by the same printer in 1557, which may be represented here. Not all sources treat this title, when found alone, as a solo edition (see Shaaber B67). *Language(s)*: French. Appraised at 18d in 1581.

138.38 Callendarium Historicum
Paul Eber. *Calendarium historicum*. Continent: date indeterminable.
Language(s): Latin. Appraised at 12d in 1581.

138.39 Opera nova de Achille
Alexander Achillinus. [*Works*]. Venice: (different houses), 1508–1568. Not appraised. Appended after the sum total. *Language(s)*: Latin.

Thomas Ruckwood. Scholar (student): Probate Inventory. 1581

GRADY A. SMITH

Thomas Ruckwood (Rookewoode, Ruckwoode) is identified only as "clerke and student of [Saint] Edmonde hall" in the inventory of his goods compiled upon his decease in 1581 (see *Alumni Oxonienses*, 3:1279 as well). He is not listed anywhere as having received even a first degree. A.B. Emden notes that a Thomas Ruckwood was one of the witnesses to the deed of sale of St. Edmund Hall on 2 February 1553 ("per me Thomam Ruckwood") (Emden 1968, 252 and 295). He also quotes a document from the following year which describes Ruckwood as one "whoys learnyng and levyng is knowne to be very evyll & nowght" (Emden 1968, 255 nn.). Emden then links that Ruckwood to the one of the current inventory: he "seems to have continued in residence until his death in 1581" (257). Whether these two Ruckwoods, however, are in fact the same person cannot be determined with certainty. There is the peculiarity of one in his forties—or even fifties in 1581—being described as a student, though the sumptuous character of the rest of Ruckwood's inventory, which, along with some rather grand apparel, reveals that his lodgings included a cockloft as well as a bed chamber, is more appropriate for a man of later years than a young man just coming up to university.

Whichever Thomas Ruckwood owned the books listed below, they attest to his interest in a clerical career, reflect skill in Greek, show an admiration for Aristotle, particularly his *Logic*, and balance collections of sermons with rhetorical works of classical and humanist authors.

Oxford University Archives, Bodleian Library: Hyp.B.18.

§

A.B. Emden. 1968. *An Oxford Hall in Medieval Times*. Oxford: Clarendon Press.

§

139.1	Terentus cum commento
139.2	faber stapulensis in Organon Aristotelis
139.3	Logica Aristotelis cum tertia recognitione
139.4	Linaceri Grammatica
139.5	vocabularius utriusque juris
139.6	Calepini dictionarium
139.7	figuri Susenbroti
139.8	Clictovius in phisica
139.9	Aristotelis Organum grece
139.10	Johannes lodovicus vives de disciplinis
139.11	theophylactus in Evangelistas
139.12	C. plinii 2i panygiris
139.13	P ovidii fastorum et de tristibus
139.14	Novum Testamentum Bezae
139.15	valerius maximus
139.16	Justini institutiones
139.17	Christoferus Ehenius de principiis juris
139.18	florius sosipatrus de arte grammatices
139.19	natura Gremium
139.20	melanthonis dialectica
139.21	A hunei dialectica
139.22	Organum aristotelis
139.23	haymonis homiliae
139.24	Quintilianus de instituendo oratore
139.25	meditationes augustini
139.26	Biblia vetus
139.27	Erasmi Roterodami Copia verborum
139.28	de ecclesia Catholica decretum
139.29	an olde booke of presentmentes
139.30	A necessarie instruction for christians
139.31	A booke of Common praier
139.32	francisci nigri grammatica
139.33	infantie utriusque linguae
139.34	opusculum de terminis et artium divisionibus
139.35	vitruvius de architectura
139.36	sermonum liber
139.37	Gabrielis Bartleti conciones
139.38	tabula martiniana
139.39	Ciceronis epistolae familiares

139.40   In Aristotelis physica et metaphysica
139.41   Justice of peace
139.42   haimones homiliae
139.43:1–16   with xvi other old bookes

§

139.1   Terentus cum commento
Publius Terentius, *Afer*. *[Works]*. Britain or Continent: date indeterminable.
STC 23885.3 *et seq*. The first edition issued from England (STC 23885) does not carry a commentary. *Language(s)*: Latin. Appraised at 20d in 1581.

139.2   faber stapulensis in Organon Aristotelis
Jacobus Faber, *Stapulensis*. *[Aristotle–Selected works–Logica: commentary]*. Continent: date indeterminable.
Language(s): Latin. Appraised at 8d in 1581.

139.3   Logica Aristotelis cum tertia recognitione
Aristotle. *[Selected works–Logica]*. Continent: date indeterminable.
Apparently, the compiler mistook the phrase *tertia recognitione* (third edition) for the title of another work. *Language(s)*: Latin (probable) Greek (perhaps). Appraised at 8d in 1581.

139.4   Linaceri Grammatica
Thomas Linacre. Probably *Rudimenta grammatices*. Translated by George Buchanan. Britain or Continent: 1533–1566.
STC 15636 *et seq*. and non-STC. Shaaber L202–27. The single edition of Linacre's *Progymnasmata grammatices vulgaria* (1512) is a remote possibility. *Language(s)*: Latin. Appraised at 6d in 1581.

139.5   vocabularius utriusque juris
Vocabularius juris utriusque. Continent: date indeterminable.
Language(s): Latin. Appraised at 6d in 1581.

139.6   Calepini dictionarium
Ambrogio Calepino. *Dictionarium*. Continent: 1502–1581.
Labarre nos. 1–139. Several vernacular languages possible. *Language(s)*: Greek Latin. Appraised at 20d in 1581.

139.7   figuri Susenbroti
Joannes Susenbrotus. *Epitome troporum ac schematum*. Britain or Continent: 1535–1577.
STC 23437 *et seq*. and non-STC. *Language(s)*: Latin. Appraised at 6d in 1581.

139.8 Clictovius in phisica
Jacobus Faber, *Stapulensis*. [*Aristotle–Physica: commentary and paraphrase*]. Commentary by Jodocus Clichtoveus. Continent: 1510–1522.
The 1510 edition also contains *De anima*. VHc, no. X (p. 390). *Language(s)*: Latin. Appraised at 12d in 1581.

139.9 Aristotelis Organum grece
Aristotle. *Organon*. Continent: date indeterminable.
Another copy at 139.22. *Language(s)*: Greek. Appraised at 8d in 1581.

139.10 Johannes lodovicus vives de disciplinis
Joannes Ludovicus Vives. *De disciplinis libri xx*. Continent: 1531–1551.
Language(s): Latin. Appraised at 6d in 1581.

139.11 theophylactus in Evangelistas
Theophylact, *Archbishop of Achrida*. [*Gospels: commentary and text*]. (*Bible–N.T.*).
Continent: date indeterminable.
Language(s): Latin. Appraised at 12d in 1581.

139.12 C. plinii 2i panygiris
Pliny, *the Younger*. *Panegyricus*. Continent: 1482–1520.
Language(s): Latin. Appraised at 6d in 1581.

139.13 P ovidii fastorum et de tristibus
Publius Ovidius Naso. [*Selected works*]. Continent: date indeterminable.
A number of editions appear with the *Fasti* and the *Tristia* leading; for five such editions, see Adams O425, O435, and O439–441. *Language(s)*: Latin. Appraised at 1d in 1581.

139.14 Novum Testamentum Bezae
[*Bible–N.T.*]. Translated and edited by Théodore de Bèze. Britain or Continent: date indeterminable.
STC 2802 *et seq.* and non-STC. The editions published in England were in Latin only. *Language(s)*: Latin Greek (perhaps). Appraised at 18d in 1581.

139.15 valerius maximus
Valerius Maximus. *Facta et dicta memorabilia*. Continent: date indeterminable.
Language(s): Latin. Appraised at 6d in 1581.

139.16 Justini institutiones
Justinian I. *Institutiones*. (*Corpus juris civilis*). Continent: date indeterminable.
Language(s): Latin. Appraised at 6d in 1581.

139.17 Christoferus Ehenius de principiis juris
Christoph Ehem. *De principiis juris libri septem*. Basle: [ex officina Isingriniana], 1556.

Language(s): Latin. Appraised at 8d in 1581.

139.18 florius sosipatrus de arte grammatices
Flavius Sosipater Charisius. *Artis grammaticae libri quinque*. Continent: 1532–1551.
Language(s): Latin. Appraised at 8d in 1581.

139.19 natura Gremium
Unidentified. Place unknown: stationer unknown, date indeterminable.
STC/non-STC status unknown. Perhaps a poorly heard or poorly written *Brevium* for *Natura brevium*. *Language(s)*: Latin (probable). Appraised at 6d in 1581.

139.20 melanthonis dialectica
Philipp Melanchthon. [*Dialectica*]. Continent: date indeterminable.
Language(s): Latin. Appraised at 6d in 1581.

139.21 A hunei dialectica
Augustinus Hunnaeus. [*Aristotle–Organon: commentary*]. Continent: 1551–1581.
Language(s): Latin. Appraised at 4d in 1581.

139.22 Organum aristotelis
Aristotle. *Organon*. Continent: date indeterminable.
Another copy, in Greek, at 139.9. *Language(s)*: Latin (probable). Appraised at 12d in 1581.

139.23 haymonis homiliae
Haymo, *Bishop of Halberstadt*. [*Homiliae*]. Continent: date indeterminable.
Perhaps this item is the *pars hiemalis* volume, and 139.42 is the *pars aestivalis* volume. *Language(s)*: Latin. Appraised at 8d in 1581.

139.24 Quintilianus de instituendo oratore
Marcus Fabius Quintilianus. *Institutiones oratoriae*. Continent: date indeterminable.
Language(s): Latin. Appraised at 14d in 1581.

139.25 meditationes augustini
Augustine, *Saint* (spurious). *Meditationes*. Continent: 1483–1578.
Language(s): Latin. Appraised at 10d in 1581.

139.26 Biblia vetus
The Bible. Britain or Continent: date indeterminable.
STC 2055 *et seq.* and non-STC. An old Bible, not the Old Testament. *Language(s)*: Latin (probable). Appraised at 12d in 1581.

139.27 Erasmi Roterodami Copia verborum
Desiderius Erasmus. *De duplici copia verborum ac rerum*. Britain or Continent: date indeterminable.

STC 10471.4 *et seq.* and non-STC. Numerous editions from 1511 according to VHc. *Language(s)*: Latin. Appraised at 4d in 1581.

139.28   de ecclesia Catholica decretum
Unidentified. Continent: date indeterminable.
The name of the reigning pope under whom this decretum was issued is needed to identify the work specifically. *Language(s)*: Latin. Appraised at 4d in 1581.

139.29   an olde booke of presentmentes
Unidentified. Provenance unknown: date indeterminable.
Probably manuscript. Either clergy benefices or civil legal presentments. *Language(s)*: English (probable) Latin (perhaps). Appraised at 4d in 1581.

139.30   A necessarie instruction for christians
Perhaps *A necessary doctrine and erudition for any christen man, sette furthe by the kynges majestie.* London: (different houses), 1543–1545.
STC 5168 *et seq.* An official publication printed in great quantity for wide distribution. See note preceding STC 5163. *Language(s)*: English. Appraised at 4d in 1581.

139.31   A booke of Common praier
[*Liturgies–Church of England–Book of Common Prayer*]. Britain: 1549–1581.
STC 16267 *et seq. Language(s)*: English. Appraised at 12d in 1581.

139.32   francisci nigri grammatica
Franciscus Niger, *Venetus. Grammatica.* Continent: 1480–1514.
Language(s): Latin. Appraised at 11d in 1581.

139.33   infantie utriusque linguae
Unidentified. Place unknown: stationer unknown, date indeterminable.
STC/non-STC status unknown. *Language(s)*: Latin. Appraised at 1d in 1581.

139.34   opusculum de terminis et artium divisionibus
Unidentified. Place unknown: stationer unknown, date indeterminable.
STC/non-STC status unknown. *Language(s)*: Latin (probable). Appraised at 4d in 1581.

139.35   vitruvius de architectura
Marcus Vitruvius Pollio. [*De architectura*]. Continent: date indeterminable.
Language(s): Latin. Appraised at 16d in 1581.

139.36   sermonum liber
Unidentified [sermons]. Place unknown: stationer unknown, date indeterminable.
STC/non-STC status unknown. *Language(s)*: Latin. Appraised at 6d in 1581.

139.37 Gabrielis Bartleti conciones
Gabriel Barletta. [*Sermones*]. Continent: date indeterminable.
Language(s): Latin. Appraised at 4d in 1581.

139.38 tabula martiniana
Martinus Polonus. *Margarita decreti, seu Tabula Martiniana*. Continent: date indeterminable.
Language(s): Latin. Appraised at 11d in 1581.

139.39 Ciceronis epistolae familiares
Marcus Tullius Cicero. *Epistolae ad familiares*. Britain or Continent: date indeterminable.
STC 5295 *et seq.* and non-STC. *Language(s)*: Latin. Appraised at 2d in 1581.

139.40 In Aristotelis physica et metaphysica
Unidentified. [*Aristotle–Metaphysica and Physica: commentary*]. Continent: date indeterminable.
These two Aristotelian texts were sometimes published together, but this could be two commentaries bound, rather than published together. *Language(s)*: Latin. Appraised at 12d in 1581.

139.41 Justice of peace
Perhaps [*Justices of Peace*]. London: date indeterminable.
STC 14862 *et seq.* But other works are possible, particularly STC 10968 *et seq.* *Language(s)*: English. Appraised at 6d in 1581.

139.42 haimones homiliae
Haymo, *Bishop of Halberstadt*. [*Homiliae*]. Continent: date indeterminable.
See 139.23, particularly the annotations. *Language(s)*: Latin. Appraised at 8d in 1581.

139.43:1–16 with xvi other old bookes
Unidentified. Places unknown: stationers unknown, dates indeterminable.
STC/non-STC status unknown. *Language(s)*: Unknown. Appraised at 20d in 1581.

John Heath. Scholar (M.A.): Inventory (against debt). 1582

RIVES NICHOLSON

John Heath (Heathe, Heithe) is identified as Master of Arts and "late of Merton College" in the inventory of his goods made in early March, 1582. There is no record of a John Heath associated with Merton in *Alumni Oxonienses,* though he may possibly be the John Heathe of St. Alban Hall, in or before 1572, who received a Master of Arts in 1578 (*Alumni Oxonienses,* 2:686), later migrating to Merton. His goods, including the books listed below, were "found in the possession of William White, Master of Arts," perhaps the William White who received the Bachelor of Arts degree from Brasenose in 1570 and the Master of Arts degree in 1573 (*Alumni Oxonienses,* 4:1617). Heath's books listed for appraisal probably did not constitute his entire library since the few titles, along with a few personal articles, were "arrested by [Master] vicechauncellor's decree for a dett of six poundes dewe" to White.

That Heath was perhaps a student of the law is about all that can be hazarded about him, since the collection is made up predominantly of legal works by Justinian; beyond that, the list is neither extensive nor idiosyncratic enough to give any clear idea of his scholarly interests or character. Aside from a reasonably valuable fifteen-volume set of the *Corpus juris civilis,* the collection includes a Latin dictionary, a work of the Jewish historian Josephus, and an unidentified text by the Catholic theologian Joannes Driedo.

Oxford University Archives, Bodleian Library: Hyp.B.13.

§

140.1   the Course of Civill Lawe in xvem volumes in 16°, videlicet 7 of the Digest, 4 of the Code, 3 of the Authentiques, & 1 of the Edictes

140.2   Dictionarium Calepini
140.3   Adagia Erasmi
140.4   Johannes Driedon, theologiae professor
140.5   Josephus de bello judaico

§

140.1 the Course of Civill Lawe in xvem volumes in 16°, videlicet 7 of the Digest, 4 of the Code, 3 of the Authentiques, & 1 of the Edictes
Justinian I. *Corpus juris civilis*. Continent: date indeterminable. *Language(s)*: Latin Greek (perhaps). Appraised at 11s in 1582.

140.2 Dictionarium Calepini
Ambrogio Calepino. *Dictionarium*. Continent: date indeterminable.
Some editions contained vernacular languages. *Language(s)*: Greek Latin. Appraised at 5s in 1582.

140.3 Adagia Erasmi
Desiderius Erasmus. *Adagia*. Continent: date indeterminable.
Language(s): Latin. Appraised at 2s in 1582.

140.4 Johannes Driedon, theologiae professor
Joannes Driedo. Unidentified. Continent: date indeterminable.
De ecclesiasticis scripturis seems to have been the most frequently published of Driedo's works, but this item could be part of his *opera* or another individually published work. *Language(s)*: Latin. Appraised at 12d in 1582.

140.5 Josephus de bello judaico
Flavius Josephus. *De bello judaico*. Continent: date indeterminable.
Language(s): Latin. Appraised at 2s 6d in 1582.

John Forster. Scholar (B.C.L.):
Probate Inventory. 1584

RIVES NICHOLSON

John Forster (Foster), "sometime fellow of New College" according to the inventory of his possessions, is no better known than many of his contemporaries at Oxford. A brief *Alumni Oxonienses* entry reveals only that he was granted the Bachelor of Civil Law degree and that his will, no longer extant, was proved at Oxford on 7 April 1584. An inventory of his books and possessions was made on 12 April 1584.

Forster's modest library is that of a dutiful scholar with a pious streak who was little inclined to stray in his reading far outside the safe confines of standard student materials in law, rhetoric, and literature. It includes the legal texts one would expect a law student to own (Justinian's *Corpus Juris Civilis* and the *Institutiones*), and a scattering of works on grammar and history. The library's most distinctive trait is perhaps its several biblical commentaries by Aquinas and a Tridentine catechism among its few works of theology, books which may indicate a conservative religious temperament.

Oxford University Archives, Bodleian Library: Hyp.B.12.

§

141.1 one Course of the Civill Law
141.2 Bibliotheca Eliotae
141.3 a peece of Scotus
141.4 Aquinas in Epistolas Pauli
141.5 Erasmi Kiliades
141.6 Theophilactus in Evangelia
141.7 Cornucopia

141.8   Osorius de nobilitate
141.9   Catechismus ad Parochos
141.10   Testamentum Novum
141.11   duo volumina Orationum Ciceronis
141.12   Rhetorica ad Herennium
141.13   Guiliandus in Johannem
141.14   Titilmanni Dialectica
141.15   Quintus Curtius anglicè
141.16   Nicephorus
141.17   Institutiones Juris Civilis
141.18   Lucanus
141.19   Vergilius cum Comment
141.20   El: [Elucidatio] Titilmannus in psalmos, 2o vol:
141.21   Aquinas in Matheum et Lucam

§

141.1   one Course of the Civill Law
Justinian I. *Corpus juris civilis.* Continent: date indeterminable.
Language(s): Latin Greek (perhaps). Appraised at 26s 8d in 1584.

141.2   Bibliotheca Eliotae
Sir Thomas Elyot. *Bibliotheca Eliotae.* London: in off. T. Bertheleti, 1542–1559. STC 7659.5 *et seq.* The manuscript entry indicates that this is not the 1538 first edition (STC 7659, *The dictionary of syr Thomas Elyot*). *Language(s)*: English Latin. Appraised at 6s 8d in 1584.

141.3   a peece of Scotus
John Duns, *Scotus.* Unidentified. Continent: date indeterminable.
A part of his multi-volumed commentary on Lombard is, perhaps, most likely to be so represented, but the *peece* does not seem very large according to the valuation. *Language(s)*: Latin. Appraised at 6d in 1584.

141.4   Aquinas in Epistolas Pauli
Thomas Aquinas, *Saint.* [*Epistles–Paul: commentary*]. Continent: date indeterminable.
Language(s): Latin. Appraised at 20d in 1584.

141.5   Erasmi Kiliades
Desiderius Erasmus. *Adagia.* Continent: date indeterminable.
Language(s): Latin. Appraised at 20d in 1584.

141.6   Theophilactus in Evangelia
Theophylact, *Archbishop of Achrida.* [*Gospels: commentary and text*]. (*Bible–N.T.*).

Continent: date indeterminable.
Language(s): Latin. Appraised at 10d in 1584.

141.7   Cornucopia
Perhaps Nicolaus Perottus. *Cornucopia*. Continent: date indeterminable.
Perottus's popular reference seems marginally more likely than the rarer works with this title by Joannes Ravisius (Textor) or Eustathius, *of Thessalonica*, but even Perottus would hardly be considered current at this date. *Language(s)*: Latin. Appraised at 6d in 1584.

141.8   Osorius de nobilitate
Jeronimo Osorio da Fonseca, *Bishop*. *De nobilitate civili libri II. De nobilitate christiana libri III*. Continent: 1542–1552.
Language(s): Latin. Appraised at 8d in 1584.

141.9   Catechismus ad Parochos
Catechismus ex decreto Concilii Tridentini. (*Councils–Trent*). Continent: 1566–1587.
The long title continues: "... ad parochos, ..." *Language(s)*: Latin. Appraised at 4d in 1584.

141.10   Testamentum Novum
[*Bible–N.T.*]. Britain or Continent: date indeterminable.
STC 2799 *et seq*. and non-STC. *Language(s)*: Latin. Appraised at 4d in 1584.

141.11   duo volumina Orationum Ciceronis
Marcus Tullius Cicero. [*Selected works–Orations*]. Britain or Continent: date indeterminable.
STC 5308 *et seq*. and non-STC. Perhaps part, since the collected orations were usually issued in three volumes. *Language(s)*: Latin. Appraised at 14d in 1584.

141.12   Rhetorica ad Herennium
Marcus Tullius Cicero (spurious). *Rhetorica ad Herennium*. Britain or Continent: date indeterminable.
STC 5323.5 *et seq*. and non-STC. *Language(s)*: Latin. Appraised at 4d in 1584.

141.13   Guiliandus in Johannem
Claudius Guilliaudus. [*John: commentary and text*]. (*Bible–N.T.*). Continent: date indeterminable.
Language(s): Latin. Appraised at 10d in 1584.

141.14   Titilmanni Dialectica
Franz Titelmann. [*Dialectica*]. Continent: date indeterminable.
Language(s): Latin. Appraised at 6d in 1584.

141.15 Quintus Curtius anglicè
Quintus Curtius Rufus. *The historie of Quintus Curcius, contayning the actes of the greate Alexander*. Translated by John Brende. London: (different houses), 1553–1584.
STC 6141.5 *et seq. Language(s)*: English. Appraised at 10d in 1584.

141.16 Nicephorus
Perhaps Nicephorus Callistus. *Ecclesiastica historia*. Continent: 1553–1574.
Nicephorus, *Blemmida* and Nicephorus, *Chartophylax* are less likely possibilities given the other books in Forster's collection. *Language(s)*: Latin. Appraised at 5s in 1584.

141.17 Institutiones Juris Civilis
Justinian I. *Institutiones*. (*Corpus juris civilis*). Continent: date indeterminable. *Language(s)*: Greek Latin. Appraised at 4d in 1584.

141.18 Lucanus
Marcus Annaeus Lucanus. *Pharsalia*. Continent: date indeterminable. *Language(s)*: Latin. Appraised at 12d in 1584.

141.19 Vergilius cum Comment
Publius Virgilius Maro. Probably [*Works*]. Britain or Continent: date indeterminable.
STC 24788 *et seq.* and non-STC. STC 24787 does not carry commentary. *Language(s)*: Latin. Appraised at 2s 6d in 1584.

141.20 El: [Elucidatio] Titilmannus in psalmos, 2o vol:
Franz Titelmann. [*Psalms: commentary and text*]. (*Bible–O.T.*). Continent: date indeterminable.
Language(s): Latin. Appraised at 2s 4d in 1584.

141.21 Aquinas in Matheum et Lucam
Thomas Aquinas, *Saint*. [*Gospels: commentary* (part)]. Continent: date indeterminable.
Aquinas's commentaries on the four gospels were not published separately. Whether this is the entire collection, with the compiler citing only Matthew and Luke, or just these two commentaries alone, separated from the whole, cannot be determined. *Language(s)*: Latin. Appraised at 20d in 1584.

Thomas Morrey. Scholar (M.A.): Probate Inventory and will. 1584

D. V. N. BAGCHI

Thomas Morrey (Morey, Morré, Norrey) was a student of Christ Church, Oxford, from 1571 until his death in 1584. He graduated Bachelor of Arts in February 1572, and Master of Arts in May 1575 (*Alumni Oxonienses*, 3:1027). In his will Morrey bequeathed to his college library copies of Calvin's commentaries on Isaiah (in one volume), on Daniel (in one volume), and on the New Testament (in two volumes), although none of the college's present holdings can positively be identified as his (see Ker 1986, 499). His only lasting memorial there is a brass plate, now in the north transept of Christ Church Cathedral, which pointedly praises his "zeal for the Lord and love of His [or 'the'] House."

Morrey's sizeable and largely theological collection is dominated by the works of Continental Calvinists, although Lutherans, English reformers, and early fathers are also present in force. By contrast, Bonaventura (in a collection of sermons and in a commentary) is the sole representative of medieval theology. From the evidence of his books, it has been suggested that Morrey was one of the best read men of his day in the Reformed tradition, in the vanguard of late sixteenth-century Oxford Protestantism (Dent 1983, 97f.). A few legal and medical works complete the library.

Oxford University Archives, Bodleian Library: Hyp.B.16.

§

Dent, C. M. 1983. *Protestant Reformers in Elizabethan Oxford*. Oxford: Oxford Univ. Press.

Ker, N.R. 1986. "Books at Christ Church 1562–1602," Appendix III in *The*

Collegiate University, ed., James K. McConica. Volume 3 of *The History of the University of Oxford*, gen. ed., T.H. Aston. Oxford: Clarendon Press, pp. 498–519.

§

142.1	Calvine upon Genesis and th'other 4 bookes of Moses
142.2	[Calvin] upon Jeremy
142.3:1	[Calvin] upon Isay and Danyell
142.3:2	[See 142.3:1]
142.4	[Calvin] upon Ezechiell
142.5	[Calvin] upon the small prophetes
142.6	[Calvin] upon the evangelistes
142.7	[Calvin] upon the epistles
142.8	[Calvin] upon Josua
142.9	[Calvin] upon the Ephesians anglice
142.10	[Calvin] upon the Psalmes
142.11	[Calvin] his Institutions
142.12	[Calvin] his epistles in folio
142.13	[Calvin] his Answears to Baldwyne
142.14	[Calvin] his examining of the Councell of Trent
142.15	Kemnisius his Examen. of the Councel of Trent
142.16	Beza his greate annotations
142.17	[Beza] de haereticis puniendis
142.18	[Beza] Opuscula, 2 volum: [volumina]
142.19	[Beza] Questiones
142.20	[Beza] Confess:
142.21	[Beza] de notis ecclesiae
142.22	Zanchius de tribus Elohim
142.23	[Zanchius] de attributis Dei
142.24	[Zanchius] Miscelanea
142.25	[Zanchius] oratio
142.26	Mercer in 5 minores prophaetas
142.27	[Mercer] in Job
142.28	[Mercer] in Proverbia, Ecclesiasten, Cantica
142.29	Bullingeri Decades
142.30	[Bullinger] Compendium Christianae religionis
142.31	Petrus Martyr in Romanos
142.32	[Petrus Martyr] in primam ad Corinthios
142.33	[Petrus Martyr] de eucharistia
142.34	[Petrus Martyr] de utraque Christi natura
142.35	[Petrus Martyr] de coelibatu
142.36	[Petrus Martyr] preces
142.37	Loniceri Exempla

142.38	Musculi loci communes
142.39	[Musculi] in Genesim
142.40	Buceri scripta anglicana
142.41	[Buceri] Colloquia Ratispo[nensia]
142.42	[Buceri] de coena
142.43	Stephani concordantiae
142.44	Wigandi Corpus Doctrinae, 2 volum: [volumina]
142.45	Tremelius his Bible
142.46	Geneva Bible
142.47	Fulke in Apocalipsin
142.48	Gualter in Marcum
142.49:1	Testamentum anglice bis
142.49:2	[See 142.49:1]
142.50	Testamentum graece
142.51	Testamentum latine
142.52	Melchior Canus
142.53	Arnobius in Psal
142.54	Pandectae Scriptuarum
142.55	Pontificum Vitae
142.56	Bertrandes tretie of the Churche
142.57	Another treteys of the Churche
142.58	Lutheri allegoriae
142.59	Coment' de Reg' adversus Machavil
142.60	Bartram de politia judaica
142.61	Castalionis diologi
142.62	Ecci Enchiridion
142.63	Corranus Ecclesiastes
142.64	Grinei Cronologia
142.65	Methodus Sarcerii
142.66	Cornerus in Psal.
142.67	Lactantius
142.68	Theodoreti decem orationes
142.69	Cipriani opera 2 volum.
142.70	Augustini De doctrina Christiana
142.71	[Augustini] De consensu evangelistarum
142.72	[Augustini] De praedestinatione sanctorum
142.73	Pasquil' [Pasquillus]
142.74	Aretius de caena
142.75	[Aretius] Examen Theologicum
142.76	Danaei 9 volumina
142.77	[Danaei] De elenchis haereticorum
142.78	Heming [Hemingius], volum. 7
142.79	Sadeel, vlum. 4
142.80	Stephani responsio ad censuras Paris.
142.81	Melanchthon in Romanos

142.82	Foxi Historia Ecclesiastica
142.83	[Foxi] De Christo grati. justificante
142.84	An Answear and Replie to the Jesuyte, 2 volumes
142.85	Praxis Curiae Romanae
142.86	Dearing against Hardinge
142.87	Whitaker against Campion
142.88	Jewell, his sermons
142.89	[Jewell] upon the Thessalonians
142.90	Piselius
142.91	Bertram de natura Christi in eucharistia
142.92	Refutatio ommispraesentiae
142.93	Menselius in Hossium
142.94	Herebrandi disputatio theologica
142.95	Luther upon the psalms of degrees
142.96	Conference
142.97	Christian Righteousnes
142.98	Excellencie of a Christian
142.99	Travers on the 111 psalm
142.100	Admonition to the parliament
142.101	Execution of Justice
142.102	Rodericke Mors
142.103	Brulifer in Bonaventuram
142.104	Bonaventura de morte
142.105	Dialogus contra papistarum tyrannidem
142.106	Catalogus
142.107	Luther, Praefac[io] in Romanos
142.108	Calfield in Marshall
142.109	Confutatio doctorum Parris
142.110	Collection of the Churche
142.111	Theses Rainoldi
142.112	Consensus Patrum
142.113	Epistol Pauli italice
142.114	Quintini sermones
142.115	Apologia Anglicana
142.116	A prayer booke
142.117	Psalmes
142.118	Calvine's catechisme
142.119	Anchor of Fayth
142.120	Deeringes lectures
142.121	Willicii Logicke
142.122	Psalmes in 16 in meeter
142.123	Plinie
142.124	Erasmi Chiliades
142.125	Wolphius upon Isocrates
142.126	Senecae Moralia

142.127   Historia Scotica
142.128   Hebrew Grammer
142.129   Greeke lexicon
142.130   Synonima Greca
142.131   Plautus
142.132   Senecae Traged
142.133   Sleidani De 4 Imperiis
142.134   Syntaxis Linguae Grecae
142.135   Similitudines
142.136   Phrigius
142.137   Velcurio
142.138   Curaeus
142.139:1 Valerius bis
142.139:2 [See 142.139:1]
142.140   Cosmographia
142.141   Metamorphoses
142.142   Institutions
142.143   Tusculan Questions
142.144   Common Lawe
142.145   Plutarchi Simili [Similia]
142.146   Praelia Anglorum
142.147   De furoribus gallicis
142.148   Testificatio Lodovici
142.149   Epistolae Plinii
142.150   Hebrew, 5 volumes
142.151   Disciplina ecclesiastica
142.152   Christian Perigrinations
142.153   De jure magistratuum
142.154   Knoxe de praedestinatione
142.155   Hessus de tuenda valitudine
142.156   The Way of Lief
142.157:1–5   Five odd bookes
142.158   Biblia latine, 5 volum [volumina]

§

142.1   Calvine upon Genesis and th'other 4 bookes of Moses
Jean Calvin. [*Pentateuch: commentary*]. Geneva: (different houses), 1563–1583.
The compiler invariably gives the titles of Calvin's works in English, but only in one case (142.10) is an item described expressly as *anglice*. Calvin's works listed here are, therefore, treated as Latin editions unless otherwise indicated by the compiler. It is assumed that a French edition would also have been designated as such; but there are no other French items in Morrey's list. The 1563 edition of Calvin's commentary on the Pentateuch contains the Biblical text as well. *Language(s)*: Latin. Appraised at 8s in 1584.

142.2 [Calvin] upon Jeremy

Jean Calvin. [*Jeremiah and Lamentations: commentary*]. Geneva: (different houses), 1563–1576.

Calvin's commentary on Jeremiah seems to have been published only with his commentary on Lamentations, in Latin editions at least. *Language(s)*: Latin. Appraised at 5s 6d in 1584.

142.3:1 [Calvin] upon Isay and Danyell

Jean Calvin. [*Isaiah: commentary*]. Geneva: (different houses), 1551–1583.

Morrey's will records that he bequeathed copies of Calvin's commentaries on Isaiah and Daniel (together with one on the New Testament) "unto the Librarye of Christ-church to the use of students [i.e., fellows?] theire." Unfortunately, no book inscribed as a bequest from Morrey has been found in the college library. See Ker 1986, 499. *Language(s)*: Latin. Appraised with one other at 6s in 1584.

142.3:2 [See 142.3:1]

Jean Calvin. [*Daniel: commentary and text*]. (*Bible–O.T*). Edited by Jean Budé and Charles Jonviller (Charles de Joan). Continent: 1561–1571.

For another example of these two titles apparently bound together, see BCI 1:485 (Bridges 14). The 1561 edition contains a polyglot text. See the annotations to 142.3:1. *Language(s)*: Latin Aramaic (perhaps) Hebrew (perhaps). Appraised with one other at 6s in 1584.

142.4 [Calvin] upon Ezechiell

Jean Calvin. [*Ezekiel: commentary*]. Edited by Jean Budé and Charles Jonviller (Charles de Joan). Geneva: (different houses), 1565–1583.

Language(s): Latin. Appraised at 18d in 1584.

142.5 [Calvin] upon the small prophetes

Jean Calvin. [*Minor prophets: commentary*]. Geneva: (different houses), 1559–1581. *Language(s)*: Latin. Appraised at 5s 6d in 1584.

142.6 [Calvin] upon the evangelistes

Jean Calvin. *Harmonia*. Geneva: (different houses), 1555–1582.
Language(s): Latin. Appraised at 6s in 1584.

142.7 [Calvin] upon the epistles

Jean Calvin. [*Epistles–Paul: commentary*]. Geneva: (different houses), 1548–1580.
Language(s): Latin. Appraised at 5s 6d in 1584.

142.8 [Calvin] upon Josua

Jean Calvin. Probably [*Joshua: commentary*]. Geneva: (different houses), 1564–1577.

Probably not STC 4394; see the annotations to 142.1. *Language(s)*: Latin. Appraised at 8d in 1584.

142.9 [Calvin] upon the Ephesians anglice

Jean Calvin. *The sermons of M. John Calvin, upon the epistle too the Ephesians. (Bible–N.T.)*. Translated by Arthur Golding. London: [T. Dawson] for L. Harison and G. Byshop, 1577.

STC 4448. *Language(s)*: English. Appraised at 2s 6d in 1584.

142.10 [Calvin] upon the Psalmes

Jean Calvin. [*Psalms: commentary*]. Geneva: (different houses), 1557–1584.

At least one edition (1578) contains the Hebrew text. *Language(s)*: Latin Hebrew (perhaps). Appraised at 2s 4d in 1584.

142.11 [Calvin] his Institutions

Jean Calvin. *Institutio Christianae religionis*. Britain or Continent: date indeterminable.

STC 4414 *et seq.* and non-STC. Possibly the Latin version published in Britain in 1576 (STC 4414), less likely an English translation. *Language(s)*: Latin English (perhaps). Appraised at 2s 4d in 1584.

142.12 [Calvin] his epistles in folio

Jean Calvin. [*Epistolae*]. Continent: date indeterminable.

Which collection that leads with *Epistolae* (*Epistolae et responsa*, *Epistolae duae de rebus hoc saeculo cognitu necessariis*, for two) cannot be determined, though the second seems not to have been published in folio. *Language(s)*: Latin. Appraised at 4s in 1584.

142.13 [Calvin] his Answears to Baldwyne

Jean Calvin. *Responsio ad Balduini convicia*. Geneva: [Jean Crespin], 1562. *Language(s)*: Latin. Appraised at 4d in 1584.

142.14 [Calvin] his examining of the Councell of Trent

Jean Calvin. *Acta synodi Tridentinae cum antidoto. (Councils–Trent)*. Geneva: [Joannes Gerardus], 1547.

Language(s): Latin. Appraised at 3d in 1584.

142.15 Kemnisius his Examen. of the Councel of Trent

Martinus Chemnitius. *Examen concilii Tridentini. (Councils–Trent)*. Frankfurt am Main (probable): (different houses), 1566–1578.

Probably not an STC book but see STC 5116. The manuscript entry poses problems for determining language; it has features of both English and Latin. Given, however, the compiler's habit of entering Latin titles in English (see the annotations to 142.1), the Latin edition is assumed to be intended here. *Language(s)*: Latin (probable) English (perhaps). Appraised at 7s 6d in 1584.

142.16 Beza his greate annotations

[*Bible–N.T.*]. Translated and annotated by Théodore de Bèze. Continent: date indeterminable.

Doubtless Bèze's annotations to the New Testament, but since they were not published separately until 1594, and since the appraisal suggests something even more grand, it is assumed that his edition of the New Testament with the *Annotationes majores* is represented here. See BCI 2:117, where a scrupulously compiled catalogue also cites Bèze's New Testament in this manner. *Language(s)*: Latin. Appraised at 10s in 1584.

142.17 [Beza] de haereticis puniendis

Théodore de Bèze. *De haereticis a civili magistratu puniendis*. Geneva: oliva Roberti Stephani, 1554.

Gardy no. 80. *Language(s)*: Latin. Appraised at 6d in 1584.

142.18 [Beza] Opuscula, 2 volum: [volumina]

Théodore de Bèze. Unidentified. Place unknown: stationer unknown, date indeterminable.

STC/non-STC status unknown. Just possibly the *Poemata*, or else the first two volumes of the *Tractationes theologicae*. See Adams B927–940 and B952–958. *Language(s)*: Latin (probable). Appraised at 9s in 1584.

142.19 [Beza] Questiones

Théodore de Bèze. *Quaestionum et responsionum christianarum libellus*. Britain or Continent: 1571–1581.

STC 2036 *et seq*. and non-STC. The English translation by Arthur Golding (STC 2037–40) is possible but unlikely, given the spelling of the entry. *Language(s)*: Latin English (perhaps). Appraised at 6d in 1584.

142.20 [Beza] Confess:

Théodore de Bèze. *Confessio christianae fidei*. Britain or Continent: 1560–1583.
STC 2006 *et seq*. and non-STC. *Language(s)*: Latin. Appraised at 3d in 1584.

142.21 [Beza] de notis ecclesiae

Théodore de Bèze. *De veris et visibilibus ecclesiae catholicae notis*. Geneva: apud Eustathium Vignon, 1579.

Gardy no. 326. *Language(s)*: Latin. Appraised at 3d in 1584.

142.22 Zanchius de tribus Elohim

Hieronymus Zanchius. *De tribus Elohim*. Frankfurt am Main: apud Georgium Corvinum, 1572–1573.

Language(s): Latin. Appraised at 4s 6d in 1584.

142.23 [Zanchius] de attributis Dei
Hieronymus Zanchius. *De natura Dei, seu de divinis attributis, libri V*. Heidelberg: excud. Jacobus Mylius, 1577.
Language(s): Latin. Appraised at 6s 6d in 1584.

142.24 [Zanchius] Miscelanea
Hieronymus Zanchius. *Miscellaneorum libri tres*. Neustadt an der Haardt: excud. Matthaeus Harnisch, 1582.
Language(s): Latin. Appraised at 4d in 1584.

142.25 [Zanchius] oratio
Hieronymus Zanchius. Perhaps *De aperiendis in ecclesia scholis oratio*. Neustadt an der Haardt: per haered. Joannis Meyer, 1579.
Language(s): Latin. Appraised at 1d in 1584.

142.26 Mercer in 5 minores prophaetas
Joannes Mercerus, *Professor of Hebrew*. [*Minor prophets: commentary and text*]. (*Bible–O.T.*). Geneva: excud. Henricus Stephanus, date indeterminable.
Dates, ranging from 1565 to 1583, are supplied by various bibliographical sources. *Language(s)*: Latin. Appraised at 4s 6d in 1584.

142.27 [Mercer] in Job
Joannes Mercerus, *Professor of Hebrew*. *Commentarii in librum Job*. Geneva: excudebat Eustathius Vignon, 1573.
May contain the text. *Language(s)*: Latin. Appraised at 3s 6d in 1584.

142.28 [Mercer] in Proverbia, Ecclesiasten, Cantica
Joannes Mercerus, *Professor of Hebrew*. *Commentarii in Salomonis Proverbia, Ecclesiasten, et Canticum canticorum*. (*Bible–O.T.*). Geneva: excudebat Eustathius Vignon, 1573.
Language(s): Latin. Appraised at 3s 6d in 1584.

142.29 Bullingeri Decades
Heinrich Bullinger. *Sermonum decades*. Zürich: Christoph Froschouer, 1549–1577.
Language(s): Latin. Appraised at 5s in 1584.

142.30 [Bullinger] Compendium Christianae religionis
Heinrich Bullinger. *Compendium christianae religionis*. Continent: 1556–1569.
Language(s): Latin. Appraised at 4d in 1584.

142.31 Petrus Martyr in Romanos
Pietro Martire Vermigli (Peter Martyr). [*Romans: commentary*]. Continent: 1558–1570.
Language(s): Latin. Appraised at 4s in 1584.

142.32 [Petrus Martyr] in primam ad Corinthios
Pietro Martire Vermigli (Peter Martyr). [*Corinthians: commentary*]. Zürich: Christoph Froschouer, 1551–1579.
Language(s): Latin. Appraised at 3s 6d in 1584.

142.33 [Petrus Martyr] de eucharistia
Pietro Martire Vermigli (Peter Martyr). Probably *Tractatio de sacramento eucharistiae, habita in universitate Oxoniensi*. Britain or Continent: 1549–1552.
STC 24673 and non-STC. Other, less likely, possibilities are *Defensio doctrinae de eucharistiae sacramento adversus S. Gardineri librum* and *Disputatio de eucharistiae sacramento*. *Language(s)*: Latin. Appraised at 4s in 1584.

142.34 [Petrus Martyr] de utraque Christi natura
Pietro Martire Vermigli (Peter Martyr). *Dialogus de utraque in Christo natura*. Zürich: excudebat Christophorus Froschouerus, 1561–1575.
Language(s): Latin. Appraised at 6d in 1584.

142.35 [Petrus Martyr] de coelibatu
Pietro Martire Vermigli (Peter Martyr). *Defensio ad Riccardi Smythaei Angli duos libellos de caelibatu sacerdotum, et votis monasticis*. Basle: apud Petrum Pernam, 1559–1570.
Language(s): Latin. Appraised at 9d in 1584.

142.36 [Petrus Martyr] preces
Pietro Martire Vermigli (Peter Martyr). *Preces sacrae ex Psalmis Davidis desumptae*. Zürich: Christoph Froschouer, 1561–1578.
The translation by Charles Glemhan, *Most godly prayers compiled out of Davids psalmes* (London: W. Seres, 1569) [STC 24671], is possible but unlikely. *Language(s)*: Latin. Appraised at 6d in 1584.

142.37 Loniceri Exempla
Andreas Hondorff. *Theatrum historicum, sive Promptuarium exemplorum*. Translated by Philipp Lonicer. Frankfurt am Main: apud Georgium Corvinum, impens. Sigismundi Feierabend, 1575.
Language(s): Latin. Appraised at 5s in 1584.

142.38 Musculi loci communes
Wolfgang Musculus. *Loci communes*. Basle: (different houses), 1560–1573.
The less popular *Loci communes sacri* of Andreas Musculus is possible but highly unlikely, given that the following entry is Wolfgang's Genesis commentary. The printer Hervagius was involved in all of the editions in this date range. *Language(s)*: Latin. Appraised at 5s 6d in 1584.

142.39 [Musculi] in Genesim
Wolfgang Musculus. [*Genesis: commentary and text*]. (*Bible–O.T.*). Basle: (different houses), 1554–1565.
Language(s): Latin. Appraised at 6s in 1584.

142.40 Buceri scripta anglicana
Martin Bucer. *Scripta anglicana fere omnia*. Basle: ex. officina P. Pernae, 1577.
Language(s): Latin. Appraised at 5s in 1584.

142.41 [Buceri] Colloquia Ratispo[nensia]
Martin Bucer. *Acta colloquii in comitiis imperii Ratisponae habiti*. Continent: 1541–1542.
Printed at Strassburg and Wesel. *Language(s)*: Latin. Appraised at 12d in 1584.

142.42 [Buceri] de coena
Martin Bucer. Probably *De vera et falsa Caenae Dominicae administratione*. Neuburg ad Danubium: apud Johannem Kilianum, 1546.
Possible, but less likely, is *Apologia Martini Buceri qua fidei suae atque doctrinae circa Christe Caenam*. *Language(s)*: Latin. Appraised at 1d in 1584.

142.43 Stephani concordantiae
Robert Estienne, *the Elder*. *Concordantiae Bibliorum utriusque Testamenti*. Continent: 1555–1581.
Printed at Antwerp and Paris. *Language(s)*: Latin. Appraised at 10s in 1584.

142.44 Wigandi Corpus Doctrinae, 2 volum: [volumina]
Johann Wigand and Matthias Richter (Matthaeus Judex). *Syntagma, seu corpus doctrinae veri et omnipotentis Dei, ex veteri Testamento tantum*. Continent: 1558–1575.
"Syntagma" in Greek characters. *Language(s)*: Latin. Appraised at 8s in 1584.

142.45 Tremelius his Bible
The Bible. Translated and edited by Joannes Immanuel Tremellius and François Du Jon, *the Elder*. Britain or Continent: date indeterminable.
STC 2056 *et seq*. and non-STC. *Language(s)*: Latin. Appraised at 9s in 1584.

142.46 Geneva Bible
The Bible. Britain or Continent: 1560–1584.
STC 2093 *et seq*. *Language(s)*: English. Appraised at 5s in 1584.

142.47 Fulke in Apocalipsin
William Fulke. *In sacram divi Joannis Apocalypsim praelectiones*. (*Bible–N.T.–Revelation*). London: praelum T. Purfoetii, 1573.
STC 11442. *Language(s)*: Latin. Appraised at 12d in 1584.

142.48 Gualter in Marcum
Rudolph Walther. [*Mark: commentary and text*]. (*Bible–N.T.*). Zürich: Christoph Froschouer, 1561–1584.
Language(s): Latin. Appraised at 18d in 1584.

142.49:1 Testamentum anglice bis
[*Bible–N.T.*]. Britain or Continent: date indeterminable.
STC 2823 *et seq. Language(s)*: English. Appraised with another at 2s 4d in 1584.

142.49:2 [See 142.49:1]
[*Bible–N.T.*]. Britain or Continent: date indeterminable.
STC 2823 *et seq. Language(s)*: English. Appraised with another at 2s 4d in 1584.

142.50 Testamentum graece
[*Bible–N.T.*]. Continent: date indeterminable.
Language(s): Greek. Appraised at 8d in 1584.

142.51 Testamentum latine
[*Bible–N.T.*]. Britain or Continent: date indeterminable.
STC 2799 *et seq.* and non-STC. *Language(s)*: Latin. Appraised at 4d in 1584.

142.52 Melchior Canus
Francisco Melchor Cano, *Bishop*. Unidentified. Continent: date indeterminable.
Language(s): Latin. Appraised at 16d in 1584.

142.53 Arnobius in Psal
Arnobius, *the Younger*. [*Psalms: commentary*]. Edited by Desiderius Erasmus. Continent: date indeterminable.
Some editions appear to contain the text. *Language(s)*: Latin. Appraised at 10d in 1584.

142.54 Pandectae Scriptuarum
Probably Otto Brunfels. *Pandectae scripturarum*. Continent: date indeterminable.
It is just possible, but highly unlikely, that the *Pandectes scripturae* of the monk Antiochus, printed by Jacques Kerver (Paris, 1543) in the translation by Godfridus Tilmann, is meant here (see Adams A1200). *Language(s)*: Latin. Appraised at 12d in 1584.

142.55 Pontificum Vitae
Unidentified. Place unknown: stationer unknown, date indeterminable.
STC/non-STC status unknown. The two most likely possibilities are Bartolomeo Platina's *Historia de vitis pontificum* and Robert Barnes's *Vitae romanorum pontificum*. *Language(s)*: Latin. Appraised at 9d in 1584.

142.56 Bertrandes tretie of the Churche
Unidentified. Continent (probable): date indeterminable.

Almost certainly not an STC book. A remote possibility is Petrus Bertrandi's *Libellus de jurisdictione ecclesiastica contra Petrum de Cugneriis*, an anti-Gallican treatise republished in Paris in 1513. *Language(s)*: Latin (probable). Appraised at 8d in 1584.

142.57 Another treteys of the Churche
Unidentified. Britain (probable): date indeterminable.

Perhaps an STC book. *Language(s)*: English (probable). Appraised at 8d in 1584.

142.58 Lutheri allegoriae
Martin Luther. *Allegoriarum, typorum et exemplorum veteris et novi testamenti libri duo*. Edited by Jacobus Hertelius. Basle: [Arnoldi Gymnici, sumptibus Joannis Oporini], 1561.

Language(s): Latin. Appraised at 8d in 1584.

142.59 Coment' de Reg' adversus Machavil
Innocent Gentillet. *Commentariorum de regno aut quovis principatu recte administrando libri tres. Adversus N. Machiavellum*. Continent: date indeterminable.

Language(s): Latin. Appraised at 12d in 1584.

142.60 Bartram de politia judaica
Bonaventure Corneille Bertram. *De politia judaica*. Geneva: apud Eustathium Vignon, 1574–1580.

Language(s): Latin. Appraised at 3d in 1584.

142.61 Castalionis diologi
Sebastian Castalio. *Dialogorum sacrorum libri quatuor*. Britain or Continent: date indeterminable.

STC 4770 *et seq*. and non-STC. *Language(s)*: Latin. Appraised at 6d in 1584.

142.62 Ecci Enchiridion
Joannes Eckius. *Enchiridion locorum communium adversus Lutheranos*. Britain or Continent: date indeterminable.

STC 7481.4 and non-STC. The inventory has the word *Pigg* crossed out and *Ecci* in its place. Eckius's fellow Catholic controversialist, Albertus Pighius, is not otherwise represented among Morrey's books. *Language(s)*: Latin. Appraised at 4d in 1584.

142.63 Corranus Ecclesiastes
Antonio de Corro. *Sapientissimi regis Salomonis . . . in Latinam linguam ab A. Corrano versa. (Bible–O.T.)*. London: [J. Charlewood for] per J. Wolfium exp. ipsius authoris, 1579.

STC 2761. *Language(s)*: Latin. Appraised at 6d in 1584.

142.64 Grinei Cronologia
Johann Jacob Grynaeus. *Chronologia brevis evangelicae historiae logicique artificii in epistola Pauli ad Romanos declaratio*. Basle: ex. off. (per) Sebastiani Henricpetri, 1580.
Language(s): Latin. Appraised at 5d in 1584.

142.65 Methodus Sarcerii
Erasmus Sarcerius. [*Methodus in praecipuos scripturae divinae locos*]. Continent: 1538–1555.
Language(s): Latin. Appraised at 6d in 1584.

142.66 Cornerus in Psal.
Christoph Corner. [*Psalms: commentary and text*]. (*Bible–O.T.*). Continent: 1564–1581.
Corner's *Cantica selecta* probably appended. *Language(s)*: Latin. Appraised at 12d in 1584.

142.67 Lactantius
Lucius Coelius Lactantius. Probably [*Works*]. Continent: date indeterminable.
Language(s): Latin. Appraised at 10d in 1584.

142.68 Theodoreti decem orationes
Theodoret, *Bishop*. *De providentia*. Continent: date indeterminable.
Probably the Leipzig, 1564 edition in the translation by Victorinus Strigelius, which has *orationes* for *sermones* in the title. *Language(s)*: Latin. Appraised at 4d in 1584.

142.69 Cipriani opera 2 volum.
Cyprian, *Saint*. [*Works*]. Continent: date indeterminable.
Language(s): Latin. Appraised at 20d in 1584.

142.70 Augustini De doctrina Christiana
Augustine, *Saint*. *De doctrina Christiana*. Continent: date indeterminable.
Language(s): Latin. Appraised at 6d in 1584.

142.71 [Augustini] De consensu evangelistarum
Augustine, *Saint*. *De consensu evangelistarum*. Continent: date indeterminable.
Language(s): Latin. Appraised at 6d in 1584.

142.72 [Augustini] De praedestinatione sanctorum
Augustine, *Saint*. *De praedestinatione sanctorum*. Britain or Continent: date indeterminable.
Language(s): Latin. Appraised at 3d in 1584.

142.73 Pasquil' [Pasquillus]
Unidentified. Place unknown: stationer unknown, date indeterminable.

STC/non-STC status unknown. There are several possibilities, including Caelius Secundus Curio's *Pasquillus ecstaticus* and the *Pasquillorum tomi duo* (which includes Curio's work) and even, though less likely, STC 17330, *The market or fayre of usurers. A newe pasquillus or dialogue. Language(s)*: Latin (probable). Appraised at 6d in 1584.

142.74 Aretius de caena
Benedictus Aretius. [*De coena Domini*]. Continent: 1578–1581.
Language(s): Latin. Appraised at 2d in 1584.

142.75 [Aretius] Examen Theologicum
Benedictus Aretius. *Examen theologicum*. Continent: 1570–1578.
Language(s): Latin. Appraised at 2d in 1584.

142.76 Danaei 9 volumina
Lambert Daneau. Unidentified. Place unknown: stationer unknown, date indeterminable.

STC/non-STC status unknown. Could be a mix of books, rather than a set, some published in England, some on the Continent. *Language(s)*: Latin (probable). Appraised at 6s 6d in 1584.

142.77 [Danaei] De elenchis haereticorum
Lambert Daneau. *Elenchi haereticorum*. Geneva: [probably] Eustathius Vignon, 1573–1582.

No stationer is given for the 1582 edition, but Vignon is the printer for all other editions. *Language(s)*: Latin. Appraised at 4d in 1584.

142.78 Heming [Hemingius], volum. 7
Niels Hemmingsen. Unidentified. Place unknown: stationer unknown, date indeterminable.

STC/non-STC status unknown. *Language(s)*: Latin (probable). Appraised at 5s in 1584.

142.79 Sadeel, vlum. 4
Antoine de La Roche de Chandieu (Antonius Sadeel). Unidentified. Place unknown: stationer unknown, date indeterminable.

STC/non-STC status unknown. *Language(s)*: Latin (probable). Appraised at 2s 6d in 1584.

142.80 Stephani responsio ad censuras Paris.
Robert Estienne, *the Elder. Ad censuras theologorum Parisiensium responsio*. Geneva: oliva Roberti Stephani, 1552.

Language(s): Latin. Appraised at 4d in 1584.

142.81 Melanchthon in Romanos

Philipp Melanchthon. [*Romans: commentary*]. Continent: date indeterminable. *Language(s)*: Latin. Appraised at 6d in 1584.

142.82 Foxi Historia Ecclesiastica

John Foxe, *the Martyrologist. Rerum in ecclesia gestarum commentarii*. Continent: 1554–1564.

Shaaber F183–186. *Language(s)*: Latin. Appraised at 3d in 1584.

142.83 [Foxi] De Christo grati. justificante

John Foxe, *the Martyrologist. De Christo gratis justificante*. London: T. Purfutius, imp. G. Byshop, 1583.

STC 11234. *Language(s)*: Latin. Appraised at 8d in 1584.

142.84 An Answear and Replie to the Jesuyte, 2 volumes

Unidentified. Britain (probable): date indeterminable.

Unidentifiable in the STC. Several books with similar titles were published at this time (including works by Haddon and Foxe, Charke, and Knox) but none in two volumes so far as can be ascertained. Probably, therefore, two separate books; see especially Charke's at STC 5005–5007. A single title, however, remains a possibility. *Language(s)*: English (probable). Appraised at 6d in 1584.

142.85 Praxis Curiae Romanae

Perhaps *Practica cancellariae apostolicae cum stylo et formis in romana curia usitatis*. (*Church of Rome*). Continent: date indeterminable.

Language(s): Latin. Appraised at 6d in 1584.

142.86 Dearing against Hardinge

Edward Dering. *A sparing restraint, of many lavishe untruthes, which M. doctor Harding dothe chalenge*. London: H. Denham for H. Toy, 1568.

STC 6725. *Language(s)*: English. Appraised at 12d in 1584.

142.87 Whitaker against Campion

William Whitaker. Perhaps *Ad rationes decem Edmundi Campiani jesuitae, responsio*. London: T. Vautrollierius, imp. T. Chardi, 1581.

STC 25358 *et seq*. Also likely is STC 25362, Whitaker's reply to Campian's response, *Responsionis ad decem illas rationes, quibus fretus E. Campianus, defensio* (1583). *Language(s)*: Latin. Appraised at 4d in 1584.

142.88 Jewell, his sermons

John Jewel, *Bishop. Certaine sermons preached before the Queenes majestie, and at Paules crosse*. Edited by John Garbrand. London: C. Barker, 1583.

STC 14596 *et seq*. Two editions in 1583. *Language(s)*: English. Appraised at 8d in 1584.

142.89 [Jewell] upon the Thessalonians
John Jewel, *Bishop*. [*Thessalonians: commentary and text*]. (*Bible–N.T.*). Edited by John Garbrand. London: (different houses), 1583–1584.
STC 14603 *et seq*. Ralph Newbery was involved in the printing of both editions. *Language(s)*: English. Appraised at 8d in 1584.

142.90 Piselius
Christoph Pezel. Unidentified. Continent: date indeterminable.
Whatever this item is, there is no reason from the rest of the list to expect it to be a German edition. *Language(s)*: Latin. Appraised at 8d in 1584.

142.91 Bertram de natura Christi in eucharistia
Ratramnus, *Monachus* (Bertramus, *Corbiensis*). *De corpore et sanguine Domini*. Continent: 1531–1579.
English translations at STC 20748.5 *et seq*. *Language(s)*: Latin. Appraised at 3d in 1584.

142.92 Refutatio ommispraesentiae
Unidentified. Continent (probable): date indeterminable.
Probably not an STC book. Presumably a Calvinist refutation of the Lutheran doctrine of the ubiquity of Christ's body. *Language(s)*: Latin. Appraised at 6d in 1584.

142.93 Menselius in Hossium
Hieronymus Menzel. *Responsio ad calumnias Osii*. Frankfurt am Main: Peter Brubach, 1558.
This response to Stanislaus Hozyusz, *Cardinal*, also appears as the lead item in a collection of Menzel's published in 1562. See Adams M1252 where he gives c.1556 as its date of publication. *Language(s)*: Latin. Appraised at 2d in 1584.

142.94 Herebrandi disputatio theologica
Jacob Heerbrand. *Disputatio theologica contra abominandum Missae pontificiae sacrificium*. Tübingen: apud Alexandrum Hockium, 1579.
Language(s): Latin. Appraised at 18d in 1584.

142.95 Luther upon the psalms of degrees
Martin Luther. *A commentarie upon the fiftene psalmes, called psalmi graduum*. (*Bible–O.T.*). Translated by Henry Bull, with an introduction by John Foxe, *the Martyrologist*. London: T. Vautrollier, 1577.
STC 16975 *et seq*. *Language(s)*: English. Appraised at 8d in 1584.

142.96 Conference
Unidentified. Britain (probable): date indeterminable.
Probably STC, but unidentifiable. Likely possibilities include STC 5005, Christianus Francke's *A conference or dialogue discovering the sect of jesuites*, in the trans-

lation by William Charke (1580); STC 15000, the second part of Andrew Kingsmill's *A most excellent and comfortable treatise* (1577); STC 20626, the often published John Rainolds's *The summe of the conference betwene J. Rainoldes and J. Hart*; and STC 25286, *The declaracyon of the procedynge of a conference, begon at Westminster the laste of Marche, 1559* (1560?). *Language(s)*: English (probable). Appraised at 4d in 1584.

142.97 Christian Righteousnes
Probably Jean de L'Espine. *An excellent treatise of christian righteousnes*. Translated by John Field, *Minister*. London: T. Vautrollier, 1577–1584.

STC 15512 *et seq. Language(s)*: English. Appraised at 1d in 1584.

142.98 Excellencie of a Christian
Pierre de La Place. *A treatise of the excellencie of a christian man*. Translated by Laurence Tomson. London: C. Barker, 1576–1577.

STC 15231 *et seq. Language(s)*: English. Appraised at 2d in 1584.

142.99 Travers on the 111 psalm
Robert Travers. *A learned and a very profitable exposition made upon the CXI. psalme*. London: Thomas Vautrollier, 1579–1583.

STC 24180 *et seq. Language(s)*: English. Appraised at 4d in 1584.

142.100 Admonition to the parliament
John Field and Thomas Wilcox. *An admonition to the parliament. (A view of popishe abuses yet remaining in the Englishe church)*. Hemel Hempstead (probable): [probably] John Stroud, 1572.

STC 10847 *et seq*. Two editions in 1572. *Language(s)*: English. Appraised at 1d in 1584.

142.101 Execution of Justice
William Cecil, *Baron Burghley*. *The execution of justice in England for maintenaunce of publique and christian peace, without any persecution for questions of religion*. London: [probably] C. Barker, 1583.

STC 4902 *et seq. Language(s)*: English. Appraised at 1d in 1584.

142.102 Rodericke Mors
Henry Brinkelow. *The complaynt of Roderyck Mors, for the redresse of certen wicked lawes*. Britain or Continent: 1542–1560 (probable).

STC 3760 *et seq*. Less likely is STC 3764, the same author's *The lamentacion of a christian, against the citie of London, made by R. Mors* (Bonn, 1542). *Language(s)*: English. Appraised at 1d in 1584.

142.103 Brulifer in Bonaventuram
Stephanus Brulefer. *Reportata in quattuor sancti Bonaventurae sententiarum libros Scoti subtilis secundi*. Basle: Jacobus [Wolff] de Pfortzheim, 1501–1507.

Language(s): Latin. Appraised at 6d in 1584.

142.104 Bonaventura de morte
Bonaventura, *Saint. Sermones de morte*. Paris: (different houses), 1494–c1510. *Language(s)*: Latin. Appraised at 1d in 1584.

142.105 Dialogus contra papistarum tyrannidem
Dialogus contra papistarum tyrannidem. London: W. S[eres], 1562.
STC 19175. Not appraised. Possibly by Walter Haddon according to the STC. *Language(s)*: Latin.

142.106 Catalogus
Unidentified. Place unknown: stationer unknown, date indeterminable.
STC/non-STC status unknown. Not appraised. Whether a catalogue of books or one of several polemical, theological works with titles beginning "Catalogus" cannot be determined. *Language(s)*: Unknown.

142.107 Luther, Praefac[io] in Romanos
Martin Luther. [*Romans: commentary*]. Translated by Justus Jonas. Continent: 1523–1524.
Published at Strassburg and Mainz. *Language(s)*: Latin. Appraised at 1d in 1584.

142.108 Calfield in Marshall
James Calfhill. *An aunswere to the Treatise of the crosse*. London: H. Denham for L. Harryson, 1565.
STC 4368. *Language(s)*: English. Appraised at 10d in 1584.

142.109 Confutatio doctorum Parris
Martin Luther. *Confutatio determinationis Doctorum Parrhisiensium, contra M.L., ex Ecclesiasticis doctoribus denuo recognita et locupleta*. Basle: Adam Petri, 1523.
Benzing no. 1485. *Language(s)*: Latin. Appraised at 4d in 1584.

142.110 Collection of the Churche
Unidentified. Britain (probable): date indeterminable.
Probably STC, but unidentifiable. Possibly related to *Collectanea de scriptoribus ecclesiasticis* (see BCI 2:233). See also STC 10394. *Language(s)*: English (probable). Appraised at 1d in 1584.

142.111 Theses Rainoldi
John Rainolds. *Sex theses de sacra scriptura, et ecclesia*. London: H. Middletonus, imp. G. Bishop, 1580.
STC 20624. *Language(s)*: Latin. Appraised at 3d in 1584.

142.112 Consensus Patrum
Perhaps Hermann Hamelmann. *Unanimis omnium patrum consensus de vera justificatione hominis coram Deo*. With a preface by Johann Wigand. Ursell: excudebat Nicolaus Henricus, 1562.

Language(s): Latin. Appraised at 18d in 1584.

142.113 Epistol Pauli italice
[*Bible–N.T.–Epistles–Paul*]. Continent: date indeterminable.
The *italice* in the manuscript entry may indicate italic font rather than Italian. *Language(s)*: Italian. Appraised at 5d in 1584.

142.114 Quintini sermones
Nicolaus, *de Aquaevilla. Sermones dominicales*. Edited by Jean Quentin. Paris: (different houses), date indeterminable.
The bibliographical sources disagree on the dates of the editions. *Language(s)*: Latin. Appraised at 2d in 1584.

142.115 Apologia Anglicana
John Jewel, *Bishop. Apologia ecclesiae anglicanae*. London: (different houses), 1562–1584.
STC 14581 *et seq. Language(s)*: Latin. Appraised at 8d in 1584.

142.116 A prayer booke
Probably [*Liturgies–Church of England–Book of Common Prayer*]. Britain: 1549–1584.
STC 16267 *et seq. Language(s)*: English (probable). Appraised at 3d in 1584.

142.117 Psalmes
[*Bible–O.T.–Psalms*]. Britain or Continent: date indeterminable.
STC 2370 *et seq*. A Latin version must be considered only a remote possibility given the context of this item. *Language(s)*: English. Appraised at 4d in 1584.

142.118 Calvine's catechisme
Jean Calvin. [*Catechism*]. Britain or Continent: 1556–1582.
STC 4380 *et seq*. As with the preceding, the manuscript entry and the context suggest an English version. *Language(s)*: English. Appraised at 6d in 1584.

142.119 Anchor of Fayth
Unidentified. Britain: date indeterminable.
Unidentifiable in the STC. STC 25763.5, published in 1628, is far too late for this book-list. Conceivably, however, an early manuscript from its author, William Willymat (Wilmot), was at Oxford during the 1580s. *Language(s)*: English. Appraised at 6d in 1584.

142.120 Deeringes lectures
Edward Dering. *XXVII. lectures, or readings, upon part of the epistle to the Hebrues*. Probably edited by John Field. London: (different houses), 1576–1583.
STC 6726 *et seq. Language(s)*: English. Appraised at 12d in 1584.

142.121   Willicii Logicke
Jodocus Willich. Probably *Erotemata dialectices*. Continent: 1540–1549. *Language(s)*: Latin. Appraised at 2d in 1584.

142.122   Psalmes in 16 in meeter
[*Bible–O.T.–Psalms*]. Translated and versified by Thomas Sternhold and John Hopkins. Britain or Continent: 1551–1583.
STC 2424 *et seq. Language(s)*: English. Appraised at 24d in 1584.

142.123   Plinie
Perhaps Pliny, *the Elder*. *Historia naturalis*. Continent: date indeterminable.
The *Epistolae* of Pliny, *the Younger*, must also be considered. The valuation is no help in determining which, since this may be a tattered copy of the *Historia naturalis*. *Language(s)*: Latin. Appraised at 12d in 1584.

142.124   Erasmi Chiliades
Desiderius Erasmus. *Adagia*. Continent: date indeterminable.
Language(s): Latin. Appraised at 3s 4d in 1584.

142.125   Wolphius upon Isocrates
Isocrates. [*Works*]. Edited by Hieronymus Wolfius. Continent: date indeterminable.
Language(s): Greek (perhaps) Latin. Appraised at 6s in 1584.

142.126   Senecae Moralia
Lucius Annaeus Seneca. [*Selected Works*]. Continent (probable): date indeterminable.
Probably not an STC book, but see STC 17498 *et seq*. Perhaps part of a two-volume edition with the tragedies in one and the works of moral philosophy in another, the second being represented here, or, alternatively, a separately issued volume; see Brunet (5:275) and Goff S368-372. The spurious *Seneca moralissmus philosophus* ... at STC 17498 *et seq*. might be intended, and the *Epistolae morales* is also possible. *Language(s)*: Latin. Appraised at 6d in 1584.

142.127   Historia Scotica
Perhaps Hector Boethius (Boece). *Scotorum historiae*. Continent: 1527–1575.
Language(s): Latin. Appraised at 4s in 1584.

142.128   Hebrew Grammer
Unidentified. Continent: date indeterminable.
The possibilities are too numerous for an attempt at identification to be worthwhile. John Udall's English translation of Martinius's grammar was not published until 1593 (and appears as STC 17523 though printed in Leyden). No Hebrew

grammar was printed in England by this date, though Ralph Baynes's Hebrew grammar was published on the Continent in 1550. *Language(s)*: Hebrew Latin (probable). Appraised at 2s in 1584.

142.129 Greeke lexicon
Unidentified. Continent: date indeterminable.
Language(s): Greek Latin (probable). Appraised at 3s 6d in 1584.

142.130 Synonima Greca
Probably Martin Ruland, *the Elder. Synonyma.* Augsburg: (different houses), 1563–1582.
Language(s): Greek Latin. Appraised at 12d in 1584.

142.131 Plautus
Titus Maccius Plautus. *Comoediae.* Continent: date indeterminable.
Language(s): Latin. Appraised at 12d in 1584.

142.132 Senecae Traged
Lucius Annaeus Seneca. *Tragoediae.* Continent: date indeterminable.
Language(s): Latin. Appraised at 8d in 1584.

142.133 Sleidani De 4 Imperiis
Joannes Philippson, *Sleidanus. De quatuor summis imperiis.* Britain or Continent: date indeterminable.
STC 19847 and non-STC. *Language(s)*: Latin. Appraised at 5d in 1584.

142.134 Syntaxis Linguae Grecae
Unidentified. Continent: date indeterminable.
Possibilities include works by Joannes Posselius and by Joannes Varennius, the titles of which match the manuscript entry, an entry that could also be simply descriptive. *Language(s)*: Greek Latin. Appraised at 3d in 1584.

142.135 Similitudines
Unidentified. Continent: date indeterminable.
A number of works might be represented by such a manuscript entry, including titles by Alardus, *of Amsterdam*, by Johann Cogler, and by Levinus Lemnius. *Language(s)*: Latin.

142.136 Phrigius
Unidentified. Continent: date indeterminable.
Perhaps Dares, *the Phrygian* or Joannes Thomas Freigius, or even Reiner Gemma, *Frisius* (see BCI 2:377, a 1598/99 entry). *Language(s)*: Unknown. Appraised at 10d in 1584.

142.137 Velcurio
Joannes Velcurio. Unidentified. Place unknown: stationer unknown, date indeterminable.
STC/non-STC status unknown. *Language(s)*: Latin. Appraised at 10d in 1584.

142.138 Curaeus
Joachim Cureus. Unidentified. Continent: date indeterminable.
Language(s): Latin (probable). Appraised at 3d in 1584.

142.139:1 Valerius bis
Unidentified. Place unknown: stationer unknown, date indeterminable.
STC/non-STC status unknown. Cornelius Valerius, Valerius Maximus, and Gaius Valerius Flaccus are likely possibilities. *Language(s)*: Latin (probable). Appraised with another at 7d in 1584.

142.139:2 [See 142.139:1]
Unidentified. Place unknown: stationer unknown, date indeterminable.
STC/non-STC status unknown. Cornelius Valerius, Valerius Maximus, and Gaius Valerius Flaccus are likely possibilities. *Language(s)*: Latin (probable). Appraised with another at 7d in 1584.

142.140 Cosmographia
Unidentified. Continent (probable): date indeterminable.
Almost certainly not an STC book. Possibilities include works by Peter Apian, Joannes Honterus, and Sebastian Muenster. *Language(s)*: Latin. Appraised at 2d in 1584.

142.141 Metamorphoses
Probably Publius Ovidius Naso. *Metamorphoses*. Britain or Continent: date indeterminable.
STC 18951 *et seq.* and non-STC. *The golden ass* of Lucius Apuleius is also possible, but less likely. *Language(s)*: Latin. Appraised at 8d in 1584.

142.142 Institutions
Unidentified. Place unknown: stationer unknown, date indeterminable.
STC/non-STC status unknown. Possibly the *Institutiones* of the *Corpus juris civilis*; but there are many other possibilities, including even Calvin. *Language(s)*: Unknown. Appraised at 12d in 1584.

142.143 Tusculan Questions
Marcus Tullius Cicero. *Quaestiones Tusculanae*. Britain or Continent: date indeterminable.
STC 5314.5 *et seq.* and non-STC. *Language(s)*: Latin. Appraised at 1d in 1584.

142.144 Common Lawe
Unidentified. Britain: date indeterminable.
Unidentifiable in the STC. *Language(s)*: English. Appraised at 14d in 1584.

142.145 Plutarchi Simili [Similia]
Plutarch. Probably *Vitae parallelae*. Continent: date indeterminable.
Language(s): Latin. Appraised at 5d in 1584.

142.146 Praelia Anglorum
Christopher Ockland. *Anglorum praelia, ab anno domini 1327 usque ad annum 1558*. London: (different houses), 1580–1582.
STC 18772 *et seq*. Henry Bynneman was involved in some manner in all five editions issued during this two-year period. *Language(s)*: Latin. Appraised at 6d in 1584.

142.147 De furoribus gallicis
François Hotman. *De furoribus Gallicis*. Britain or Continent: 1573.
STC 13844 *et seq*. Imprinted Edinburgh, but actually Basle and London. *Language(s)*: Latin. Appraised at 3d in 1584.

142.148 Testificatio Lodovici
Louis I, *Prince de Condé. Literae . . . Testificatio causarum quae eum arma sumere coegerunt* [and other works]. Edited by Henri Estienne. Geneva (probable): Henricus Stephanus (probable), c.1569.
Whether the entire collection of letters or just a separated *Testificatio* cannot be determined. *Language(s)*: Latin. Appraised at 2d in 1584.

142.149 Epistolae Plinii
Pliny, *the Younger*. *Epistolae*. Continent: date indeterminable.
Language(s): Latin. Appraised at 4d in 1584.

142.150 Hebrew, 5 volumes
Unidentified. Continent: date indeterminable.
Language(s): Hebrew. Appraised at 3s in 1584.

142.151 Disciplina ecclesiastica
Walter Travers. *Ecclesiastica disciplina*. Heidelberg: Michael Schirat, 1574.
Falsely imprinted as Rupellae: excudebat Adamus de Monte. *Language(s)*: Latin. Appraised at 6d in 1584.

142.152 Christian Perigrinations
Unidentified. Britain (probable): stationer unknown, date indeterminable.
Probably STC, but unidentifiable. This item probably represents a work with a metaphorical title relating to Christian life, but a pilgrims' guide is a possibility, though very remote. *Language(s)*: English (probable). Appraised at 2d in 1584.

142.153 De jure magistratuum
Théodore de Bèze. *De jure magistratuum in subditos*. Lyon: apud Joannem Mareschallum, 1576.
Published anonymously. Gardy no. 303. *Language(s)*: Latin. Appraised at 2d in 1584.

142.154 Knoxe de praedestinatione
John Knox. *An answer to a great nomber of blasphemous cavillations written by an anabaptist and adversarie to Gods eternal predestination*. Geneva: J. Crespin, 1560.
STC 15060. *Language(s)*: English. Appraised at 2d in 1584.

142.155 Hessus de tuenda valitudine
Helius Eobanus, *Hessus*. [*De tuenda bona valetudine*]. Continent: date indeterminable.
Language(s): Latin. Appraised at 3d in 1584.

142.156 The Way of Lief
Niels Hemmingsen. *The way of lyfe*. London: [W. How for] R. Jones, 1578 (probable).
STC 13067 *et seq*. *Language(s)*: English. Appraised at 4d in 1584.

142.157:1–5 Five odd bookes
Unidentified. Places unknown: stationers unknown, dates indeterminable.
STC/non-STC status unknown. Possibly blank books or manuscripts. *Language(s)*: Unknown. Appraised at 5d in 1584.

142.158 Biblia latine, 5 volum [volumina]
The Bible. Britain or Continent: date indeterminable.
STC 2056 *et seq*. and non-STC. *Language(s)*: Latin. Appraised at 5s in 1584.

Anthony Tye. Scholar (M.A.): Probate Inventory. 1584

LEE PIEPHO

Anthony Tye (Tie), a fellow of Oriel College, died intestate in May of 1584 (Richards and Salter 1926, 180) and was buried in St. Mary's, Oxford (*Alumni Oxonienses*, 4:1526). Originally from the diocese of Exeter (Richards and Salter 1926, 163), Tye was admitted to Corpus Christi College in 1561 (*Alumni Oxonienses*, 4:1526). He supplicated for the Bachelor of Arts degree in April 1570 (*Alumni Oxonienses*, 4:1526) and on 13 April 1571 was admitted as a probationary fellow to Oriel (Richards and Salter 1926, 163). There was a fellowship for Devon at the college (Salter and Lobel 1954, 119), and in October 1573 he was licensed for the Master of Arts degree (*Alumni Oxonienses*, 4:1526). Several times during the early 1580s he served as dean at the college (Richards and Salter 1926, 177, 179).

The presence in Tye's book-list of Duns Scotus's *Quaestiones* on Aristotle's *Metaphysics* (143.15) indicates the Scholastic heritage that lingered on at Oxford as at Cambridge (BCI, 1:xxxii–xxiii). Taken as a whole, however, his collection shows the effect of the "floodtide of humanism" that swept through Oxford during the sixteenth century (McConica, 703). In particular it buttresses McConica's conclusion (712) for an increased interest in Greek at the University. Early Christian writers such as Apollinarius are included (143.39), but Tye's collection is striking for its range of ancient Greek authors. It offers, for example, one of the rare recorded instances of ownership of an edition of Maximus, *of Tyre* (143.53), a work that appears in only two other personal libraries in the universities by the 1580s, in Cambridge in 1589 (BCI, 2:535) and in Oxford in 1577 (PLRE 127.137). There were other, later works in Greek, including the *Transformationum congeries* of Antonius, *Liberalis* (143.41; an important source for the study of Ovid's *Metamorphoses*), published with several other works (by Apollonius, *Dyscolus* and Antigonus, *of Carystus*, among other writers), some or all of which may have been separated from the single title listed by the compiler at 4*d*.

Tye's book-list dramatically shows how Greek was being used to deepen the study of subjects that earlier in the century had been learned largely by means of Latin texts. In rhetoric, for instance, his library contained Cicero's *Opera* (143.14), but he went well beyond Roman oratory and owned a copy of the complete works of Demosthenes (143.60). And to his copy of Schorus's *Phrases* (143.33), Tye added not only Zenobius's *Compendium veterum proverbiorum* (143.79; found in earlier inventories at Cambridge [BCI, 2:811]), but also Michael Neander's Graeco-Latin collection of Isocratean phrases (143.30) and Henri Estienne's compilation of maxims and parodies of ancient Greek writers (143.74).

The same pervasive presence of Greek texts related to rhetoric marks Tye's studies in logic and (to the extent that he pursued them) theology and the early church fathers. The bias of his arts studies helps to explain the paucity of works by the Latin fathers. Nonetheless, besides the Bible, Tye read Theophylact in Latin and Eusebius, Justin, *Martyr*, and Apollinarius, all only in Greek. More interesting is his ownership of Ammonius's commentary on Aristotle's *Categories* (143.61). McConica has remarked on a revival of Aristotelianism at Oxford in the last quarter of the sixteenth century, a revival to which Ammonius's commentary contributed. More than any other book in Tye's collection, the presence of Ammonius reminds us of a kind of eclectic Aristotelianism that, shaped by ancient and humanist commentaries, McConica finds to have been basic to the intellectual culture of Elizabethan Oxford (McConica, 707-8).

Tye's Hebrew texts were limited exclusively to the Bible. He owned one of the relatively few editions of Genesis printed in Hebrew (143.26) during the sixteenth century as well as an edition of the Hebrew psalms (143.75). At the same time, his larger philological interests are indicated by his ownership of two Hebrew grammars: Sebastian Muenster's popular text (143.38) as well as the grammar of Campensis (143.77).

Tye's book-list reflects an interest in astronomy as well as astrology. He owned an edition of Girolamo Cardano's commentary on Ptolemy (143.89) which may have contained his notorious horoscope of Jesus Christ (Shumaker 1982, 53–90, esp. 68–69). Moreover, Tye's reading in the subject was sophisticated and wide-ranging. Reflecting the overlapping claims of astronomy and astrology, his collection contained, for instance, Cardano's *De restitutione* (143.95) in an edition that conspicuously mixes the two subjects (Shumaker 1972, 37), and he owned a copy of Simler's book on astronomy (143.54), a very rare book today that had only one edition during Tye's lifetime.

Finally, while there is no record that he formally studied medicine at Oxford, Tye's library contained a large and expensive collection of medical books. Copies of Hippocrates, Galen, and Celsus perhaps reflect no more than a humanist's interest in their contributions to Graeco-Roman culture, but a few of the items, such as two treatises on urines (143.91 and 143.100), are more specialized, and Tye may have been planning to seek the university's licence in medicine.

Oxford University Archives, Bodleian Library: Hyp.B.19.

§

Richards, G.C. and H. E. Salter, eds. 1926. *The Dean's Register of Oriel, 1446–1661.* Oxford: The Oxford Historical Society.

Salter, H.E. and Lobel, Mary D., eds. 1954. *The Victoria History of the County of Oxford.* Volume 3. Oxford: Oxford Univ. Press.

Shumaker, Wayne. 1972. *The Occult Sciences in the Renaissance.* Berkeley/Los Angeles: Univ. of California Press.

Shumaker, Wayne. 1982. *Renaissance Curiosa.* Binghamton, NY: Medieval and Renaissance Texts and Studies.

§

143.1	Thesaurus Step*** [Stephani] **** 3us [tribus] Volum: [Voluminibus]
143.2	Cooperi dictionarium
143.3	Erasmus in nov** [novum] **stamentum [testamentum]
143.4	Plutarchi moral: gra* [graecae]
143.5	Plutarchi vitae gra:
143.6	Homeri Illias cum interpr: grae:
143.7	Budeus de Asse
143.8:1	Theophilactus in evangel: et acta Apost:
143.8:2	[See 143.8:1]
143.9	Ducherius in tres dec: [decades] livii
143.10	Lucanus cum Comment:
143.11	Orationes Oratorum Veterum grae:
143.12	Justinus martyr grae:
143.13	Thucitides grae:
143.14	Opera Ciceronis 2bus volum:
143.15	Scotus in metaphi: eiusdem castiga:
143.16	Appianus Sophista
143.17	Lavinius in Metamorph: Ovidii
143.18	Virgilius cum coment:
143.19	Helliodorus
143.20	Johan: Ruffensis adversus Eliodocosomp: [Oecolampadium]
143.21	Scalliger poeta et historicus
143.22	Alexander Brassicanus
143.23	Chalimici himni
143.24	Nonnius poeta
143.25	Foxius in Christo crucifixo
143.26	Genesis hebra:
143.27	Biblion

143.28	Palmirius in Acad: quaestiones
143.29	Arist: de repub: [republica]
143.30	Isocrates grae: phrasiol:
143.31	Euripides poeta lat:
143.32	Martynus Baldeus in polytic: Arist:
143.33	Scori phrases
143.34	Homeri Ilias Lat:
143.35	Crucii Grammat: grae: 2bus volum:
143.36	AEsopus grae: et Latin:
143.37	Strozius poeta latin:
143.38	Munsteri gram: haebr:
143.39	Apolinarius in psalmos grae:
143.40	Apollogi Juelli
143.41	Antonin: in Metamorph: grae
143.42	Philippus Decius de reg* [regulis] juris
143.43	Euripedes Resus
143.44	Homeri Ilias grae:
143.45	Sturmius ad Jacobum Cammerarium
143.46	Ciceronis Epistolae
143.47	Arist: Ethica
143.48	Arist: de Anima
143.49	Theophocles grae:
143.50	Valerius de re dialectica
143.51	Jodocus Radius
143.52	Luciani opera grae:
143.53	Maximus Tyrius ph: [philosophus] plat: [platonicus]
143.54	Simlerus de princ: Astro:
143.55	Clenardi gram:
143.56	Apthonius
143.57	Eschili tragoed: grae:
143.58	AEneus Silvius
143.59	Sansonus
143.60	Orationes Demosth: grae: 2bus vol:
143.61	Ammonius in Praed: grae:
143.62	Epigram: Veterum poet:
143.63	The franch scholemaster
143.64	Sebastiani Quaestura
143.65	Justiniani lib: 4°
143.66	Sophocles grae:
143.67	Alcimus de Origine mundi
143.68	Pandecta legis Evangel: bis
143.69	[See 143.68]
143.70	Themistius grae:
143.71	Theaparipha in englishe
143.72	liber psalmorum lat:

143.73   Claudiani poetae opera
143.74   Henrici Stephani parad* morales
143.75   psalmi haebr:
143.76   Epistolae Cipri:
143.77   Campensis gram: haeb:
143.78   Hesiodus grae:
143.79   Zenobii Compend***
143.80   Euzebius grae:
143.81   A booke of Pre****es in englishe
143.82   A note Booke of *hisick [phisick] unbound
143.83:1–22   xxii litle volumes in greke
143.84:1:1–14   xiiii Paper bookes in written hand grae: et lat: and A eneologie written
143.84:2   [See 143.83:1:1–14]
143.85:A   Sceggius in physica Arist:
143.85:B   [See 143.85:A]
143.86   Epitome Galeni
143.87   Jacobi Wickeri Syntaxis
143.88   Johan: Fernel de medicina
143.89   Cardanus de Astrorum judiciis
143.90   Cornelius Celsus de re medica
143.91   The judiciall of urines in englishe
143.92   Petri Alcionii de Exilio oratio
143.93   Quintus Serenus de re medica
143.94   Heronimi Thriveri in hip: Aphori:
143.95   Cardanus de restitutione temp:
143.96   Nicolaus medicus
143.97   Hippo: de flatibus
143.98   Otho Brunfelsius de remediis morborum
143.99   Alexander de Secretis
143.100   Actuarius de Urinis
143.101   Fernelius de roe [ratione] medendi
143.102   Aretius medicus
143.103   Ruffus de medicamentis purgantibus
143.104   Plinius Secundus de nat: Hist:
143.105   Simplicius in 8° physic:
143.106   Toleti in physica

§

143.1   Thesaurus Step*** [Stephani] **** 3us [tribus] Volum: [Voluminibus]
Probably Henri Estienne. *Thesaurus graecae linguae.* Geneva: excudebat Henricus Stephanus, 1572–c.1580.
Tye's collection contains so many Greek texts that one would expect this to be

an edition of Estienne's great Greek dictionary. The entry could, however, refer to the *Thesaurus linguae latinae* of Robert Estienne, *the Elder*. Printed in four volumes, the Greek dictionary was listed in a 1589 inventory in three volumes valued at 33s 4d (see BCI 2:719). There, and here, it is either a broken or rebound set. The lacuna in the entry has been appropriately filled in on this assumption. *Language(s)*: Greek Latin. Appraised at 24s in 1584.

143.2   Cooperi dictionarium

Thomas Cooper, *Bishop. Thesaurus linguae Romanae et Britannicae*. London: (different houses), 1565–1578.

STC 5686 *et seq*. A 1584 edition was entered in the *Stationers Register* on 30 December of that year, too late to appear in this inventory. *Language(s)*: English Latin. Appraised at 15s in 1584.

143.3   Erasmus in nov** [novum] **stamentum [testamentum]

Desiderius Erasmus. [*New Testament: commentary*]. Continent: date indeterminable.

Language(s): Latin. Appraised at 2s in 1584.

143.4   Plutarchi moral: gra* [graecae]

(Plutarch). *Moralia*. Continent: date indeterminable.

Language(s): Greek. Appraised at 6s in 1584.

143.5   Plutarchi vitae gra:

Plutarch. *Vitae parallelae*. Continent: date indeterminable.

The appraisal suggests that this is probably a complete edition. *Language(s)*: Greek. Appraised at 6s in 1584.

143.6   Homeri Illias cum interpr: grae:

Homer. *Iliad*. Continent: date indeterminable.

Language(s): Greek Latin. Appraised at 3s in 1584.

143.7   Budeus de Asse

Gulielmus Budaeus. *De asse et partibus eius*. Continent: date indeterminable.

Language(s): Latin. Appraised at 18d in 1584.

143.8:1   Theophilactus in evangel: et acta Apost:

Theophylact, *Archbishop of Achrida*. [*Gospels: commentary and text*]. (*Bible–N.T.*). Continent: date indeterminable.

There is no record of a combined edition of Theophylact's commentaries on the Gospels and Acts having been issued. Whether the two are bound together here or simply grouped by the compiler cannot be determined. *Language(s)*: Latin. Appraised with one other at 6s in 1584.

143.8:2 [See 143.8:1]

Theophylact, *Archbishop of Achrida*. [*Acts: commentary and text*]. (*Bible–N.T.*). Continent: date indeterminable.

See the annotations to the preceding (143.8:1). *Language(s)*: Latin. Appraised with one other at 6s in 1584.

143.9 Ducherius in tres dec: [decades] livii

Titus Livius. [*Historiae Romanae decades–Selected works*]. Continent (probable): date indeterminable.

Almost certainly not an STC book. The entry appears to refer to a commentary on or an edition of Livy's history by Gilbertus Ducherius, but although Ducherius served as an editor of Pliny, *the Elder* and Caesar's *Commentaries* nowhere is he mentioned as an editor of Livy (see CTC 2:336–340 and 3:445–449). Conceivably this is an untraced edition or, perhaps, the compiler conflated two items. *Language(s)*: Latin. Appraised at 16d in 1584.

143.10 Lucanus cum Comment:

Marcus Annaeus Lucanus. *Pharsalia*. Continent: date indeterminable. *Language(s)*: Latin. Appraised at 12d in 1584.

143.11 Orationes Oratorum Veterum grae:

Multiple. *Oratorum veterum orationes*. Edited by Henri Estienne, with Latin translations by various authors. Geneva: excud. Henricus Stephanus, 1575.

Besides Estienne, the Latin translations are by Hieronymus Wolf, Dionysius Lambinus, and Claude Groulart, *Baron de Monville*. *Language(s)*: Greek Latin. Appraised at 6s 8d in 1584.

143.12 Justinus martyr grae:

Justinus, *Martyr*. [*Works*]. Edited by Robert Estienne, *the Elder*. Paris: ex officina Roberti Stephani, 1551.

Language(s): Greek. Appraised at 3s 4d in 1584.

143.13 Thucitides grae:

Thucydides. *De bello peloponnesiaco*. Continent: date indeterminable. *Language(s)*: Greek. Appraised at 5s in 1584.

143.14 Opera Ciceronis 2bus volum:

Marcus Tullius Cicero. [*Works*]. Continent: date indeterminable. *Language(s)*: Latin. Appraised at 9s in 1584.

143.15 Scotus in metaphi: eiusdem castiga:

John Duns, *Scotus*. [*Aristotle–Metaphysica: commentary*]. Edited by Maurice O'Fihely (Mauritius de Portu Hibernicus). Venice: Bonetus Locatellus for Octavianus Scotus, 1497–1501.

These two editions by O'Fihely (Hibernicus) carried his annotations (*Castigationes*) as well. The 1501 edition was published by the Heirs of Octavianus Scotus. *Language(s)*: Latin. Appraised at 2s in 1584.

143.16 Appianus Sophista
Appian, *of Alexandria*. [*Historia Romana*]. Continent: date indeterminable. *Language(s)*: Latin (probable) Greek (perhaps). Appraised at 4d in 1584.

143.17 Lavinius in Metamorph: Ovidii
Publius Ovidius Naso. *Metamorphoses*. Edited by Petrus Lavinius. Continent: date indeterminable.
Appraised at 10d in 1584.

143.18 Virgilius cum coment:
Publius Virgilius Maro. [*Works*]. Britain or Continent: date indeterminable. STC 24788 *et seq.* and non-STC. At this valuation, more likely a Continental folio edition than one of the modest octavo or sextodecimo editions printed in England. *Language(s)*: Latin. Appraised at 6s 8d in 1584.

143.19 Helliodorus
Heliodorus. *Historia Aethiopica*. Continent: date indeterminable. *Language(s)*: Latin Greek (perhaps). Appraised at 12d in 1584.

143.20 Johan: Ruffensis adversus Eliodocosomp: [Oecolampadium]
John Fisher, *Saint and Cardinal*. *De veritate corporis et sanguinis Christi in eucharistia*. Cologne: (different houses), 1527.
The manuscript entry *Eliodecosomp* is doubtless a misreading for or a mishearing of "Oecolampadius," the German reformer against whom Fisher, *Archbishop of Rochester*, wrote on the eucharist. The long title continues "... adversus Johannem Oecolampadium." Shaaber F71–73 and Klaiber no. 1189. *Language(s)*: Latin. Appraised at 16d in 1584.

143.21 Scalliger poeta et historicus
Julius Caesar Scaliger. *Poetices libri septem*. Lyon: (different houses), 1561–1581. *Language(s)*: Latin. Appraised at 18d in 1584.

143.22 Alexander Brassicanus
Joannes Alexandrus Brassicanus. Unidentified. Continent: date indeterminable.
Brassicanus compiled a collection of proverbs and wrote a commentary on a declamation by Poliziano. He was also an editor as well as a poet. *Language(s)*: Latin. Appraised at 10d in 1584.

143.23 Chalimici himni
Callimachus. [*Hymni*]. Continent: date indeterminable. *Language(s)*: Latin (probable) Greek (perhaps). Appraised at 6d in 1584.

143.24 Nonnius poeta
Nonnus, *Panopolitanus*. Unidentified. Continent: date indeterminable.
Either his *Dionysiaca* or his verse paraphrase of St. John's Gospel. *Language(s)*: Greek (probable) Latin (perhaps). Appraised at 8d in 1584.

143.25 Foxius in Christo crucifixo
John Foxe, *the Martyrologist. De Christo crucifixo concio*. Translated into Latin by Foxe. Britain: apud J. Dayum, 1575.
STC 11247. This is the Latin version of Foxe's *Sermon of Christ crucified*, printed first in English in 1570 (STC 11242). DNB (7:585) states that an edition was published at Frankfurt in 1575; that edition is not found in Shaaber or elsewhere. *Language(s)*: Latin. Appraised at 6d in 1584.

143.26 Genesis hebra:
[*Bible–O.T.–Genesis*]. Continent: date indeterminable.
Language(s): Hebrew. Appraised at 8d in 1584.

143.27 Biblion
The Bible. Continent: date indeterminable.
Tye's copy may have contained only the New Testament, particularly at this low valuation, which had several editions in Greek before 1584 (see DM, nos. 4597–4645 passim). This manuscript entry was inserted in a different hand. *Language(s)*: Greek (probable). Appraised at 4d in 1584.

143.28 Palmirius in Acad: quaestiones
Aulus Antonius Palmyraenus. *In academicas quaestiones Ciceronis scholion*. Basle: (stationer unknown), 1544.
Language(s): Latin. Appraised at 12d in 1584.

143.29 Arist: de repub: [republica]
Aristotle. *Politica*. Continent: date indeterminable.
Language(s): Latin (probable) Greek (perhaps). Appraised at 6d in 1584.

143.30 Isocrates grae: phrasiol:
Michael Neander, *of Sorau*, editor. [*Phraseologia Isocratis graecolatina*]. Phrases from Isocrates selected and translated by Neander. Basle: ex officina Oporiniana, 1558 (probable).
Language(s): Greek Latin. Appraised at 12d in 1584.

143.31 Euripides poeta lat:
Euripides. [*Works*]. Continent: date indeterminable.
Language(s): Latin. Appraised at 12d in 1584.

143.32 Martynus Baldeus in polytic: Arist:
Unidentified. [*Aristotle–Politica: commentary*]. Continent (probable): date indeterminable.
Almost certainly not an STC book. No "Martynus Baldeus" appears in any of the Aristotle bibliographies. Martin Borrhaus wrote on the *Politica*; see Adams B2514. *Language(s)*: Latin (probable). Appraised at 6d in 1584.

143.33 Scori phrases
Antonius Schorus. *Phrases linguae latinae*. Continent: date indeterminable.
Language(s): Latin. Appraised at 16d in 1584.

143.34 Homeri Ilias Lat:
Homer. *Iliad*. Continent: date indeterminable.
Language(s): Latin. Appraised at 12d in 1584.

143.35 Crucii Grammat: grae: 2bus volum:
Martin Crusius. *Grammatica graeca, cum latina congruens*. Continent: date indeterminable.
Language(s): Greek Latin. Appraised at 2s in 1584.

143.36 AEsopus grae: et Latin:
Aesop. *Fabulae*. Continent: date indeterminable.
Language(s): Greek Latin. Appraised at 6d in 1584.

143.37 Strozius poeta latin:
Tito Vespasiano Strozzi and Ercole Strozzi. *Strozzi poetae pater et filius*. Continent: date indeterminable.
Renaissance editions of Strozzi's poetry also include poems by his son Ercole.
Language(s): Latin. Appraised at 6d in 1584.

143.38 Munsteri gram: haebr:
Sebastian Muenster. [*Grammatica hebraica*]. Continent: date indeterminable.
Language(s): Hebrew Latin. Appraised at 4d in 1584.

143.39 Apolinarius in psalmos grae:
Apollinarius, *Bishop*. [*Psalms: commentary and text*]. (*Bible–O.T.*). Paris: (different houses), 1552–1580.
Language(s): Greek Latin (perhaps). Appraised at 6d in 1584.

143.40 Apollogi Juelli
John Jewel, *Bishop*. *Apologia ecclesiae anglicanae*. London: (different houses), 1562–1584.
STC 14581 *et seq*. *Language(s)*: Latin. Appraised at 12d in 1584.

143.41 Antonin: in Metamorph: grae
Antoninus, *Liberalis. Transformationum congeries* [and other works]. Translated and edited by Gulielmus Xylander. Basle: per Thomam Guarinum, 1568.

A collection, if whole, that also includes *De mirabilibus et longaevis libellus* and the *Olympiades* of Phlegon, *of Tralles*, the *Historiae mirabiles* of Apollonius, *Dyscolus*, the *Mirabilium narrationum congeries* of Antigonus, *of Carystus*, and the *Meditationes* of Marcus Aurelius Antoninus. *Language(s)*: Greek Latin. Appraised at 4d in 1584.

143.42 Philippus Decius de reg* [regulis] juris
Felippo Decio. *De regulis juris*. Continent: date indeterminable. *Language(s)*: Latin. Appraised at 12d in 1584.

143.43 Euripedes Resus
Euripides (attributed). *Rhesus*. Continent: date indeterminable.

Before Tye's death there is no separate publication of *Rhesus* recorded in the basic sources. Copies appear at PLRE 67.122 (1558) and PLRE 121.19 (1577), and there are four appearances in BCI, all of which, along with this entry, suggest one or more lost editions of the play. *Language(s)*: Latin (probable) Greek (perhaps). Appraised at 10d in 1584.

143.44 Homeri Ilias grae:
Homer. *Iliad*. Continent: date indeterminable. *Language(s)*: Greek. Appraised at 12d in 1584.

143.45 Sturmius ad Jacobum Cammerarium
Joannes Sturmius. *Luctus ad Joachimum Camerarium* [and other works]. Strassburg: in aedibus W. Rihelius, 1542.

Language(s): Latin. Appraised at 3d in 1584.

143.46 Ciceronis Epistolae
Marcus Tullius Cicero. [*Selected works–Epistolae*]. Continent: date indeterminable.

Conceivably the popular *Epistolae ad familiares*, and if so, then an STC edition would be possible. *Language(s)*: Latin. Appraised at 10d in 1584.

143.47 Arist: Ethica
Aristotle. *Ethica*. Britain or Continent: date indeterminable.

STC 752 *et seq*. and non-STC. *Language(s)*: Latin (probable) Greek (perhaps). Appraised at 6d in 1584.

143.48 Arist: de Anima
Aristotle. *De anima*. Continent: date indeterminable. *Language(s)*: Latin (probable) Greek (perhaps). Appraised at 6d in 1584.

143.49 Theophocles grae:
Unidentified. Continent (probable): date indeterminable.

Probably not an STC book. No "Theophocles" can be found in the basic sources. Perhaps a slip for Theophrastus, or even Theophylactus. Both writers were issued in Greek. Also, conceivably a mishearing of Sophocles, whose tragedies, in Greek, appear elsewhere in the collection. *Language(s)*: Greek. Appraised at 3d in 1584.

143.50 Valerius de re dialectica
Cornelius Valerius. *Tabulae totius dialectices*. Continent: date indeterminable. *Language(s)*: Latin. Appraised at 4d in 1584.

143.51 Jodocus Radius
Perhaps Jodocus Badius, *Ascensius*. Unidentified. Continent: date indeterminable.

Badius was an editor and an author as well as a printer. *Language(s)*: Latin. Appraised at 4d in 1584.

143.52 Luciani opera grae:
Lucian, *of Samosata*. [*Works*]. Continent: date indeterminable. *Language(s)*: Greek. Appraised at 14d in 1584.

143.53 Maximus Tyrius ph: [philosophus] plat: [platonicus]
Maximus, *of Tyre*. *Sermones*. Continent. date indeterminable. *Language(s)*: Latin (probable) Greek (perhaps). Appraised at 10d in 1584.

143.54 Simlerus de princ: Astro:
Josias Simler. *De principiis astronomiae libri duo*. Zürich: apud Froschouerum juniorem, 1559.
Language(s): Latin. Appraised at 2d in 1584.

143.55 Clenardi gram:
Nicolaus Clenardus. Probably [*Institutiones linguae graecae*]. Britain or Continent: date indeterminable.

STC 5400.5 and non-STC. In light of the Hebrew texts in Tye's collection, Clenard's *Tabula in grammaticen hebraeam* must be considered a possibility. *Language(s)*: Greek Latin. Appraised at 4d in 1584.

143.56 Apthonius
Aphthonius, *Sophista*. *Progymnasmata*. Britain or Continent: date indeterminable. STC 699 *et seq*. and non-STC. *Language(s)*: Latin. Appraised at 4d in 1584.

143.57 Eschili tragoed: grae:
Aeschylus. [*Works*]. Continent: date indeterminable.
Language(s): Greek. Appraised at 14d in 1584.

143.58 AEneus Silvius
Pius II, *Pope* (Aeneas Silvius, *Piccolomini*). Unidentified. Place unknown: stationer unknown, date indeterminable.
STC/non-STC status unknown. The appraisal suggests a modest edition, not one of the folio volumes of Piccolomini's collected works. *Language(s)*: Latin (probable). Appraised at 2d in 1584.

143.59 Sansonus
Perhaps Franciscus Sanson, *de Senis*. *Quaestiones super Physicam Aristotelis*. Continent: c.1486–1496.
Given the other commentaries on Aristotle's *Physica* in Tye's collection, this rare work is a possibility. At nearly a century old, a copy of Sanson's work, published only in folio, would probably be tattered, accounting for the low valuation. *Language(s)*: Latin. Appraised at 12d in 1584.

143.60 Orationes Demosth: grae: 2bus vol:
Demosthenes. [*Works*]. Continent: date indeterminable.
Language(s): Greek. Appraised at 5s in 1584.

143.61 Ammonius in Praed: grae:
Ammonius, *Hermeae*. [*Aristotle–Categoriae: commentary*]. Venice: (different houses), 1545–1546.
Includes Aristotle's text. *Language(s)*: Greek. Appraised at 2d in 1584.

143.62 Epigram: Veterum poet:
Multiple. *Anthologia graeca*. Continent: date indeterminable.
This often published collection sometimes carried the title *Epigrammata veterum poetarum*. *Language(s)*: Greek Latin. Appraised at 2d in 1584.

143.63 The franch scholemaster
Claude Desainliens (Claude Holyband). *The French schoolemaister*. London: W. How for A. Veale, 1573–1582?
STC 6748 *et seq*. In dialogue form, with French and English on facing pages. *Language(s)*: English French. Appraised at 3d in 1584.

143.64 Sebastiani Quaestura
Sebastian Corradus. [*Quaestura*]. Continent: 1537–1556.
Language(s): Latin. Appraised at 10d in 1584.

143.65 Justiniani lib: 4°
Justinian I. *Institutiones*. Continent: date indeterminable.
Justinian's *Institutiones* often bore the title *Institutionum libri IIII* and 4° in the manuscript entry probably refers to that title, or a part identified as book four, not the format. *Language(s)*: Latin Greek (perhaps). Appraised at 8d in 1584.

143.66 Sophocles grae:
Sophocles. [*Works*]. Continent: date indeterminable.
Language(s): Greek. Appraised at 8d in 1584.

143.67 Alcimus de Origine mundi
Alcimus Ecdicius Avitus. *De origine mundi* [and other works]. Continent: date indeterminable.
Language(s): Latin. Appraised at 8d in 1584.

143.68 Pandecta legis Evangel: bis
Simon Du Corroy. *Pandecta legis evangelicae*. Continent: 1547–1555.
Language(s): Latin. Appraised, with one other, at 12d in 1584.

143.69 [See 143.68]
Simon Du Corroy. *Pandecta legis evangelicae*. Continent: 1547–1555.
Language(s): Latin. Appraised, with one other, at 12d in 1584.

143.70 Themistius grae:
Themistius. Unidentified. Continent: date indeterminable.
Language(s): Greek. Appraised at 6d in 1584.

143.71 Theaparipha in englishe
Perhaps *The volume of the bokes called Apocripha*. (*Bible–O.T.*). Translated by Richard Taverner. London: J. Day and W. Seres, 1549.
STC 2087.5. This conjectural identification assumes that the manuscript entry is a mishearing or a miswriting of "the apocrypha." DMH no. 82. *Language(s)*: English. Appraised at 8d in 1584.

143.72 liber psalmorum lat:
[*Bible–O.T.–Psalms*]. Britain or Continent: date indeterminable.
STC 2354 *et seq*. and non-STC. Tye's copy might have included Coverdale's English version (STC 2368). *Language(s)*: Latin. Appraised at 4d in 1584.

143.73 Claudiani poetae opera
Claudius Claudianus. [*Works*]. Continent: date indeterminable.
Language(s): Latin. Appraised at 4d in 1584.

143.74 Henrici Stephani parad* morales
Henri Estienne. *Parodiae morales*. Geneva (probable): excudebat Henricus Stephanus, 1575.
Language(s): Greek Latin. Appraised at 6d in 1584.

143.75 psalmi haebr:
[*Bible–O.T.–Psalms*]. Continent: date indeterminable.
Language(s): Hebrew. Appraised at 4d in 1584.

143.76   Epistolae Cipri:
Cyprian, *Saint*. [*Epistolae*]. Continent: date indeterminable. *Language(s)*: Latin. Appraised at 2d in 1584.

143.77   Campensis gram: haeb:
Joannes Campensis. [*Grammatica hebraica*]. Continent: 1520–1553. Based on the Hebrew grammar of Elias, *Levita*. *Language(s)*: Hebrew Latin. Appraised at 4d in 1584.

143.78   Hesiodus grae:
Hesiod. [*Works*]. Continent: date indeterminable. *Language(s)*: Greek. Appraised at 1d in 1584.

143.79   Zenobii Compend***
Zenobius. [*Compendium veterum proverbiorum*]. Continent: 1497–1535. *Language(s)*: Greek. Appraised at 2d in 1584.

143.80   Euzebius grae:
Eusebius, *Pamphili, Bishop*. Unidentified. Continent: date indeterminable.
The vagueness of the entry makes it impossible to determine if this is a copy of Eusebius' *Evangelica praeparatio*, *Evangelica demonstratio*, or *Historia ecclesiastica*, all of which were issued in Greek editions. *Language(s)*: Greek. Appraised at 2s in 1584.

143.81   A booke of Pre****es in englishe
A book of precedents. London: (different houses), 1543–1583.
STC 3327 *et seq*. Several editions include a preface by Thomas Phaer, and the work as a whole is often ascribed to him (STC, 2:233). *Language(s)*: English. Appraised at 2d in 1584.

143.82   A note Booke of *hisick [phisick] unbound
Unidentified. Provenance unknown: date indeterminable.
Manuscript. *Language(s)*: Unknown. Appraised at 8d in 1584.

143.83:1–22   xxii litle volumes in greke
Unidentified. Places unknown: stationers unknown, dates indeterminable. STC/non-STC status unknown. *Language(s)*: Greek. Appraised at 10d in 1584.

143.84:1:1–14   xiiii Paper bookes in written hand grae: et lat: and A geneologie written
Unidentified. Provenances unknown: date indeterminable.
Manuscripts. Probably personal notebooks. *Language(s)*: Greek Latin. Appraised as a group with another manuscript at 18d in 1584.

143.84:2   [See 143.83:1:1–14]
Unidentified [*genealogy*]. Provenance unknown: date indeterminable.

Manuscript. Perhaps a genealogy of Tye's family. *Language(s)*: Unknown. Appraised with fourteen notebooks at 18d in 1584.

143.85:A Sceggius in physica Arist:
Jacob Schegk, *the Elder*. *In octo Physicorum, sive de auditione physica libros Aristotelis, commentaria*. Basle: per Joannem Hervagium, 1546 (composite publication). Sole edition. *Language(s)*: Latin. Appraised [a composite volume] at 4s in 1584.

143.85:B [See 143.85:A]
Jacob Schegk, *the Elder*. *Commentarius in III libros De anima*. [Composite publication].
Language(s): Latin. Appraised [a composite volume] at 4s in 1584.

143.86 Epitome Galeni
Galen. [*Works–Epitome*]. Continent: date indeterminable.
Language(s): Latin. Appraised at 2s 8d in 1584.

143.87 Jacobi Wickeri Syntaxis
Hanss Jacob Wecker. [*Medicinae utriusque syntaxes*]. Continent: 1562–1583. In table form. *Language(s)*: Latin. Appraised at 4s in 1584.

143.88 Johan: Fernel de medicina
Joannes Fernelius. *Medicina*. Continent: 1554–1565.
Language(s): Latin. Appraised at 3s in 1584.

143.89 Cardanus de Astrorum judiciis
Girolamo Cardano. *In Cl. Ptolemaei de astrorum judiciis*. Continent: 1554–1578. Published with other of Cardano's works, which varied with the editions. *Language(s)*: Latin. Appraised at 3s in 1584.

143.90 Cornelius Celsus de re medica
Aulus Cornelius Celsus. [*De re medica*]. Continent: date indeterminable.
Language(s): Latin. Appraised at 2s 6d in 1584.

143.91 The judiciall of urines in englishe
Joannes Vasseus. *Here beginnith a litel treatise conteyninge the jugement of urynes*. Translated by Humphrey Llwyd. London: Richard Tottyl, 1553.
STC 24595. An English translation of Vasseus' *De judiciis urinarum*. *Language(s)*: English. Appraised at 4d in 1584.

143.92 Petri Alcionii de Exilio oratio
Pietro Alcionio. *De exilio*. Continent: 1522–1546.
Language(s): Latin. Appraised at 4d in 1584.

143.93 Quintus Serenus de re medica
Quintus Serenus Sammonicus. [*De re medica*]. Continent: date indeterminable. *Language(s)*: Latin. Appraised at 12d in 1584.

143.94 Heronimi Thriveri in hip: Aphori:
Hieremias Triverius (Brachelius). *Commentarii in VII libros Aphorismorum Hippocratis*. Lyon: apud haeredes Jacobi Juntae, 1551.
Language(s): Latin. Appraised at 20d in 1584.

143.95 Cardanus de restitutione temp:
Girolamo Cardano. *Libellus de restitutione temporum et motum coelestium*. Continent: date indeterminable.
This seems to have been published only with other works, which varied with the collections. *Language(s)*: Latin. Appraised at 2s in 1584.

143.96 Nicolaus medicus
Unidentified. Place unknown: stationer unknown, date indeterminable.
STC/non-STC status unknown. Among the several possibilities are: Nicolaus Taurellus, Nicolaus Piso, and Nicolaus Biesius. *Language(s)*: Latin (probable). Appraised at 7d in 1584.

143.97 Hippo: de flatibus
Hippocrates. *De flatibus*. Paris: (different houses), 1525–1557.
Language(s): Latin Greek (perhaps). Appraised at 3d in 1584.

143.98 Otho Brunfelsius de remediis morborum
Otto Brunfels. *Iatrion medicamentorum simplicium*. Strassburg (probable): [Georg Ulricher], 1533?
The entry indicates that this is (as a fuller version of its title indicates) *Iatrion medicamentorum simplicium, continens remedia omnium morborum quae tam hominibus quam pecudibus accidere possunt*. *Language(s)*: Latin. Appraised at 8d in 1584.

143.99 Alexander de Secretis
Alessio, *Piemontese, pseudonym* (Girolamo Ruscelli). *De secretis*. Translated by Hanss Jacob Wecker. Continent: date indeterminable.
Language(s): Latin. Appraised at 2d in 1584.

143.100 Actuarius de Urinis
Joannes Actuarius. *De urinis*. Continent: date indeterminable.
Language(s): Latin. Appraised at 6d in 1584.

143.101 Fernelius de roe [ratione] medendi
Joannes Fernelius. *Therapeutices universalis seu medendi rationis libri septem*. Continent: date indeterminable.
Language(s): Latin. Appraised at 8d in 1584.

143.102 Aretius medicus
Aretaeus, *Cappadox*. Unidentified. Continent: date indeterminable.
Language(s): Latin (probable) Greek (perhaps). Appraised at 6d in 1584.

143.103 Ruffus de medicamentis purgantibus
Rufus, *of Ephesus*. *De medicamentis purgantibus*. Continent: date indeterminable.
This text seems only to have appeared in a variety of collections. *Language(s)*: Latin (probable) Greek (perhaps). Appraised at 18d in 1584.

143.104 Plinius Secundus de nat: Hist:
Pliny, *the Elder*. *Historia naturalis*. Continent: date indeterminable.
Language(s): Latin. Appraised at 18d in 1584.

143.105 Simplicius in 8° physic:
Simplicius, *of Cilicia*. [*Aristotle–Physica: commentary*]. Continent: date indeterminable.
Language(s): Latin (probable) Greek (perhaps). Appraised at 5s in 1584.

143.106 Toleti in physica
Franciscus Toletus, *Cardinal*. [*Aristotle–Physica: commentary*]. Continent: date indeterminable.
Some editions also carry Toletus' commentary on Aristotle's *De generatione et corruptione*. *Language(s)*: Latin. Appraised at 2s 8d in 1584.

John Haynes. Scholar (M.A.): Probate Inventory. 1585

RUDOLPH P. ALMASY

John Haynes (Hayne, Heney, Heyney), born in 1562 in Gloucestershire, matriculated from St. Mary Hall, Oxford, on 28 May 1580 at the age of eighteen. He earned the B.A. on 22 February 1582 and the M.A. on 2 June 1584 as "Heyney" (*Alumni Oxonienses*, 2:681). At the time of his death on 16 December 1585, he was still associated with St. Mary Hall. The inventory of his belongings, including books, was compiled by Haynes's brother, Oliver, on 12 January 1586.

Haynes appears to have been a student of theology—and probably a Calvinist at that—since a good third of his books are theological in nature, patristic and reformed. Yet, over a short period of time (he died at twenty-three), he gathered a great many of the classical authors central to the canon and to the rhetoric course, and he seems to have had an abiding interest in belletristic classical texts with a library that included Aesop, Catullus, Demosthenes, Juvenal, Lucian, Lucretius, and Ovid along with a solid representation of the ancient dramatists: Aeschylus, Euripides, Sophocles, and Terence. There seems also to have been an interest in history and natural philosophy; the books on logic indicate that he still retained texts both from the B.A. and from the M.A. syllabus.

Oxford University Archives, Bodleian Library: Hyp.B.13.

§

144.1	Tullie's workes in folio, ii volumes
144.2	Scapula
144.3	a Greecke gramer
144.4	ethica Aristoi greca:
144.5	florilegium grece

144.6	Tullie's epistole
144.7	Calvin Institu
144.8	Juvenall
144.9	scolia in Euripidem
144.10	Crustostomus in epistolas Pauli, duo volumina
144.11	Cesars coment:
144.12	regium rusticum
144.13	Defe: orthodoxii Fidei
144.14	athanasii grece
144.15	marcellinus
144.16	Melanthon in Topica
144.17	Jecstius titelmns
144.18	tragediae Euripidis
144.19	dialogi gre:
144.20	tragediae Sophoclis
144.21	Terens
144.22	Ambrosius in paul: epist:
144.23	Livinus Lemnius de complec:
144.24	Suonima Rulandi
144.25	Aristo: Topica
144.26	sententiae lumbardi
144.27	exemeron wolpigangi
144.28	alius gellius
144.29	epistolae olynthii
144.30	tractus de eccl
144.31	Mallius
144.32:1	comentaria Bedae, bis
144.32:2	[See 144.32:1]
144.33	pupilla oculii
144.34	ovide metamorph:
144.35	haymo'
144.36	Porphurius
144.37	fox de xpo
144.38	sdus [secundus] scotii
144.39	opuscula Ancelmi
144.40	opuscula Barnar:
144.41	Gecinus
144.42	origen: duo vol
144.43	calepinus
144.44	laurentius valla
144.45	Scotus in phisica
144.46	faber stapulen:
144.47	opera Augustini Aurelii
144.48	picus mirandula

144.49	thomae Aquin. quae.
144.50	florilegium grece
144.51	textus Sententiarum
144.52:1–3	iii paper bookes
144.53	loci cummunes
144.54	a confutacion of the Familie of Love
144.55	flores doctorum
144.56	Osculi tragediae
144.57	Lucretius
144.58	Jewell's Apologie
144.59	Ovid' Metamorphos
144.60	Cattulus
144.61	Clendarde's gramar
144.62	Epitome Fidei
144.63	Ove de tristibus
144.64	Testamentum grece
144.65	Eutropius
144.66	Rudimenta Fidei
144.67	esopi fabulae
144.68	Diodor: sic:
144.69	a psalm book in Duch
144.70	Demothens olyn
144.71:1–20	xx other bookes in the stode [study?]

§

144.1   Tullie's workes in folio, ii volumes

Marcus Tullius Cicero. [*Works*]. Continent: date indeterminable.

A two-volume, folio edition of Cicero's works was published in Paris in 1527, but the entry could refer to any two volumes of several multi-volume, folio editions. *Language(s)*: Latin. Appraised at 20s in 1585.

144.2   Scapula

Joannes Scapula. *Lexicon graecolatinum novum*. Basle: ex off. Hervagiana, per Eusebium Episcopium, 1580.

Language(s): Greek Latin. Appraised at 12s in 1585.

144.3   a Greecke gramer

Unidentified. Place unknown: stationer unknown, date indeterminable.

STC/non-STC status unknown. Perhaps a copy of the *Compendium grammaticae graecae* by Jacobus Ceporinus (see STC 4913, printed in 1585), but probably, at this valuation, one of the many Greek grammars published on the Continent. *Language(s)*: Greek. Appraised at 2s 6d in 1585.

144.4 ethica Aristoi greca:
Aristotle. *Ethica*. Continent: date indeterminable.
Language(s): Greek. Appraised at 2s in 1585.

144.5 florilegium grece
Probably *Anthologia graeca*. Continent: date indeterminable.
Epigrammata graeca is a less likely possibility with this entry. See 144.50. *Language(s)*: Greek. Appraised at 20d in 1585.

144.6 Tullie's epistole
Marcus Tullius Cicero. [*Selected works–Epistolae*]. Continent (probable): date indeterminable.
Probably not an STC book, but see STC 5295 *et seq*. If the popular *Epistolae ad familiares*, this could be an edition published in England. *Language(s)*: Latin. Appraised at 20d in 1585.

144.7 Calvin Institu
Jean Calvin. *Institutio Christianae religionis*. Britain or Continent: date indeterminable.
STC 4414 and non-STC. An English translation is only a remote possibility in this collection, particularly in the context of this item's location in the list. *Language(s)*: Latin. Appraised at 3s in 1585.

144.8 Juvenall
Decimus Junius Juvenalis. Probably [*Works*]. Continent: date indeterminable.
Language(s): Latin. Appraised at 2s 6d in 1585.

144.9 scolia in Euripidem
Arsenios, *Archbishop of Monemvasia* (Aristobulus), compiler. *Scholia in septem Euripidis tragoedias*. Continent: 1534–1544.
Language(s): Greek. Appraised at 8d in 1585.

144.10 Crustostomus in epistolas Pauli, duo volumina
John, *Chrysostom, Saint*. [*Epistles–Paul: commentary and text*]. (*Bible–N.T.*). Continent: date indeterminable.
Whether a two-volume edition or two volumes of a larger set cannot be known. *Language(s)*: Latin. Appraised at 4s in 1585.

144.11 Cesars coment:
Caius Julius Caesar. *Commentarii*. Britain or Continent: date indeterminable.
STC 4332 and non-STC. The manuscript entry could indicate an English edition. *Language(s)*: Latin English (perhaps). Appraised at 16d in 1585.

144.12 regium rusticum
Unidentified. Place unknown: stationer unknown, date indeterminable.

STC/non-STC status unknown. *Language(s)*: Latin (probable). Appraised at 12d in 1585.

144.13 Defe: orthodoxii Fidei
Jean Calvin. *Defensio orthodoxae fidei de sacra Trinitate*. Geneva: oliva Roberti Stephani, 1554.
Language(s): Latin. Appraised at 16d in 1585.

144.14 athanasii grece
Athanasius, *Saint. Dialogi V, de sancta Trinitate*. Leipzig: (imprim. Andreas Schneider, typis Voegelianis), 1573.
The only work of Athanasius published solely in Greek by the date of this inventory. It also appeared in a Greek-Latin edition in 1570. *Language(s)*: Greek. Appraised at 16d in 1585.

144.15 marcellinus
Probably Marcellinus Ammianus. *Res gestae*. Continent: date indeterminable.
A remote possibility is Valerio Marcellini's *Il Diameroni* (1564). *Language(s)*: Latin. Appraised at 12d in 1585.

144.16 Melanthon in Topica
Marcus Tullius Cicero. *Topica*. Edited, with commentary, by Philipp Melanchthon. Continent: date indeterminable.
Language(s): Latin. Appraised at 12d in 1585.

144.17 Jecstius titelmns
Perhaps Tilemannus Heshusius, *Bishop*. Unidentified. Continent: date indeterminable.
Heshusius, *Bishop of Samland*, wrote theological works, biblical commentaries, and controversialist tracts against the Calvinists. *Language(s)*: Latin. Appraised at 12d in 1585.

144.18 tragediae Euripidis
Euripides. [*Works*]. Continent: date indeterminable.
Language(s): Latin (probable) Greek (perhaps). Appraised at 16d in 1585.

144.19 dialogi gre:
Perhaps Lucian, *of Samosata*. Unidentified. Britain or Continent: date indeterminable.
STC/non-STC status unknown. What arrangement of *Dialogues*—whether collected or selected, if indeed this is Lucian—cannot be determined. *Language(s)*: Latin (probable) Greek (perhaps). Appraised at 16d in 1585.

144.20 tragediae Sophoclis
Sophocles. [*Works*]. Continent: date indeterminable.

Language(s): Latin (probable) Greek (perhaps). Appraised at 10d in 1585.

144.21 Terens
Publius Terentius, *Afer*. [*Works*]. Britain or Continent: date indeterminable. STC 23885 *et seq.* and non-STC. *Language(s)*: Latin. Appraised at 6d in 1585.

144.22 Ambrosius in paul: epist:
Ambrose, Saint. [*Epistles–Paul: commentary and text*]. (*Bible–N.T.*). Edited by Desiderius Erasmus. Continent: 1530–1540.
Language(s): Latin. Appraised at 6d in 1585.

144.23 Livinus Lemnius de complec:
Levinus Lemnius. *De habitu et constitucione corporis*. Continent: 1561–1582.
Language(s): Latin. Appraised at 12d in 1585.

144.24 Suonima Rulandi
Martin Ruland, *the Elder*. *Synonyma*. Continent: 1563–1585.
Language(s): Greek Latin. Appraised at 16d in 1585.

144.25 Aristo: Topica
Aristotle. *Topica*. Continent: date indeterminable.
Language(s): Latin (probable) Greek (perhaps). Appraised at 3d in 1585.

144.26 sententiae lumbardi
Peter Lombard. *Sententiarum libri IIII*. Continent: date indeterminable. Another copy at 144.51. *Language(s)*: Latin. Appraised at 8d in 1585.

144.27 exemeron wolpigangi
Wolfgang Fabricius Capito. *Hexameron Dei opus explicatum*. Strassburg: per Wendelinum Rihelium, 1539.
Language(s): Latin. Appraised at 6d in 1585.

144.28 alius gellius
Aulus Gellius. *Noctes Atticae*. Continent: date indeterminable.
Language(s): Latin. Appraised at 12d in 1585.

144.29 epistolae olynthii
Demosthenes. Perhaps [*Works*]. Continent: date indeterminable.
No edition of the *Olynthiacs* and the epistles alone can be found; perhaps then this is an edition of the *opera* with the compiler giving fragmentary information.
Language(s): Latin (probable) Greek (perhaps). Appraised at 10d in 1585.

144.30 tractus de eccl
Philippe de Mornay. *Tractatus de ecclesia*. Continent: 1579–1585.
Language(s): Latin. Appraised at 12d in 1585.

144.31 Mallius
Jacob Sprenger and Heinrich Kraemer. *Malleus maleficarum*. Continent: date indeterminable.
Language(s): Latin. Appraised at 2d in 1585.

144.32:1 comentaria Bedae, bis
Beda, *the Venerable*. Unidentified. Continent: date indeterminable.
Could be a two-volume edition of Bede's commentaries, but it is treated here as two discrete editions. See Adams B454–457 at least. *Language(s)*: Latin. Appraised with one other at 6d in 1585.

144.32:2 [See 144.32:1]
Beda, *the Venerable*. Unidentified. Continent: date indeterminable.
See note to preceding. *Language(s)*: Latin. Appraised with one other at 6d in 1585.

144.33 pupilla oculii
Joannes de Burgo. *Pupilla oculi*. Britain or Continent: 1510–1527.
STC 4115 and non-STC. *Language(s)*: Latin. Appraised at 2d in 1585.

144.34 ovide metamorph:
Publius Ovidius Naso. *Metamorphoses*. Britain or Continent: date indeterminable.
STC 18951 *et seq.* and non-STC. Another copy at 144.59; one could be English. *Language(s)*: Latin (probable) English (perhaps). Appraised at 2d in 1585.

144.35 haymo'
Haymo, *Bishop of Halberstadt*. Unidentified. Continent: date indeterminable.
Language(s): Latin (probable). Appraised at 6d in 1585.

144.36 Porphurius
Porphyrius, *of Tyre*. Unidentified. Continent: date indeterminable.
Language(s): Latin. Appraised at 2d in 1585.

144.37 fox de xpo
John Foxe, *the Martyrologist*. Unidentified. London: date indeterminable.
Unidentifiable in the STC. Surely either STC 11234 *De Christo gratis justificante* (1582) or STC 11247 *De Christo crucifixo* (1571), but which cannot be determined from the truncated manuscript entry. *Language(s)*: Latin. Appraised at 12d in 1585.

144.38 sdus [secundus] scotii
John Duns, *Scotus*. [*Sentences II: commentary*]. Continent: date indeterminable.
Language(s): Latin. Appraised at 12d in 1585.

144.39 opuscula Ancelmi
Anselm, *Saint, Archbishop of Canterbury*. [*Selected works–Opuscula*]. Continent: 1544–1549.
Language(s): Latin. Appraised at 10d in 1585.

144.40 opuscula Barnar:
Bernard, *Saint. Opuscula*. Continent: 1478–1503.
Language(s): Latin. Appraised at 2s in 1585.

144.41 Gecinus
Unidentified. Place unknown: stationer unknown, date indeterminable. STC/non-STC status unknown. Conceivably something by Joannes Gerson, especially since it is in the midst of a number of theological works. *Language(s)*: Latin (probable). Appraised at 12d in 1585.

144.42 origen: duo vol
Origen. Probably [*Works*]. Continent: date indeterminable.
Several two-volume printings appeared (1512, 1536, 1557, 1571, 1574) mostly in Paris or Basle. *Language(s)*: Latin. Appraised at 4s in 1585.

144.43 calepinus
Ambrogio Calepino. *Dictionarium*. Continent: date indeterminable.
Several vernacular languages are possible. *Language(s)*: Greek Latin. Appraised at 3s 4d in 1585.

144.44 laurentius valla
Laurentius Valla. Unidentified. Continent: date indeterminable.
Likely the often-issued *Elegantiae*. *Language(s)*: Latin. Appraised at 6d in 1585.

144.45 Scotus in phisica
John Duns, *Scotus*. Probably [*Aristotle–Unidentified: commentary*]. Continent: date indeterminable.
Scotus's commentary on Aristotle's *Physica* seems not to have been published under his name until the seventeenth century (see Shaaber D278–279), though Harris (323) cites a reference to a 1504 Venice edition not now found in any extant bibliographical source. A commentary published under the name of Marsilius, *ab Inghen* and attributed to Scotus (with dates of editions variously given as 1513, 1516, and 1518) would probably not be so identified by the compiler here. Perhaps a more likely possibility is Matthaeus Silvagius, *Lectura seu expositio brevis super VIII libros physicorum Aristotelis cum aliquibus adnotationibus de mente Doctoris Subtilis* (Venice, 1542). Probably even more likely, however, is the compiler's truncating the title of Scotus's widely published commentary on Aristotle's *Metaphysica*, a possibility so strong that the item must remain unidentified here. *Language(s)*: Latin. Appraised at 6d in 1585.

144.46 faber stapulen:
Jacobus Faber, *Stapulensis*. Unidentified. Continent: date indeterminable. *Language(s)*: Latin. Appraised at 12d in 1585.

144.47 opera Augustini Aurelii
Augustine, *Saint*. [*Works*]. Continent: date indeterminable. *Language(s)*: Latin. Appraised at 2s in 1585.

144.48 picus mirandula
Giovanni Pico della Mirandola, *Count*. Unidentified. Continent (probable): date indeterminable.
Probably not an STC book but see STC 19898. Probably an edition of one of Pico's Latin works, though it could be the English *Here is conteyned the lyfe of J. Picus Erle of Myrandula* (STC 19897.7–19898). *Language(s)*: Latin (probable). Appraised at 18d in 1585.

144.49 thomae Aquin. quae.
Thomas Aquinas, *Saint*. [*Quaestiones*]. Continent: date indeterminable.
Whether the *Quaestiones disputatae* or the *Quaestiones quodlibetales* cannot be determined. *Language(s)*: Latin. Appraised at 2s 6d in 1585.

144.50 florilegium grece
Probably *Anthologia graeca*. Continent: date indeterminable.
See 144.5. *Language(s)*: Greek. Appraised at 6d in 1585.

144.51 textus Sententiarum
Peter Lombard. *Sententiarum libri IIII*. Continent: date indeterminable. *Language(s)*: Latin. Appraised at 12d in 1585.

144.52:1–3 iii paper bookes
Unidentified. Provenances unknown. Dates indeterminable.
Manuscripts. Assumed to be notebooks, not blank books. *Language(s)*: Unknown. Three books appraised at 12d in 1585.

144.53 loci cummunes
Unidentified. Place unknown: stationer unknown, date indeterminable.
STC/non-STC status unknown. *Language(s)*: Latin. Appraised at 2s 6d in 1585.

144.54 a confutacion of the Familie of Love
William Wilkinson. *A confutation of certaine articles delivered unto the Familye of Love*. London: J. Daye, 1579.
STC 25665. Another possibility for this entry is STC 15040, John Knewstub's *A confutation of monstrous and horrible heresies, taught by H. N.* (1579), printed in London by Thomas Dawson. *Language(s)*: English. Appraised at 8d in 1585.

144.55 flores doctorum
Thomas, *Hibernicus*. [*Flores omnium fere doctorum*]. Continent: date indeterminable.
Language(s): Latin. Appraised at 12d in 1585.

144.56 Osculi tragediae
Aeschylus. [*Works*]. Continent: date indeterminable.
Language(s): Latin (probable) Greek (perhaps). Appraised at 6d in 1585.

144.57 Lucretius
Titus Lucretius Carus. *De rerum natura*. Continent: date indeterminable.
Language(s): Latin. Appraised at 6d in 1585.

144.58 Jewell's Apologie
John Jewel, *Bishop*. *An apologie, or aunswer in defence of the Church of England*. London: R. Wolfe, 1562–1564.
STC 14590 *et seq*. The entry indicates the English, not the Latin, version.
Language(s): English. Appraised at 6d in 1585.

144.59 Ovid' Metamorphos
Publius Ovidius Naso. *Metamorphoses*. Britain or Continent: date indeterminable.
STC 18951 *et seq*. and non-STC. Another copy at 144.34; one could be English.
Language(s): Latin (probable) English (perhaps). Appraised at 2d in 1585.

144.60 Cattulus
Caius Valerius Catullus, Albius Tibullus and Sextus Propertius. Probably [*Works*]. Continent: date indeterminable.
The roles of Tibullus and Propertius depend, of course, on the item being identified as above. *Language(s)*: Latin. Appraised at 4d in 1585.

144.61 Clendarde's gramar
Nicolaus Clenardus. [*Institutiones linguae graecae*]. Continent: date indeterminable.
Language(s): Greek Latin. Appraised at 6d in 1585.

144.62 Epitome Fidei
Unidentified. Continent (probable): date indeterminable.
Almost certainly not an STC book. Several catechistic epitomes might be so listed. *Language(s)*: Latin. Appraised at 10d in 1585.

144.63 Ove de tristibus
Publius Ovidius Naso. *Tristia*. Britain or Continent: date indeterminable.
STC 18976.4 *et seq*. and non-STC. *Language(s)*: Latin. Appraised at 8d in 1585.

144.64 Testamentum grece
[*Bible–N.T.*]. Continent: date indeterminable.
The first English printing of a Greek New Testament was in 1587, too late for this inventory. *Language(s)*: Greek. Appraised at 20d in 1585.

144.65 Eutropius
Flavius Eutropius. [*Historia Romana*]. Continent: date indeterminable.
There is no reason to think that this would be the 1564 English translation of the *Breviarium*. *Language(s)*: Latin. Appraised at 6d in 1585.

144.66 Rudimenta Fidei
Jean Calvin. [*Catechism*]. Britain or Continent: date indeterminable.
STC 4375 *et seq.* and non-STC. *Language(s)*: Greek Latin. Appraised at 8d in 1585.

144.67 esopi fabulae
Aesop. *Fabulae*. Britain or Continent: date indeterminable.
STC 168 *et seq.* and non-STC. *Language(s)*: Latin (probable) Greek (perhaps). Appraised at 8d in 1585.

144.68 Diodor: sic:
Diodorus, *Siculus. Bibliotheca historica*. Continent: date indeterminable.
The 1569 English edition of selections is hardly likely in this collection. *Language(s)*: Latin. Appraised at 6d in 1585.

144.69 a psalm book in Duch
[*Bible–O.T.–Psalms*]. Britain or Continent: date indeterminable.
STC 2738.7 and non-STC. A German (commonly given as "Dutch") translation is a possibility. *Language(s)*: Dutch. Appraised at 2s in 1585.

144.70 Demothens olyn
Demosthenes. *Olynthiacae orationes tres*. Continent: date indeterminable.
STC 6577 is *Selected works* with the *Olynthiacs* leading, which this could be. *Language(s)*: Greek Latin (probable). Appraised at 4d in 1585.

144.71:1–20 xx other bookes in the stode [study?]
Unidentified. Places unknown: stationers unknown, dates indeterminable.
STC/non-STC status unknown. *Language(s)*: Unknown. Twenty books appraised at 5s in 1585.

Thomas Hill. Scholar (Probable): Probate Inventory. 1585

JOCELYN SHEPPARD

Thomas Hill, whose goods were inventoried in 1585 upon his decease, is not listed by Foster in the *Alumni Oxonienses*, and the index to Oxford University wills (Griffiths 1862, p. 30) does not associate Hill with any college or degree, providing only that his will was proved on 8 February 1585. Contributing additional doubts about Hill's scholarly status is that only one of the four persons compiling the inventory can be identified for certain as an Oxford scholar, Simon Vincent, B.A. 1587 and M.A. 1591. Since Vincent was granted his Bachelor of Arts degree from New College, of the several Thomas Hills listed in Foster, the one recorded as having received his B.A. degree also from New College (1581) would be the most likely candidate to have had connections with Vincent. This New College Hill is, however, listed as having been licensed to practice medicine in 1591, years after the Hill of the current list died. Perhaps two Thomas Hills are conflated in the Foster entry. To add to the problem of identity is the question about the date of the inventory. Recorded at the end of the manuscript inventory, the preface to which provides the date 6 February 1585, is the statement that the inventory was "Exhibitum octavo Februarii 1584." The two dates, both old style, conflict (in new style, the dates are, respectively, 1586 and 1585). No datable book in Hill's collection, however, is later than 1584, providing marginal support for the date at the end of the inventory, 1584. The year of the inventory is, therefore, assumed to be 1584, old style, providing the manuscript with a date 1585, new style.

Despite the absence of external evidence, Hill appears to have been a scholar on the basis of his collection of books, which is comprised mainly of standard classical works in literature, rhetoric, philosophy, logic, and history, with a good deal of theology, mostly reformist. Hill apparently read Greek, but his books are overwhelmingly in Latin and issued from Continental presses. Even the single book in English in Hill's collection has a Continental association. A book of meditations, it is a popular translation of a work by the Lutheran Hebraist, Johann

Habermann (Joannes Avenarius), not a native collection of prayers. The only entry that is not academic, though hardly unusual to find in a scholar's inventory, is located in the midst of his personal possessions: three sets of song books.

Oxford University Archives, Bodleian Library: Hyp.B.13.

§

Griffiths, John. 1862. *An Index to Wills Proved in the Court of the Chancellor of the University of Oxford.* Oxford: at the Univ. Press.

§

145.1	Calvini Institutio
145.2	dialectica Tolleti
145.3	Problemata Aristotelis
145.4	flores doctorum
145.5	Albertus Magnus
145.6	Ethica Aristotelis cum annotationibus Lambini
145.7	Josephus de antiquitatibus
145.8	cathena aurea in psalmos
145.9	Tolleti physica
145.10	Posselii sintaxis
145.11	postilla Himingii
145.12	a bible
145.13	Donatus in Ethicam Aristotelis
145.14	Lycosthenis appo
145.15	lexicon grecum
145.16	Johannes de sacra
145.17	Demochares in Topica
145.18	Plutarchi moralia
145.19	Wildenburgius
145.20	Ramus
145.21	testamentum greco-latinum
145.22	Homerus grece
145.23	Foxius in Ethica
145.24	Sophocles
145.25	Stanihurst
145.26	dialectica Titlemanni
145.27	commentarii Cesaris
145.28	Justinus
145.29	Ovidius de fastis
145.30	Ceporini grammatica

145.31	orationes Eschinis et Demostenis
145.32	Physica Aristotelis
145.33	dialectica Aristotelis
145.34	catechismus grec:latt
145.35	Dictis Cretensis
145.36	Mathisii epitome
145.37	Epistolae familiares Ciceronis
145.38	Textoris epitheta
145.39	orationes Isocratis
145.40	Rodolphus Agricola
145.41	dialogi Luciani
145.42	sententiae Ciceronis
145.43	grammatica Clenardi
145.44	rhetorica Valerii
145.45	orationes Ciceronis
145.46	Canisii catechismus
145.47	Manutii phrases
145.48	Littleton's Tenures
145.49	Tusculanae Questiones
145.50	Mantuanus
145.51	Margarita Theolog'
145.52	The Enimie of Securitie
145.53	Testamentum Bezae
145.54	Titlemanni physica
145.55	Fenestella

§

145.1   Calvini Institutio

Jean Calvin. *Institutio Christianae religionis*. Britain or Continent: date indeterminable.

STC 4414 and non-STC. *Language(s)*: Latin. Appraised at 2s 6d in 1585.

145.2   dialectica Tolleti

Franciscus Toletus, *Cardinal*. [*Aristotle–Selected works–Logica: commentary*]. Continent: 1575–1583.

Language(s): Latin. Appraised at 16d in 1585.

145.3   Problemata Aristotelis

Aristotle (spurious). *Problemata*. Britain or Continent: date indeterminable.
STC 761. *Language(s)*: Latin. Appraised at 10d in 1585.

145.4   flores doctorum

Thomas, *Hibernicus*. [*Flores omnium fere doctorum*]. Continent: date indeterminable.

Language(s): Latin. Appraised at 12d in 1585.

145.5 Albertus Magnus
Albertus Magnus. Unidentified. Place unknown: stationer unknown, date indeterminable.
STC/non-STC status unknown. *Language(s)*: Latin (probable). Appraised at 6d in 1585.

145.6 Ethica Aristotelis cum annotationibus Lambini
Aristotle. *Ethica*. Translated, with commentary, by Dionysius Lambinus. Continent: 1558–1566.
The 1566 edition also contains commentary by Theodor Zwinger. *Aureliensis* 108.350, 108.360, 108.496, 108.503. *Language(s)*: Latin. Appraised at 20d in 1585.

145.7 Josephus de antiquitatibus
Flavius Josephus. *Antiquitates Judaicae*. Continent: date indeterminable.
Language(s): Latin. Appraised at 12d in 1585.

145.8 cathena aurea in psalmos
Franciscus de Puteo, *Carthusian*. *Cathena aurea super psalmos*. Continent: date indeterminable.
Language(s): Latin. Appraised at 20d in 1585.

145.9 Tolleti physica
Franciscus Toletus, *Cardinal*. [*Aristotle–Physica: commentary*]. Continent: 1574–1578.
Some editions were published in composite volumes with his commentary on *De generatione et corruptione*. *Language(s)*: Latin. Appraised at 2s 4d in 1585.

145.10 Posselii sintaxis
Joannes Posselius. *Syntaxis linguae graecae*. Continent: date indeterminable.
Language(s): Greek Latin. Appraised at 6d in 1585.

145.11 postilla Himingii
Niels Hemmingsen. [*Gospels (liturgical): commentary*]. Continent: date indeterminable.
Language(s): Latin. Appraised at 12d in 1585.

145.12 a bible
The Bible. Britain or Continent: date indeterminable.
STC 2063 *et seq*. Bibles in languages other than English were sometimes entered in inventories in English. *Language(s)*: English (probable). Appraised at 8s in 1585.

145.13 Donatus in Ethicam Aristotelis
Donatus Acciaiolus. [*Aristotle–Ethica: commentary*]. Continent: date indeterminable. Editions from 1478. *Language(s)*: Latin. Appraised at 12d in 1585.

145.14 Lycosthenis appo
Conrad Lycosthenes (Conrad Wolffhart). *Apophthegmata.* Britain or Continent: date indeterminable.
STC 17003.3 and non-STC. *Language(s)*: Latin. Appraised at 12d in 1585.

145.15 lexicon grecum
Unidentified [dictionary]. Continent: date indeterminable.
Language(s): Greek Latin. Appraised at 2s 6d in 1585.

145.16 Johannes de sacra
John Holywood (Joannes Sacrobosco). *Sphaera mundi.* Continent: date indeterminable.
Language(s): Latin. Appraised at 4d in 1585.

145.17 Demochares in Topica
Antoine de Mouchy (Demochares). *In octo libros Topicorum Aristotelis hypomnema.* Paris: ex officina Simon Colinaeus, 1535.
Language(s): Latin. Appraised at 8d in 1585.

145.18 Plutarchi moralia
Plutarch. *Moralia.* Continent: date indeterminable.
Language(s): Latin (probable) Greek (perhaps). Appraised at 2s in 1585.

145.19 Wildenburgius
Hieronymus Wildenbergius. Probably [*Aristotle–Unidentified: commentary*]. Continent: date indeterminable.
Language(s): Latin. Appraised at 3d in 1585.

145.20 Ramus
Pierre de La Ramée. Unidentified. Place unknown: stationer unknown, date indeterminable.
STC/non-STC status unknown. *Language(s)*: Latin (probable). Appraised at 3d in 1585.

145.21 testamentum greco-latinum
[*Bible–N.T.*]. Continent: date indeterminable.
Language(s): Greek Latin. Appraised at 20d in 1585.

145.22 Homerus grece
Homer. Probably [*Works*]. Continent: date indeterminable.
Language(s): Greek. Appraised at 8d in 1585.

145.23 Foxius in Ethica
Sebastiano Fox Morzillo. *Ethices philosophiae compendium*. Continent: 1554–1561.
Treats both Aristotle and Plato. *Language(s)*: Latin. Appraised at 6d in 1585.

145.24 Sophocles
Sophocles. Probably [*Works*]. Continent: date indeterminable.
Language(s): Greek (perhaps) Latin (perhaps). Appraised at 2d in 1585.

145.25 Stanihurst
Richard Stanyhurst. Unidentified. Place unknown: stationer unknown, date indeterminable.
STC/non-STC status unknown. *Language(s)*: Latin. Appraised at 4d in 1585.

145.26 dialectica Titlemanni
Franz Titelmann. [*Dialectica*]. Continent: date indeterminable.
Language(s): Latin. Appraised at 6d in 1585.

145.27 commentarii Cesaris
Caius Julius Caesar. *Commentarii*. Britain or Continent: date indeterminable.
STC 4332 and non-STC. *Language(s)*: Latin. Appraised at 6d in 1585.

145.28 Justinus
Trogus Pompeius and Justinus, *the Historian*. [*Epitomae in Trogi Pompeii historias*]. Britain or Continent: date indeterminable.
STC 24287 *et seq.* and non-STC. Justinus, *Martyr* is but a remote possibility. *Language(s)*: Latin. Appraised at 6d in 1585.

145.29 Ovidius de fastis
Publius Ovidius Naso. *Fasti*. Britain or Continent: date indeterminable.
STC 18947.5 and non-STC. *Language(s)*: Latin. Appraised at 6d in 1585.

145.30 Ceporini grammatica
Jacobus Ceporinus. *Compendium grammaticae graecae*. Britain or Continent: date indeterminable.
STC 4913 and non-STC. *Language(s)*: Greek Latin. Appraised at 4d in 1585.

145.31 orationes Eschinis et Demostenis
Aeschines and Demosthenes. [*Selected works–Orations*]. Continent: date indeterminable.
Language(s): Latin. Appraised at 6d in 1585.

145.32 Physica Aristotelis
Aristotle. *Physica*. Britain or Continent: date indeterminable.
STC 758 and non-STC. The sole edition from England is the compendium of

Andreas Gerardus, *Hyperius*. *Language(s)*: Latin (probable) Greek (perhaps). Appraised at 12d in 1585.

145.33   dialectica Aristotelis
Perhaps John Case. [*Aristotle-Selected works–Logica: commentary*]. Britain or Continent: 1580–1584.
STC 4762. *Language(s)*: Latin. Appraised at 12d in 1585.

145.34   catechismus grec:latt
Unidentified [catechism]. Place unknown: stationer unknown, date indeterminable.
STC/non-STC status unknown. Calvin and Nowell's catechisms were both published in Greek-Latin editions by the date of this inventory. *Language(s)*: Greek Latin. Appraised at 8d in 1585.

145.35   Dictis Cretensis
Dictys, *Cretensis. De bello Troiano*. Continent: date indeterminable.
Often published with, even conflated with, the work of Dares, *the Phrygian. Language(s)*: Latin. Appraised at 4d in 1585.

145.36   Mathisii epitome
Gerardus Matthisius (Geldrensis). Perhaps *Epitoma Aristoteleae logicae graecolatina*. Cologne: [see annotation], 1569.
The form of the manuscript entry and, to a lesser extent, the context of the list, suggest this over his epitome of the *Philosophia naturalis* (*De natura libri VIII in epitomam contracti* . . .). The stationer is not provided by the bibliographical sources that list this now rare work. *Language(s)*: Latin. Appraised at 6d in 1585.

145.37   Epistolae familiares Ciceronis
Marcus Tullius Cicero. *Epistolae ad familiares*. Britain or Continent: date indeterminable.
STC 5295 *et seq*. and non-STC. *Language(s)*: Latin. Appraised at 4d in 1585.

145.38   Textoris epitheta
Joannes Ravisius (Textor). *Epitheta*. Continent: date indeterminable.
Language(s): Latin. Appraised at 3d in 1585.

145.39   orationes Isocratis
Isocrates. Probably [*Selected works–Orations*]. Continent: date indeterminable.
A copy of the complete works (*Orationes et Epistolae*) could be intended here. *Language(s)*: Greek (perhaps) Latin (perhaps). Appraised at 12d in 1585.

145.40   Rodolphus Agricola
Rodolphus Agricola. Probably *De inventione dialectica*. Continent: date indeterminable.

Overwhelmingly, his most frequently published work. *Language(s)*: Latin. Appraised at 12d in 1585.

145.41   dialogi Luciani
Lucian, *of Samosata*. Unidentified. Place unknown: stationer unknown, date indeterminable.

STC/non-STC status unknown. What arrangement of the *Dialogues* (whether collected or selected) cannot be determined. *Language(s)*: Greek (perhaps) Latin (perhaps). Appraised at 8d in 1585.

145.42   sententiae Ciceronis
Marcus Tullius Cicero. [*Selections*]. Britain or Continent: date indeterminable.

STC 5318.3 *et seq*. and non-STC. STC imprints include selections from Demosthenes and Terence. *Language(s)*: Latin. Appraised at 4d in 1585.

145.43   grammatica Clenardi
[*Institutiones linguae graecae*]. Britain or Continent: date indeterminable.

STC 5400.5 and non-STC. *Language(s)*: Greek Latin. Appraised at 3d in 1585.

145.44   rhetorica Valerii
Cornelius Valerius. *In universam bene dicendi rationem tabula*. Britain or Continent: date indeterminable.

STC 24584 and non-STC. *Language(s)*: Latin. Appraised at 2d in 1585.

145.45   orationes Ciceronis
Marcus Tullius Cicero. [*Selected works–Orations*]. Britain or Continent: date indeterminable.

STC 5308 *et seq*. and non-STC. *Language(s)*: Latin. Appraised at 20d in 1585.

145.46   Canisii catechismus
Petrus Canisius, *Saint*. [*Summa doctrinae christianae*]. Continent: date indeterminable.

Language(s): Latin. Appraised at 2d in 1585.

145.47   Manutii phrases
Aldo Manuzio, *the Younger*. *Purae, elegantes et copiosae latinae linguae phrases*. Britain or Continent: date indeterminable.

STC 17278.8 *et seq*. and non-STC. The English editions carry English translations. *Language(s)*: Latin English (perhaps). Appraised at 4d in 1585.

145.48   Littleton's Tenures
Sir Thomas Littleton. [*Tenures*]. Britain or Continent: date indeterminable.

STC 15719 *et seq*. All editions, except an early folio edition published in Rouen, unlikely here, were printed in London. *Language(s)*: English (probable) Law French (perhaps). Appraised at 3d in 1585.

145.49 Tusculanae Questiones
Marcus Tullius Cicero. *Quaestiones Tusculanae*. Britain or Continent: date indeterminable.
STC 5314.5 *et seq.* and non-STC. *Language(s)*: Latin. Appraised at 2d in 1585.

145.50 Mantuanus
Baptista Spagnuoli (Mantuanus). Unidentified. Place unknown: stationer unknown, date indeterminable.
STC/non-STC status unknown. *Language(s)*: Latin. Appraised at 2d in 1585.

145.51 Margarita Theolog'
Johann Spangenberg. *Margarita theologica*. Britain or Continent: date indeterminable.
STC 23001 *et seq.* and non-STC. *Language(s)*: Latin. Appraised at 3d in 1585.

145.52 The Enimie of Securitie
Johann Habermann (Joannes Avenarius). *The enemy of security*. Translated by Thomas Rogers, *M.A*. London: Henry Denham, 1579–1583.
STC 12582.2 *et seq. Language(s)*: English. Appraised at 10d in 1585.

145.53 Testamentum Bezae
[*Bible–N.T.*]. Translated and edited by Théodore de Bèze. Britain or Continent: date indeterminable.
STC 2802 *et seq.* and non-STC. The editions published in England were in Latin only. *Language(s)*: Latin Greek (probable). Appraised at 12d in 1585.

145.54 Titlemanni physica
Franz Titelmann. [*Aristotle–Selected works–Philosophia naturalis: commentary*]. Continent: 1530–1582.
Language(s): Latin. Appraised at 10d in 1585.

145.55 Fenestella
Andreas Dominicus Floccus (Lucius Fenestella). Probably *De magistratibus sacerdotiisque Romanorum*. Continent: date indeterminable.
Language(s): Latin. Appraised at 2d in 1585.

Thomas Tatham. Scholar (M.A.): Probate Inventory. 1586

JULIETTE M. CUNICO and DAVID C. MCPHERSON

Thomas Tatham (Tatam, Tatta) apparently spent his entire scholarly career at Merton College, Oxford. He received his Bachelor of Arts degree on 23 February 1569 and his Master of Arts degree on 7 October 1573, and supplicated for his Bachelor of Civil Law degree on 13 June 1584. He was a fellow of the college from 1569 to 1586 when he died (*Alumni Oxonienses*, 3:1457).

Tatham's books, unlike those of many scholars represented in the Oxford inventories, are generally grouped according to subject. The heaviest concentrations are in law (both civil and canon) and theology, but philosophy (chiefly the usual Cicero and Aristotle), Greek and Roman classics, politics, rhetoric, orations, medicine, the occult, geography, and arithmetic are also represented.

A comparison of the libraries of Thomas Tatham and John Tatham (d.1576; PLRE 112, Volume 4), who was at Merton when Thomas became a fellow, reveals remarkable overlapping, with at least one-fourth of Thomas Tatham's books also found in John Tatham's library; approximately forty more titles were possibly owned by both (the manuscript entries of this smaller group are not specific enough to make a definite connection; e.g., "hemingius"). That two individuals with the same surname possessed so many of the same titles must be more than a coincidence. Although we have not been able to determine that the two men were related, we nonetheless conjecture that portions of John Tatham's library passed to Thomas Tatham. Accordingly, the identifiable items in Thomas Tatham's inventory that also appear in John Tatham's inventory are so cited in the annotations.

Oxford University Archives, Bodleian Library: Hyp.B.19.

§

146.1	Corpus Juris civilis cum glossa 5 voluminibus
146.2	corpus panormitani 4tour voluminibus
146.3	felinus duobus
146.4	Repertorium corseti
146.5	Corpus Juris civilis cum glossa 5 volumes
146.6:1	minsingerus in Inst et wesembesius in paratitla
146.6:2	[See 146.6:1]
146.7	nizolius
146.8	Casus longi
146.9	phisica aristotelis cum commento
146.10	officina textoris
146.11	canonicu in phisic aristotelis
146.12	Egidius in phisica
146.13	Cornucopiae
146.14	consilia matrimonialia
146.15	corpus Juris
146.16	de conjecturis ult'
146.17	alphabetum aureum
146.18	Institutions Juris civilis
146.19	methodus lagi
146.20	hemingius
146.21	didaci covaruvias
146.22	Inst Juris canonici lancelotti
146.23	Rebuffus de decimis
146.24	Sebastianus brant
146.25	pract lanfranci
146.26	Const linwod
146.27	hemingius de repudio
146.28	Brisonius de ritu nuptiarum
146.29	manutius de legibus
146.30	corpus canonicum 4tor
146.31	Const linwodi 8°
146.32	edict princ: romanorum
146.33	oldendorpius
146.34:A	heningius de libellis formandis
146.34:B	[See 146.34:A]
146.35	Inst hopperi
146.36	Tractatus benef
146.37	viglius in inst
146.38	natura brevium
146.39	Gronds of the laws
146.40	Index Juris
146.41	vocabulorum Juris
146.42	Inst: accursii
146.43	titulorum Juris brant

146.44	reformatio Legum
146.45	flores senece
146.46	simon simonius de nobilitate
146.47	carpentarii epistola
146.48	alcinous de exilio
146.49	poemata pithagorice
146.50	Cato
146.51	Campanus
146.52	facetiarum bebelii
146.53	sententiae vet poeta
146.54	Regulae chitrei
146.55	parabolae erasmi
146.56	flores poetarum
146.57	Agrippa de vanit sient
146.58	Strigelius in ethica
146.59	erasmus de Lingua
146.60	Bonfinius de conJugale
146.61	Ethica melanthonis
146.62	sent aristotelis
146.63	gnomologia platonis
146.64	sent Ciceronis
146.65	flores aristotelis
146.66	vives de officio mariti
146.67	officia Ciceronis
146.68	ethika aristotelis grece
146.69	orat Ciceronis 8o stepha
146.70	philosophia ciceronis
146.71	Apohthegmata licosthenis
146.72	Beroaldus
146.73	Ethica aristotelis 4to
146.74	piscatius de lusu alaee
146.75	wolphius in officia &c Ciceronis
146.76	Paulus Jovius in 16°
146.77	cronica Carionis
146.78	comment: Cesaris
146.79	Epit vit plut
146.80	methodu Bodini
146.81	mores gentium
146.82	dictis Cretensis
146.83	philostratus
146.84	Justinus
146.85	salustius
146.86	hist: fabritii
146.87	officia Ciceronis
146.88	simbola heroica

146.89	elianus de varia hist
146.90	Cronologia Chitrei
146.91	Chitreus de lection his
146.92	valeris maximus
146.93	de statu galliae
146.94	humfred de vit Juelli
146.95	french littlton
146.96	perionus de vitis apost
146.97	panormitanus de ordine
146.98	libbllus [libellus] suppilorum
146.99	sleidanus de 4tor imperiis
146.100	viperanus de scribenda hist
146.101	de moribus turcarum
146.102	epistole Japanice
146.103	Chitreus de scribenda hist
146.104	fenestella
146.105	hist' fran' spirae
146.106	comines de bello neapol
146.107	cronographia pantaleonis
146.108	Rhet wilichii
146.109	Arith tonstalli
146.110	durandus de arte testandi
146.111	inst juris Civilis
146.112	Salust
146.113	Epistolae Ciceronis
146.114	agripa de occult philosophia
146.115	2 virgilius
146.116	[See 146.115]
146.117	Illiades homeri grece
146.118	Idem latine
146.119	aphthonius
146.120	plautus
146.121	pallingenius
146.122	Ramus in georgica virgilli
146.123	epigrammata martialis
146.124	lucanus
146.125	persius
146.126	alqwot Germanorum carminum
146.127	politica aristotelis
146.128	dialogi luciani
146.129	clark de aulico
146.130	viperanus de rege et regno
146.131	machivell de principe
146.132	Loritius de principe
146.133	foxius de regis institutione

146.134   Brentius de republ[i]ca
146.135   dialectica Rami
146.136   dialectica perioni
146.137   dialect melant
146.138   dialectica rodolph
146.139   dialet titelmanni
146.140   wilichii logica
146.141   nunii logica
146.142   lexicon dassipodii
146.143   ode rami
146.144   grammatica Clenardi gre 4to
146.145   Grammatica tremelli
146.146   Grammatica melancthonis
146.147   epito pagnini Lex
146.148   Grammatica clenardi
146.149   Idem ecolampadii
146.150   Grammatica heb Clenardi
146.151   Elucidarius poeticus
146.152   ortagraphia manuti
146.153   Idem nemi
146.154   de verbis anomolis
146.155   Grammatica gazae
146.156:1 grammer frenc and dut [dutch]
146.156:2 [See 146.156:1]
146.157   Enchiridion ad copiam
146.158   phrase scori
146.159   adagia erasmi
146.160   manutii phrases
146.161   Epistole sadeleti
146.162   Colloquium
146.163   copia verborum
146.164   vives de exert ling
146.165   Epistole manutii
146.166   Epistole plinii
146.167   Epistole Ciceronis
146.168   Idem ad atticum
146.169   orat longolii
146.170   Elegant valla
146.171   orat Isocrat gre et lat
146.172   opera Ciceronis
146.173   epistole Simach
146.174   Brandolinus de conscribendis
146.175   epistolae ascam
146.176   epistole bunelli
146.177   orat muret

146.178 moriae encomium gre lat
146.179 Rhetorica Crusii
146.180 demosthenis olinthice
146.181 Erasmi ciceronianus
146.182 de falsa legat gre
146.183:1 2 esckines et demostenis orat gre
146.183:2 [See 146.183:1]
146.184 orat hironimi faleti
146.185 orat perpiniani
146.186 orat perionii
146.187 Isocratis archidamus
146.188 sambucus de Imitatione
146.189 demosthenis contr leptinem
146.190 Isocrates ad demonicum
146.191 Isocratis evagoras
146.192 oratio humfredi ad reginam
146.193 Rhetorica aristotelis
146.194 Rhetorica talei
146.195 Riccius de imitatione
146.196 Rami Rhetorica
146.197 Trapezutii Retorica
146.198 Gorsius de figuris
146.199 Toxitus ad Herennium
146.200:1 Epitome susenbrot e strebeus
146.200:2 [See 146.200:1]
146.201 Sturmius de periodis
146.202 Aphthonius
146.203 Sturmii parti
146.204 erasmus de conscribiendis
146.205 hermogenis grece
146.206 Galenus de simp medicament
146.207 practica gordonii
146.208 methodus fernelii
146.209 Erithreus de elocutione
146.210 fuctii methodus
146.211 Paraselus de tartaro
146.212 Rhetorica ciceronis
146.213 alexandrinus de sanit tuenda
146.214 Cardanus de varietate
146.215 Idem de subtilitate
146.216 themistius
146.217 marsilius fisinus
146.218 foxii philosophia natur
146.219 peucerus de divinationibus
146.220 agrippa de occulta philosophia

146.221 liber phisicorum
146.222 Rhetorica vivis
146.223 Regulae medicinales
146.224 Lmnius [Lemnius] de humano corpore
146.225 de gubernanda sanit
146.226 Lemnius de astrologia
146.227 phisica melancthonis
146.228 Gwintherus de balneis
146.229 melancthon de anima
146.230 pantapolion pictorii
146.231 Lavaterus de spectris
146.232 mizaldus
146.233 Trithemius de 7 Secundis
146.234 Beverus d in phisicam aristotelis
146.235 valerius de sphera
146.236:1 bis 2 daneus de venefisis
146.236:2 [See 146.236:1]
146.237 abstract of statuts
146.238 practica de ferariis
146.239 flaminius
146.240 Ethica valerii
146.241 Cureus de sensibus
146.242 mathisii epitome
146.243 Geometiae elementa
146.244 Cosmographiae instit
146.245 Theorice purbachii
146.246 arithmetica tonstalli
146.247 Cosmographia Gemme frisii
146.248 Chiromantia indaginis
146.249:1 2 hunter cosmograph
146.249:2 [See 146.249:1]
146.250 arithmetica peltarii
146.251 valerius de sphera
146.252 problemata aristotelis
146.253 dinis de regulis Juris
146.254:1–2 2 Coppi bookes
146.255 Ramus in Cicer de fato
146.256 de causis affetionum
146.257 magiae naturalis
146.258 hasfardus de sanit tuenda
146.259 Gwido de Inditiis
146.260 Boetii arithmetica
146.261 homilia clitovii
146.262 andradius in chemnitium
146.263 Loci communes Cani

146.264	preces privatae
146.265	Sermones
146.266	liber de animalibus
146.267	ecclesiastica dissiplina
146.268	elenchus hereticorum
146.269	Lavaterus de cena domini
146.270:1	bis Genesis heb
146.270:2	[See 146.270:1]
146.271	hemingius de pastore
146.272	montensis de eucaristia
146.273	Bullingerus de fine mundi
146.274	daneus de heresibus
146.275	vives de fide Christiana
146.276	Catheckismus noeli
146.277	Imagines mortis
146.278	Gerson de imit Chrsti [Christi]
146.279	Sanderus de honor imagines
146.280	parchment book
146.281	Bertram de poltia Judaica
146.282	Simlerus de presentia Cristi
146.283	Examen theologicum
146.284	nesechius de Caena domini
146.285	Chitreus de studio thel
146.286	herborn in 70 psalmum
146.287:1	erasmus de rat studii theologice
146.287:2	[See 146.287:1]
146.288	hiperius de Christiana Religione
146.289	Catologus autorum veteris test
146.290	Chitreus de studio
146.291	apologia Ecclesia ang
146.292	Cathechis palatinatus
146.293	Loci melantonis
146.294	de ritibus et inst ecl tigurine
146.295	Beza in selnecerum
146.296	Latomas de theologo
146.297	petrus martir in smitheum
146.298	Qwestiones thomae
146.299	philo de mund fabricatione
146.300	confessio Bezae
146.301	kempisius de imitando Cristo
146.302	Rivius de consol egrotantibus
146.303	Basilius magnus de stult moi
146.304	Ridleus de cena domini
146.305	Epista lutheri
146.306	Sermones dominicales

146.307	aureum opus de contritione
146.308	aretius defentio gentilis
146.309	Speculum morale
146.310	Biblia stephani
146.311	decades bullingeri
146.312	Sermones parisiensis
146.313	Loci marlorati
146.314	bis Biblia castalionis
146.315	Kemnitius
146.316	Loci communes musculi
146.317	Sintagma wigandi
146.318	hierarchia caelestis
146.319:1	Calvinus in Genesim et in psalmos
146.319:2	[See 146.319:1]
146.320	paraphras erasmi
146.321	aretius in epistolas
146.322	Gregorius in cantica
146.323	erasmus in Ecclesiast
146.324	hiperii opuscula
146.325	Idem methodus
146.326	Lactantius
146.327	Lombardus
146.328	Test bezae
146.329	biblia
146.330	2a pars hiperii opuscula
146.331	flores doctorum
146.332	hiperius de ratione studii
146.333	postilla spangembergii
146.334	postilla wigandi
146.335	postilla gresseri
146.336	homer
146.337	Loci martiris
146.338	dialogi cast
146.339	Compendia pindari
146.340:1	2 decadum bulingeri
146.340:2	[See 146.340:1]
146.341	eusebius de preparta evange
146.342	flaminis in psalmum
146.343	philo Judeus de antiquit
146.344	osorius de gloria
146.345	Idem de regis inst
146.346	Idem de Justitia
146.347	Idem in haddonum
146.348	Speculum durandi
146.349	prateolus de vitis hereticorum

146.350   mercurialis
146.351   Calvinus in esiam
146.352   aretius in Johannem
146.353:1 Idem in marcum et lucam
146.353:2 [See 146.353:1]
146.354   Idem in matheum
146.355   problemat aretii 3bus
146.356   Idem in acta
146.357   historia ecclesiast Cristophersoni
146.358   epiphanius
146.359   Baldus
146.360 multiple   a certay company of english bookes
146.361 multiple   bookes for master Rape

§

146.1   Corpus Juris civilis cum glossa 5 voluminibus
Justinian I. *Corpus juris civilis*. Continent: date indeterminable.
One of three copies; see 146.5 and 146.15. Note the differences in appraised values. *Language(s)*: Latin. Appraised at 20s in 1586.

146.2   corpus panormitani 4tour voluminibus
Nicolaus Tudeschis (Panormitanus). [*Decretales: commentary*]. (*Corpus juris canonici*). Continent: date indeterminable.
Language(s): Latin. Appraised at 12s in 1586.

146.3   felinus duobus
Probably Felino Maria Sandeo. [*Decretales: commentary*]. (*Corpus juris canonici–Liber Extra*). Continent: date indeterminable.
Two volumes. Originally appraised at 8s, which is struck out. *Language(s)*: Latin. Appraised at 13s 4d in 1586.

146.4   Repertorium corseti
Antonius Corsettus. *Repertorium in opera Nicolae de Tudeschis*. Continent: date indeterminable.
Language(s): Latin. Appraised at 3s in 1586.

146.5   Corpus Juris civilis cum glossa 5 volumes
Justinian I. *Corpus juris civilis*. Continent: date indeterminable.
The phrase *cum glossa* in the entry replaces *notis*, which was struck out. One of three copies; see 146.1 and 146.15. Note the differences in appraised values. *Language(s)*: Latin. Appraised at 40s in 1586.

146.6:1 minsingerus in Inst et wesembesius in paratitla
Joachim Mynsinger. *Apotelesma.* (*Corpus juris civilis–Institutiones*). Continent: date indeterminable.
Language(s): Latin. Appraised with one other at 8s in 1586.

146.6:2 [See 146.6:1]
Matthaeus Wesenbecius. [*Digesta: commentary*]. Continent: date indeterminable. This commentary on the *Digest* commonly went by the name *Paratitla*. *Language(s)*: Latin. Appraised with one other at 8s in 1586.

146.7 nizolius
Marius Nizolius. [*Observationes*]. Continent: date indeterminable.
Also found in the library of John Tatham, PLRE 112. *Language(s)*: Latin. Appraised at 2s in 1586.

146.8 Casus longi
Unidentified. Continent: date indeterminable.
Either Guido or Bernardus Bottonus; the first, on civil law, is perhaps marginally more likely than the second, on canon law. *Language(s)*: Latin. Appraised at 1s in 1586.

146.9 phisica aristotelis cum commento
Aristotle. *Physica*. Continent (probable): date indeterminable.
Probably not an STC book, but see STC 758. The paraphrase, with commentary, by Andreas Gerardus, *Hyperius* (London, 1583) is a remote possibility. *Language(s)*: Latin Greek (perhaps). Appraised at 6d in 1586.

146.10 officina textoris
Joannes Ravisius (Textor). [*Officina*]. Continent: date indeterminable.
Language(s): Latin. Appraised at 10d in 1586.

146.11 canonicu in phisic aristotelis
Joannes, *Canonicus*. [*Aristotle–Physica: commentary*]. Britain or Continent: date indeterminable.
STC 14621 and non-STC. Also found in the library of John Tatham, PLRE 112. *Language(s)*: Latin. Appraised at 4d in 1586.

146.12 Egidius in phisica
Aegidius Columna, *Romanus*. [*Aristotle–Physica: commentary*]. Continent: date indeterminable.
Language(s): Latin. Appraised at 4d in 1586.

146.13 Cornucopiae
Unidentified. Place unknown: stationer unknown, date indeterminable.
STC/non-STC status unknown. Perhaps one of the works of Nicolas Perottus,

or conceivably Joannes Ravisius, *Textor*. *Language(s)*: Unknown. Appraised at 18d in 1586.

146.14 consilia matrimonialia
Consilia matrimonialia. Edited by Giovanni Battista Ziletti. Continent: date indeterminable.
Language(s): Latin. Appraised at 5s in 1586.

146.15 corpus Juris
Justinian I. *Corpus juris civilis*. Continent: date indeterminable.
One of three copies; see 146.1 and 146.5. Note the differences in appraised values. *Language(s)*: Latin. Appraised at 12s in 1586.

146.16 de conjecturis ult'
Probably Francesco Mantica, *Cardinal*. *Tractatus de conjecturis ultimarum voluntatum*. Continent: date indeterminable.
Andreas Osiander's *Conjecturae de ultimis temporibus*, a theological work, is considerably less likely to appear in the law section of Tatham's collection. *Language(s)*: Latin. Appraised at 6s in 1586.

146.17 alphabetum aureum
Petrus Ravennas (Pietro Tommai). *Alphabetum aureum utriusque juris*. Continent: 1508–1517.
Language(s): Latin. Appraised at 3d in 1586.

146.18 Institutions Juris civilis
Justinian I. *Institutiones*. (*Corpus juris civilis*). Continent: date indeterminable.
Tatham owned another copy; see 146.111. *Language(s)*: Latin. Appraised at 4d in 1586.

146.19 methodus lagi
Conradus Lagus (Conrad Haas). *Methodicus juris utriusque traditio*. Continent: date indeterminable.
Language(s): Latin. Appraised at 4d in 1586.

146.20 hemingius
Niels Hemmingsen. Unidentified. Place unknown: stationer unknown, date indeterminable.
STC/non-STC status unknown. Most of Hemmingsen's works are theological, though in this legal section of the collection, one of his works on law must be considered a possibility. *Language(s)*: Latin. Appraised at 4d in 1586.

146.21 didaci covaruvias
Diego Covarruvias a Leyva, *Bishop of Segovia*. Unidentified. Continent: date indeterminable.
Language(s): Latin. Appraised at 6d in 1586.

146.22 Inst Juris canonici lancelotti
Giovanni Paolo Lancelotto. *Institutiones juris canonici*. Continent: date indeterminable.
Also found in the library of John Tatham, PLRE 112. *Language(s)*: Latin. Appraised at 12d in 1586.

146.23 Rebuffus de decimis
Petrus Rebuffus. *Tractatus de decimis tam feudalibus, quam aliis*. Continent: date indeterminable.
Not an STC book, but see STC 7262. *Language(s)*: Latin. Appraised at 8d in 1586.

146.24 Sebastianus brant
Sebastian Brant. Unidentified. Place unknown: stationer unknown, date indeterminable.
STC/non-STC status unknown. Probably one of Brant's legal works rather than his now-famous *Ship of Fools*. This section of the library is mostly legal, and Tatham owned another of Brant's books on law (see 146.43). *Language(s)*: Latin. Appraised at 2d in 1586.

146.25 pract lanfranci
Lanfrancus de Oriano. [*Practica Lanfranci*]. Continent: date indeterminable. *Language(s)*: Latin. Appraised at 6d in 1586.

146.26 Const linwod
William Lyndewode, *Bishop*. *Constitutiones provinciales*. Britain or Continent: 1483–1525.
STC 17102 *et seq*. Tatham owned two copies; see 146.31. This entry probably represents one of the folio editions, which were printed up until 1525. Tatham's other copy of Lyndewode is an octavo. *Language(s)*: Latin. Appraised at 3s in 1586.

146.27 hemingius de repudio
Niels Hemmingsen. *Libellus de conjugio, repudio, et divortio*. Leipzig: imprim. Joannes Steinman, 1573–1581.
Language(s): Latin. Appraised at 6d in 1586.

146.28 Brisonius de ritu nuptiarum
Barnabé Brisson. *De ritu nuptiarum liber singularis*. Continent: date indeterminable.
Language(s): Latin. Appraised at 3d in 1586.

146.29 manutius de legibus
Paolo Manuzio. *Antiquitatum Romanarum liber de legibus*. Continent: date indeterminable.
Language(s): Latin. Appraised at 3d in 1586.

146.30 corpus canonicum 4tor
Corpus juris canonici. Continent: date indeterminable.
Language(s): Latin. Appraised at 6s 8d in 1586.

146.31 Const linwodi 8°
William Lyndewode, Bishop. *Constitutiones provinciales.* London: (different houses), 1496–1557.
STC 17102 *et seq.* See notes to 146.26, where there is listed another copy. Also found in the library of John Tatham, PLRE 112. *Language(s)*: Latin. Appraised at 4d in 1586.

146.32 edict princ: romanorum
Franciscus Balduinus. *Ad edicta veterum principum Rom. de christianis.* Basle: per Joannem Oporinum, 1557.
Language(s): Latin. Appraised at 1d in 1586.

146.33 oldendorpius
Johann Oldendorp. Unidentified. Continent: date indeterminable.
Language(s): Latin. Appraised at 1d in 1586.

146.34:A heningius de libellis formandis
Henning Goeden. *Ordinis judiciarii processus.* Continent: 1538–1582 (composite publication).
Language(s): Latin. Appraised [a composite volume] at 4d in 1586.

146.34:B [See 146.34:A]
Denari Odofredus (Bononiensis). *Summa de libellis formandis.* [Composite publication]
Language(s): Latin. Appraised [a composite volume] at 4d in 1586.

146.35 Inst hopperi
Joachim Hopper. *Institutiones imperiales. (Corpus juris civilis).* Cologne: apud haered. Joannis Quentelii et Gervinium Calenium, 1560–1565.
Also found in the library of John Tatham, PLRE 112. Language(s): Latin. Appraised at 5d in 1586.

146.36 Tractatus benef
Unidentified. Continent (probable): date indeterminable.
Almost certainly not an STC book. Numerous possibilities. *Language(s)*: Latin. Appraised at 1d in 1586.

146.37 viglius in inst
Nicolaus Vigelius. *Institutionum juris publici libri III.* Basle: ex officina Oporiniana, 1572.
Language(s): Latin. Appraised at 3d in 1586.

146.38 natura brevium
Natura brevium. London: (different houses), date indeterminable.
STC 18385 *et seq.* From 1494 in Law French; from 1530 in English. *Language(s)*: English (probable) Law French (probable). Appraised at 2d in 1586.

146.39 Gronds of the laws
Institutions, or principall groundes of the lawes and statutes of England. (England–Statutes–Institutions). London: (different houses), 1543–1580.
STC 9292 *et seq. Language(s)*: English. Appraised at 3d in 1586.

146.40 Index Juris
Justinian I. [*Corpus juris civilis–Index*]. Continent: date indeterminable. *Language(s)*: Latin. Appraised at 2d in 1586.

146.41 vocabulorum Juris
Anonymous. *Vocabularius juris utriusque.* Continent: date indeterminable. *Language(s)*: Latin. Appraised at 4d in 1586.

146.42 Inst: accursii
Justinian I. *Institutiones.* (*Corpus juris civilis*). With commentary by Franciscus Accursius. Continent: date indeterminable.
The *glossa ordinaria* of Accursius was commonly printed with the *Institutiones.* *Language(s)*: Latin. Appraised at 8d in 1586.

146.43 titulorum Juris brant
Sebastian Brant. [*Expositiones omnium titulorum juris tam civilis quam canonici*]. Continent: date indeterminable.
See 146.24. *Language(s)*: Latin. Appraised at 3d in 1586.

146.44 reformatio Legum
Thomas Cranmer, *Archbishop* (with Walter Haddon, Richard Cox and others). *Reformatio legum ecclesiasticarum.* Edited by John Foxe, *the Martyrologist.* London: ex off. J. Daii, 1571.
STC 6006. Also found in the library of John Tatham, PLRE 112. *Language(s)*: Latin. Appraised at 4d in 1586.

146.45 flores senece
Lucius Annaeus Seneca. [*Selections–Flores selecti*]. Continent: date indeterminable.
Language(s): Latin. Appraised at 1d in 1586.

146.46 simon simonius de nobilitate
Simon Simonius. *De vera nobilitate.* Leipzig: (Joannes Rhamba excud.), 1572. *Language(s)*: Latin. Appraised at 3d in 1586.

146.47 carpentarii epistola
Pierre Charpentier. *Epistola ad Franciscum Portum*. Continent: 1572–1573.
Language(s): Latin. Appraised at 1d in 1586.

146.48 alcinous de exilio
Pietro Alcionio. *De exilio*. Continent: 1522–1546.
Language(s): Latin. Appraised at 2d in 1586.

146.49 poemata pithagorice
Pythagoras. [*Carmina aurea*]. Continent: date indeterminable.
Often printed with the poems of Phocylis and Theognis. *Language(s)*: Greek Latin. Appraised at 3d in 1586.

146.50 Cato
Unidentified. Place unknown: stationer unknown, date indeterminable.
STC/non-STC status unknown. The *Disticha* of Dionysius Cato and the *De re rustica* of Marcus Portius Cato are equal candidates, though perhaps the *Disticha* is marginally more likely. *Language(s)*: Latin. Appraised at 1d in 1586.

146.51 Campanus
Perhaps Joannes Antonius Campanus. Unidentified. Continent: date indeterminable.
Language(s): Latin. Appraised at 1d in 1586.

146.52 facetiarum bebelii
Heinrich Bebel. *Facetiae*. Continent: date indeterminable.
Also found in the library of John Tatham, PLRE 112. *Language(s)*: Latin. Appraised at 3d in 1586.

146.53 sententiae vet poeta
Georg Meier, *Professor at Wittenberg*. *Sententiae veterum poetarum*. Continent: date indeterminable.
Language(s): Latin (probable) Greek (perhaps). Appraised at 2d in 1586.

146.54 Regulae chitrei
David Chytraeus. *Regulae vitae*. Continent: date indeterminable.
Language(s): Latin. Appraised at 2d in 1586.

146.55 parabolae erasmi
Desiderius Erasmus. *Parabolae sive similia*. Continent: date indeterminable.
Language(s): Latin. Appraised at 2d in 1586.

146.56 flores poetarum
Flores poetarum. Continent: date indeterminable.
Language(s): Latin. Appraised at 4d in 1586.

146.57 Agrippa de vanit sient
Henricus Cornelius Agrippa. *De incertitudine et vanitate scientiarum*. Continent: date indeterminable.
Also found in the library of John Tatham, PLRE 112. *Language(s)*: Latin. Appraised at 6d in 1586.

146.58 Strigelius in ethica
Victorinus Strigelius. [*Aristotle–Ethica: commentary*]. Continent: 1572–1586. *Language(s)*: Latin. Appraised at 12d in 1586.

146.59 erasmus de Lingua
Desiderius Erasmus. *Lingua*. Continent: date indeterminable.
Language(s): Latin. Appraised at 3d in 1586.

146.60 Bonfinius de conJugale
Antonius Bonfinius. *Symposion trimeron*. Edited by Joannes Leunclavius. Basle: ex officina Oporiniana, 1572.
The long title includes *de virginitate et pudicitia conjugale*. Also found in the library of John Tatham, PLRE 112. *Language(s)*: Latin. Appraised at 4d in 1586.

146.61 Ethica melanthonis
Philipp Melanchthon. [*Aristotle–Ethica: commentary*]. Continent: date indeterminable.
Language(s): Latin. Appraised at 4d in 1586.

146.62 sent aristotelis
Aristotle. [*Selections*]. Continent: date indeterminable.
Language(s): Latin. Appraised at 2d in 1586.

146.63 gnomologia platonis
Plato. [*Selections*]. Continent: date indeterminable.
Language(s): Latin (probable) Greek (perhaps). Appraised at 3d in 1586.

146.64 sent Ciceronis
Marcus Tullius Cicero. [*Selections*]. Britain or Continent: date indeterminable. STC 5318.3 *et seq.* and non-STC. The STC editions are not limited to Cicero. Also found in the library of John Tatham, PLRE 112. *Language(s)*: Latin. Appraised at 4d in 1586.

146.65 flores aristotelis
Aristotle. *Flores illustriores Aristotelis*. Probably edited and compiled by Jacques Bouchereau. Continent: date indeterminable.
Also found in the library of John Tatham, PLRE 112. *Language(s)*: Latin. Appraised at 12d in 1586.

146.66   vives de officio mariti
Joannes Ludovicus Vives. *De officio mariti*. Continent: date indeterminable.
Also found in the library of John Tatham, PLRE 112. *Language(s)*: Latin. Appraised at 8d in 1586.

146.67   officia Ciceronis
Marcus Tullius Cicero. *De officiis*. Continent: date indeterminable.
Tatham owned a second copy of this work; see 146.87. Also found in the library of John Tatham, PLRE 112. *Language(s)*: Latin. Appraised at 8d in 1586.

146.68   ethika aristotelis grece
Aristotle. *Ethica*. Continent: date indeterminable.
Language(s): Greek. Appraised at 12d in 1586.

146.69   orat Ciceronis 8o stepha
Marcus Tullius Cicero. [*Selected Works–Orations*]. Edited by Robert Estienne. Paris: ex officina Roberti Stephani, 1543.
One or more of the three volumes of orations; perhaps the entire Stephanus edition in which the *Orationes* lead. See Adams C1643. *Language(s)*: Latin. Appraised at 3s in 1586.

146.70   philosophia ciceronis
Marcus Tullius Cicero. [*Selected works–Philosophica*]. Continent: date indeterminable.
Language(s): Latin. Appraised at 12d in 1586.

146.71   Apohthegmata licosthenis
Conrad Lycosthenes (Conrad Wolffhart). *Apophthegmata*. Britain or Continent: date indeterminable.
STC 17003.3 and non-STC. Also found in the library of John Tatham, PLRE 112. *Language(s)*: Latin. Appraised at 14d in 1586.

146.72   Beroaldus
Unidentified. Place unknown: stationer unknown, date indeterminable.
STC/non-STC status unknown. Either Philippus Beroaldus or Matthaeus Beroaldus. STC 1968.3 *et seq*. is a remote possibility, but it must be considered. *Language(s)*: Latin (probable) English (perhaps). Appraised at 4d in 1586.

146.73   Ethica aristotelis 4to
Aristotle. *Ethica*. Britain or Continent: date indeterminable.
STC 752 and non-STC. The only quarto edition to appear in England was published in 1479, unlikely to be represented here. Also found in the library of John Tatham, PLRE 112. *Language(s)*: Latin (probable) Greek (perhaps). Appraised at 14d in 1586.

146.74 piscatius de lusu alaee

Pascasius Justus. *Alea, sive de curanda ludendi in pecuniam cupiditate*. Basle: Joannes Oporinus, 1561.

This unusual work was also found in the library of John Tatham, PLRE 112. *Language(s)*: Latin. Appraised at 10d in 1586.

146.75 wolphius in officia &c Ciceronis

Hieronymus Wolfius. *In Officia Catonem Laelium Paradoxa et Scipionis Somnium commentarii*. Basle: ex off. Hervagiana, per Eusebium Episcopum, 1569-1584.

Language(s): Latin. Appraised at 3s 4d in 1586.

146.76 Paulus Jovius in 16°

Paolo Giovio, *Bishop*. Unidentified. Continent: date indeterminable.

His widely published *Historiarum sui temporis* was published in sextodecimo, as this book was. *Language(s)*: Latin. Appraised at 2s 6d in 1586.

146.77 cronica Carionis

Johann Carion. *Chronica*. Continent: date indeterminable.

Language(s): Latin. Appraised at 10d in 1586.

146.78 comment: Cesaris

Caius Julius Caesar. *Commentarii*. Britain or Continent: date indeterminable. STC 4332 and non-STC. *Language(s)*: Latin. Appraised at 3d in 1586.

146.79 Epit vit plut

Plutarch. [*Vitae parallelae–Epitome*]. Continent: date indeterminable.

Language(s): Latin. Appraised at 6d in 1586.

146.80 methodu Bodini

Jean Bodin, *Bishop*. *Methodus ad facilem historiarum cognitionem*. Continent: date indeterminable.

Language(s): Latin. Appraised at 16d in 1586.

146.81 mores gentium

Joannes Boemus. [*Omnium gentium mores, leges et ritus*]. Continent: date indeterminable.

Also found in the library of John Tatham, PLRE 112. *Language(s)*: Latin. Appraised at 6d in 1586.

146.82 dictis Cretensis

Dictys, *Cretensis*. *De bello troiano*. Continent: date indeterminable.

Often published with, and even conflated with, the works of Dares, *the Phrygian*. *Language(s)*: Latin. Appraised at 3d in 1586.

146.83 philostratus
Philostratus. Perhaps *De vita Apollonii Tyanei*. Continent: date indeterminable. The life of Apollonius is Philostratus's most frequently reprinted work. *Language(s)*: Latin (probable) Greek (perhaps). Appraised at 3d in 1586.

146.84 Justinus
Trogus Pompeius and Justinus, *the Historian*. [*Epitomae in Trogi Pompeii historias*]. Britain or Continent: date indeterminable.

STC 24287 *et seq*. and non-STC. Possibly Justinus, *Saint and Martyr*, but this book is in the history section of the library. Also found in the library of John Tatham, PLRE 112. *Language(s)*: Latin. Appraised at 3d in 1586.

146.85 salustius
Caius Sallustius Crispus. Unidentified. Place unknown: stationer unknown, date indeterminable.

STC/non-STC status unknown. Which combination of Sallust's works cannot be determined. See 146.112 for another copy of Sallust. *Language(s)*: Latin. Appraised at 4d in 1586.

146.86 hist: fabritii
Probably Franciscus Fabricius, *Marcoduranus. M. Tullii Ciceronis historia*. Continent: date indeterminable.

The titles of two other works by Georgius Fabricius have some form of the word *history* in them, but neither deals with Roman history nor with Cicero. Since the entry prior to this is a book on Roman history, and since the following entry is Cicero, the book by Franciscus Fabricius seems the best possibility. *Language(s)*: Latin. Appraised at 3d in 1586.

146.87 officia Ciceronis
Marcus Tullius Cicero. *De officiis*. Continent: date indeterminable.

See 146.67 for another copy. Also found in the library of John Tatham, PLRE 112. *Language(s)*: Latin. Appraised at 6d in 1586.

146.88 simbola heroica
Claude Paradin. *Symbola*. Continent: date indeterminable.

First published in French as *Devises heroiques*, but this is presumably the Latin translation. *Language(s)*: Latin. Appraised at 4d in 1586.

146.89 elianus de varia hist
Claudius Aelianus. *Varia historia*. Continent: date indeterminable. *Language(s)*: Latin. Appraised at 3d in 1586.

146.90 Cronologia Chitrei
David Chytraeus. *Chronologia historiae Herodoti et Thucydidis*. Continent: date indeterminable.

Language(s): Latin. Appraised at 2d in 1586.

146.91 Chitreus de lection his
David Chytraeus. *De lectione historiarum.* Continent: date indeterminable. *Language(s)*: Latin. Appraised at 3d in 1586.

146.92 valeris maximus
Valerius Maximus. *Facta et dicta memorabilia.* Continent: date indeterminable. Also found in the library of John Tatham, PLRE 112. *Language(s)*: Latin. Appraised at 4d in 1586.

146.93 de statu galliae
Pierre de La Place. *De statu religionis et reipublicae in regno Galliae.* Continent: date indeterminable.
Also found in the library of John Tatham, PLRE 112. *Language(s)*: Latin. Appraised at 4d in 1586.

146.94 humfred de vit Juelli
Laurence Humphrey. *Joannis Juelli Angli, episcopi Sarisburiensis vita et mors, eiusque verae doctrinae defensio.* London: apud J. Dayum, 1573.
STC 13963. *Language(s)*: Latin. Appraised at 12d in 1586.

146.95 french littlton
Sir Thomas Littleton. [*Tenures*]. Britain or Continent: date indeterminable.
STC 15719 *et seq. Language(s)*: English (probable) Law French (perhaps). Appraised at 3d in 1586.

146.96 perionus de vitis apost
Joachim Perion. *De rebus gestis vitisque Apostolorum.* Continent: 1552–1569. *Language(s)*: Latin. Appraised at 3d in 1586.

146.97 panormitanus de ordine
Joannes de Urbach. *Processus judiciarius.* Continent: date indeterminable.
At this time, usually attributed to Nicolaus Tudeschis, *Panormitanus. Language(s)*: Latin. Appraised at 2d in 1586.

146.98 libbllus [libellus] suppilorum
Unidentified. Place unknown: stationer unknown, date indeterminable.
STC/non-STC status unknown. A number of possibilities, including Osorio da Fonseca's *In Gualterum Haddonum magistrum libellorum supplicum* (see 146.347) and STC 18440, *Libellus supplex imperatoriae majestati . . . nomine Belgarum ex inferiori Germania* (1530). *Language(s)*: Latin. Appraised at 10d in 1586.

146.99 sleidanus de 4tor imperiis
Joannes Philippson, *Sleidanus. De quatuor summis imperiis.* Britain or Continent: date indeterminable.
STC 19847 *et seq.* and non-STC. *Language(s)*: Latin. Appraised at 3d in 1586.

146.100   viperanus de scribenda hist

Giovanni Antonio Viperano. *De historia scribenda liber.* Antwerp: ex officina Christopheri Plantini, 1569.

Issued with the same author's *De rege, et regno liber* (also owned by Tatham; see 146.130), but this work was also published separately. Also found in the library of John Tatham, PLRE 112. *Language(s)*: Latin. Appraised at 2d in 1586.

146.101   de moribus turcarum

Bartholomaeus Georgievits. *De Turcarum moribus epitome.* Continent: date indeterminable. 1552–1578.

Language(s): Latin. Appraised at 2d in 1586.

146.102   epistole Japanice

Anonymous. *Epistolae japanicae, de multorum gentilium in variis insulis ad Christi fidem per Societatis Jesu theologos conversione.* (*Jesuits*). Louvain: apud Rutgerum Velpium, 1569–1570.

Language(s): Latin. Appraised at 7d in 1586.

146.103   Chitreus de scribenda hist

David Chytraeus. *De scribenda historia.* Continent: date indeterminable.

Published in compilations of writings on history, Chytraeus's work seems not to have been appeared alone. *Language(s)*: Latin. Appraised at 1d in 1586.

146.104   fenestella

Andreas Dominicus Floccus (Lucius Fenestella). Probably *De magistratibus sacerdotiisque Romanorum.* Continent: date indeterminable.

Language(s): Latin. Appraised at 2d in 1586.

146.105   hist' fran' spirae

Caelius Secundus Curio. *Francisci Spierae historia, a quatuor summis viris.* Basle: [Joannes Oporinus], 1550.

Language(s): Latin. Appraised at 2d in 1586.

146.106   comines de bello neapol

Philippe de Comines. [*Memoires*]. Translated by Joannes Philippson, *Sleidanus.* Continent: date indeterminable.

The long title continues: *sive . . . De Carolo octavo Galliae rege, et bello Neapolitano. Language(s)*: Latin. Appraised at 4d in 1586.

146.107   cronographia pantaleonis

Heinrich Pantaleon. *Chronographia ecclesiae christianae.* Continent: date indeterminable.

Also found in the library of John Tatham, PLRE 112. *Language(s)*: Latin. Appraised at 12d in 1586.

146.108 Rhet wilichii

Jodocus Willich. *De pronuntiatione rhetorica*. Continent: date indeterminable. *Language(s)*: Latin. Appraised at 1d in 1586.

146.109 Arith tonstalli

Cuthbert Tunstall, *Bishop*. *De arte supputandi libri quattuor*. Britain or Continent: 1522–1551.

STC 24319 and non-STC. See 146.246 for another copy. Also found in the library of John Tatham, PLRE 112. *Language(s)*: Latin. Appraised at 2d in 1586.

146.110 durandus de arte testandi

Johann Dilectus Durans. *De arte testandi, et cautelis ultimarum voluntatum*. Continent: date indeterminable.

Language(s): Latin. Appraised at 4d in 1586.

146.111 inst juris Civilis

Justinian I. *Institutiones*. (*Corpus juris civilis*). Continent: date indeterminable. See 146.18 for another copy. *Language(s)*: Latin. Appraised at 6d in 1586.

146.112 Salust

Caius Sallustius Crispus. Unidentified. Place unknown: stationer unknown, date indeterminable.

STC/non-STC status unknown. Which combination of Sallust's works cannot be determined. See 146.85 for another copy of Sallust. *Language(s)*: Latin. Appraised at 6d in 1586.

146.113 Epistolae Ciceronis

Marcus Tullius Cicero. [*Selected works–Epistolae*]. Continent: date indeterminable.

Possibly the *Epistolae ad familiares* only. See 146.167 for another copy. Also found in the library of John Tatham, PLRE 112. *Language(s)*: Latin. Appraised at 12d in 1586.

146.114 agripa de occult philosophia

Henricus Cornelius Agrippa. *De occulta philosophia*. Continent: date indeterminable.

Also found in the library of John Tatham, PLRE 112. *Language(s)*: Latin. Appraised at 2s in 1586.

146.115 2 virgilius

Publius Virgilius Maro. Probably [*Works*]. Britain or Continent: date indeterminable.

STC 24787 *et seq*. and non-STC. Conceivably two volumes, but the marginal note (2) more likely indicates two copies; see 146.249:1 and 146.254:1 for other instances of this scribal habit. *Language(s)*: Latin. Appraised at 3d in 1586.

146.116 [See 146.115]
Publius Virgilius Maro. Probably [*Works*]. Britain or Continent: date indeterminable.
STC 24787 *et seq.* and non-STC. See the annotations to the preceding. *Language(s)*: Latin. Appraised at 3d in 1586.

146.117 Illiades homeri grece
Homer. *Iliad*. Continent: date indeterminable.
Also found in the library of John Tatham, PLRE 112. *Language(s)*: Greek. Appraised at 3d in 1586.

146.118 Idem latine
Homer. *Iliad*. Continent: date indeterminable.
Also found in the library of John Tatham, PLRE 112. *Language(s)*: Latin. Appraised at 10d in 1586.

146.119 aphthonius
Aphthonius, *Sophista*. *Progymnasmata*. Britain or Continent: date indeterminable.
STC 699 *et seq.* and non-STC. See 146.202 for another copy. Also found in the library of John Tatham, PLRE 112. *Language(s)*: Latin (probable) Greek (perhaps). Appraised at 2d in 1586.

146.120 plautus
Titus Maccius Plautus. *Comoediae*. Continent: date indeterminable.
Language(s): Latin. Appraised at 6d in 1586.

146.121 pallingenius
Marcellus Palingenius (Pietro Angelo Manzolli [Stellatus]). *Zodiacus vitae*. Britain or Continent: date indeterminable.
STC 19138.5 *et seq.* and non-STC. English translations by Barnaby Googe begin 1560; London Latin editions begin 1569. *Language(s)*: Latin (probable) English (perhaps). Appraised at 4d in 1586.

146.122 Ramus in georgica virgilli
Pierre de la Ramée. [*Virgilius–Georgics: commentary*]. Continent: date indeterminable.
Virgil's text is included (see Ong, nos. 479–483). *Language(s)*: Latin. Appraised at 8d in 1586.

146.123 epigrammata martialis
Marcus Valerius Martialis. *Epigrammata*. Continent: date indeterminable.
Also found in the library of John Tatham, PLRE 112. *Language(s)*: Latin. Appraised at 3d in 1586.

146.124 lucanus
Marcus Annaeus Lucanus. *Pharsalia*. Continent: date indeterminable.
Also found in the library of John Tatham, PLRE 112. *Language(s)*: Latin. Appraised at 3d in 1586.

146.125 persius
Aulus Persius Flaccus. [*Works*]. Continent: date indeterminable.
Language(s): Latin. Appraised at 3d in 1586.

146.126 alqwot Germanorum carminum
Illustrium aliquot Germanorum carminum liber. Basle (probable): (stationer unknown), 1573.
The book carries a false imprint: *Vilnae*; Petrus Pernam is sometimes supplied as the printer. *Language(s)*: Latin. Appraised at 1d in 1586.

146.127 politica aristotelis
Aristotle. *Politica*. Continent: date indeterminable.
Language(s): Latin (probable) Greek (perhaps). Appraised at 12d in 1586.

146.128 dialogi luciani
Lucian, *of Samosata*. Unidentified. Place unknown: stationer unknown, date indeterminable.
STC/non-STC status unknown. Whether collected or selected dialogues cannot be determined. *Language(s)*: Latin (probable) Greek (perhaps). Appraised at 2d in 1586.

146.129 clark de aulico
Baldassare Castiglione, *Count*. *De curiali sive aulico libri quatuor ex Italico sermone in Latinum conversi*. Translated by Bartholomew Clerke. London: (different houses), 1571–1585.
STC 4782 *et seq*. *Language(s)*: Latin. Appraised at 10d in 1586.

146.130 viperanus de rege et regno
Giovanni Antonio Viperano. *De rege, et regno liber*. Antwerp: ex officina Christopheri Plantini, 1569.
The Plantin press issued this work with the same author's *De historia scribenda liber*, which is also in Tatham's collection, and this may have separated from that volume since it was not issued separately, though the *De historia scribenda liber* was. Perhaps, however, the composite volume is listed here, and a single edition of the other is at 146.100. This title is also found in the library of John Tatham, PLRE 112. *Language(s)*: Latin. Appraised at 3d in 1586.

146.131 machivell de principe
Niccolò Macchiavelli. *De principe*. Translated by Telius Sylvester. Continent: date indeterminable.

The use of the word *de* as opposed to *il* points toward this being a Latin translation from the Italian. *Language(s)*: Latin. Appraised at 3d in 1586.

146.132   Loritius de principe
Reinhard Lorich (Hadamarius). *De institutione principum loci communes*. Frankfurt am Main: (different houses), 1538–1563.
All editions were published by either Christian Egenolph or his heirs. *Language(s)*: Latin. Appraised at 2d in 1586.

146.133   foxius de regis institutione
Sebastiano Fox Morzillo. *De regni regisque institutione*. Antwerp: (different houses), 1556–1566.
Also found in the library of John Tatham, PLRE 112. *Language(s)*: Latin. Appraised at 10d in 1586.

146.134   Brentius de republca [republica]
Johann Brentz, *the Elder*. *De administranda pie republica*. Continent: 1527–1553. *Language(s)*: Latin. Appraised at 2d in 1586.

146.135   dialectica Rami
Pierre de La Ramée. [*Dialectica*]. Britain or Continent: date indeterminable.
STC 15241.7 *et seq*. and non-STC. Also found in the library of John Tatham, PLRE 112. *Language(s)*: Latin. Appraised at 6d in 1586.

146.136   dialectica perioni
Joachim Perion. *De dialectica*. Continent: date indeterminable.
Also found in the library of John Tatham, PLRE 112. *Language(s)*: Latin. Appraised at 3d in 1586.

146.137   dialect melant
Philipp Melanchthon. [*Dialectica*]. Continent: date indeterminable.
Also found in the library of John Tatham, PLRE 112. *Language(s)*: Latin. Appraised at 4d in 1586.

146.138   dialectica rodolph
Probably Caspar Rhodolphus. [*Dialectica*]. Continent: date indeterminable.
Rodolphus Agricola's *De inventione dialectica* is another possibility. *Language(s)*: Latin. Appraised at 2d in 1586.

146.139   dialet titelmanni
Franz Titelmann. [*Dialectica*]. Continent: date indeterminable.
Language(s): Latin. Appraised at 3d in 1586.

146.140   wilichii logica
Jodocus Willich. *Erotemata dialectices*. Continent: date indeterminable.
Language(s): Latin. Appraised at 10d in 1586.

146.141 nunii logica
Petrus Nunius Velius. *Dialecta libri tres*. Continent: 1570–1578.
Language(s): Latin. Appraised at 2d in 1586.

146.142 lexicon dassipodii
Petrus Dasypodius. *Dictionarium Latin-germanicum*. Continent: date indeterminable.
See 146.156:1. *Language(s)*: German Latin. Appraised at 8d in 1586.

146.143 ode rami
Gabriel Harvey. *Ode natalitia, vel opus eius feriae quae S. Stephani protomartyris nomine celebrata est. In memoriam P. Rami*. London: T. Vautrollerius, 1575.
STC 12902.5. *Language(s)*: Latin. Appraised at 10d in 1586.

146.144 grammatica Clenardi gre 4to
Nicolaus Clenardus. [*Institutiones linguae graecae*]. Continent: date indeterminable.
STC 5400.5 (dated 1582) is an octavo. Tatham may have owned the octavo as well; see 146.148 for another copy. *Language(s)*: Greek Latin. Appraised at 2s in 1586.

146.145 Grammatica tremelli
Grammatica chaldaea et syra. Geneva (probable): Henricus Stephanus, 1569.
Language(s): Chaldaic Latin Syriac. Appraised at 2s in 1586.

146.146 Grammatica melancthonis
Phillipp Melanchthon. Unidentified. Continent: date indeterminable.
The *Grammatica graeca* and the *Grammatica latina* are equal candidates. *Language(s)*: Latin Greek (perhaps). Appraised at 3d in 1586.

146.147 epito pagnini Lex
Sanctes Pagninus. *Thesauri linguae sanctae epitome*. Antwerp: Christopher Plantin, 1570–1578.
Language(s): Hebrew Latin. Appraised at 13d in 1586.

146.148 Grammatica clenardi
Nicolaus Clenardus. [*Institutiones linguae graecae*]. Britain or Continent: date indeterminable.
STC 5400.5 and non-STC. Tatham owned another copy, a quarto, of this work; see 146.144. *Language(s)*: Greek Latin. Appraised at 2d in 1586.

146.149 Idem ecolampadii
Joannes Oecolampadius. *Graecae literaturae dragmata*. Continent: date indeterminable.
Language(s): Greek Latin. Appraised at 2d in 1586.

146.150 Grammatica heb Clenardi
Nicolaus Clenardus. *Tabula in grammaticen hebraeam*. Continent: date indeterminable.
Language(s): Hebrew Latin. Appraised at 2d in 1586.

146.151 Elucidarius poeticus
Probably Hermann Torrentinus. [*Elucidarius carminum*]. Continent: date indeterminable.
Torrentinus's widely published work is considered more likely than either the work of Robert Estienne or that of Johann Gast, each of which carries the same title. The two must, however, remain possibilities. *Language(s)*: Latin. Appraised at 2d in 1586.

146.152 ortagraphia manuti
Aldo Manuzio, *the Elder* (Aldus Manutius). Perhaps *Orthographia et flexus dictionum graecarum omnium apud Statium*. Continent: date indeterminable.
Aldo Manuzio, *the Younger* also published works on orthography, and this entry could refer to one of those. Those by *the Younger* seem to be versions of (or in any case indebted to) *the Elder*'s work. *Language(s)*: Greek Latin. Appraised at 1d in 1586.

146.153 Idem nemi
Joannes Nemius. *Orthographiae ratio*. Antwerp: ex officina Christopheri Plantini, 1572.
Language(s): Latin. Appraised at 2d in 1586.

146.154 de verbis anomolis
Gulielmus Morelius. *De verbis anomalis*. Continent: date indeterminable.
Language(s): Greek Latin. Appraised at 3d in 1586.

146.155 Grammatica gazae
Theodorus, *Gaza*. [*Institutiones grammaticae*]. Continent: date indeterminable.
Language(s): Greek Latin. Appraised at 2d in 1586.

146.156:1 grammer frenc and dut [dutch]
Unidentified. Place unknown: stationer unknown, date indeterminable.
STC/non-STC status unknown. A puzzling manuscript entry. It suggests a single work, but a French-German (or French-Dutch) grammar would be an extremely unusual book to be in an English library. Further, if two books (perhaps bound together) as thought likely, whether the second is a German grammar or a Dutch grammar cannot be determined by the word *dut* [Dutch] which could represent either language at this time, but German is more likely given the German-Latin dictionary in this collection (see 146.142). Several French grammars were published in England; see STC 7377 *et seq.*, as well as the collection of grammars following STC 11375. *Language(s)*: French. Appraised with one other at 3d in 1586.

146.156:2 [See 146.156:1]
   Unidentified. Continent: date indeterminable.
   See the annotations to the preceding, as well as 146.142. *Language(s)*: German/probable Dutch/perhaps. Appraised with one other at 3d in 1586.

146.157   Enchiridion ad copiam
   Theodoricus Morellus. *Enchiridion ad verborum copiam.* Continent: date indeterminable.
   Language(s): Latin. Appraised at 1d in 1586.

146.158   phrase scori
   Antonius Schorus. *Phrases linguae latinae.* Continent: date indeterminable.
   Language(s): Latin. Appraised at 8d in 1586.

146.159   adagia erasmi
   Desiderius Erasmus. *Adagia.* Continent: date indeterminable.
   Also found in the library of John Tatham, PLRE 112. *Language(s)*: Latin. Appraised at 6d in 1586.

146.160   manutii phrases
   Aldo Manuzio, *the Younger. Purae, elegantes et copiosae latinae linguae phrases.* Continent: date indeterminable.
   STC 17278.8 *et seq.* and non-STC. The English issues, which began in 1573, carry an English translation. Also found in the library of John Tatham, PLRE 112. *Language(s)*: Latin. Appraised at 4d in 1586.

146.161   Epistole sadeleti
   Jacobus Sadoletus. [*Epistolae*]. Continent: date indeterminable.
   Also found in the library of John Tatham, PLRE 112. *Language(s)*: Latin. Appraised at 6d in 1586.

146.162   Colloquium
   Probably Desiderius Erasmus. *Colloquia.* Britain or Continent: date indeterminable.
   STC 10450.6 *et seq.* and non-STC. Also found in the library of John Tatham, PLRE 112. *Language(s)*: Latin. Appraised at 3d in 1586.

146.163   copia verborum
   Probably Desiderius Erasmus. *De duplici copia verborum ac rerum.* Britain or Continent: date indeterminable.
   STC 10471.4 *et seq.* and non-STC. Works by other authors are possible, but the title is also found in the library of John Tatham, PLRE 112. *Language(s)*: Latin. Appraised at 2d in 1586.

146.164 vives de exert ling

Joannes Ludovicus Vives. [*Familiarum colloquiorum formulae, sive linguae latinae exercitatio*]. Continent: date indeterminable.

Language(s): Latin. Appraised at 2d in 1586.

146.165 Epistole manutii

Paolo Manuzio. Probably [*Epistolae*]. Britain or Continent: date indeterminable.

STC 17286 *et seq.* and non-STC. His *Epistolae clarorum virorum selectae* is less likely. Also found in the library of John Tatham, PLRE 112. *Language(s)*: Latin. Appraised at 8d in 1586.

146.166 Epistole plinii

Pliny, *the Younger*. *Epistolae*. Continent: date indeterminable.

Also found in the library of John Tatham, PLRE 112. *Language(s)*: Latin. Appraised at 2d in 1586.

146.167 Epistole Ciceronis

Marcus Tullius Cicero. [*Selected works–Epistolae*]. Continent: date indeterminable.

Cicero's popular *Epistolae ad familiares* is possible. See 146.113 for another copy. Also found in the library of John Tatham, PLRE 112. *Language(s)*: Latin. Appraised at 12d in 1586.

146.168 Idem ad atticum

Marcus Tullius Cicero. *Epistolae ad Atticum*. Continent: date indeterminable.

Language(s): Latin. Appraised at 6d in 1586.

146.169 orat longolii

Christophorus Longolius. *Orationes duae pro defensione sua*. Continent: 1524–1539.

Language(s): Latin. Appraised at 6d in 1586.

146.170 Elegant valla

Laurentius Valla. *Elegantiae*. Continent: date indeterminable.

Also found in the library of John Tatham, PLRE 112. *Language(s)*: Latin. Appraised at 6d in 1586.

146.171 orat Isocrat gre et lat

Isocrates. [*Selected works–Orations*]. Continent: date indeterminable.

Language(s): Greek Latin. Appraised at 20d in 1586.

146.172 opera Ciceronis

Marcus Tullius Cicero. [*Works*]. Britain or Continent: date indeterminable.

STC 5266.4 and non-STC. Also found in the library of John Tatham, PLRE 112. *Language(s)*: Latin. Appraised at 12d in 1586.

146.173   epistole Simach
Quintus Aurelius Symmachus. [*Epistolae*]. Continent: date indeterminable. *Language(s)*: Latin. Appraised at 4d in 1586.

146.174   Brandolinus de conscribendis
Aurelius Brandolinus (Lippus). *De rationi scribendi*. Britain or Continent: 1549–1579.
STC 3542 and non-STC. Also found in the library of John Tatham, PLRE 112. *Language(s)*: Latin. Appraised at 8d in 1586.

146.175   epistolae ascam
Roger Ascham. *Familiarium epistolarum libri tres*. Edited by Edward Grant. London: (different houses), 1576–1581.
STC 826 *et seq*. Francis Coldock was involved with the publication of all editions. *Language(s)*: Latin. Appraised at 7d in 1586.

146.176   epistole bunelli
Pierre Bunel. [*Epistolae*]. Continent: 1551–1568.
Some editions also contain letters by Manutius. Also found in the library of John Tatham, PLRE 112. *Language(s)*: Latin. Appraised at 1d in 1586.

146.177   orat muret
Marcus Antonius Muretus. [*Selected works–Orations*]. Continent: date indeterminable.
Language(s): Latin. Appraised at 4d in 1586.

146.178   moriae encomium gre lat
Desiderius Erasmus. *Moriae encomium*. Continent: date indeterminable.
Also found in the library of John Tatham, PLRE 112. *Language(s)*: Greek Latin. Appraised at 6d in 1586.

146.179   Rhetorica Crusii
Probably Philipp Melanchthon. [*Rhetorica*]. Edited by Martin Crusius. Continent: date indeterminable.
See BCI 2:540. *Language(s)*: Latin. Appraised at 12d in 1586.

146.180   demosthenis olinthice
Demosthenes. *Olynthiacae orationes tres*. Continent: date indeterminable.
Probably not an STC book, but see STC 6577. STC 6577 is selected works, but leads with this title. *Language(s)*: Latin (probable) Greek (perhaps). Appraised at 3d in 1586.

146.181   Erasmi ciceronianus
Desiderius Erasmus. *De recta pronuntiatione* [and other works]. Continent: 1528–1558.

Date range is taken from VHe. Language(s): Greek Latin. Appraised at 4d in 1586.

146.182   de falsa legat gre
Demosthenes. *De falsa legatione*. Continent: date indeterminable.
Language(s): Greek. Appraised at 4d in 1586.

146.183:1   2 esckines et demostenis orat gre
Aeschines and Demosthenes. [*Selected works–Orations*]. Continent: date indeterminable.
Language(s): Greek. Appraised with one other at 4d in 1586.

146.183:2   [See 146.183:1]
Aeschines and Demosthenes. [*Selected works–Orations*]. Continent: date indeterminable.
Language(s): Greek. Appraised with one other at 4d in 1586.

146.184   orat hironimi faleti
Girolamo Falletti. *Orationes XII*. Venice: [Aldine Press], 1558.
Language(s): Latin. Appraised at 8d in 1586.

146.185   orat perpiniani
Petrus Joannes Perpinianus. [*Orationes*]. Continent: date indeterminable.
Probably part of a collection since his *Orationes* seems not to have been published solo until 1587. Also found in the library of John Tatham, PLRE 112. *Language(s)*: Latin. Appraised at 2d in 1586.

146.186   orat perionii
Joachim Perion. Unidentified. Continent: date indeterminable.
Several possibilities; see, e.g., Adams P693–95 and P705. *Language(s)*: Latin. Appraised at 2d in 1586.

146.187   Isocratis archidamus
Isocrates. *Archidamus*. Translated by Victorinus Strigelius. Leipzig: in officina Voegeliniana, 1564.
Language(s): Greek Latin. Appraised at 1d in 1586.

146.188   sambucus de Imitatione
Joannes Sambucus. *Tres dialogi de imitatione Ciceroniana*. Continent: 1561–1563.
Each edition contains at least one other work. *Language(s)*: Latin. Appraised at 4d in 1586.

146.189   demosthenis contr leptinem
Demosthenes. *Adversus Leptinem*. Continent: date indeterminable.
Language(s): Latin (probable) Greek (perhaps). Appraised at 1d in 1586.

146.190 Isocrates ad demonicum
Isocrates. *Ad Demonicum*. Continent: date indeterminable.
Language(s): Latin (probable) Greek (perhaps). Appraised at 1d in 1586.

146.191 Isocratis evagoras
Isocrates. *Evagoras*. Continent: date indeterminable.
Evagoras appeared only in collections at this time. Probably separated here, which would be consistent with the low valuation. *Language(s)*: Latin (probable) Greek (probable). Appraised at 1d in 1586.

146.192 oratio humfredi ad reginam
Laurence Humphrey. Unidentified. London: (different houses), 1572–1575. Unidentifiable in the STC. Two such speeches were made, one published in 1572, the other in 1575. See STC 13959–13560. *Language(s)*: Latin. Appraised at 2d in 1586.

146.193 Rhetorica aristotelis
Aristotle. *Rhetorica*. Continent: date indeterminable.
Also found in the library of John Tatham, PLRE 112. *Language(s)*: Latin (probable) Greek (perhaps). Appraised at 4d in 1586.

146.194 Rhetorica talei
Audomarus Talaeus (Omer Talon). *Rhetorica*. Continent: date indeterminable.
Language(s): Latin. Appraised at 2d in 1586.

146.195 Riccius de imitatione
Bartholomaeus Riccius. *De imitatione libri tres*. Continent: date indeterminable.
Language(s): Latin. Appraised at 3d in 1586.

146.196 Rami Rhetorica
Pierre de La Ramée. Unidentified. Continent: date indeterminable.
There are several possibilities for this entry, including Ramus's *Rhetoricae distinctiones in Quintilianum* and *Scholae rhetoricae*, as well as Audomarus Talaeus's *Rhetoricae libri duo Petri Rami praelectionibus illustrati*. *Language(s)*: Latin. Appraised at 2d in 1586.

146.197 Trapezutii Retorica
Georgius Trapezuntius. [*Rhetorica*]. Continent: date indeterminable.
Language(s): Latin. Appraised at 8d in 1586.

146.198 Gorsius de figuris
Jacobus Gorscius. *De figuris, tum grammaticis, tum rhetoricis, libri V*. Cracow: in officina typographica Matthaei Siebeneycher, 1560.
Also found in the library of John Tatham, PLRE 112. *Language(s)*: Latin. Appraised at 6d in 1586.

146.199 Toxitus ad Herennium
Michael Toxites. [*Cicero (spurious)–Rhetorica ad Herennium: commentary and text*]. Basle: Joannes Oporinus (with other houses), 1556–1568.
Language(s): Latin. Appraised at 8d in 1586.

146.200:1 Epitome susenbrot e strebeus
Joannes Susenbrotus. *Epitome troporum ac schematum*. Britain or Continent: date indeterminable.
STC 23437 *et seq.* and non-STC. The detached *e* in the manuscript entry is assumed to be a truncated *et*, for Strebaeus did not edit Susenbrotus's *Epitome*. Two works entered, perhaps bound, together. *Language(s)*: Latin. Appraised with one other at 4d in 1586.

146.200:2 [See 146.200:1]
Jacobus Lodovicus Strebaeus. Unidentified. Continent: date indeterminable.
Located in a rhetoric section and entered by the compiler with the preceding, this is probably one of Strebaeus's books on rhetoric. *Language(s)*: Latin. Appraised with one other at 4d in 1586.

146.201 Sturmius de periodis
Joannes Sturmius. *De periodis*. Strassburg: (different houses), 1550–1567.
This work was issued both singly and in a composite volume. Also found in the library of John Tatham, PLRE 112. *Language(s)*: Latin Greek (perhaps). Appraised at 8d in 1586.

146.202 Aphthonius
Aphthonius, *Sophista*. *Progymnasmata*. Britain or Continent: date indeterminable.
STC 699 et seq. and non-STC. Numerous editions exist in Latin, Greek, and English. See 146.119 for another copy. Also found in the library of John Tatham, PLRE 112. *Language(s)*: Latin (probable) Greek (perhaps). Appraised at 8d in 1586.

146.203 Sturmii parti
Joannes Sturmius. *In partitiones oratorias Ciceronis dialogi*. Continent: date indeterminable.
Also found in the library of John Tatham, PLRE 112. *Language(s)*: Latin. Appraised at 8d in 1586.

146.204 erasmus de conscribiendis
Desiderius Erasmus. *De conscribendis epistolis*. Britain or Continent: date indeterminable.
STC 10496 and non-STC. Also found in the library of John Tatham, PLRE 112. *Language(s)*: Latin. Appraised at 5d in 1586.

146.205   hermogenis grece
Hermogenes. [*Rhetorica*]. Continent: date indeterminable.
Either his popular *Ars rhetorica*, alone or with other rhetorical texts, or some other collection of his rhetorical works. Both were often accompanied by rhetorical texts by other authors. *Language(s)*: Greek. Appraised at 8d in 1586.

146.206   Galenus de simp medicament
Galen. *De simplicium medicamentorum facultatibus*. Continent: date indeterminable.
Perhaps selected works with this title leading. *Language(s)*: Latin. Appraised at 6d in 1586.

146.207   practica gordonii
Bernardus de Gordonio. [*Practica, seu Lilium medicinae*]. Continent: date indeterminable.
Also found in the library of John Tatham, PLRE 112. *Language(s)*: Latin. Appraised at 20d in 1586.

146.208   methodus fernelii
Joannes Fernelius. *Febrium curandarum methodus generalis*. Continent: 1577–1579.
Language(s): Latin. Appraised at 12d in 1586.

146.209   Erithreus de elocutione
Valentinus Erythraeus. *De elocutione*. Strassburg: excudebat J. Rihelius, 1567.
Language(s): Latin. Appraised at 5d in 1586.

146.210   fuctii methodus
Leonard Fuchs. [*Methodus seu ratio compendiaria perveniendi ad medicinam*]. Continent: date indeterminable.
Many variants of the title exist. *Language(s)*: Latin. Appraised at 8d in 1586.

146.211   Paraselus de tartaro
Paracelsus. *De tartaro libri septem perquam utiles*. Basle: [Petrus Perna], 1568–1570.
Language(s): Latin. Appraised at 6d in 1586.

146.212   Rhetorica ciceronis
Marcus Tullius Cicero. [*Selected works–Rhetorica*]. Continent: date indeterminable.
Also found in the library of John Tatham, PLRE 112. *Language(s)*: Latin. Appraised at 10d in 1586.

146.213   alexandrinus de sanit tuenda
Julius Alexandrinus. *Salubrium sive de sanitate tuenda*. Cologne: apud Gervinum Calenium et haeredes Quentelios, 1575.

Language(s): Latin. Appraised at 5s in 1586.

146.214   Cardanus de varietate
Girolamo Cardano. *De rerum varietate*. Continent: 1557–1581.
A continuation of *De subtilitate*, which follows this item. Also found in the library of John Tatham, PLRE 112. *Language(s)*: Latin. Appraised at 16d in 1586.

146.215   Idem de subtilitate
Girolamo Cardano. *De subtilitate*. Continent: 1550–1582.
Also found in the library of John Tatham, PLRE 112. *Language(s)*: Latin. Appraised at 12d in 1586.

146.216   themistius
Themistius. Unidentified. Continent: date indeterminable.
Language(s): Latin (probable) Greek (perhaps). Appraised at 8d in 1586.

146.217   marsilius fisinus
Marsilio Ficino. Unidentified. Continent: date indeterminable.
Language(s): Latin. Appraised at 6d in 1586.

146.218   foxii philosophia natur
Sebastiano Fox Morzillo. *De naturae philosophia, seu de Platonis et Aristotelis consensione*. Continent: date indeterminable.
Also found in the library of John Tatham, PLRE 112. *Language(s)*: Latin. Appraised at 6d in 1586.

146.219   peucerus de divinationibus
Kaspar Peucer. *Commentarius de praecipuis divinationum generibus*. Wittenberg: (different houses), 1533–1580.
Also found in the library of John Tatham, PLRE 112. *Language(s)*: Latin. Appraised at 12d in 1586.

146.220   agrippa de occulta philosophia
Cornelius Henricus Agrippa. *De occulta philosophia*. Continent: date indeterminable.
Also found in the library of John Tatham, PLRE 112. *Language(s)*: Latin. Appraised at 20d in 1586.

146.221   liber phisicorum
Unidentified. Place unknown: stationer unknown, date indeterminable.
STC/non-STC status unknown. Aristotle's *Physica* or one of the many commentaries on the *Physica* is probably represented here, but other works are possible. *Language(s)*: Latin. Appraised at 6d in 1586.

146.222 Rhetorica vivis

Joannes Ludovicus Vives. Probably *De ratione dicendi. De consultatione praeceptiones*. Continent: 1533–1537.

Also found in the library of John Tatham, PLRE 112. *Language(s)*: Latin. Appraised at 3d in 1586.

146.223 Regulae medicinales

Unidentified. Continent (probable): date indeterminable.

Almost certainly not an STC book. *Language(s)*: Latin (probable). Appraised at 10d in 1586.

146.224 Lmnius [Lemnius] de humano corpore

Levinus Lemnius. Probably *De habitu et constitucione corporis*. Continent: 1561–1582.

The title of a 1564 Italian translation reads: *Della complessione del corpo humano libri due*, but there is no evidence from the rest of Tatham's collection that he read Italian. *Language(s)*: Latin. Appraised at 5d in 1586.

146.225 de gubernanda sanit

Joannes Kastzschius. *De gubernanda sanitate*. Frankfurt am Main: apud haeredes Christiani Egenolphi, 1557–1570.

Language(s): Latin. Appraised at 1d in 1586.

146.226 Lemnius de astrologia

Levinus Lemnius. *Libelli tres (De astrologia, De praefixo cuique vitae termino, De honesto animi et corporis oblectamento)*. Antwerp: apud Martinum Nutium, 1554.

Language(s): Latin. Appraised at 10d in 1586.

146.227 phisica melancthonis

Philipp Melanchthon. Probably [*Aristotle–Physica: commentary*]. Continent: date indeterminable.

Melanchthon also published *Orationes* on physics in 1542 and 1550 (Keen, 170, 162). Also found in the library of John Tatham, PLRE 112. *Language(s)*: Latin. Appraised at 3d in 1586.

146.228 Gwintherus de balneis

Joannes Guinterius (Andernacus). *Commentarius de balneis, et aquis medicatis*. Strassburg: excudebat Theodosius Rihelius, 1565.

Language(s): Latin. Appraised at 3d in 1586.

146.229 melancthon de anima

Philipp Melanchthon. [*Liber de anima*]. Continent: date indeterminable.

Language(s): Latin. Appraised at 3d in 1586.

146.230 pantapolion pictorii
Georg Pictorius. [*Pantapolion, continens omnium ferme quadrupedum*]. Basle: per Henricum Petri, 1563.
Language(s): Latin. Appraised at 4d in 1586.

146.231 Lavaterus de spectris
Ludwig Lavater. *De spectris*. Geneva: 1570–1581.
Language(s): Latin. Appraised at 6d in 1586.

146.232 mizaldus
Antoine Mizauld. Unidentified. Continent: date indeterminable.
Language(s): Latin. Appraised at 3d in 1586.

146.233 Trithemius de 7 Secundis
Johann von Tritheim. *De septem secundeis*. Continent: 1522–1567.
Language(s): Latin. Appraised at 4d in 1586.

146.234 Beverus d in phisicam aristotelis
Joannes Beverus. [*Aristotle–Physica: commentary*]. Louvain: ex officina Bartholomaei Gravii, 1567–1577.
Language(s): Latin. Appraised at 2s in 1586.

146.235 valerius de sphera
Cornelius Valerius. *De sphaera*. Antwerp: (different houses), 1561–1585.
See 146.251 for another copy. *Language(s)*: Latin. Appraised at 2d in 1586.

146.236:1 bis 2 daneus de venefisis
Lambert Daneau. *De veneficis quas sortiarios vocant*. Continent: 1574–1581.
Language(s): Latin. Appraised with one other at 4d in 1586.

146.236:2 [See 146.236:1]
Lambert Daneau. *De veneficis quas sortiarios vocant*. Continent: 1574–1581.
Language(s): Latin. Appraised with one other at 4d in 1586.

146.237 abstract of statuts
An abstract of all the penall statutes. (*England–Statutes–Abridgements and Extracts*). Ferdinand Pulton. London: (different houses), 1577–1586.
STC 9526.7 *et seq*. Appraisal first given as 3s. *Language(s)*: English. Appraised at 4d in 1586.

146.238 practica de ferariis
Joannes Matthaeus Ferrarius, *de Gradi*. *Practica*. Continent: date indeterminable,
Not appraised. *Language(s)*: Latin.

146.239 flaminius
Unidentified. Continent (probable): date indeterminable.
Almost certainly not an STC book. *Language(s)*: Latin (probable). Appraised at 3d in 1586.

146.240 Ethica valerii
Cornelius Valerius. *Ethicae, seu De moribus philosophiae brevis et perspicua descriptio*. Continent: 1566–1582.
Language(s): Latin. Appraised at 2d in 1586.

146.241 Cureus de sensibus
Joachim Cureus. [*Aristotle–De sensu et sensibilibus: commentary*]. Wittenberg: (different houses), 1567–1584.
Language(s): Latin. Appraised at 6d in 1586.

146.242 mathisii epitome
Gerardus Matthisius (Geldrensis). Unidentified. Continent: date indeterminable.
Matthisius published epitomes of Aristotle's logic and natural philosophy. *Language(s)*: Latin Greek (perhaps). Appraised at 1d in 1586.

146.243 Geometiae elementa
Euclid. *Elementa*. Continent: date indeterminable.
Language(s): Latin (probable) Greek (perhaps). Appraised at 1d in 1586.

146.244 Cosmographiae instit
Unidentified. Continent (probable): date indeterminable.
Probably not an STC book. The entry *institutio* is most likely a scribal error for "introductio," which would allow several possibilities; see Adams C2722–24, as well as Peter Apian's *Cosmographia*, also published under the title *Cosmographiae introductio*. *Language(s)*: Latin. Appraised at 1d in 1586.

146.245 Theorice purbachii
Georg Purbach. *Novae theoricae planetarum*. Continent: date indeterminable.
Language(s): Latin. Appraised at 4d in 1586.

146.246 arithmetica tonstalli
Cuthbert Tunstall, *Bishop*. *De arte supputandi libri quattuor*. Britain or Continent: 1522–1551.
STC 24319 and non-STC. For another copy, see 146.109. Also found in the library of John Tatham, PLRE 112. *Language(s)*: Latin. Appraised at 3d in 1586.

146.247 Cosmographia Gemme frisii
Reiner Gemma, *Frisius*. *De principiis astronomiae et cosmographiae, deque usu globi*. Continent: 1530–1578.

Language(s): Latin. Appraised at 8d in 1586.

146.248   Chiromantia indaginis
Joannes ab Indagine. [*Chiromantia*]. Continent: date indeterminable.
Language(s): Latin. Appraised at 3d in 1586.

146.249:1   2 hunter cosmograph
Joannes Honterus. [*Rudimenta cosmographica*]. Continent: date indeterminable.
Language(s): Latin. Appraised with one other at 3d in 1586.

146.249:2   [See 146.249:1]
Joannes Honterus. [*Rudimenta cosmographica*]. Continent: date indeterminable.
Language(s): Latin. Appraised with one other at 3d in 1586.

146.250   arithmetica peltarii
Reiner Gemma, *Frisius*. *Arithmetica practicae methodus facilis*. Edited by Jacques Peletier. Continent: date indeterminable.
Language(s): Latin. Appraised at 3d in 1586.

146.251   valerius de sphera
Cornelius Valerius. *De sphaera*. Antwerp: (different houses), 1561–1585.
See 146.235 for another copy. *Language(s)*: Latin. Appraised at 2d in 1586.

146.252   problemata aristotelis
Aristotle (spurious). *Problemata*. Britain or Continent: date indeterminable.
STC 761 and non-STC. Also found in the library of John Tatham, PLRE 112.
Language(s): Latin. Appraised at 6d in 1586.

146.253   dinis de regulis Juris
Dinus de Mugello. *De regulis juris*. Continent: date indeterminable.
Also found in the library of John Tatham, PLRE 112. *Language(s)*: Latin. Appraised at 4d in 1586.

146.254:1–2   2 Coppi bookes
Unidentified. Provenances unknown: dates indeterminable.
Manuscripts. *Language(s)*: Unknown. Appraised as a pair at 3d in 1586.

146.255   Ramus in Cicer de fato
Pierre de La Ramée. [*Cicero–De fato: commentary*]. Continent: 1550–1583.
See Ong, nos. 190–195. *Language(s)*: Latin. Appraised at 2d in 1586.

146.256   de causis affetionum
Unidentified. Continent (probable): date indeterminable.
An initial *Idem* is struck through in the manuscript entry. *Language(s)*: Latin. Appraised at 1d in 1586.

146.257 magiae naturalis
Giovanni Battista della Porta. *Magia naturalis*. Continent: date indeterminable. *Language(s)*: Latin. Appraised at 2d in 1586.

146.258 hasfardus de sanit tuenda
Joannes Hasfurtus, *Virdungus* (Johann Virdung). Unidentified. Continent: date indeterminable.

Hasfurtus seems not to have written a work with this title, nor does he appear as an editor of the various *De sanitate tuenda*s published during this period. *Language(s)*: Latin. Appraised at 1d in 1586.

146.259 Gwido de Inditiis
Unidentified. Continent: date indeterminable.

Perhaps a legal tract by Guido de Zesaria or Guido de Suzaria. See the list following Adams S2127. *Language(s)*: Latin. Appraised at 2s in 1586.

146.260 Boetii arithmetica
Anicius M.T.S. Boethius. *Arithmetica*. Continent: date indeterminable.

Also found in the library of John Tatham, PLRE 112. *Language(s)*: Latin. Appraised at 6d in 1586.

146.261 homilia clitovii
Jodocus Clichtoveus. [*Homiliae*]. Continent: date indeterminable.

Also found in the library of John Tatham, PLRE 112. *Language(s)*: Latin. Appraised at 4d in 1586.

146.262 andradius in chemnitium
Diogo de Paiva de Andrade de Payva, *the Elder. Defensio Tridentiae fidei. (Councils–Trent)*. Continent: 1578–1580.

Responding to the *Examen concilii Tridentini* by Martinus Chemnitius; see 146.315. *Language(s)*: Latin. Appraised at 12d in 1586.

146.263 Loci communes Cani
Francisco Melchor Cano, *Bishop. De locis theologicis*. Continent: 1563–1585. *Language(s)*: Latin. Appraised at 20d in 1586.

146.264 preces privatae
Preces privatae. London: William Seres, 1564–1574.

STC 20378 *et seq. Language(s)*: Latin. Appraised at 6d in 1586.

146.265 Sermones
Unidentified [sermons]. Place unknown: stationer unknown, date indeterminable.

STC/non-STC status unknown. *Language(s)*: Latin. Appraised at 5d in 1586.

146.266 liber de animalibus
Aristotle. *Historia animalium*. Continent: date indeterminable.
The title is sometimes given as *De animalibus historia*. *Language(s)*: Latin (probable) Greek (perhaps). Appraised at 8d in 1586.

146.267 ecclesiastica dissiplina
Walter Travers. *Ecclesiastica disciplina*. Heidelberg: Michael Schirat, 1574. Shaaber T110. False imprint *Rupellae, Adamus de Monte*. Also found in the library of John Tatham, PLRE 112. *Language(s)*: Latin. Appraised at 8d in 1586.

146.268 elenchus hereticorum
Lambert Daneau. *Elenchi haereticorum*. Geneva: Eustathius Vignon, 1573–1580. *Language(s)*: Latin. Appraised at 4d in 1586.

146.269 Lavaterus de cena domini
Ludwig Lavater. *Historia de origine et progressu controversiae sacramentariae, de coena Domini*. Zürich: excudebat Christophorus Froschouerus, 1563.
Language(s): Latin. Appraised at 2d in 1586.

146.270:1 bis Genesis heb
[*Bible–O.T.–Genesis*]. Continent: date indeterminable.
May be two volumes of one edition. *Language(s)*: Hebrew. Appraised with one other at 3d in 1586.

146.270:2 [See 146.270:1]
[*Bible–O.T.–Genesis*]. Continent: date indeterminable.
May be the second volume of a single edition. *Language(s)*: Hebrew. Appraised with one other at 3d in 1586.

146.271 hemingius de pastore
Niels Hemmingsen. *Pastor, sive pastoris optimus vivendi agendique modus*. Continent: date indeterminable.
Also found in the library of John Tatham, PLRE 112. *Language(s)*: Latin. Appraised at 3d in 1586.

146.272 montensis de eucaristia
Jodocus Harchius (Montensis). *De eucharistiae mysterio*. Basle: per Petrum Perna, 1573.
Language(s): Latin. Appraised at 4d in 1586.

146.273 Bullingerus de fine mundi
Heinrich Bullinger. *De fine seculi et juditio venturo Domini nostri Jesu Christi*. Basle: per Joannem Oporinum, 1557.
One assumes a rephrasing by the compiler (or dictator). *Language(s)*: Latin. Appraised at 3d in 1586.

146.274 daneus de heresibus
Augustine, *Saint. De haeresibus.* Edited by Lambert Daneau. Geneva: Eustathius Vignon, 1576–1578.
Language(s): Latin. Appraised at 12d in 1586.

146.275 vives de fide Christiana
Joannes Ludovicus Vives. *De veritate fidei christianae.* Continent: 1543–1568.
Language(s): Latin. Appraised at 4d in 1586.

146.276 Catheckismus noeli
Alexander Nowell. *Catechismus.* London: (different houses), 1570–1580.
STC 18701 *et seq. Language(s)*: Latin Greek (perhaps). Appraised at 2d in 1586.

146.277 Imagines mortis
[*Imagines mortis*]. (*Dance of Death*). Latin translation by Georg Aemilius; possibly one of the editions with woodcuts or designs by Hans Holbein. Continent: date indeterminable.
Language(s): Latin. Appraised at 3d in 1586.

146.278 Gerson de imit Chrsti [Christi]
Thomas, *à Kempis. De imitatione Christi.* Continent: date indeterminable.
The work had been attributed to Joannes Gerson. Another copy is at 146.301. Also found in the library of John Tatham, PLRE 112. *Language(s)*: Latin. Appraised at 6d in 1586.

146.279 Sanderus de honor imagines
Nicholas Sanders. *De typica et honoraria sacrarum imaginum adoratione libri duo.* Louvain: apud Joannem Foulerum, 1569.
Shaaber S20. Also found in the library of John Tatham, PLRE 112. *Language(s)*: Latin. Appraised at 6d in 1586.

146.280 parchment book
Unidentified. Provenance unknown: date indeterminable.
Manuscript. *Language(s)*: Unknown. Appraised at 6d in 1586.

146.281 Bertram de poltia Judaica
Bonaventure Corneille Bertram. *De politia judaica.* Geneva: apud Eustathium Vignon, 1574–1580.
Language(s): Latin. Appraised with the next at 6d in 1586.

146.282 Simlerus de presentia Cristi
Josias Simler. *De vera Jesu Christi secundum humanam naturam in his terris praesentia.* Zürich: ex officina Froschouiana, 1574–1578.
Language(s): Latin. Appraised with the preceding at 6d in 1586.

146.283 Examen theologicum
Benedictus Aretius. *Examen theologicum.* Continent: 1570–1584. *Language(s)*: Latin. Appraised at 2d in 1586.

146.284 nesechius de Caena domini
Théodore de Bèze. *Adversus sacramentariorum errorem pro vera Christi praesentia in coena Domini.* [Geneva: J. Stoer], 1574.
Published under the pseudonym of N. Nesekius, with a false imprint of *Theopoli* (God's city); the publisher was not identified, but it was Jacobus Stoer. *Language(s)*: Latin. Appraised at 2d in 1586.

146.285 Chitreus de studio thel
David Chytraeus. *De studio theologiae recte inchoando.* Continent: date indeterminable.
See 146.290 for another likely copy. *Language(s)*: Latin. Appraised at 3d in 1586.

146.286 herborn in 70 psalmum
Nikolaus Herborn. *In psalmum septuagesima octavum enarratio lamentatoria, pro miseranda populi Christiani de populatione.* Cologne: Peter Quentel, 1529.
The manuscript entry appears to read 7 with a superscript *0*; Herborn's commentary is on Psalm 78. *Language(s)*: Latin. Appraised at 2d in 1586.

146.287:1 erasmus de rat studii theologice
Desiderius Erasmus. *De ratione studii.* Continent: date indeterminable.
See the next record. *Language(s)*: Latin. Appraised with one other at 2d in 1586.

146.287:2 [See 146.287:1]
Unidentified. Continent: date indeterminable.
The *theologice* in the manuscript entry at 146.287:1 may be the compiler conflating Erasmus's *De ratione studii* with his *Ratio verae theologiae* or with the *De theologo sive De ratione studii theologici* of Andreas Gerardus, *Hyperius*, one of whose works follows this item. The stray word may, however, be some other completely indecipherable garble. *Language(s)*: Latin. Appraised with one other at 2d in 1586.

146.288 hiperius de Christiana Religione
Andreas Gerardus, *Hyperius. Elementa christianae religionis.* Basle: per Thomam Guarinum, 1563.
See the annotations to the preceding. *Language(s)*: Latin. Appraised at 2d in 1586.

146.289 Catologus autorum veteris test
Matthias Flacius, *Illyricus. Catalogus testium veritatis.* Continent: date indeterminable.

Language(s): Latin. Appraised at 1d in 1586.

146.290 Chitreus de studio
David Chytraeus. *De studio theologiae recte inchoando*. Continent: date indeterminable.
Another copy is at 146.285; this could, perhaps, be Chytraeus's *Oratorio de studio theologicae*. *Language(s)*: Latin. Appraised at 1d in 1586.

146.291 apologia Ecclesia ang
John Jewel, *Bishop*. *Apologiae ecclesiae anglicanae*. Britain or Continent: 1562–1586.
STC 14581 *et seq.* and non-STC. *Language(s)*: Latin. Appraised at 3d in 1586.

146.292 Cathechis palatinatus
Catechesis religionis christianae: quae in ecclesiis et scholis Palatinatus traditur. (*Heidelberg catechism*). Continent: date indeterminable.
Language(s): Greek Latin. Appraised at 2d in 1586.

146.293 Loci melantonis
Philipp Melanchthon. [*Loci communes theologici*]. Continent: date indeterminable.
Language(s): Latin. Appraised at 2d in 1586.

146.294 de ritibus et inst ecl tigurine
De ritibus et institutis ecclesiae tigurinae opusculum. (*Zürich*). Zürich (probable): (stationer unknown), 1559.
Language(s): Latin. Appraised at 1d in 1586.

146.295 Beza in selnecerum
Théodore de Bèze. Unidentified. Geneva: 1571–1578.
Which of Bèze's works against Nicolas Selneccer cannot be determined, but all Latin versions were published in Geneva in octavo; see Gardy nos. 291–292 and 294–295. *Language(s)*: Latin. Appraised at 1d in 1586.

146.296 Latomas de theologo
Jacobus Latomus, *the Elder*. Unidentified. Continent: date indeterminable.
Either his *Articulorum doctrinae Fratris Martini Lutheri per theologos Louvanienses damnatorum ratio* or his *De trium linguarum et studii theologici ratione dialogus*. *Language(s)*: Latin. Appraised at 2d in 1586.

146.297 petrus martir in smitheum
Pietro Martire Vermigli (Peter Martyr). *Defensio ad Riccardi Smythaei Angli duos libellos de caelibatu sacerdotum, et votis monasticis*. Basle: apud Petrum Pernam, 1559–1570.
Language(s): Latin. Appraised at 2d in 1586.

146.298 Qwestiones thomae
Thomas Aquinas, *Saint.* [*Quaestiones*]. Continent: date indeterminable.
This could be either the *Quaestiones disputatae* or *Quaestiones quodlibetales*, but at this low valuation, probably a part or a selection of one. *Language(s)*: Latin. Appraised at 3d in 1586.

146.299 philo de mund fabricatione
Philo, *Judaeus. Libri Quatuor. Primus de mundi fabricatione, secundus de decem praeceptis, tertius de magistratu seu principe deligendo, quartus de officio judices.* Translated by John Christopherson, *Bishop.* Antwerp: excud. Joannes Verwithhaghen, 1553. *Language(s)*: Latin. Appraised at 6d in 1586.

146.300 confessio Bezae
Théodore de Bèze. *Confessio christianae fidei.* Britain or Continent: 1560–1583. STC 2006 *et seq.* and non-STC. *Language(s)*: Latin. Appraised at 8d in 1586.

146.301 kempisius de imitando Cristo
Thomas, *à Kempis. De imitatione Christi.* Continent: date indeterminable. Another copy at 146.278. *Language(s)*: Latin. Appraised at 3d in 1586.

146.302 Rivius de consol egrotantibus
Joannes Rivius. *De consolandis aegrotantibus.* Basle: Joannes Oporinus, 1546 (probable)–1557.
Language(s): Latin. Appraised at 3d in 1586.

146.303 Basilius magnus de stult moi
Basil, *Saint, the Great.* Unidentified. Continent: date indeterminable.
The manuscript entry is nonsense, but if the last glyph is read as *rone* (i.e., *r[ati]one*), which is possible, then either Basil's *De ratione vitae solitariae* or his *De instituenda studiorum ratione* would be possible. *Language(s)*: Latin. Appraised at 3d in 1586.

146.304 Ridleus de cena domini
Nicholas Ridley. *De coena Dominica assertio.* Geneva: apud Joannem Crispinum, 1556.
Shaaber R78. Originally in English (STC 21046). *Language(s)*: Latin. Appraised at 2d in 1586.

146.305 Epista lutheri
Martin Luther. Unidentified. Continent: date indeterminable.
Several possibilities. *Language(s)*: Latin. Appraised at 1d in 1586.

146.306 Sermones dominicales
Unidentified [sermons]. Continent: date indeterminable.
Language(s): Latin. Appraised at 1d in 1586.

146.307 aureum opus de contritione
Joannes Ludovicus Vivaldus. *Aureum opus de veritate contritionis*. Continent: date indeterminable.
Language(s): Latin. Appraised at 2d in 1586.

146.308 aretius defentio gentilis
Benedictus Aretius. *Valentini Gentilis capitis supplicio Bernae affecti brevis historia*. Geneva: ex officina Francisci Perrini, 1567.
Two editions in one year. Also found in the library of John Tatham, PLRE 112.
Language(s): Latin. Appraised at 8d in 1586.

146.309 Speculum morale
Unidentified. Continent: date indeterminable.
Either the anonymous early-fourteenth-century compilation, drawn primarily from Augustine, published alongside the three genuine parts of Vincentius, *Bellovacensis*'s (Vincent *de Beauvais*) *Speculum major*, or the *Speculum morale totius sacrae scripturae* of Joannes Vitalis de Furno. *Language(s)*: Latin. Appraised at 6d in 1586.

146.310 Biblia stephani
The Bible. Continent: Robertus Stephanus, date indeterminable.
Could be either Robertus Stephanus. *Language(s)*: Latin (probable) Greek (perhaps) Hebrew (perhaps). Appraised at 6s in 1586.

146.311 decades bullingeri
Heinrich Bullinger. *Sermonum decades*. Continent: date indeterminable,
See 146.340:1–2. Also found in the library of John Tatham, PLRE 112. *Language(s)*: Latin. Appraised at 5s in 1586.

146.312 Sermones parisiensis
Gulielmus, *Parisiensis, Professor*. [*Gospels and Epistles (liturgical): commentary and text*]. Continent: date indeterminable.
Language(s): Latin. Appraised at 20d in 1586.

146.313 Loci marlorati
Augustine Marlorat. [*Thesaurus sacrae scripturae*]. Britain or Continent: 1574–1575.
STC 17409 and non-STC. A marginal cross marks this entry. *Language(s)*: Latin. Appraised at 20d in 1586.

146.314 bis Biblia castalionis
The Bible. Translated by Sebastian Castalio. Basle: (different houses), 1551–1573.
Probably volumes one and two, not two copies. Also found in the library of John Tatham, PLRE 112. *Language(s)*: Latin. Appraised at 5s in 1586.

146.315 Kemnitius
Martinus Chemnitius. Unidentified. Continent (probable): date indeterminable.
Almost certainly not an STC book. At this valuation, probably either his *Loci* or his *Examen concilii Tridentini*, both published in folio editions. Tatham owned Paiva de Andrade's response to Chemnitz on the Council of Trent; see 146.262. On the other hand, there are several *loci* in this section and Chemnitz's *Loci* was published in several folio volumes. *Language(s)*: Latin. Appraised at 6s 8d in 1586.

146.316 Loci communes musculi
Probably Wolfgang Musculus. *Loci communes*. Continent: date indeterminable.
The less popular *Loci communes sacri* of Andreas Musculus is another possibility. Also found in the library of John Tatham, PLRE 112. *Language(s)*: Latin. Appraised at 4s in 1586.

146.317 Sintagma wigandi
Johann Wigand and Matthias Richter (Matthias Judex). *Syntagma, seu corpus doctrinae veri et omnipotentis Dei, ex veteri Testamento tantum*. Continent: date indeterminable.
On the title page, the word *Syntagma* is written in Greek letters. *Language(s)*: Latin. Appraised at 6s in 1586.

146.318 hierarchia caelestis
Dionysius Areopagita. [*Works*]. Continent: date indeterminable.
De caelesti hierarchia never appeared solo and leads in *Works*. *Language(s)*: Latin. Appraised at 12d in 1586.

146.319:1 Calvinus in Genesim et in psalmos
Jean Calvin. [*Genesis: commentary*]. Geneva: Robertus Stephanus, *the Elder*, 1554.
The two works were not published in one edition. *Language(s)*: Latin. Appraised with one other at 5s in 1586.

146.319:2 [See 146.319:1]
Jean Calvin. [*Psalms: commentary and text*]. (*Bible–O.T.*). Geneva: 1557–1584.
One edition contains the Hebrew text. *Language(s)*: Latin (probable) Hebrew (perhaps). Appraised with one other at 5s in 1586.

146.320 paraphras erasmi
Desiderius Erasmus. [*New Testament: paraphrase* (part)]. (*Bible–N.T.*). Continent: date indeterminable.
The valuation does not suggest the entire work. *Language(s)*: Latin. Appraised at 16d in 1586.

146.321 aretius in epistolas
Benedictus Aretius. *Commentarii in omnes epistolas Pauli, et Canonicas, itemque in*

Apocalypsin. Morges: excudebat Joannis Le Preux, 1583.
Language(s): Latin. Appraised at 8s in 1586.

146.322   Gregorius in cantica
Gregory I, *Saint, Pope*. [*Song of Solomon: commentary and text*]. (*Bible–O.T*). Continent: date indeterminable.
Language(s): Latin. Appraised at 8d in 1586.

146.323   erasmus in Ecclesiast
Desiderius Erasmus. *Ecclesiastes, sive de ratione concionandi*. Continent: 1535–1554.
The date range is based on VHe. *Language(s)*: Latin. Appraised at 12d in 1586.

146.324   hiperii opuscula
Andreas Gerardus, *Hyperius*. *Opuscula theologica*. Basle: ex officina Oporiniana, 1570.
The manuscript entry is taken to be the first of two parts; see 146.330. *Language(s)*: Latin. Appraised at 16d in 1586.

146.325   Idem methodus
Andreas Gerardus, *Hyperius*. *Methodus theologiae sive loci communes*. Basle: Oporinus, 1567–1574.
Language(s): Latin. Appraised at 12d in 1586.

146.326   Lactantius
Lucius Coelius Lactantius. Probably [*Works*]. Continent: date indeterminable.
A cross marks this entry. Also found in the library of John Tatham, PLRE 112.
Language(s): Latin. Appraised at 14d in 1586.

146.327   Lombardus
Peter Lombard. Probably *Sententiarum libri IIII*. Continent: date indeterminable.
A cross marks this entry. Also found in the library of John Tatham, PLRE 112.
Language(s): Latin. Appraised at 20d in 1586.

146.328   Test bezae
[*Bible–N.T.*]. Translated and edited by Théodore de Bèze. Britain or Continent: date indeterminable.
STC 2802 *et seq*. and non-STC. A Greek or Greek-Latin edition is possible.
Language(s): Latin. Appraised at 2s in 1586.

146.329   biblia
The Bible. Britain or Continent: date indeterminable.
STC 2055 *et seq*. and non-STC. *Language(s)*: Latin. Appraised at 8d in 1586.

146.330   2a pars hiperii opuscula
Andreas Gerardus, *Hyperius. Opuscula theologica.* Basle: ex officina Oporiniana, 1571.
See 146.324. *Language(s)*: Latin. Appraised at 12d in 1586.

146.331   flores doctorum
Thomas, *Hibernicus.* [*Flores omnium fere doctorum*]. Continent: date indeterminable.
See Shaaber T40 *et seq. Language(s)*: Latin. Appraised at 12d in 1586.

146.332   hiperius de ratione studii
Andreas Gerardus, *Hyperius. De theologo, sive De ratione studii theologici.* Continent: 1556–1582.
Also found in the library of John Tatham, PLRE 112. *Language(s)*: Latin. Appraised at 14d in 1586.

146.333   postilla spangembergii
Johann Spangenberg. [*Gospels and Epistles (liturgical): commentary and text*]. Continent: date indeterminable.
Language(s): Latin. Appraised at 2s in 1586.

146.334   postilla wigandi
Johann Wigand. [*Postilla*]. Ursell: Nikolaus Henricus, 1565–1569.
Language(s): Latin. Appraised at 20d in 1586.

146.335   postilla gresseri
Daniel Greiser. *Enarratio brevis et orthodoxa evangeliorum dominicalium et festorum aliquot.* Frankfurt am Main: Peter Brubach, 1567.
A Frankfurt 1586 second edition is probably too late for this collection. *Language(s)*: Latin. Appraised at 10d in 1586.

146.336   homer
Homer. Probably [*Works*]. Continent: date indeterminable.
Also found in the library of John Tatham, PLRE 112. *Language(s)*: Latin (probable) Greek (perhaps). Appraised at 3d in 1586.

146.337   Loci martiris
Pietro Martire Vermigli (Peter Martyr). *Loci communes.* Britain or Continent: 1576–1583.
STC 24667 *et seq.* and non-STC. Also found in the library of John Tatham, PLRE 112. *Language(s)*: Latin. Appraised at 5s in 1586.

146.338   dialogi cast
Sebastian Castalio. *Dialogorum sacrorum libri quatuor.* Britain or Continent: date indeterminable.
STC 4770 *et seq.* and non-STC. *Language(s)*: Latin. Appraised at 2d in 1586.

146.339 Compendia pindari
Ulrich Pinder. *Compendium breve de bone valetudinis cura*. Place not given: stationer unknown, 1510.
Printed with works by two others. *Language(s)*: Latin. Appraised at 3d in 1586.

146.340:1 2 decadum bulingeri
Heinrich Bullinger. *Sermonum decades*. Continent: date indeterminable.
The compiler habitually places the number of multiple copies in the margin, as a 2 is written here. This manuscript entry could, however, represent *Sermonum decades duae*. The following (146.340:2), therefore, would not be listed. See 146.311. Also found in the library of John Tatham, PLRE 112. *Language(s)*: Latin. Appraised with one other at 6d in 1586.

146.340:2 [See 146.340:1]
Heinrich Bullinger. *Sermonum decades*. Continent: date indeterminable.
See the annotations to the preceding. *Language(s)*: Latin. Appraised with one other at 6d in 1586.

146.341 eusebius de preparta evange
Eusebius, *Pamphili, Bishop*. *De evangelica praeparatione*. Continent: date indeterminable.
Language(s): Latin. Appraised at 6d in 1586.

146.342 flaminis in psalmum
Marco Antonio Flaminio. [*Psalms: commentary and text*]. (*Bible–O.T.*). Continent: date indeterminable.
See 146.239. A less likely possibility for this entry is his paraphrase of the Psalms. *Language(s)*: Latin. Appraised at 4d in 1586.

146.343 philo Judeus de antiquit
Philo, *Judaeus*. [*Selected works*]. Edited by Joannes Sichardus. Basle: per (excud.) Adamum Petrum, 1527.
Libri antiquitatum is the lead title in this collection and seems not to have been published alone. *Language(s)*: Latin. Appraised at 6d in 1586.

146.344 osorius de gloria
Jeronimo Osorio da Fonseca, *Bishop*. *De gloria*. Florence: apud Laurentium Torrentinum, 1552.
His more widely published *Selected works* with *De gloria* leading is also possible, especially at this date. *Language(s)*: Latin. Appraised at 10d in 1586.

146.345 Idem de regis inst
Jeronimo Osorio da Fonseca, *Bishop*. *De regis institutione et disciplina*. Continent: 1571–1582.
Also found in the library of John Tatham, PLRE 112. *Language(s)*: Latin. Appraised at 12d in 1586.

146.346 Idem de Justitia
Jeronimo Osorio da Fonseca, *Bishop. De justitia*. Continent: 1564–1586.
Also found in the library of John Tatham, PLRE 112. *Language(s)*: Latin. Appraised at 10d in 1586.

146.347 Idem in haddonum
Jeronimo Osorio da Fonseca, *Bishop. In Gualterum Haddonum magistrum libellorum supplicum libri tres*. Continent: 1567–1585.
See 146.98. Also found in the library of John Tatham, PLRE 112. *Language(s)*: Latin. Appraised at 10d in 1586.

146.348 Speculum durandi
Gulielmus Durandus I, *Bishop of Mende. Speculum juris*. Continent: date indeterminable.
Language(s): Latin. Appraised at 16d in 1586.

146.349 prateolus de vitis hereticorum
Gabriel Du Preau (Prateolus). *De vitis, sectis, et dogmatibus omnium haereticorum, elenchus alphabeticus*. Continent: 1569–1583.
Language(s): Latin. Appraised at 2s in 1586.

146.350 mercurialis
Hieronymus Mercurialis. Unidentified. Continent: date indeterminable.
Language(s): Latin. Appraised at 4d in 1586.

146.351 Calvinus in esiam
Jean Calvin. *[Isaiah: commentary]*. Geneva: (different houses), 1551–1583.
Language(s): Latin. Appraised at 4d in 1586.

146.352 aretius in Johannem
Benedictus Aretius. *Commentarii in Evangelium secundum Joannem*. Lausanne: Franciscus Le Preux, 1578–1579.
Language(s): Latin. Appraised at 20d in 1586.

146.353:1 Idem in marcum et lucam
Benedictus Aretius. *Commentarii in Evangelium secundum Marcum*. Lausanne: Franciscus Le Preux, 1577–1579.
Since the works were not published together, this entry represents two separate volumes, perhaps bound together, listed as one. *Language(s)*: Latin. Appraised with one other at 18d in 1586.

146.353:2 [See 146.353:1]
Benedictus Aretius. *Commentarii in Evangelium secundum Lucam*. Lausanne: Franciscus Le Preux, 1577–1579.
See the annotations to the preceding. *Language(s)*: Latin. Appraised with one other at 18d in 1586.

146.354   Idem in matheum
Benedictus Aretius. *Commentarii in Evangelium secundum Matthaeum*. Continent: 1577–1580.
Language(s): Latin. Appraised at 20d in 1586.

146.355   problemat aretii 3bus
Benedictus Aretius. [*Problemata theologica*]. Continent: date indeterminable.
Language(s): Latin. Appraised at 4s in 1586.

146.356   Idem in acta
Benedictus Aretius. [*Acts: commentary*]. Continent: 1579–1584.
Language(s): Latin. Appraised at 16d in 1586.

146.357   historia ecclesiast Cristophersoni
Eusebius, *Pamphili, Bishop*. *Historia ecclesiastica*. Translated and edited by John Christopherson, *Bishop*. Continent: 1569–1581.
At this valuation, probably one of the folio copies issued from 1570 to 1581. See Shaaber C285–C288. *Language(s)*: Latin. Appraised at 8s in 1586.

146.358   epiphanius
Epiphanius, *Bishop of Constantia*. Unidentified. Continent: date indeterminable.
See Adams E249–59. The bulk of Epiphanius's works concerns heresy; his *Contra octoginta haeresis* enjoyed the most printings. Other works include *De prophetarum vita et interitu*, *Oratio de fide catholica*, and a collection of sermons. *Language(s)*: Latin. Appraised at 4s in 1586.

146.359   Baldus
Probably Baldus de Ubaldis. Unidentified. Continent: date indeterminable.
Language(s): Latin (probable). Appraised at 5s in 1586.

146.360 multiple   a certay company of english bookes
Unidentified. Britain: date indeterminable.
Unidentifiable in the STC. *Language(s)*: English. Appraised as a group at 15s in 1586.

146.361 multiple   bookes for master Rape
Unidentified. Places unknown: stationers unknown, dates indeterminable.
STC/non-STC status unknown. *Language(s)*: Unknown. Appraised as a group at 3s in 1586.

Thomas Newby. Scholar (M.A.): Probate Inventory. 1587

DAVID GALBRAITH

Thomas Newby (Newbie), from Leicestershire, matriculated from Lincoln College 17 December 1579, aged eighteen. He supplicated for his Bachelor of Arts degree on 19 February 1583 and received it on 16 March 1583. He became a fellow of Lincoln College 4 July 1582. He supplicated for his M.A. 2 July 1585 and received that degree on 7 July 1585. He died on 6 November 1587. The inventory of his goods, including his books, is dated 23 April 1588 (Clark, 2:ii.89 and 2:iii.111–12; *Alumni Oxonienses*, 3:1059).

Among the forty-five entries of books in the inventory are found many common items, including Bibles, editions of classical authors, and copies of texts such as Erasmus's *De copia*. His library also includes a significant number of works of biblical scholarship and theological controversy.

More unusual, however, particularly in a library of this relatively modest size, is the number of titles in Hebrew listed in the inventory. In comparison, the only other near-contemporary Oxford inventories with a similar number of Hebrew titles, Thomas Morrey's (1584) and Edward Higgins's (1588), contain, respectively, more than four and eight times the number of books that Newby owned. See PLRE 142 for Morrey's book-list and PLRE 149 for Higgins's. Newby's library includes a Hebrew Bible (147.3), editions of Proverbs (147.29) and Hosea (147.40), a lexicon (147.28), and two grammars (147.30 and 147.35). The latter are two of the most important aids for the study of the language in the period: Petrus Martinius's *Grammatica hebraica* and Nicolaus Clenardus's *Tabula in grammaticen hebraeam*.

Oxford University Archives, Bodleian Library: Hyp.B.16.

§

147.1	a Byble in octavo in Lattin
147.2	an englishe byble
147.3	an part Ebrue byble
147.4	a paper booke
147.5	Margareta philo: Duobus volu:
147.6	Arristotle, Organum 4°
147.7	Bezae testa grecae-Latt.
147.8	zegaden Loci com:
147.9	Analisis Typica
147.10	Bilson in 4°
147.11	Arist: Metaphas 4°
147.12	Arist: ethica 4°
147.13	Cristostomus in episto: ad rom:
147.14	Calvin Inst: 8°
147.15	postilla in Evang: Hemintii 8°
147.16	Whitacar against renolds
147.17	Petrus Hisp. fo.
147.18	Consilii tridentini
147.19	osorius de gloria
147.20	The hermo: of Confession
147.21	osorius in haddo:
147.22	Lactantius de vera relig:
147.23	Silva Sino:
147.24	Hiperii phis:
147.25	A Concordans
147.26	Apthonius
147.27	Horatius
147.28	Lexicon hab:
147.29	prov: sal Haeb
147.30	Martinius gra: Haeb:
147.31	Copia Verbo:
147.32	A booke of presidentes
147.33	Claudius emblemata
147.34	Gramatica graeca
147.35	Clenardi gram: Haebr:
147.36:1–2	ii sermons in Englishe
147.37	An Astrolo: Discourse
147.38	Jacobs Journey
147.39	D. Raynoldes orat:
147.40	Oseus in Ebrue
147.41	speculum pontifi:
147.42	Terentius
147.43	An Eng: Lett: [Lecture] and a Catach:
147.44	Shepres vers
147.45	A copye booke

§

147.1   a Byble in octavo in Lattin
The Bible. Continent: date indeterminable.
Language(s): Latin. Appraised at 3s in 1588.

147.2   an englishe byble
The Bible. Britain or Continent: date indeterminable.
STC 2063 *et seq. Language(s)*: English. Appraised at 2s 6d in 1588.

147.3   an part Ebrue byble
Probably [*Bible–O.T.* (part)]. Continent: date indeterminable.
The word "part" was inserted by the compiler after the initial entry. *Language(s)*: Hebrew. Appraised at 5s 6d in 1588.

147.4   a paper booke
Unidentified. Provenance unknown: date indeterminable.
Manuscript. Perhaps a notebook. *Language(s)*: Unknown. Appraised at 12d in 1588.

147.5   Margareta philo: Duobus volu:
Gregor Reisch. *Margarita philosophica.* Continent: date indeterminable.
Language(s): Latin. Appraised at 4s in 1588.

147.6   Arristotle, Organum 4°
Aristotle. *Organon.* Continent: date indeterminable.
Language(s): Latin (probable) Greek (perhaps). Appraised at 20d in 1588.

147.7   Bezae testa grecae-Latt.
[*Bible–N.T.*]. Translated and edited by Théodore de Bèze. Geneva: Henricus Stephanus, 1565–1580.
DM nos. 4629–4630, 4632, 4641. Ulrich Fugger was involved in the publication of the 1565 edition, at least. *Language(s)*: Greek Latin. Appraised at 2s 6d in 1588.

147.8   zegaden Loci com:
Stephanus Kis (Stephanus Szegedinus). *Theologiae sincerae loci communes.* Basle: ex off. Pernea, per Conradum Waldkirch, 1585.
See 147.41. *Language(s)*: Latin. Appraised at 4s 6d in 1588.

147.9   Analisis Typica
Probably Moses Pflacher. *Analysis typica omnium cum veteris tum novi Testamenti librorum historicorum.* Britain or Continent: 1587.
STC 19826 and non-STC. Editions in 1587 from London (quarto) and Basle (folio); the valuation (which could be either *ixs* or *xs*) may suggest the Basle edition. *Language(s)*: Latin. Appraised at 10s in 1588.

147.10 Bilson in 4°

Thomas Bilson, *Bishop*. *The true difference betweene christian subjection and unchristian rebellion*. Oxford: J. Barnes, 1585.

STC 3071. The London, 1586 edition was in octavo. *Language(s)*: English. Appraised at 2s 8d in 1588.

147.11 Arist: Metaphas 4°

Aristotle. *Metaphysica*. Continent: date indeterminable.

Language(s): Latin (probable) Greek (perhaps). Appraised at 12d in 1588.

147.12 Arist: ethica 4°

Aristotle. *Ethica*. Britain or Continent: date indeterminable.

STC 752 and non-STC. STC 752, the 1479 edition, is not likely intended here. *Language(s)*: Latin (probable) Greek (perhaps). Appraised at 16d in 1588.

147.13 Cristostomus in episto: ad rom:

John, *Chrysostom, Saint*. *In epistolam ad Romanos homiliae octo priores*. Translated by Germanus Brixius. Basle: ex (in) off. Frobeniana (per Hieronymum Frobenium ac Nicolaum Episcopium), 1533.

This is the only recorded solo edition. *Language(s)*: Latin. Appraised at 8d in 1588.

147.14 Calvin Inst: 8°

Jean Calvin. *Institutio Christianae religionis*. Britain or Continent: date indeterminable.

STC 4414 *et seq.* and non-STC. The first English translation issued in octavo format appeared in 1578. *Language(s)*: Latin (probable) English (perhaps). Appraised at 3s in 1588.

147.15 postilla in Evang: Hemintii 8°

Niels Hemmingsen. *[Gospels (liturgical): commentary]*. Continent: date indeterminable.

Language(s): Latin. Appraised at 10d in 1588.

147.16 Whitacar against renolds

William Whitaker. *An aunswere to a certaine booke, written by M. W. Rainoldes*. Britain: 1585.

STC 25364 *et seq*. There were three editions of Whitaker's reply to William Rainolds (STC 20632) published in 1585, one printed in Cambridge (STC 25364) and two in London (STC 25364a and 25364b). The Continental edition (in Latin) did not appear until 1612 (see Shaaber W56). *Language(s)*: English. Appraised at 12d in 1588.

147.17 Petrus Hisp. fo.

John XXI, *Pope* (Petrus, *Hispanus*). Unidentified. Continent: date indeterminable.

The compiler struck out *8*. Both the *Summa logicales* and the *Thesaurus pauperum* were issued in folio editions. All English editions of the *Thesaurus pauperum*, the only work of his to be published in England, were in the octavo format. *Language(s)*: Latin. Appraised at 12d in 1588.

147.18 Consilii tridentini
Probably *Acta Concilii Tridentini*. (*Councils–Trent*). Continent: 1546–1569. *Language(s)*: Latin. Appraised at 20d in 1588.

147.19 osorius de gloria
Jeronimo Osorio da Fonseca, *Bishop*. [*Selected works*]. Britain or Continent: date indeterminable.

STC 18884 and non-STC. The single solo edition of *De gloria* (Florence, 1552) is not as likely as one of the numerous editions of Osorio's selected works with *De gloria* leading, including an edition published in England in 1580. *Language(s)*: Latin. Appraised at 12d in 1588.

147.20 The hermo: of Confession
An harmony of the confessions of the faith of the christian and reformed churches. (*Reformed Churches*). Compiled by J.F. Salvart. Cambridge: T. Thomas, pr. to the Univ. of Cambridge, 1586.

STC 5155. *Language(s)*: English. Appraised at 18d in 1588.

147.21 osorius in haddo:
Jeronimo Osorio da Fonseca, *Bishop*. *In Gualterum Haddonum magistrum libellorum supplicum libri tres*. Continent: 1567–1576.

The manuscript entry does not suggest the 1568 English translation (STC 18889) published in Louvain. *Language(s)*: Latin. Appraised at 10d in 1588.

147.22 Lactantius de vera relig:
Lucius Coelius Lactantius. [*Works*]. Continent: date indeterminable.

The compiler was probably reading from Book IV, which is sub-titled "De vera sapientia et religione." *Language(s)*: Latin. Appraised at 8d in 1588.

147.23 Silva Sino:
Simon Pelegromius. *Synonymorum sylva olim a Simone Pelegromio collecta, nunc è Belgarum sermone in Anglicanum transfusa, et redacta per H. F. Accesserunt huic editioni synonyma quaedam poetica*. London: T. Vautrollerius, 1580–1585.

STC 19556 *et seq*. *Language(s)*: English Latin. Appraised at 14d in 1588.

147.24 Hiperii phis:
Andreas Gerardus, *Hyperius*. [*Aristotle–Physica: paraphrase*]. Britain or Continent: 1574–1585.

STC 758 and non-STC. *Language(s)*: Latin. Appraised at 10d in 1588.

147.25 A Concordans
Unidentified [Biblical concordance]. Place unknown: stationer unknown, date indeterminable.
STC/non-STC status unknown. STC 17300, Marbecke's concordance, is a possibility. *Language(s)*: Latin (probable) English (perhaps). Appraised at 8d in 1588.

147.26 Apthonius
Aphthonius, *Sophista. Progymnasmata.* Britain or Continent: date indeterminable.
STC 699 *et seq.* and non-STC. *Language(s)*: Latin (probable) Greek (perhaps). Appraised at 6d in 1588.

147.27 Horatius
Quintus Horatius Flaccus. Probably [*Works*]. Britain or Continent: date indeterminable.
STC 13784 and non-STC. *Language(s)*: Latin. Appraised at 5d in 1588.

147.28 Lexicon hab:
Unidentified [dictionary]. Continent: date indeterminable.
Muenster's and Pagninus's are among the most likely to be represented here. *Language(s)*: Hebrew Latin. Appraised at 20d in 1588.

147.29 prov: sal Haeb
[*Bible–O.T.–Proverbs*]. Continent: date indeterminable.
Language(s): Hebrew. Appraised at 12d in 1588.

147.30 Martinius gra: Haeb:
Petrus Martinius. [*Grammatica hebraica*]. Continent: 1567–1585.
Language(s): Hebrew Latin. Appraised at 8d in 1588.

147.31 Copia Verbo:
Desiderius Erasmus. *De duplici copia verborum ac rerum.* Britain or Continent: date indeterminable.
STC 10471.4 *et seq.* and non-STC. *Language(s)*: Latin. Appraised at 2d in 1588.

147.32 A booke of presidentes
Anonymous. *A book of precedents.* London: (different houses), 1543–1584.
STC 3327 *et seq. Language(s)*: English. Appraised at 4d in 1588.

147.33 Claudius emblemata
Andrea Alciati. *Emblemata.* Edited, with a commentary, by Claude Mignault. Continent: 1571–1584.
Language(s): Latin. Appraised at 8d in 1588.

147.34 Gramatica graeca
Unidentified [grammar]. Britain or Continent: date indeterminable.
STC 12188 and non-STC. Edward Grant's 1575 Greek grammar is the sole possibility from England. *Language(s)*: Greek Latin. Appraised at 3d in 1588.

147.35 Clenardi gram: Haebr:
Nicolaus Clenardus. *Tabula in grammaticen hebraeam*. Continent: 1529–1581.
According to *Aureliensis* (see 141.176), this text was first published in 1529 and reprinted nineteen times by 1581. *Language(s)*: Hebrew Latin. Appraised at 3d in 1588.

147.36:1–2 ii sermons in Englishe
Unidentified [sermons]. Britain (probable): dates indeterminable.
Unidentifiable in the STC. *Language(s)*: English. Appraised at 2d in 1588.

147.37 An Astrolo: Discourse
Richard Harvey. *An astrological discourse upon the conjunction of Saturne and Jupiter*. London: H. Bynneman (with the assent of R. W[atkins]), 1583.
STC 12909.7 *et seq*. Multiple editions and issues in 1583. *Language(s)*: English Latin. Appraised at 2d in 1588.

147.38 Jacobs Journey
John Overton. *Jacobs troublesome journey to Bethel*. Oxford: J. Barnes, 1586.
STC 18924. The STC entry identifies this text as a commentary on Genesis 33:1–4. *Language(s)*: English. Appraised at 2d in 1588.

147.39 D. Raynoldes orat:
John Rainolds. *Joannis Rainoldi orationes duae: ex iis quas habuit in collegio Corporis Christi, anno 1576*. Oxford: ex off. J. Barnesii, 1587.
STC 20612. *Language(s)*: Latin. Appraised at 3d in 1588.

147.40 Oseus in Ebrue
[*Bible–O.T.–Hosea*]. Continent: date indeterminable.
See Adams B1289 for a Hebrew text of Hosea. *Language(s)*: Hebrew. Appraised at 10d in 1588.

147.41 speculum pontifi:
Probably Stephanus Kis (Stephanus Szegedinus). *Speculum romanorum pontificum*. Basle (probable): [Konrad von Waldkirch], 1584–1586.
Another work by Kis appears in Newby's library (see 147.8). *Language(s)*: Latin. Appraised at 8d in 1588.

147.42 Terentius
Publius Terentius, *Afer*. [*Works*]. Britain or Continent: date indeterminable.
STC 23885 *et seq*. and non-STC. *Language(s)*: Latin. Appraised at 3d in 1588.

147.43 An Eng: Lett: [Lecture] and a Catach:
Perhaps John Baker, *Minister. Lectures of J. B(aker) upon the xii. articles of our christian faith. Also a briefe confession.* London: C. Barker, 1581–1584.
STC 1219 *et seq.* The "briefe confession" is by John Hooper, *Bishop. Language(s)*: English. Appraised at 3d in 1588.

147.44 Shepres vers
John Shepery. *Hyppolitus Ovidianae Phaedrae respondens.* Edited by George Edrichus. Oxford: J. Barnesius, typog. Oxoniensis, 1586 (probable).
STC 22405. *Language(s)*: Latin. Appraised at 1d in 1588.

147.45 A copye booke
Unidentified. Provenance unknown: date indeterminable.
Manuscript. Likely a personal book of some kind such as a commonplace book or an account book. *Language(s)*: Unknown. Appraised at 4d in 1588.

Robert Dowe. Scholar (B.C.L.): Probate Inventory. 1588

RICHARD OVENDEN

Robert Dowe (Dove, Dow) was born in 1553, the son of Robert Dowe (1517–1612), a wealthy and successful London merchant. The Dowe family lived in London, his mother being a daughter of another wealthy London merchant, Nicholas Bull. Robert was their eldest son, although they had had at least four other boys by 1568 (London and Rawlins 1963, 41), and he is not to be confused with the Robert Dowe (b. 1551) who was the son of Christopher Dowe, and who married one Luce Smith sometime before 1587 (London and Rawlins 1963, 42).

The elder Dowe was one of the senior figures in the Merchant Taylors' Company, which was in itself one of the most powerful institutions in the City of London at the time. He was Warden of the Merchant Taylors' Company in 1571 and 1575, and was Master in 1578. The Company erected a monument to him in 1622 in St Botolph's Aldgate, in honor of his numerous benefactions. Robert senior (who outlived his son) distinguished himself by a large variety of charitable bequests, both small and large. He gave money to prisoners at Newgate and elsewhere; he helped the poor of St Botolph's Aldgate and gave money to the poor of his own Guild (Clode 1888, 157–169). He gave £50 for building work in 1596 and over £16 for the purchase of books on canon and civil law to St John's College Oxford, which was closely connected to the Merchant Taylors' (see Stevenson and Salter 1939, 296 and 298). He also gave a thirteenth-century manuscript to the College in 1600 (see Alexander and Temple 1939, no. 219).

For most of his life Robert Dowe senior was a major benefactor to Merchant Taylors' School, founded in 1561. His sons John and Henry were sent there (see Hart 1936, 9) and, in addition to significant benefactions, he was instrumental in having the Statutes revised (see Draper 1962, 40). Despite this family association, Robert junior does not appear in the School records, which are unreliable until the early seventeenth century, when his father instituted the School's Probation Books (Mateer 1986–87, 1–2), but given the other family connections, it is highly likely that Robert received his early education at the School. From here he seems to have foregone the family connections with St John's College Oxford, and entered Corpus Christi College as a gentleman-commoner sometime before September 1573, for which date there survives a letter from Dowe to William Cecil, Lord Burghley from the College (BL, Lansdowne MS xvii, no. 77). The letter is the only evidence for his residence in the College, and as he does not appear in the College Registers, his exact status at Corpus remains something of a mystery.

The first facts of which we can be sure are that he supplicated for the degree of Bachelor of Arts on 12 October 1573, was admitted to the degree on 14 January 1574 (and is listed in the Faculty of Arts Admission Register with other Corpus men) (Mateer 1986–87, 3), and determined later in the same year (again listed with the other Corpus determiners). After some obsequious lobbying of Burghley he managed to further his academic career, being elected a probationary Fellow of All Souls on 28 November 1575, and was admitted to the College as a Student of Laws on 14 January 1577. He supplicated for the Baccalaureate of Civil Law on 28 March 1579, and was admitted to the degree on 26 April 1583 (Hart 1936, 36). He was appointed Bursar of Laws at All Souls in November 1585, a position which he held until October 1587. He died on 10 November 1588, and an inventory of goods, including books, was compiled on 1 March 1589.

Robert's younger brother Henry entered Christ Church on 22 April 1576, and was evidently a student of great promise, as his admission to the College had been on the orders of Elizabeth I, but Henry soon fell ill, and despite receiving care from his elder brother at All Souls, he died on 23 October 1578. Robert and others penned lamentations on his passing, which are inscribed on his memorial in Christ Church Cathedral. In 1581 Dowe can again be found penning Latin verse, this time in memory of Sir William Cordell, Master of the Rolls, and presumably because of Cordell's interest in Merchant Taylors' School (Mateer 1986–87, 3).

Perhaps the most interesting of all of Dowe's contacts whilst at Oxford are those which he made with the Sidney family. The first of these connections is the record of payments "To Sr Dowe for teaching him to write . . . 5s" in the account book of Robert Dorsett of expenses for Robert Sidney whilst at Oxford, on 25 June 1575 (HMC 1925, 1:268–269). Dowe also published a funerary poem "Clarissimi Equitis Philippi Sidnei Memoriae Sacrum" which appeared in a volume of verse in 1575 under the title *Equitis D. Philippi Sidnei* and edited by William Gager (STC 22551; Dowe's verse appears on sigs. Dv-D2v). These verses indicate that Dowe had more than a passing acquaintance with Sidney. The other verses in the volume do not give nearly so much personal detail, nor do they indicate, as Dowe's does, that Sidney held such a deep interest in European political affairs. Dowe's verse also suggests that Sidney might have been considered a successor to the crown of Poland upon the death of Stephan Báthory, had he not predeceased him in 1586. Sidney certainly visited Eastern Europe on his extended period in Europe from 1572 to 1575 (Osborn 1972, 245–46, and Gömöri 1991, 23–33) The poem also makes it clear that Dowe had met Báthory in Poland, and it has been suggested that Dowe visited Poland as a member of a trade delegation connected with the Merchant Taylors which was led by John Herbert (see Zins 1974, 89–95 and 294–296). Further evidence of such a journey is found among his possessions, which include a "Polish gowne" and a "grogram gowne" and several books with Polish connections, in particular Cromer's *Polonia*. The Bursars' books at All Souls suggest that he was not present for the period from March 1583 until March 1586, and he was granted leave of absence from College in March and December 1584, each time for one year (Upton 1989, 141).

Robert Dowe, like numerous other educated Englishmen, was deeply moved by the death of Sidney. Not only did he pen the verses in his memory which were printed in Oxford by Gager, but he copied numerous poems together with music by William Byrd into five manuscript part-books now in the library of Christ Church Oxford. These anthologies contain several pieces connected with Sidney, including two elegies, one of which may have been penned by Edward Dyer. This collection is one of the earliest and most authoritative of the works of Byrd, and shows that Dowe must not only have had access to either the composer himself, or someone closely connected with him who may well have shared manuscript copies of the music with Dowe (Woudhuysen 1996, 255–257).

The music books are no doubt the "songe bookes" which feature at the end of the book-list proper in his probate inventory. The bindings as they survive have been lettered "G.T." on the front boards, referring to one Giles Thomson, who may have known Dowe either through Merchant Taylors' School, where he was a pupil, or at All Souls, where he was a Fellow. Either way, Thomson owned not only these manuscript volumes, but also several printed books which are now in the library of St George's Chapel, and it has been suggested that he acquired these books from the sale of Dowe's goods and chattels (Mateer 1986–87, 4).

But music was not the only subject matter that Dowe was interested in. He made copies of sermons, speeches, and letters related to religious, legal, and political matters, roughly covering the period 1560–81, and now in the Bodleian (MS Top.Oxon.e.5, SC 28841), and his book list, a substantial one, indicates wide-ranging interests. The unusual manuscript entry "Italian poettes" reflects, on the basis of surviving Oxford book-lists, a unique interest in this genre for Oxford scholars and conceivably may even reveal an additional connection with Sidney.

Finally, the inventory, despite its clear hand, offers a number of peculiar entries even by the vagaries of sixteenth-century spelling. The extant manuscript, with its scribally embellished preface and uniform script, gives evidence of being fair copy, and the legible but garbled entries may have resulted from misreadings made during transcription of an original, sometimes indecipherable list. See, for example, 148.260, 148.265, 148.269 and a pair of uniformly odd misspellings of Susenbrotus (148.70 and 148.189). Mistranscription in copying may also be responsible for the entries at 148.151, 148.217, 148.253, and 148.293, which resist identification as written, however legibly.

Oxford University Archives, Bodleian Library: Hyp.B.12.

§

Alexander, J.J.G., and Elzbieta Temple. 1985. *Illuminated Manuscripts in Oxford College Libraries, The University Archives and the Taylor Institution*. Oxford: Oxford Univ. Press.

Clode, Charles M. 1888. *The Early History of the Guild of Merchant Taylors'*. London: Harrison and Sons.

Draper, F.W.M. 1962. *Four Centuries of Merchant Taylors' School 1561–1961*. London: Oxford Univ. Press.

Gömöri, George. 1991. "Sir Philip Sidney's Hungarian and Polish Connections." *Oxford Slavonic Papers*, n.s. 24: 23–33.

Hart, E.P., ed. 1934. *Merchant Taylors' School Register 1561–1934*. London: Printed for the Merchant Taylors' Company by the Eastern Press.

HMC 1925. *Report on the Manuscripts of Lord de L'Isle and Dudley preserved at Penshurst Place*. London: His Majesty's Stationery Office.

London, H. Stanford, and S.W. Rawlins, eds. 1963. *Visitation of London 1568*. Publications of the Harleian Society 109–110. London: Harleian Society.

Mateer, David. 1986–87. "Oxford, Christ Church Music MSS 984–8: An Index and Commentary." *Research Chronicle of the Royal Musical Association*, 20: 1–18.

Osborn, James M. 1972. *Young Philip Sidney 1572–1577*. New Haven and London: Yale Univ. Press for the Elizabethan Club.

Stevenson, W.H., and H.E. Salter. 1939. *The Early History of St John's College Oxford*. Oxford Historical Society, n.s. 1.

Upton, C.A. 1989. " 'Speaking Sorrow': The English University Anthologies of 1587 on the Death of Philip Sidney in the Low Countries," in *Academic Relations Between the Low Countries and the British Isles 1450–1700: Proceedings of the First Conference of Belgian, British, and Dutch Historians of Universities held in Ghent*, ed. H. De Ridder-Symoens and J.M. Fletcher. *Studia Historica Gandensia* 273. Gent: Rijksuniversiteit te Gent, pp. 131–141.

Woudhuysen, Henry. 1996. *Sir Philip Sidney and the Circulation of Manuscripts 1558–1640*. Oxford: Clarendon Press.

Zins, Henryk. 1974. *Polska w oczach Anglików XIV–XVI w.* Warsaw: Państwowy Instytut Wydawniczy.

§

148.1	Gasparus Defensus Caroli 5ti
148.2	Guichiartinus de repub. [republica]
148.3	Bembi Historia
148.4	De Bello Coloniensi
148.5	Calepinus auctus et recognitus
148.6	Corpus Juris Civilis uno vol
148.7	Fenestella de magistratibus
148.8	Ptolomaeus
148.9	Belaius de rebus Gallicis
148.10	de sphaera
148.11	Litterae principis Bur ad Car
148.12	Moslan
148.13	C. Ortelii tabulae
148.14	Seneca
148.15	Cornelius Tacitus
148.16	Funxii Chronologia
148.17	T. Livius
148.18	Bodinus de repub.
148.19	Lucan
148.20	Demosthenis Olynth.
148.21	Mureti Orationes
148.22	Longolii Epistolae
148.23	Officia Ciceronis
148.24	Cato
148.25	Pausanias folio
148.26	Xenophon graece et latine
148.27	Historia Scanderbegi
148.28	Zwingeri tabulae in ethicam Aristotelis
148.29	Strebaeus de oratore
148.30	Buchanani Historia Scot.
148.31	Velcurii Physica
148.32	Aesopi Fabulae
148.33	Rami Logica
148.34	Italian Grammar
148.35	Epitome Physice
148.36	Opera Ciceronis in folio
148.37	Turnebi Adversaria
148.38	Dionisius graece
148.39	Martiall wth a comment
148.40	Hardinge against Jewell
148.41	Philippus Commineus
148.42	L. Apuleius
148.43	Athenagoras

148.44	Terence wth a comment
148.45	Calvini Inst. [Institutio]
148.46	A commentarie uppon Tullie ad Atticum
148.47	Duraeus against Whittaker
148.48	Biblia latina
148.49	Zwinger uppon Aristotle's Ethics
148.50	Lambinus super Horatio
148.51	Jewelli Vita
148.52	Organon Aristotelis
148.53	Children's Dictionarie
148.54	Aristotelis Politica
148.55	Foxius Phy[Philosophia]
148.56	Tullies Epist
148.57	Sententiae et Exempla Ebor
148.58	Quintilian 2 vol
148.59	Manutius ad Atticum
148.60	Replie to the aunswere by Whittaker
148.61	Euclides graece
148.62	Ciceronis Philipica
148.63	Erasmus de figuris
148.64	Quintilian
148.65	Erasmus de pronunciatione linguae latinae
148.66	Victorii Casi graece
148.67	Euclides graece
148.68	Hezeus Psalter
148.69	Valerii Dialectica
148.70	Susambroti Figurae
148.71	Assertio Arthuri
148.72	Ovid de tristibus
148.73	Aristotelis Retorica
148.74	Terence
148.75	Salust
148.76	Periphrasis Erasmi
148.77	Strabo
148.78	Commentarius in Physicam
148.79	Gyraldi Dialogismus
148.80	Smithius de emend linguae ang
148.81	Symon Symonii philoso
148.82	Lyndani Tabulae
148.83	Euripedes Hecuba
148.84	Hegendorphinus in Topica
148.85	Bax Arithmetica
148.86	Ortodoxae Explicationes
148.87	Daneaus in Genebrardum
148.88	Poselii Syntaxis

148.89	Whittaker in Campianum
148.90	Mustellae loci communes
148.91	Calvini Inst:
148.92	Beza Testamentum grae et lat
148.93	Doctor Bylson
148.94	Nowells Catechisme
148.95	Testamentum Erasmi
148.96	Vutableri annot in phy
148.97	Theses Reginaldi
148.98	Hyperii Theologia
148.99	Vita Basilidis
148.100	Davidis Psalmi
148.101	Testamentum latinum
148.102	Praecationes Roffensis
148.103	Testamentum Italicum
148.104	Calvini Catechismus graece et latine
148.105	Tremelii Biblia
148.106	Phrases Scoci
148.107	Talei Retorica
148.108	Grammatica Linacri
148.109	Vivis Dialogi
148.110	Vivis de causis corruptionis artium
148.111	Vivis de anima
148.112	Plinii Epistolae
148.113	Middendorpius de academiis
148.114	Epistolae Principum
148.115	Bembi Epistolae
148.116	Aschami Epistolae
148.117	Brandolini de epistoliis conscribendis
148.118	Tullii Epistolae Familiares
148.119	Christophori Lexicon
148.120	Morae Epistolae
148.121	Smithius de pronunciacione linguae graecae
148.122	Clenardi Grammatica
148.123	Spicelegium
148.124	Leonardi Meditationes
148.125	Institutiones Justiniani
148.126	Stephanus de abusu linguae graecae
148.127	Varrinaei Syntaxis
148.128	Poselius
148.129	Isocrates graece
148.130	Fortescue in commendatione legum Angliae
148.131	Doctor & the Student
148.132	Abridgment of the Statutes
148.133	Summa Angelica

148.134	Summa Roscelli
148.135	Ars Notariatus
148.136	Duraeus de beneficiis
148.137	Silva Nuptialis
148.138	Vocabularius Utriusque Juris
148.139	Lagii Methodus
148.140	Aristotelis Organum
148.141	Lypsius Epistles
148.142	Sigonius de antiquo iure Italiae
148.143	Flaminius de Roma triumphante
148.144	Vita Jewelli
148.145	Scheperi Hypolita
148.146	Synopsis
148.147	Vita Casparis
148.148	Jovii Opera
148.149	Surii Chronicon
148.150	Genebrardi chronologia
148.151	Caius Kemmisius
148.152	Confessio Augustiniana
148.153	Osorius in Haddonum
148.154	Osorius de regum institutione
148.155	Osorius in Isaiam
148.156	Osorius de rebus Emanuelis
148.157	Osorius de sapientia
148.158	Osorius de gloria
148.159	Osorius de justitia
148.160	Chromeri Polonia
148.161	Camdeni Brittannia
148.162	Mori Utopia
148.163:1	Metropolis Grantii et Saxonia
148.163:2	[See 148.163:1]
148.164	Antemachevile
148.165	Matchevile de Principe
148.166	Virginius
148.167	Secelius de republica Galliae
148.168	Narratio Rerum ab Adventu Johannis Austriaci
148.169	Causa Ruentis Reipublicae
148.170	Demosthenis Heraliptimen
148.171	The Praise of Follie
148.172	Querela in Albana
148.173	Dialectica Legalis
148.174	Vindiciae contra Tyrannos
148.175	Homeri Odyssea
148.176	Ovid de tristibus
148.177	Tullie's Philosophie

148.178	Kytraeus de ratione dicendi
148.179	Pomponius Mela
148.180	Tullie's Philosophie
148.181	Jesneri Appendix
148.182	Oedorus
148.183	Ethica Aristotelis
148.184	Musarum Lachrimae
148.185	Euripidis Tragaedia
148.186	Gentilis Opera
148.187	Ramus in Physicam
148.188	Ramus in Metaphysicam
148.189	Susambrotus
148.190	Sebastiani Questura
148.191	Heraclis Philosophia
148.192	Cooper
148.193	Navis Stultifera
148.194	Cornucopia
148.195	Exposit. Tit.
148.196	A Booke of Presidentes
148.197	Crispinus
148.198	Institutiones Justiniani
148.199	Caelius
148.200	Erasmi Epistolae
148.201	Barete Dictionarie
148.202	Westenbecius
148.203	Angeli Politiani Opera
148.204	Methodus Vigeliae
148.205	Corpus Civile cum Glossa
148.206	Heywood
148.207	Budaei Forensia
148.208	Nizolius
148.209	An olde booke
148.210	Dion Caseus
148.211	Trebelius Polis
148.212	Stanihurstus de rebus Hybernia
148.213	Posceuius de Societate Jesu
148.214	Terence wth a Comment
148.215	Plautus wth a comment
148.216	Virgill
148.217	Tabule Crassentini
148.218	Mureti orat:
148.219	Symbola Heroica
148.220	Crinitus de honesta disciplina
148.221	Macrobius
148.222	Tullies' Historie

148.223 Carion's Chronicle fo.
148.224 Lucian's Woorke
148.225 Luciani Dialogi
148.226 L. Florus
148.227 Herodotus
148.228:1 Justinus et Salustius
148.228:2 [See 148.228:1]
148.229 Caesar's comment:
148.230 Bodini Methodus
148.231 Thuscidides
148.232 Carion wth out Melangthon
148.233 Laertius
148.234 Textors Officina
148.235 Carions Chronicles .3. Vol
148.236 Civill Converse
148.237 Plutarchi Opera grae:
148.238 Plutarchi Opera lat:
148.239 Plutarchi Moralia
148.240 Horace
148.241 Claudianus
148.242 Juvenall
148.243 Aeliani Varia Historia
148.244 Petrarch de remediis utriusque fortunae
148.245 Erasmi lingua
148.246 Erasmi adagia
148.247 dictionarium poeticum
148.248 Ovid de tristibus
148.249 Valerius maximus
148.250 Ovides Epistles
148.251:1 Ovidii metamor. bis.
148.251:2 [See 148.251:1]
148.252 Francis Frankius
148.253 Petrus Kyralonus
148.254 Bezae Poemata
148.255 Pallingenius
148.256 Seneca
148.257 Hieronimus
148.258 Italian poettes
148.259 Syntagmata Juris
148.260 Archyfremus
148.261 Dispauterius
148.262 Aristotelis Ethica graece
148.263 Jo. Lucenbergius
148.264 Textors Epistles
148.265 Crinaeus de mundo

148.266	Symon Symonis
148.267	Schola Salerna
148.268	Epit Plutarchi
148.269	Locuinas de complexionibus
148.270	Schola Salerna, lat
148.271	Foxius, Eth:
148.272	Daneus Eth:
148.273	Dialectica Perionii
148.274	cut. super eth. Arist
148.275	Arist. Organon
148.276	Phy: Titelmanni
148.277	Rodolphi dialect:
148.278	Rami logica
148.279	Titelmanni dialect:
148.280	Foxii Physica
148.281	Ramus in Bucolica Virgillii
148.282	Rami Dialectica
148.283	Ramus Animadversiones
148.284	Ramus in 8 orat: Cic:
148.285	Arisst: phy.
148.286	Arist: Organon
148.287	Car. de Sensibus
148.288	Peuserus de divinatione
148.289	Gratalarus
148.290	Albertus de secretis
148.291	Symon Symonius de nobilitate
148.292	Sygonius
148.293	Poserius
148.294	Cane Loci Communes
148.295	Dialogus de religione
148.296	Stapletoni Speculum
148.297	Actus consilii Tridentini
148.298	censura Coloniensis
148.299	Choserii Enchiridion
148.300	Catechismus Tridentinus
148.301	Diacosiomartirion
148.302	multiple his songe bookes

§

148.1   Gasparus Defensus Caroli 5ti

Gaspar de Baeza. *In Caroli quinti Augusti hispaniae regis illustrem constitutionem.* Granada: apud Hugo Menam, 1566.

Language(s): Latin. Appraised at 10d in 1589.

148.2 Guichiartinus de repub. [republica]
Probably Francesco Guicciardini. Unidentified. Continent: date indeterminable.
Something of Ludovico Guicciardini's is also possible. *Language(s)*: Latin. Appraised at 8d in 1589.

148.3 Bembi Historia
Pietro Bembo. *Historiae Venetae libri XII*. Edited by Giovanni della Casa. Continent: 1551.
There were Latin editions in both Paris and Venice in 1551. The Italian editions of 1552 and 1570 are almost certainly not referred to by this entry. *Language(s)*: Latin. Appraised at 12d in 1589.

148.4 De Bello Coloniensi
Michael ab Isselt. *De bello Coloniensi*. Cologne: apud (excud.) Godefridum Kempensem, 1584–1586.
Language(s): Latin. Appraised at 12d in 1589.

148.5 Calepinus auctus et recognitus
Ambrogio Calepino. *Dictionarium*. Continent: 1502–1586.
Some editions contain several vernacular languages by the date of this inventory. *Language(s)*: Greek Latin. Appraised at 6s 8d in 1589.

148.6 Corpus Juris Civilis uno vol
Justinian I. *Corpus juris civilis*. Continent: date indeterminable.
This entry may represent an edition of the *Corpus* in a single volume, or possibly a stray volume from any of the multi-volume editions. The appraisal, one of the highest in the collection, is, however, extremely high for a single, stray volume. *Language(s)* : Greek Latin. Appraised at 20s in 1589.

148.7 Fenestella de magistratibus
Andreas Dominicus Floccus (Lucius Fenestella). *De magistratibus sacerdotiisque Romanorum*. Continent: date indeterminable.
Language(s): Latin. Appraised at 2d in 1589.

148.8 Ptolomaeus
Claudius Ptolemy. Unidentified. Continent (probable): date indeterminable.
Probably not an STC book. The *Geographia* is the most likely candidate. *Language(s)*: Latin (probable). Appraised at 13s in 1589.

148.9 Belaius de rebus Gallicis
Martin du Bellay. *Commentariorum de rebus Gallicis libri decem*. Translated by Hugues Sureau. Frankfurt am Main: (different houses), 1573–1575.
Andreas Wechel was involved in the printing of all editions. *Language(s)*: Latin. Appraised at 5s in 1589.

148.10 de sphaera

Unidentified. Place unknown: stationer unknown, date indeterminable.

STC/non-STC status unknown. Possibilities include works by George Buchanan, John Holywood (Joannes Sacrobosco), Proclus, and Rembert Dodoens. *Language(s)*: Latin. Appraised at 2d in 1589.

148.11 Litterae principis Bur ad Car

Louis I, *Prince de Condé. Literae.* Geneva (probable): [Henricus Stephanus], 1569c.

This entry may possibly refer to Girolamo Ruscelli's *Lettere di principi... Lib. 1 Nuovamente mandato in luce da Girolamo Ruscelli, all Illmo et Revmo Cardinal Carlo Borromeo* (Venice, 1562). *Language(s)*: Latin. Appraised at 2d in 1589.

148.12 Moslan

Perhaps Petrus Schade, *Mosellanus.* Unidentified. Place unknown: stationer unknown, date indeterminable.

STC/non-STC status unknown. *Language(s)*: Latin. Appraised at 1d in 1589.

148.13 C. Ortelii tabulae

Abraham Ortelius. *Theatrum orbis terrarum.* Continent: date indeterminable.

Despite the *C* in the manuscript entry, doubtless Ortelius. *Language(s)*: Latin. Appraised at 20s in 1589.

148.14 Seneca

Lucius Annaeus Seneca. [*Works*]. Paris: apud Jacobum Dupuys, 1587.

In a contemporary Oxford binding, decorated with Ker, Centerpiece i and Ornament 50, with MS pastedowns from a text of the *Summa Roffredi* (Ker 1417). The greater appraised value for this item (as opposed to 148.256) is no doubt a reflection of its recent publication date. *Language(s)*: Latin. Appraised at 18s in 1589. *Current location*: Windsor, St. George's Chapel, XV.g(6).

148.15 Cornelius Tacitus

Publius Cornelius Tacitus. [*Works*]. Edited by Justus Lipsius. Antwerp: apud Christophorum Plantinum, 1585.

Language(s): Latin. Appraised at 6s in 1589. *Current location*: Windsor, St. George's Chapel, T1.

148.16 Funxii Chronologia

Johann Funck. *Chronologia.* Continent: date indeterminable.
Language(s): Latin. Appraised at 5s in 1589.

148.17 T. Livius

Titus Livius. [*Historiae Romanae decades*]. Britain or Continent: date indeterminable.

STC 16611.5 *et seq.* and non-STC. *Language(s)*: Latin. Appraised at 9s in 1589.

148.18   Bodinus de repub.
Jean Bodin, *Bishop. De republica*. Continent: apud Jacobum Du-Puys, 1586.
Two editions in the same year, Paris and Lyon. *Language(s)*: Latin. Appraised at 10s in 1589.

148.19   Lucan
Marcus Annaeus Lucanus. *Pharsalia*. Britain or Continent: date indeterminable.
STC 16882 and non-STC. *Language(s)*: Latin. Appraised at 5d in 1589.

148.20   Demosthenis Olynth.
Demosthenes. *Olynthiacae orationes tres*. Britain or Continent: date indeterminable.
Some editions were issued with the *Philippicae* and other orations, including the 1571 edition published in London. *Language(s)*: Latin (probable) Greek (perhaps). Appraised at 4d in 1589.

148.21   Mureti Orationes
Marcus Antonius Muretus. [*Selected works–Orations*]. Continent: date indeterminable.
Language(s): Latin. Appraised at 12d in 1589.

148.22   Longolii Epistolae
Christophorus Longolius. [*Epistolae*]. Continent: date indeterminable.
Language(s): Latin. Appraised at 8d in 1589.

148.23   Officia Ciceronis
Marcus Tullius Cicero. *De officiis*. Continent: date indeterminable.
Language(s): Latin. Appraised at 6d in 1589.

148.24   Cato
Dionysius Cato. [*Disticha*]. Britain or Continent: date indeterminable.
STC 4839.4 *et seq.* and non-STC. May also refer to the works of Marcus Portius Cato, but he seems not to have been published alone at this time. *Language(s)*: Latin. Appraised at 1d in 1589.

148.25   Pausanias folio
Pausanias. [*Graeciae descriptio*]. Continent: date indeterminable.
Language(s): Latin Greek (perhaps). Appraised at 4s in 1589.

148.26   Xenophon graece et latine
Xenophon. [*Works*]. Continent: date indeterminable.
Language(s) : Greek Latin. Appraised at 7s in 1589.

148.27 Historia Scanderbegi
Marino Barlezio. [*Historia de vita et gestis Scanderbegi*]. Continent: c.1510–1537. *Language(s)*: Latin. Appraised at 3s in 1589.

148.28 Zwingeri tabulae in ethicam Aristotelis
Theodor Zwinger. [*Aristotle–Ethica: commentary*]. The text is translated by Dionysius Lambinus. Basle: (different houses), 1566–1582.
Another copy at 148.49. *Language(s)*: Latin. Appraised at 4s in 1589.

148.29 Strebaeus de oratore
Jacobus Lodovicus Strebaeus. Unidentified. Continent: date indeterminable. Could refer to editions of his *De partitione oratoria M.T. Ciceronis commentariis illustratus*, *De verborum electione et collocatione oratoria*, or *In dialogos Ciceronis de oratore commentaria*. *Language(s)*: Latin. Appraised at 12d in 1589.

148.30 Buchanani Historia Scot.
George Buchanan. *Rerum Scoticarum historia*. Britain or Continent: 1582–1584. STC 3391 *et seq.* and non-STC. Some editions also contained his *De Jure Regni apud Scotos*. *Language(s)*: Latin. Appraised at 7s in 1589.

148.31 Velcurii Physica
Joannes Velcurio. [*Aristotle–Physica: commentary*]. Britain or Continent: 1537–1589.
STC 24632 and non-STC. *Language(s)*: Latin. Appraised at 8d in 1589.

148.32 Aesopi Fabulae
Aesop. *Fabulae*. Britain or Continent: date indeterminable.
STC 168 *et seq.* and non-STC. *Language(s)*: Latin (probable) Greek (perhaps). Appraised at 3d in 1589.

148.33 Rami Logica
Pierre de La Ramée. [*Dialectica*]. Britain or Continent: date indeterminable.
STC 15241.7 *et seq.* and non-STC. Perhaps one of the later editions with *Logica* prominently on the title pages. Other copies at 148.278 and 148.282. *Language(s)*: Latin. Appraised at 14d in 1589.

148.34 Italian Grammar
Unidentified [grammar]. Place unknown: stationer unknown, date indeterminable.
Unidentifiable in the STC. The possibilities are STC 15469 and STC 24020; STC 6758 cannot be ruled out, nor can a Continental publication. *Language(s)*: English Italian. Appraised at 4d in 1589.

148.35 Epitome Physice
Unidentified. Continent (probable): date indeterminable.

Probably not an STC book. An epitome of Aristotle's *Physica*? *Language(s)*: Latin. Appraised at 2d in 1589.

148.36 Opera Ciceronis in folio
Marcus Tullius Cicero. [*Works*]. Continent: date indeterminable. *Language(s)*: Latin. Appraised at 9s in 1589.

148.37 Turnebi Adversaria
Adrianus Turnebus. *Adversariorum*. Continent: date indeterminable. *Language(s)*: Latin. Appraised at 3s in 1589.

148.38 Dionisius graece
Unidentified. Continent: date indeterminable.
Works by Dionysius, *of Halicarnassus*, Dionysius, *Periegetes*, and Dionysius, *Areopagita* are all possibilities for this entry. *Language(s)*: Greek. Appraised at 3s 4d in 1589.

148.39 Martiall wth a comment
Marcus Valerius Martialis. Unidentified. Continent: date indeterminable.
Doubtless the *Epigrammata*, but whether selected or collected cannot be determined, though perhaps the latter more likely would carry commentary. *Language(s)*: Latin. Appraised at 1d in 1589.

148.40 Hardinge against Jewell
Thomas Harding. Unidentified. Continent: date indeterminable.
Unidentifiable in the STC. One of several possible reponses in the series of polemical treatises between John Jewel, *Bishop of Salisbury* and Harding (STC 12758 *et seq.*), some of which were substantial volumes. Given the appraised value of this item, two different works entitled *A Rejoindre to M. Jewels Replie* (STC 12760–12761) are likely candidates. *Language(s)*: English. Appraised at 2s 4d in 1589.

148.41 Philippus Commineus
Philippe de Comines. [*Memoires*]. Continent: date indeterminable.
Comines was published in English, Italian, French, and German, but this item almost certainly refers to one of the Latin editions. *Language(s)*: Latin (probable). Appraised at 10d in 1589.

148.42 L. Apuleius
Lucius Apuleius. *Metamorphoses*. Venice: in aed. Aldi, et Andreae soc., 1521.
Language(s): Latin. Appraised at 12d in 1589. *Current location*: New College, Oxford.

148.43 Athenagoras
Athenagoras. Unidentified. Continent (probable): date indeterminable.

Probably not an STC book, but see STC 886, *De resurrectione mortuorum* or that work in a composite volume with the *Apologia pro Christianis*. *Language(s)*: Latin (probable) Greek (perhaps). Appraised at 3d in 1589.

148.44 Terence wth a comment
Publius Terentius, *Afer*. [*Works*]. Britain or Continent: date indeterminable.
STC 23885.3 *et seq.* and non-STC. *Language(s)*: Latin. Appraised at 4s in 1589.

148.45 Calvini Inst. [Institutio]
Jean Calvin. *Institutio Christianae religionis*. Britain or Continent: date indeterminable.
STC 4414 *et seq.* and non-STC. *Language(s)*: Latin. Appraised at 3s in 1589.

148.46 A commentarie uppon Tullie ad Atticum
Unidentified. [*Cicero–Epistolae ad Atticum: commentary*]. Continent: date indeterminable.
Language(s): Latin. Appraised at 18d in 1589.

148.47 Duraeus against Whittaker
John Durie, *Jesuit*. *Confutatio responsionis Gulielmus Whitaker*. Continent: 1582–1585.
Part of a long-running controversy between the Jesuit Edmund Campian and William Whitaker, Regius Professor of Divinity at Cambridge. Here the Scottish Jesuit Durie takes up Campian's position against Whitaker. Of the two editions, the 1585 Ingolstadt included a reply to STC 25362, in which Whitaker had answered the earlier 1582 Paris edition. See 148.89. *Language(s)*: Latin. Appraised at 2s 4d in 1589.

148.48 Biblia latina
The Bible. Britain or Continent: date indeterminable.
STC 2055 *et seq.* and non-STC. *Language(s)*: Latin. Appraised at 2s 6d in 1589.

148.49 Zwinger uppon Aristotle's Ethics
Theodor Zwinger. [*Aristotle–Ethica: commentary*]. The text is translated by Dionysius Lambinus. Basle: (different houses), 1566–1582.
Another copy at 148.28. *Language(s)*: Latin. Appraised at 3s in 1589.

148.50 Lambinus super Horatio
Dionysius Lambinus. Probably [*Horace–Unidentified: commentary*]. Continent: date indeterminable.
But perhaps an edition of Horace with a commentary by Lambinus. *Language(s)*: Latin. Appraised at 8d in 1589.

148.51 Jewelli Vita
Laurence Humphrey. *Joannis Juelli Angli, episcopi Sarisburiensis vita et mors, eiusque verae doctrinae defensio*. London: apud J. Dayum, 1573.

STC 13963. A postscript on the Jewel-Harding controversy by the Regius Professor of Divinity at Oxford, on the Anglican side. Includes memorial verses. Another copy at 148.144. *Language(s)*: Latin. Appraised at 12d in 1589.

148.52   Organon Aristotelis
Aristotle. *Organon*. Continent: date indeterminable.
Other copies at 148.140, 148.275, and 148.286. *Language(s)*: Latin (probable) Greek (perhaps). Appraised at 8d in 1589.

148.53   Children's Dictionarie
Perhaps John Withals. *A shorte dictionarie for yonge begynners*. London: (different houses), 1553–1586.
STC 25874 *et seq*. Just possibly one of the dictionaries or lexicons by one of the brothers Stephanus. See BCI 1:507 (no. 548), Lorkyn 1591, "a Dictionarie for children," also appraised at 2d. *Language(s)*: English. Appraised at 2d in 1589.

148.54   Aristotelis Politica
Aristotle. *Politica*. Continent: date indeterminable.
Language(s): Latin (probable) Greek (perhaps). Appraised at 16d in 1589.

148.55   Foxius Phy[Philosophia]
Sebastiano Fox Morzillo. *De naturae philosophia, seu de Platonis et Aristotelis consensione*. Continent: 1551–1560.
See 148.280 for another copy. *Language(s)*: Latin. Appraised at 12d in 1589.

148.56   Tullies Epist
Marcus Tullius Cicero. Probably [*Selected works–Epistolae*]. Continent: date indeterminable.
Conceivably the *Epistolae ad familiares*, which was published in England as well as on the Continent. *Language(s)*: Latin. Appraised at 3d in 1589.

148.57   Sententiae et Exempla Ebor
Lucius Andreas Resendius (Andreas Eborensis). *Sententia et exempla ex probatissimis quibusque scriptoris collecta*. Continent: date indeterminable.
Language(s): Latin. Appraised at 8d in 1589.

148.58   Quintilian 2 vol
Marcus Fabius Quintilianus. Unidentified. Continent: date indeterminable.
There were two-volume editions of Quintilian's *Works, Institutiones Oratoriae*, and *Selected works*. See 148.64. *Language(s)*: Latin. Appraised at 20d in 1589.

148.59   Manutius ad Atticum
Paolo Manuzio. [*Cicero–Epistolae ad Atticum: commentary*]. Continent: date indeterminable.
More than likely one of the many Aldine editions from Venice, but there was

at least one edition from Frankfurt, with additional material (1580). See Adams M464. *Language(s)*: Latin. Appraised at 16d in 1589.

148.60   Replie to the aunswere by Whittaker
William Rainolds. *A refutation of sundry reprehensions, cavils, and false sleightes, by which M. Whitaker laboureth to deface the late English translation, and catholike annotations of the new Testament*. Paris: [for R. Verstegan?], 1583.

STC 20632. A response to William Whitaker's criticism of Gregory Martin's annotated version of the Geneva Bible (STC 2884) and his *Discouerie of the manifold corruptions of the holy scriptures by the heretikes of our daies* (STC 17503). *Language(s)*: English. Appraised at 12d in 1589.

148.61   Euclides graece
Euclid. Probably *Elementa*. Continent: date indeterminable. See 148.67. *Language(s)*: Greek. Appraised at 10d in 1589.

148.62   Ciceronis Philipica
Marcus Tullius Cicero. *Philippicae*. Britain or Continent: date indeterminable. STC 5311 and non-STC. *Language(s)*: Latin. Appraised at 3d in 1589.

148.63   Erasmus de figuris
Desiderius Erasmus. *De octo partium orationis constructione*. Continent: 1514–1563.

The *De constructionis figuris* formed part of the *De octo partium orationis constructione* usually in the version of Joannes Sulpitius, but latterly by Gerardus Listius. The main work was originally written by William Lily but was edited and amended extensively by Erasmus. Date range is from VHe. *Language(s)*: Latin. Appraised at 2d in 1589.

148.64   Quintilian
Marcus Fabius Quintilianus. Unidentified. Continent: date indeterminable. See 148.58. *Language(s)*: Latin. Appraised at 10d in 1589.

148.65   Erasmus de pronunciatione linguae latinae
Desiderius Erasmus. *De recta pronuntiatione* [and other works]. Continent: 1528–1558.

Date range is from VHe. *Language(s)*: Greek Latin. Appraised at 3d in 1589.

148.66   Victorii Casi graece
Unidentified. Continent (probable): date indeterminable.

Almost certainly not an STC book. Perhaps something of Petrus Victorius, *the Elder*, who edited several editions of Aristotle in Greek. Joannes Caselius may be represented by the *Casi* in the manuscript entry; he edited some of Victorius's works, but none of those in Greek, apparently. *Language(s)*: Greek. Appraised at 12d in 1589.

148.67 Euclides graece
Euclid. Probably *Elementa*. Continent: date indeterminable.
See 148.61. *Language(s)*: Greek. Appraised at 4d in 1589.

148.68 Hezeus Psalter
[*Bible–O.T.–Psalms*]. Translated by Helius Eobanus, *Hessus*. Britain or Continent: 1537–1581.
STC 2356 *et seq.* and non-STC. *Language(s)*: Latin. Appraised at 8d in 1589.

148.69 Valerii Dialectica
Cornelius Valerius. *Tabulae totius dialectices*. Continent: date indeterminable.
Language(s): Latin. Appraised at 3d in 1589.

148.70 Susambroti Figurae
Joannes Susenbrotus. Probably *Epitome troporum ac schematum*. Britain or Continent: date indeterminable.
STC 23437 *et seq.* and non-STC. *Language(s)*: Latin. Appraised at 1d in 1589.

148.71 Assertio Arthuri
John Leland. *Assertio inclytissimi Arturii regis Britanniae*. London: [R. Wolfe] ap. J. Herford, 1544.
STC 15440. *Language(s)*: Latin. Appraised at 6d in 1589.

148.72 Ovid de tristibus
Publius Ovidius Naso. *Tristia*. Britain or Continent: date indeterminable.
STC 18976.4 *et seq.* and non-STC. May also represent a composite edition, with *Tristia* leading. Other copies at 148.176 and 148.248. *Language(s)*: Latin. Appraised at 1d in 1589.

148.73 Aristotelis Retorica
Aristotle. *Rhetorica*. Continent: date indeterminable.
Language(s): Latin (probable) Greek (perhaps). Appraised at 3d in 1589.

148.74 Terence
Publius Terentius, *Afer*. [*Works*]. Britain or Continent: date indeterminable.
STC 23885 *et seq.* and non-STC. *Language(s)*: Latin. Appraised at 3d in 1589.

148.75 Salust
Caius Sallustius Crispus. Unidentified. Place unknown: stationer unknown, date indeterminable.
STC/non-STC status unknown. *Language(s)*: Latin. Appraised at 8d in 1589.

148.76 Periphrasis Erasmi
Desiderius Erasmus. [*New Testament: paraphrase* (part)]. (*Bible–N.T.*). Continent: date indeterminable.

The valuation is too low for this to be complete. *Language(s)*: Latin. Appraised at 4d in 1589.

148.77   Strabo
Strabo. [*Geographia*]. Continent: date indeterminable.
Language(s): Latin. Appraised at 3s in 1589.

148.78   Commentarius in Physicam
Unidentified. Probably [*Aristotle–Physica: commentary*]. Place unknown: stationer unknown, date indeterminable.
STC/non-STC status unknown. *Language(s)*: Latin (probable). Appraised at 2s in 1589.

148.79   Gyraldi Dialogismus
Lilius Gregorius Giraldus. *Suarum quorundam annotationum dialogismi XXX*. Venice: apud Gualterum Scottum, 1552–1553.
The 1553 edition contains notes on the life and work of Giraldus by Laurentius Frizzolius. *Language(s)*: Latin. Appraised at 8d in 1589.

148.80   Smithius de emend linguae ang
Sir Thomas Smith, *Doctor of Civil Laws. De recta et emendata linguae Anglicae scriptione, dialogus*. Paris: ex off. R. Stephani, 1568.
STC 22856.5. *Language(s)*: English Latin. Appraised at 4d in 1589.

148.81   Symon Symonii philoso
Simon Simonius. [*Aristotle–De sensuum instrumentis: commentary. Aristotle–De memoria et reminiscentia: commentary*]. Geneva: apud Joan. Crispinum, 1566.
Language(s): Greek Latin. Appraised at 12d in 1589.

148.82   Lyndani Tabulae
Willelmus Lindanus, *Bishop. Tabulae vigentium nunc atque grassantium passim haereseon*. Continent: 1558–1562.
Language(s): Latin. Appraised at 3d in 1589.

148.83   Euripedes Hecuba
Euripides. *Hecuba*. Continent: date indeterminable.
Selected works with Hecuba leading also a possibility. *Language(s)*: Latin (probable) Greek (perhaps). Appraised at 2d in 1589.

148.84   Hegendorphinus in Topica
Marcus Tullius Cicero. *Topica*. Commentary by Christoph Hegendorff. Paris: Ex officina R. Stephani, 1528.
The only edition with Hegendorff's *Scholia*. *Language(s)*: Latin. Appraised at 2d in 1589.

148.85 Bax Arithmetica
Gaspar Lax. *Arithmetica speculativa*. Paris: impressa opera ac characteribus Nicolai de la barre expensis Hemundi le fevre, 1515.
Language(s): Latin. Appraised at 4d in 1589.

148.86 Ortodoxae Explicationes
Diogo de Paiva de Andrade, *the Elder*. *Orthodoxarum explicationum libri decem*. Continent: 1564.
By a Spanish Jesuit. *Language(s)*: Latin. Appraised at 16d in 1589.

148.87 Daneaus in Genebrardum
Lambert Daneau. *Ad novas Gulielmi Genebrardi calumnias*. Geneva: apud Eustathium Vignon, 1578.
On the Trinity. *Language(s)*: Latin. Appraised at 3d in 1589.

148.88 Poselii Syntaxis
Joannes Posselius. *Syntaxis linguae graecae*. Continent: 1565–1587.
Language(s): Greek Latin. Appraised at 4d in 1589.

148.89 Whittaker in Campianum
William Whitaker. *Ad rationes decem Edmundi Campiani jesuitae, responsio*. London: (different houses), 1581–1583.
STC 25358 *et seq*. A response to the *Rationes decem* of Edmund Campian, secretly printed at Stonor Park in 1581 and distributed on the benches of St. Mary's Church in Oxford. See 148.47 for another work in this controversy. *Language(s)*: Latin. Appraised at 6d in 1589.

148.90 Mustellae loci communes
Probably Wolfgang Musculus. *Loci communes*. Continent: date indeterminable.
The less widely published *Loci communes sacri* of Andreas Musculus is also possible. *Language(s)*: Latin. Appraised at 2s 6d in 1589.

148.91 Calvini Inst:
Jean Calvin. *Institutio Christianae religionis*. Britain or Continent: date indeterminable.
STC 4414 and non-STC. *Language(s)*: Latin. Appraised at 2s 6d in 1589.

148.92 Beza Testamentum grae et lat
[*Bible–N.T.*]. Translated and edited by Théodore de Bèze. Britain or Continent: 1565–1589.
STC 2810 and non-STC. *Language(s)*: Greek Latin. Appraised at 3s in 1589.

148.93 Doctor Bylson
Thomas Bilson, *Bishop*. *The true difference betweene christian subjection and unchristian rebellion*. Britain: 1585–1586.

STC 3071 *et seq. Language(s)*: English. Appraised at 20d in 1589.

148.94 Nowells Catechisme
Alexander Nowell. *Catechismus*. London: (different houses), 1570–1586.

STC 18701 *et seq.* Probably the Larger Catechism, in either Latin or Greek, or conceivably the Shorter (STC 18711–18711b) or the Middle Catechisms (STC 18712–18733.3). *Language(s)*: Latin (probable) English (perhaps) Greek (perhaps). Appraised at 4d in 1589.

148.95 Testamentum Erasmi
[*Bible–N.T.*]. Edited by Desiderius Erasmus. Britain or Continent: date indeterminable.

STC 2800 and non-STC. *Language(s)*: Latin Greek (perhaps). Appraised at 11d in 1589.

148.96 Vutableri annot in phy
Franciscus Vatablus. Unidentified. Continent: date indeterminable.

Various possibilities: something of Vatablus's alone (Adams V302, e.g.) or his revised edition of Faber's paraphrase of the *Philosophia naturalis*. *Language(s)*: Latin. Appraised at 8d in 1589.

148.97 Theses Reginaldi
Unidentified. Continent (probable): date indeterminable.
Language(s): Latin (probable). Appraised at 3d in 1589.

148.98 Hyperii Theologia
Andreas Gerardus, *Hyperius*. Unidentified. Continent: date indeterminable.

There are at least four works by Gerardus that might be entered as *Theologica*, none published in England. *Language(s)*: Latin. Appraised at 16d in 1589.

148.99 Vita Basilidis
Paul Oderborn. *Joannis Basilidis magni Muscoviae ducis vita*. Wittenberg: excudebant haeredes Joannis Cratonis, 1585.

Language(s): Latin. Appraised at 9d in 1589.

148.100 Davidis Psalmi
[*Bible–O.T.–Psalms*]. Britain or Continent: date indeterminable.

Possibly STC 2354 *et seq.* and non-STC. *Language(s)*: Latin. Appraised at 3d in 1589.

148.101 Testamentum latinum
[*Bible–N.T.*]. Britain or Continent: date indeterminable.

STC 2799 *et seq.* and non-STC. *Language(s)*: Latin. Appraised at 3d in 1589.

148.102 Praecationes Roffensis
Psalmi seu precationes ex variis scripturae locis collectae. (Bible–Selections). Compiled by John Fisher, *Saint and Cardinal*. Britain or Continent: 1525–1572.
   STC 2994 *et seq.* and non-STC. See Shaaber F83–89 for the several Continental editions. The English translation at STC 3001.7 is a remote possibility; Fisher's treatise on the "seven penytencyall psalmes" (STC 10902) is even less likely, but still possible. *Language(s)*: Latin. Appraised at 3d in 1589.

148.103 Testamentum Italicum
[*Bible–N.T.*]. Continent: date indeterminable.
Language(s): Italian (probable). Appraised at 12d in 1589.

148.104 Calvini Catechismus graece et latine
Jean Calvin. [*Catechism*]. Continent: 1563–1589.
Language(s): Greek Latin. Appraised at 4d in 1589.

148.105 Tremelii Biblia
The Bible. Edited by Joannes Immanuel Tremellius and François Du Jon, *the Elder*. Britain or Continent: date indeterminable.
   STC 2056 *et seq.* and non-STC. *Language(s)*: Latin. Appraised at 9s in 1589.

148.106 Phrases Scoci
Antonius Schorus. *Phrases linguae latinae*. Continent: date indeterminable.
Language(s): Latin. Appraised at 4d in 1589.

148.107 Talei Retorica
Aldomarus Talaeus (Omer Talon). *Rhetorica*. Continent: date indeterminable.
   Ramus had a major role in the composition of the *Rhetorica. Language(s)*: Latin. Appraised at 2d in 1589.

148.108 Grammatica Linacri
Thomas Linacre. Probably *Rudimenta grammatices*. Translated by George Buchanan. Britain or Continent: 1525 (probable)–1566.
   STC 15636 *et seq.* and non-STC. This entry may also represent the *Progymnasmata grammatices vulgaria* of 1512 (STC 15635). Some editions also contain grammatical texts by Vives. *Language(s)*: Latin. Appraised at 10d in 1589.

148.109 Vivis Dialogi
Joannes Ludovicus Vives. [*Familiarium colloquiorum formulae, sive linguae latinae exercitatio*]. Continent: date indeterminable.
Language(s): Latin. Appraised at 4d in 1589.

148.110 Vivis de causis corruptionis artium
Joannes Ludovicus Vives. *De disciplinis libri xx*. Continent: date indeterminable.

The third part of the *De disciplinis libri xx* is entitled *De causis corruptionis artium*; the compiler likely was reading from the open book. *Language(s)*: Latin. Appraised at 12d in 1589.

148.111   Vivis de anima
Joannes Ludovicus Vives. *De anima et vita libri tres* [and other works]. Continent: 1538–1563.
Language(s): Latin. Appraised at 18d in 1589.

148.112   Plinii Epistolae
Pliny, the Younger. *Epistolae*. Continent: date indeterminable.
Language(s): Latin. Appraised at 2d in 1589.

148.113   Middendorpius de academiis
Jacob Middendorp. [*De celebrioribus universi terrarum orbis academiis*]. Cologne: (different houses), 1567–1583.
Language(s): Latin. Appraised at 3d in 1589.

148.114   Epistolae Principum
Girolamo Donzellini. *Epistolae principum rerum publicarum ac sapientum virorum*. Venice: apud J. Zilettum, 1574.
Language(s): Latin. Appraised at 10d in 1589.

148.115   Bembi Epistolae
Pietro Bembo. [*Epistolae*]. Continent: date indeterminable.
Language(s): Latin. Appraised at 12d in 1589.

148.116   Aschami Epistolae
Roger Ascham. *Familiarium epistolarum libri tres*. London: (different houses), 1576–1581.
STC 826 *et seq*. Francis Coldock was involved in the publication of all three editions represented in the date range. *Language(s)*: Latin. Appraised at 12d in 1589.

148.117   Brandolini de epistoliis conscribendis
Aurelius Brandolinus (Lippus). Probably *De ratione scribendi*. Britain or Continent: 1549–1573.
STC 3542 and non-STC. The *De epistoliis conscribendis libelli* by Vives, Erasmus, and Christoph Hegendorff, among others, were included in the compilation that leads with *De ratione scribendi* as the first item. *Language(s)*: Latin. Appraised at 7d in 1589.

148.118   Tullii Epistolae Familiares
Marcus Tullius Cicero. *Epistolae ad familiares*. Britain or Continent: date indeterminable.
STC 5295 *et seq*. and non-STC. *Language(s)*: Latin. Appraised at 10d in 1589.

148.119   Christophori Lexicon
Unidentified [dictionary]. Continent (probable): date indeterminable. Probably not an STC book. *Language(s)*: Latin (probable). Appraised at 6d in 1589.

148.120   Morae Epistolae
Sir Thomas More. Unidentified. Place unknown: stationer unknown, date indeterminable.
STC/non-STC status unknown. STC 18088 and Shaaber M217 are both possibilities. *Language(s)*: Latin. Appraised at 4d in 1589.

148.121   Smithius de pronunciacione linguae graecae
Sir Thomas Smith, *Doctor of Civil Laws*. *De recta et emendata linguae graecae pronuntiatione epistola*. Paris: ex off. R. Stephani, 1568.
STC 22856.5. *Language(s)*: Greek Latin. Appraised at 4d in 1589.

148.122   Clenardi Grammatica
Nicolaus Clenardus. [*Institutiones linguae graecae*]. Britain or Continent: 1530–1589.
STC 5400.5 *et seq.* and non-STC. See also 148.124. *Language(s)*: Greek Latin. Appraised at 4s in 1589.

148.123   Spicelegium
Unidentified. Continent: date indeterminable.
Possibilities include Herman Buschius's *Spicilegium philosophorum* (1501–1515); Lucio Scoppa's *Spicilegium seu thesaurus latinae linguae atque italicae* (Venice, 1558), which is a distinct possibility given Dowe's interest in grammar and the Italian language; and the edition of Herodotus issued by the Wechel press at Frankfurt in 1584, which contained a work entitled *Spicilegium* by Friedrich Sylburg. *Language(s)*: Latin (probable). Appraised at 12d in 1589.

148.124   Leonardi Meditationes
Probably Nicolaus Clenardus. [*Institutiones linguae graecae*]. Continent: date indeterminable.
Assumed to be a mishearing or mistranscription in fair copy of "Cleonardus." See also 148.122. *Language(s)*: Greek Latin. Appraised at 4d in 1589.

148.125   Institutiones Justiniani
Justinian I. *Institutiones*. (*Corpus juris civilis*). Continent: date indeterminable. *Language(s)*: Greek Latin. Appraised at 16d in 1589.

148.126   Stephanus de abusu linguae graecae
Henri Estienne. *De abusu linguae graecae*. Geneva (probable): excudebat Henricus Stephanus, 1563–1573.
Language(s): Greek Latin. Appraised at 3d in 1589.

148.127 Varrinaei Syntaxis
Joannes Varennius. *Syntaxis linguae graecae*. Continent: date indeterminable.
Language(s): Greek Latin. Appraised at 2d in 1589.

148.128 Poselius
Joannes Posselius. *Syntaxis linguae graecae*. Continent: 1565–1587.
Language(s): Greek Latin. Appraised at 2d in 1589.

148.129 Isocrates graece
Isocrates. Unidentified. Continent: date indeterminable.
Language(s): Greek. Appraised at 18d in 1589.

148.130 Fortescue in commendatione legum Angliae
Sir John Fortescue. *Prenobilis militis, cognomento Forescu, . . . de politica administratione, et legibus civilibus Anglie, commentarius*. London: tipis E. Whitechurche, et veneunt in ed. H. Smyth, 1543?
STC 11193. *Language(s)*: Latin. Appraised at 6d in 1589.

148.131 Doctor & the Student
Christopher Saint German. [*Doctor and student*]. London: (different houses), 1530?–1580.
STC 21561 *et seq. Language(s)*: English. Appraised at 6d in 1589.

148.132 Abridgment of the Statutes
[*Abbreviamentum statutorum*]. (*England–Statutes–Abridgements and Extracts*). London: (different houses), 1481?–1551.
STC 9513 *et seq. Language(s)*: English Latin Law French. Appraised at 3s in 1589.

148.133 Summa Angelica
Angelus de Clavasio. *Summa Angelica*. Continent: date indeterminable.
Language(s): Latin. Appraised at 3d in 1589.

148.134 Summa Roscelli
Baptista Trovamala (Baptista de Salis). [*Summa roselle de casibus conscientie*]. Continent: date indeterminable.
Language(s): Latin. Appraised at 12d in 1589.

148.135 Ars Notariatus
Ars notariatus. Continent: date indeterminable.
Language(s): Latin. Appraised at 10d in 1589.

148.136 Duraeus de beneficiis
Franciscus Duarenus. *De sacris ecclesiae ministeriis ac beneficiis libri VIII*. Britain or Continent: 1551–1585.

STC 7262 and non-STC. *Language(s)*: Latin. Appraised at 10d in 1589.

148.137 Silva Nuptialis
Matthaeus Silvagius. [*Selected works*]. Venice: in aedibus Francisci Bindonei et Maphei Pasinei, 1542.

The collection leads with *De nuptiis animae cum sponso eius Christo*. *Language(s)*: Latin. Appraised at 14d in 1589.

148.138 Vocabularius Utriusque Juris
Anonymous. *Vocabularius juris utriusque*. Continent: date indeterminable. *Language(s)*: Latin. Appraised at 1d in 1589.

148.139 Lagii Methodus
Conradus Lagus (Conrad Haas). *Methodus juris utriusque traditio*. Continent: 1543–1566.

Language(s): Latin. Appraised at 2s in 1589.

148.140 Aristotelis Organum
Aristotle. *Organon*. Continent: date indeterminable.

Other copies at 148.52, 148.275, and 148.286. *Language(s)*: Latin (probable) Greek (perhaps). Appraised at 2s 6d in 1589.

148.141 Lypsius Epistles
Justus Lipsius. Unidentified. Place unknown: stationer unknown, date indeterminable.

STC/non-STC status unknown. The *Epistolarum selectarum* (published in England in 1586, STC 15697) or the *Epistolicarum quaestionum libri V*, of which there were several editions printed by Plantin in Antwerp, 1577–1585. Neither was issued in an English version suggested, perhaps, by the manuscript entry. *Language(s)*: Latin. Appraised at 3s in 1589.

148.142 Sigonius de antiquo iure Italiae
Carlo Sigonio. *De antiquo jure italiae libri tres*. Venice: apud J. Ziletum, 1560.

Editions were issued in composite form with other works. *Language(s)*: Latin. Appraised at 12d in 1589.

148.143 Flaminius de Roma triumphante
Flavio Biondo. *Roma triumphans*. Continent: date indeterminable.

Early editions, including incunabula, appear solo; this may, then, be a composite volume with other of Biondo's works. *Language(s)*: Latin. Appraised at 8d in 1589.

148.144 Vita Jewelli
Laurence Humphrey. *Joannis Juelli Angli, episcopi Sarisburiensis vita et mors, eiusque verae doctrinae defensio*. London: apud J. Dayum, 1573.

STC 13963. Another copy at 148.51. *Language(s)*: Latin. Appraised at 10d in 1589.

148.145 Scheperi Hypolita

John Shepery. *Hyppolitus Ovidianae Phaedrae respondens*. Edited by George Edrichus. Oxford: J. Barnesius typog. Oxoniensis, 1586 (probable).

STC 22405. An imaginary reply of Hippolytus to the temptations and complaints of Phaedra, in Ovidian elegiacs. *Language(s)*: Latin. Appraised at 2d in 1589.

148.146 Synopsis

Unidentified. Place unknown: stationer unknown, date indeterminable.

STC/non-STC status unknown. *Language(s)*: Unknown. Appraised at 2d in 1589.

148.147 Vita Casparis

Jean de Serres. *Gasparis Colinii Castilloni, magni quondam Franciae Amerallii, vita*. Place unknown: stationer unknown, 1575.

Geneva is sometimes supplied as the place of publication. Also attributed to François and Jean Hotman. *Language(s)*: Latin. Appraised at 2d in 1589.

148.148 Jovii Opera

Paolo Giovio, *Bishop*. [*Works*]. Basle: ex Perniana officina sumptibus H. Petri et P. Pernae, 1578.

Language(s): Latin. Appraised at 9s in 1589.

148.149 Surii Chronicon

Laurentius Surius. *Commentaria brevis rerum in orbe gestarum*. Continent: 1566–1586.

Language(s): Latin. Appraised at 4s in 1589.

148.150 Genebrardi chronologia

Chronologia hebraeorum major. (*Seder 'Olam*). Translated by Gilbertus Genebrardus, *Archbishop*. Continent: 1578–1584.

This entry may also refer to the *Chronographia* of Genebrardus, of which there were editions from 1567–1585. *Language(s)*: Hebrew Latin. Appraised at 2s in 1589.

148.151 Caius Kemmisius

Unidentified. Place unknown: stationer unknown, date indeterminable.

STC/non-STC status unknown. Perhaps something by or related to Martinus Chemnitius, including Diogo de Paiva de Andrade's *Contra Kemnisium pro Tridentino consilio*. *Language(s)*: Latin (probable). Appraised at 7s 6d in 1589.

148.152 Confessio Augustiniana
Augustine, *Saint. Confessiones.* Continent: date indeterminable.
Language(s): Latin. Appraised at 3s in 1589.

148.153 Osorius in Haddonum
Jeronimo Osorio da Fonseca, *Bishop. In Gualterum Haddonum magistrum libellorum supplicum libri tres.* Continent: 1567–1585.
There was an English edition published in Louvain in 1568 (STC 18889). *Language(s)*: Latin. Appraised at 8d in 1589.

148.154 Osorius de regum institutione
Jeronimo Osorio da Fonseca, *Bishop. De regis institutione et disciplina.* Continent: 1571–1589.
Language(s): Latin. Appraised at 12d in 1589.

148.155 Osorius in Isaiam
Jeronimo Osorio da Fonseca, *Bishop.* [*Isaiah: commentary and paraphrase*]. (*Bible–O.T.*). Continent: 1577–1584.
Language(s): Latin. Appraised at 12d in 1589.

148.156 Osorius de rebus Emanuelis
Jeronimo Osorio da Fonseca, *Bishop. De rebus Emmanuelis regis Lusitaniae.* Continent: 1571–1586.
Language(s): Latin. Appraised at 20d in 1589.

148.157 Osorius de sapientia
Jeronimo Osorio da Fonseca, *Bishop. De vera sapientia.* Continent: 1578–1582.
Language(s): Latin. Appraised at 10d in 1589.

148.158 Osorius de gloria
Jeronimo Osorio da Fonseca, *Bishop.* Probably [*Selected works*]. Britain or Continent: 1571–1584.
STC 18884 *et seq.* and non-STC. This often-published collection (with two editions from English presses) leads with Osorio's *De gloria*, and is more likely represented here than the single solo edition of *De gloria* (Florence, 1552). *Language(s)*: Latin. Appraised at 12d in 1589.

148.159 Osorius de justitia
Jeronimo Osorio da Fonseca, *Bishop. De justitia.* Continent: 1564–1586.
Language(s): Latin. Appraised at 12d in 1589.

148.160 Chromeri Polonia
Martin Cromer, *Bishop.* Unidentified. Continent: date indeterminable.
There are three different works, or collections, on Poland that could be represented by such a manuscript entry. *Language(s)*: Latin. Appraised at 6d in 1589.

148.161 Camdeni Brittannia
William Camden. *Britannia sive florentissimorum regnorum Angliae, Scotiae, Hiberniae chorographica descriptio*. London: [Eliot's Court Press] per R. Newbery, 1586–1587. STC 4503 *et seq. Language(s)*: Latin. Appraised at 16d in 1589.

148.162 Mori Utopia
Sir Thomas More. *Utopia*. Continent (probable): date indeterminable.
Probably not an STC book, but see STC 18094. An English version is possible, the title being the same as the Latin original; see 148.171 for an English translation of *Moriae encomium*, which was published with the Latin version. *Language(s)*: Latin (probable). Appraised at 8d in 1589.

148.163:1 Metropolis Grantii et Saxonia
Albert Krantz. *Ecclesiastica historia sive Metropolis*. Continent: date indeterminable.
Language(s): Latin. Appraised with another at 3s 6d in 1589.

148.163:2 [See 148.163:1]
Albert Krantz. *Saxonia*. Continent: date indeterminable.
Language(s): Latin. Appraised with another at 3s 6d in 1589.

148.164 Antemachevile
Innocent Gentillet. *Commentariorum de regno aut quovis principatu recte administrando libri tres. Adversus N. Machiavellum*. Continent: date indeterminable.
Language(s): Latin. Appraised at 18d in 1589.

148.165 Matchevile de Principe
Niccolò Macchiavelli. *De principe*. Translated by Sylvester Telius. Continent: date indeterminable.
Language(s): Latin. Appraised at 4d in 1589.

148.166 Virginius
Unidentified. Place unknown: stationer unknown, date indeterminable.
STC/non-STC status unknown. The context of the collection here suggests a historical work, perhaps Polydore Vergil, perhaps even Thomas Hariot's treatment of Virginia (STC 12785). *Language(s)*: Latin (probable). Appraised at 8d in 1589.

148.167 Secelius de republica Galliae
Claude de Seyssel, *Bishop of Marseilles*. *De republica Galliae*. Translated and edited by Joannes Philippson, *Sleidanus*. Strassburg: (different houses), 1548–1562.
Also contains *Summa doctrina Platonis de repub. et legibus*. Sleidan's version is only a partial rendering of Seyssel's *La grant monarchie de France*. *Language(s)*: Latin. Appraised at 6d in 1589.

148.168 Narratio Rerum ab Adventu Johannis Austriaci

Hannardus de Gameren, *Mosaeus. Vera et simplex narratio eorum quae ab adventu D. Joannis Austriaci supremi in Belgio gesta sunt.* Luxembourg: apud Martinum Marchant, 1578.

A piece of propaganda (perpetrated by the Spanish) on behalf of Don John of Austria (the son of Charles V). The idea was that John would advance into Flanders, defeat the English, put Mary back on the throne of Scotland, marry her, and take the kingdoms of Scotland and England as his prize. *Language(s)*: Latin. Appraised at 6d in 1589.

148.169 Causa Ruentis Reipublicae

Unidentified. Continent (probable): date indeterminable.

Almost certainly not an STC book. A work entitled *Concio sanctissimi prophetae Esaiae imaginem reipublicae ad interitum ruentis loculentur expingens heroico carmine reddita ab Henrico Merbomio* was published at Helmstadt in 1595. *Language(s)*: Latin (probable). Appraised at 3d in 1589.

148.170 Demosthenis Heraliptimen

Demosthenes. *Adversus Leptinem.* Continent: date indeterminable.
Language(s): Latin (probable) Greek (perhaps). Appraised at 3d in 1589.

148.171 The Praise of Follie

Desiderius Erasmus. *The praise of folie.* Translated by Sir Thomas Chaloner, *the Elder.* London: (different houses), 1549–1577.

STC 10500 *et seq. Language(s)*: English. Appraised at 3d in 1589.

148.172 Querela in Albana

Unidentified. Continent (probable): date indeterminable.

Probably not an STC book. *Language(s)*: Latin (probable). Appraised at 1d in 1589.

148.173 Dialectica Legalis

Perhaps Christoph Hegendorff. *Dialecticae legalis libri quinque.* Continent: date indeterminable.

This entry might possibly refer to the *Legalis dialectica* of Pietro Gambini, published in Bologna, 1524. *Language(s)*: Latin. Appraised at 2d in 1589.

148.174 Vindiciae contra Tyrannos

Hubert Languet (Stephanus Junius Brutus, *pseudonym*). *Vindiciae contra tyrannos.* Continent: 1579–1580.

STC 15211 and non-STC. Also attributed to Philippe de Mornay, Beza, and Hotman. The title page attributes the work to Stephanus Junius Brutus. *Language(s)*: Latin. Appraised at 3d in 1589.

148.175 Homeri Odyssea
Homer. *Odyssey*. Continent: date indeterminable.
Language(s): Latin (probable) Greek (perhaps). Appraised at 10d in 1589.

148.176 Ovid de tristibus
Publius Ovidius Naso. *Tristia*. Britain or Continent: date indeterminable.
STC 18976.4 *et seq.* and non-STC. May also represent a composite edition, with *Tristia* leading. Other copies at 148.72 and 148.248. *Language(s)*: Latin. Appraised at 1d in 1589.

148.177 Tullie's Philosophie
Marcus Tullius Cicero. [*Selected works–Philosophica*]. Continent: date indeterminable.
See 148.180. *Language(s)*: Latin. Appraised at 6d in 1589.

148.178 Kytraeus de ratione dicendi
David Chytraeus. *De ratione discendi*. Wittenberg: (different houses), 1562–1586.
Language(s): Latin. Appraised at 3d in 1589.

148.179 Pomponius Mela
Pomponius Mela. *De orbis situ*. Continent (probable): date indeterminable.
Probably not an STC book, but see STC 17785. *Language(s)*: Latin (probable) English (perhaps). Appraised at 3d in 1589.

148.180 Tullie's Philosophie
Marcus Tullius Cicero. [*Selected works–Philosophica*]. Continent: date indeterminable.
See 148.177. *Language(s)*: Latin. Appraised at 8d in 1589.

148.181 Jesneri Appendix
Conrad Gesner. *Appendix bibliothecae*. Zürich: apud Christophorum Froschouerum, 1555.
Language(s): Latin. Appraised at 13d in 1589.

148.182 Oedorus
Unidentified. Continent (probable): date indeterminable.
Probably not an STC book. Possibilities include works by Georg Eder, Caesar Odo, or Geraldus Odonis. *Language(s)*: Latin (probable). Appraised at 6s 8d in 1589.

148.183 Ethica Aristotelis
Aristotle. *Ethica*. Britain or Continent: date indeterminable.
Possibly STC 752 *et seq.* and non-STC. *Language(s)*: Latin (probable) Greek (perhaps). Appraised at 6d in 1589.

148.184 Musarum Lachrimae
Gabriel Harvey. *Smithus; vel musarum lachrymae*. London: ex off. typ. H. Binnemani, 1578.
STC 12905. Verses on the death of Sir Thomas Smith. *Language(s)*: Latin. Appraised at 3d in 1589.

148.185 Euripidis Tragaedia
Euripides. Probably [*Works*]. Continent: date indeterminable.
Language(s): Latin (probable) Greek (perhaps). Appraised at 12d in 1589.

148.186 Gentilis Opera
Albericus Gentilis. Unidentified. Place unknown: stationer unknown, date indeterminable.
STC/non-STC status unknown. Albericus Gentilis was appointed to the Chair of Civil Law in Oxford in 1586. *Language(s)*: Latin. Appraised at 4d in 1589.

148.187 Ramus in Physicam
Pierre de La Ramée. [*Aristotle–Physica: commentary*]. Continent: 1565–1583.
Language(s): Latin. Appraised at 6d in 1589.

148.188 Ramus in Metaphysicam
Pierre de La Ramée. [*Aristotle–Metaphysics: commentary*]. Continent: 1566–1583.
Language(s): Latin. Appraised at 6d in 1589.

148.189 Susambrotus
Joannes Susenbrotus. Unidentified. Place unknown: stationer unknown, date indeterminable.
STC/non-STC status unknown. His *Epitome troporum ac schematum* was published more often than his *Grammaticae artis institutio*, including five times in England before the date of this inventory. *Language(s)*: Latin. Appraised at 1d in 1589.

148.190 Sebastiani Questura
Unidentified. Continent (probable): date indeterminable.
Probably not an STC book. *Language(s)*: Latin (probable). Appraised at 12d in 1589.

148.191 Heraclis Philosophia
Hierocles, *of Alexandria*. [*Pythagoras–Carmina aurea: commentary and text*]. Continent: date indeterminable.
A widely published work that sometimes included, mistakenly, the work of the first-century stoic with the same name as the platonist, fifth-century author of this work. *Language(s)*: Latin Greek (perhaps). Appraised at 3d in 1589.

148.192 Cooper
Probably Thomas Cooper, *Bishop. Thesaurus linguae Romanae et Britannicae*. London: (different houses), 1565–1584.
STC 5686 *et seq. Language(s)*: English Latin. Appraised at 12s in 1589.

148.193 Navis Stultifera
Sebastian Brant. *Stultifera navis*. Britain or Continent: date indeterminable.
STC 3546 and non-STC. Some editions are diglot. *Language(s)*: Latin English (perhaps). Appraised at 1d in 1589.

148.194 Cornucopia
Unidentified. Place unknown: stationer unknown, date indeterminable.
STC/non-STC status unknown. This entry might refer to one of the works of Nicolas Perottus, or conceivably Joannes Ravisius, *Textor*. *Language(s)*: Unknown. Appraised at 3s in 1589.

148.195 Exposit. Tit.
Probably Sebastian Brant. [*Titulorum omnium juris tam civilis quam canonici expositiones*]. Continent: date indeterminable.
Could possibly be Alexander Alesius's *Epistolae ad Titum expositio* (Leipzig, 1552) but given Dowe's interests, the legal work is more likely. *Language(s)*: Latin. Appraised at 2d in 1589.

148.196 A Booke of Presidentes
A book of precedents. London: (different houses), 1543–1589.
STC 3327 *et seq*. Most likely an edition after 1546 as the title page changed from *New book* to *Booke of presidentes*. *Language(s)*: English. Appraised at 6d in 1589.

148.197 Crispinus
Perhaps Jean Crespin. *Lexicon graecolatinum*. Britain or Continent: 1553–1583.
STC 6037 and non-STC. Conceivably, the *Altercatio synagoge* of Gilbert Crispin (1537–1540). *Language(s)*: Greek Latin. Appraised at 4s in 1589.

148.198 Institutiones Justiniani
Justinian I. *Institutiones. (Corpus juris civilis)*. Continent: date indeterminable. *Language(s)*: Greek Latin. Appraised at 6d in 1589.

148.199 Caelius
Unidentified. Continent (probable): date indeterminable.
Almost certainly not an STC book, but see STC 14717. Among the many possibilities are Caelius Aurelianus, Caelius Secundus Curio, and conceivably *The true historie of the Christen departynge of ... Martyne Luther ... collected by ... Michael Celius ....* *Language(s)*: Latin (probable). Appraised at 9s in 1589.

148.200 Erasmi Epistolae
Desiderius Erasmus. [*Epistolae*]. Continent: date indeterminable. *Language(s)*: Latin. Appraised at 8d in 1589.

148.201 Barete Dictionarie
John Baret. *An alvearie or triple [quadruple] dictionarie.* London: (different houses), 1574 (probable)–1580.
STC 1410 *et seq.* The "*quadruple*" *dictionary* adds Greek to the languages treated. Henry Denham was involved in both editions. *Language(s)*: English French Latin Greek (perhaps). Appraised at 4s in 1589.

148.202 Westenbecius
Matthaeus Wesenbecius. Unidentified. Continent: date indeterminable.
Conceivably the *In pandectas juris civilis et codicis Justinianaei lib. IIX commentarii,* the *Tractatus de feudis,* the *Tractatus et responsa quae vulgo consilia juris appellantur,* or the *Responsorium juris, quae vulgo consilia appellantur, pars II.* *Language(s)*: Latin (probable). Appraised at 5s in 1589.

148.203 Angeli Politiani Opera
Angelus Politianus (Angelo Ambrogini). [*Works*]. Continent: date indeterminable.
Language(s): Latin. Appraised at 3s 6d in 1589.

148.204 Methodus Vigeliae
Nicolaus Vigelius. Unidentified. Continent: date indeterminable.
This entry may represent either the *Methodus universi juris civilis absolutissima,* the *Methodus juris controversi,* or the *Juris civilis totius methodus.* *Language(s)*: Latin. Appraised at 7s in 1589.

148.205 Corpus Civile cum Glossa
Justinian I. *Corpus juris civilis.* Continent: date indeterminable.
Language(s): Greek Latin. Appraised at 40s in 1589.

148.206 Heywood
John Heywood. Unidentified. London: date indeterminable.
Unidentifiable in the STC. *Language(s)*: English. Appraised at 6d in 1589.

148.207 Budaei Forensia
Gulielmus Budaeus. *Forensia.* Continent: 1544–1558.
Also issued with the *Annotationes in Pandectas* (e.g., Adams B3091). *Language(s)*: Latin. Appraised at 2s in 1589.

148.208 Nizolius
Marius Nizolius. [*Observationes*]. Continent: date indeterminable.
Language(s): Latin. Appraised at 4s in 1589.

148.209 An olde booke
Unidentified. Place unknown: stationer unknown, date indeterminable.

STC/non-STC status unknown. If a manuscript, just possibly Bodleian MS Top. Oxon. e. 5 (*SC* 28841), a compilation in Latin and English by Dowe on various subjects. *Language(s)*: Unknown. Appraised at 4d in 1589.

148.210 Dion Caseus
Dion Cassius. Probably *Scriptores historiae Augustae* (part). Edited by Joannes Baptista Egnatius. Paris: ex officina Roberti Stephani, 1544.

Because of the next item, this entry is taken to represent the first volume of Estienne's edition of the *Scriptores*, the only one, it appears, to lead with Dion Cassius in the first volume and Trebellius Pollio in the second. *Language(s)*: Latin. Appraised at 12d in 1589.

148.211 Trebelius Polis
Trebellius Pollio. Probably *Scriptores historiae Augustae* (part). Edited by Joannes Baptista Egnatius. Paris: ex officina Roberti Stephani, 1544.

The companion volume to the preceding; see the annotation to 148.210. *Language(s)*: Latin. Appraised at 16d in 1589.

148.212 Stanihurstus de rebus Hybernia
Richard Stanyhurst and Giraldus, *Cambrensis*. *De rebus in Hibernia gestis libri quattuor*. Continent: apud Christophorum Plantin, 1584.

The early history of Ireland down to the time of Henry II, with extracts from Giraldus, *Cambrensis*. This work also part three of the first volume of Holinshed's *Chronicles*. There were two editions in 1584, both printed in Leyden, but some copies received a title page with Plantin's Antwerp imprint. *Language(s)*: Latin. Appraised at 12d in 1589.

148.213 Posceuius de Societate Jesu
Probably Antonio Possevino. Unidentified. Continent (probable): date indeterminable.

Probably not an STC book. The compiler of the inventory probably misread a title page such as: *Antonii Possevini Societatis Jesu Moscovia* (1587). See 148.293. *Language(s)*: Latin. Appraised at 3d in 1589.

148.214 Terence wth a Comment
Publius Terentius, *Afer*. [*Works*]. Britain or Continent: date indeterminable.

STC 23885.3 *et seq.* and non-STC. *Language(s)*: Latin. Appraised at 12d in 1589.

148.215 Plautus wth a comment
Titus Maccius Plautus. *Comoediae*. Continent: date indeterminable. *Language(s)*: Latin. Appraised at 3s 4d in 1589.

148.216 Virgill
Publius Virgilius Maro. Probably [*Works*]. Britain or Continent: date indeterminable.
STC 24787 *et seq.* and non-STC. *Language(s)*: Latin. Appraised at 12d in 1589.

148.217 Tabule Crassentini
Unidentified. Continent (probable): date indeterminable.
Probably not an STC book. *Language(s)*: Latin (probable). Appraised at 3d in 1589.

148.218 Mureti orat:
Marcus Antonius Muretus. Probably [*Selected works–Orations*]. Continent: date indeterminable.
Could, however, be a single oration. *Language(s)*: Latin. Appraised at 4d in 1589.

148.219 Symbola Heroica
Claude Paradin. *Symbola.* Translated by Joannes Gubernator. Continent: date indeterminable.
Probably one of Plantin's editions, although another Latin edition was published in 1563 by the widow of Joannes Steelsius and printed by Joannes Latius (Hans de Laet). Works by others were added to the various editions. *Language(s)*: Latin. Appraised at 4d in 1589.

148.220 Crinitus de honesta disciplina
Petrus Crinitus. *De honesta disciplina* [and other works]. Continent: date indeterminable.
Language(s): Latin. Appraised at 8d in 1589.

148.221 Macrobius
Ambrosius Aurelius Theodosius Macrobius. Probably *In somnium Scipionis*. Continent: date indeterminable.
Some editions carry the *Saturnalia. Language(s)*: Latin. Appraised at 10d in 1589.

148.222 Tullies' Historie
Franciscus Fabricius, *Marcoduranus. M. Tullii Ciceronis historia*. Cologne: apud Maternum Cholinum, 1564–1587.
The compiler, who on occasion enters a Latin title in English (see the next and 148.264), may have simply miscopied "historia." *Language(s)*: Latin. Appraised at 4d in 1589.

148.223 Carion's Chronicle fo.
Johann Carion. *Chronica*. Continent: date indeterminable.
The single English edition, which the manuscript entry seems to suggest, is in quarto, not folio. *Language(s)*: Latin. Appraised at 3s in 1589.

148.224 Lucian's Woorke
Lucian, *of Samosata*. [*Works*]. Continent: date indeterminable.
Language(s): Latin (probable) Greek (perhaps). Appraised at 5s in 1589.

148.225 Luciani Dialogi
Lucian, *of Samosata*. Unidentified. Place unknown: stationer unknown, date indeterminable.
STC/non-STC status unknown. Editions of the *Dialogues* were published in Greek, Latin, and Greek and Latin, and consisted of collections of dialogues, or individual dialogues, of which almost any combination could be represented by this entry. *Language(s)*: Latin (probable) Greek (perhaps). Appraised at 3d in 1589.

148.226 L. Florus
Lucius Annaeus Florus. [*Epitomae de Tito Livio bellorum omnium annorum*]. Continent: date indeterminable.
Language(s): Latin. Appraised at 3d in 1589.

148.227 Herodotus
Herodotus. [*Historiae*]. Continent: date indeterminable.
English version (1582) only remotely possible. *Language(s)*: Latin (probable) Greek (perhaps). Appraised at 8d in 1589.

148.228:1 Justinus et Salustius
Trogus Pompeius and Justinus, *the Historian*. [*Epitomae in Trogi Pompeii historias*]. Britain or Continent: date indeterminable.
STC 24287 *et seq*. and non-STC. Assumed to be bound with the next. *Language(s)*: Latin. Appraised with another at 10d in 1589.

148.228:2 [See 148.228:1]
Caius Sallustius Crispus. Unidentified. Place unknown: stationer unknown, date indeterminable.
STC/non-STC status unknown. Assumed to be bound with the preceding. *Language(s)*: Latin. Appraised with another at 10d in 1589.

148.229 Caesar's comment:
Caius Julius Caesar. *Commentarii*. Britain or Continent: date indeterminable.
STC 4332 and non-STC. *Language(s)*: Latin. Appraised at 12d in 1589.

148.230 Bodini Methodus
Jean Bodin, *Bishop. Methodus ad facilem historiarum cognitionem*. Continent: 1566–1583.
Language(s): Latin. Appraised at 10d in 1589.

148.231 Thuscidides
Thucydides. *De bello peloponnesiaco*. Continent: date indeterminable.
The English translation is much less likely. *Language(s)*: Latin (probable) Greek (perhaps). Appraised at 3s in 1589.

148.232 Carion wth out Melangthon
Johann Carion. *Chronica*. Continent: date indeterminable.
The editions with Melanchthon's augmentations begin in 1558, but there were editions without Melanchthon up to 1584. Perhaps a loose volume from a larger set at 148.235. *Language(s)*: Latin. Appraised at 4d in 1589.

148.233 Laertius
Diogenes Laertius. [*De vita et moribus philosophorum*]. Continent: date indeterminable.
The numerous editions were issued in Latin, Greek, and Greek and Latin. *Language(s)*: Latin (probable) Greek (perhaps). Appraised at 3s in 1589.

148.234 Textors Officina
Joannes Ravisius, (Textor). [*Officina*]. Continent: date indeterminable. *Language(s)*: Latin. Appraised at 16d in 1589.

148.235 Carions Chronicles .3. Vol
Johann Carion. *Chronica*. Continent: date indeterminable.
See 148.232. *Language(s)*: Latin. Appraised at 3s in 1589.

148.236 Civill Converse
Stefano Guazzo. *Civile conversation*. London: (different houses), 1581–1586.
STC 12422 *et seq*. Originally written in Italian; one of these two editions was translated from a French edition, the other directly from the Italian. *Language(s)*: English. Appraised at 9d in 1589.

148.237 Plutarchi Opera grae:
Plutarch. [*Works*]. Continent: date indeterminable.
Language(s): Greek Latin (perhaps). Appraised at 10s in 1589.

148.238 Plutarchi Opera lat:
Plutarch. [*Works*]. Continent: date indeterminable.
Language(s): Latin. Appraised at 10s in 1589.

148.239 Plutarchi Moralia
Plutarch. *Moralia*. Continent: date indeterminable.
Language(s): Latin (probable) Greek (perhaps). Appraised at 5s in 1589.

148.240 Horace
Quintus Horatius Flaccus. Probably [*Works*]. Britain or Continent: date indeterminable.

STC 13784 *et seq.* and non-STC. *Language(s)*: Latin. Appraised at 10d in 1589.

148.241 Claudianus
Claudius Claudianus. Probably [*Works*]. Continent: date indeterminable. *Language(s)*: Latin. Appraised at 3d in 1589.

148.242 Juvenall
Decimus Junius Juvenalis. Probably [*Works*]. Continent: date indeterminable. *Language(s)*: Latin. Appraised at 3d in 1589.

148.243 Aeliani Varia Historia
Claudius Aelianus. *Varia historia*. Continent: date indeterminable. *Language(s)*: Latin (probable) Greek (perhaps). Appraised at 4d in 1589.

148.244 Petrarch de remediis utriusque fortunae
Francesco Petrarca. [*De remediis*]. Continent: date indeterminable. *Language(s)*: Latin. Appraised at 12d in 1589.

148.245 Erasmi lingua
Desiderius Erasmus. *Lingua*. Continent: date indeterminable. *Language(s)*: Latin. Appraised at 3d in 1589.

148.246 Erasmi adagia
Desiderius Erasmus. *Adagia*. Continent: date indeterminable. Conceivably the *Epitome*. *Language(s)*: Latin. Appraised at 20d in 1589.

148.247 dictionarium poeticum
Hermann Torrentinus. [*Elucidarius carminum*]. Continent: date indeterminable. *Language(s)*: Latin. Appraised at 10d in 1589.

148.248 Ovid de tristibus
Publius Ovidius Naso. *Tristia*. Britain or Continent: date indeterminable.
STC 18976.4 *et seq.* and non-STC. May also represent a composite edition, with *Tristia* leading. Other copies at 148.72 and 148.176. *Language(s)*: Latin. Appraised at 8d in 1589.

148.249 Valerius maximus
Valerius Maximus. *Facta et dicta memorabilia*. Continent: date indeterminable. *Language(s)*: Latin. Appraised at 4d in 1589.

148.250 Ovides Epistles
Publius Ovidius Naso. *Heroides*. Britain or Continent: date indeterminable.
STC 18939.5 *et seq.* and non-STC. Given the manuscript entry, the English translation of Turberville, known as *The heroycall epistles* (1567–1584), is a possibility. *Language(s)*: Latin (probable) English (perhaps). Appraised at 4d in 1589.

148.251:1 Ovidii metamor. bis.
Publius Ovidius Naso. *Metamorphoses*. Britain or Continent: date indeterminable.
STC 18951.5 *et seq.* and non-STC. This manuscript entry suggests a Latin edition. *Language(s)*: Latin. Appraised with another at 12d in 1589.

148.251:2 [See 148.251:1]
Publius Ovidius Naso. *Metamorphoses*. Britain or Continent: date indeterminable.
STC 18951.5 *et seq.* and non-STC. This manuscript entry suggests a Latin edition. *Language(s)*: Latin. Appraised with another at 12d in 1589.

148.252 Francis Frankius
Probably Francesco Franchini, *Bishop*. *Poemata*. Continent: 1554–1558.
Just conceivably the *In Francisci Franciae delphini et Mariae Scotorum reginae nuptias carmen* or even something of Francis I (see Adams F913–F915). *Language(s)*: Latin. Appraised at 3d in 1589.

148.253 Petrus Kyralonus
Unidentified. Continent (probable): date indeterminable.
Probably not an STC book. A garbled Petrus Chrysologus? *Language(s)*: Unknown. Appraised at 10d in 1589.

148.254 Bezae Poemata
Théodore de Bèze. *Poemata*. Continent: 1548–1589.
Language(s): Latin. Appraised at 12d in 1589.

148.255 Pallingenius
Marcellus Palingenius (Pietro Angelo Manzolli [Stellatus]). *Zodiacus vitae*. Britain or Continent: date indeterminable.
STC 19138.5 *et seq.* and non-STC. *Language(s)*: Latin (probable) English (perhaps). Appraised at 8d in 1589.

148.256 Seneca
Lucius Annaeus Seneca. Perhaps [*Works*]. Continent: date indeterminable.
See 148.14. *Language(s)*: Latin. Appraised at 6d in 1589.

148.257 Hieronimus
Jerome, *Saint*. Unidentified. Continent: date indeterminable.
Probably not an STC book. Only English versions of Jerome were published in England; the manuscript entry suggests Latin, but an English title remains possible. *Language(s)*: Latin (probable). Appraised at 10d in 1589.

148.258 Italian poettes
Unidentified. Continent: date indeterminable.
Language(s): Italian. Appraised at 20d in 1589.

148.259 Syntagmata Juris
Petrus Gregorius, *Tholosanus*. *Syntagma juris universi atque legum*. Lyon: (different houses), 1582–1587.
Language(s): Latin. Appraised at 17s in 1589.

148.260 Archyfremus
Joannes, *de Altavilla*. *Archithrenius*. Edited by Jodocus Badius, *Ascensius*. Paris: vaenundatur in aedibus Ascensianis, 1517.
Language(s): Latin. Appraised at 2d in 1589.

148.261 Dispauterius
Jean Despautère. Unidentified. Place unknown: stationer unknown, date indeterminable.
STC/non-STC status unknown. *Language(s)*: Latin. Appraised at 4d in 1589.

148.262 Aristotelis Ethica graece
Aristotle. *Ethica*. Continent: date indeterminable.
Language(s): Greek. Appraised at 2s 6d in 1589.

148.263 Jo. Lucenbergius
Unidentified. Continent (probable): date indeterminable.
Almost certainly not an STC book. Bernardus de Lutzenburgo or Mameranus Lucemburgus might be intended except for the "Jo." in the manuscript entry.
Language(s): Latin (probable). Appraised at 4s in 1589.

148.264 Textors Epistles
Joannes Ravisius, (Textor). *Epistolae*. Britain or Continent: date indeterminable.
STC 20761.2 and non-STC. *Language(s)*: Latin. Appraised at 12d in 1589.

148.265 Crinaeus de mundo
Simon Grynaeus. [*Aristotle (spurious)–De mundo: commentary*]. (Pseudo-) Aristotle's text is translated by Gulielmus Budaeus. Continent: 1533–1541.
Some sources give 1542 as the date of the second edition. *Language(s)*: Latin. Appraised at 6d in 1589.

148.266 Symon Symonis
Simon Simonius. Unidentified. Continent: date indeterminable.
Many of the editions of this author were printed in Poland. *Language(s)*: Latin. Appraised at 10d in 1589.

148.267 Schola Salerna
[*Regimen sanitatis Salernitatum*]. (*Salerno*). Britain or Continent: date indeterminable.
STC 21596 *et seq*. and non-STC. Given the presence of 148.270 in this inven-

tory, this entry may represent one of the Latin–English editions. *Language(s)*: Latin English (perhaps). Appraised at 3d in 1589.

148.268   Epit Plutarchi
Plutarch. [*Vitae parallelae–Epitome*]. Continent: date indeterminable. *Language(s)*: Latin. Appraised at 6d in 1589.

148.269   Locuinas de complexionibus
Levinus Lemnius. *De habitu et constitucione corporis*. Continent: 1561–1587. *Language(s)*: Latin. Appraised at 6d in 1589.

148.270   Schola Salerna, lat
[*Regimen sanitatis Salernitatum*]. (*Salerno*). Continent: date indeterminable. See 148.267 for a possible English-Latin edition. *Language(s)*: Latin. Appraised at 8d in 1589.

148.271   Foxius, Eth:
Sebastiano Fox Morzillo. *Ethices philosophiae compendium*. Continent: 1554–1561. Includes extracts from Plato and Aristotle and others. *Language(s)*: Latin. Appraised at 10d in 1589.

148.272   Daneus Eth:
Lambert Daneau. *Ethices christianae libri tres*. Geneva: apud Eustathium Vignon, 1577–1589.
Language(s): Latin. Appraised at 20d in 1589.

148.273   Dialectica Perionii
Joachim Perion. *De dialectica*. Continent: 1544–1554.
Language(s): Latin. Appraised at 4d in 1589.

148.274   cut. super eth. Arist
Cuthbert Tunstall, *Bishop*. *Compendium et synopsis in decem libros ethicorum Aristotelis*. Paris: ex officina Michaëlis Vasconsani, 1554.
Language(s): Latin. Appraised at 7d in 1589.

148.275   Arist. Organon
Aristotle. *Organon*. Continent: date indeterminable.
Other copies at 148.52, 148.140, and 148.286. *Language(s)*: Latin (probable) Greek (perhaps). Appraised at 8d in 1589.

148.276   Phy: Titelmanni
Franz Titelmann. [*Aristotle–Selected works–Philosophia naturalis: commentary*]. Continent: date indeterminable.
Language(s): Latin. Appraised at 8d in 1589.

148.277 Rodolphi dialect:
Probably Caspar Rhodolphus. [*Dialectica*]. Continent: date indeterminable. Rodolphus Agricola's *De inventione dialectica* is a possibility. *Language(s)*: Latin. Appraised at 10d in 1589.

148.278 Rami logica
Pierre de La Ramée. [*Dialectica*]. Britain or Continent: date indeterminable. STC 15241.7 *et seq.* and non-STC. This work was known as the *Logica* on title pages between 1583 and 1587. Other copies at 148.33 and 148.282. *Language(s)*: Latin. Appraised at 6d in 1589.

148.279 Titelmanni dialect:
Franz Titelmann. [*Dialectica*]. Continent: date indeterminable. *Language(s)*: Latin. Appraised at 6d in 1589.

148.280 Foxii Physica
Probably Sebastiano Fox Morzillo. *De naturae philosophia, seu de Platonis et Aristotelis consensione*. Continent: 1554–1560.
See 148.55 for another copy. *Language(s)*: Latin. Appraised at 6d in 1589.

148.281 Ramus in Bucolica Virgillii
Pierre de La Ramée. [*Virgilius–Bucolics: commentary and text*]. Continent: 1555–1582.
Language(s): Latin. Appraised at 12d in 1589.

148.282 Rami Dialectica
Pierre de La Ramée. [*Dialectica*]. Britain or Continent: date indeterminable. STC 15241.7 *et seq.* and non-STC. Other copies at 148.33 and 148.278. *Language(s)*: Latin. Appraised at 4d in 1589.

148.283 Ramus Animadversiones
Pierre de La Ramée. [*Aristotelicae animadversiones*]. Continent: date indeterminable.
Language(s): Latin. Appraised at 10d in 1589.

148.284 Ramus in 8 orat: Cic:
Pierre de La Ramée. [*Cicero–Selected works–Orations: commentary*]. Basle: per Petrum Pernam, 1575–1580.
Also contains the *Vita Rami* of Thomas Freig. *Language(s)*: Latin. Appraised at 2s in 1589.

148.285 Arisst: phy.
Aristotle. *Physica*. Continent: date indeterminable.
Language(s): Latin (probable) Greek (perhaps). Appraised at 2s in 1589.

148.286 Arist: Organon
Aristotle. *Organon.* Continent: date indeterminable.
Other copies at 148.52, 148.140, and 148.275. *Language(s)*: Latin (probable) Greek (perhaps). Appraised at 18d in 1589.

148.287 Car. de Sensibus
Probably Joachim Cureus. [*Aristotle–De sensu et sensibilibus: commentary*]. Continent: 1567–1584.
Another likely error in copying, "a" for "u". *Language(s)*: Latin. Appraised at 12d in 1589.

148.288 Peuserus de divinatione
Kaspar Peucer. *Commentarius de praecipuis divinationum generibus.* Wittenberg: (different houses), 1553–1580.
Language(s): Latin. Appraised at 16d in 1589.

148.289 Gratalarus
Unidentified. Continent (probable): date indeterminable.
Probably not an STC book. Either something by Antonius Gratarolus or Gulielmus Gratarolus, the latter more likely. *Language(s)*: Latin (probable). Appraised at 20d in 1589.

148.290 Albertus de secretis
Albertus Magnus. *De secretis mulierum et virorum.* Britain or Continent: date indeterminable.
STC 258 and non-STC. Various editions, including STC 258, include *De virtutibus herbarum*. *Language(s)*: Latin. Appraised at 4d in 1589.

148.291 Symon Symonius de nobilitate
Simon Simonius. *De vera nobilitate.* Leipzig: excudebat Joannes Rhamba, 1572. *Language(s)*: Latin. Appraised at 6d in 1589.

148.292 Sygonius
Carlo Sigonio. Unidentified. Continent: date indeterminable.
Language(s): Latin. Appraised at 2s 6d in 1589.

148.293 Poserius
Unidentified. Place unknown: stationer unknown, date indeterminable.
STC/non-STC status unknown. Perhaps another miscopying of Possevinus; see 148.213. *Language(s)*: Latin (probable). Appraised at 3s in 1589.

148.294 Cane Loci Communes
Francisco Melchor Cano, *Bishop. De locis theologicis.* Continent: 1563–1585. *Language(s)*: Latin. Appraised at 20d in 1589.

148.295 Dialogus de religione
Perhaps Joannes, *Arundinensis. De religione sacrosancta dialogus.* Cologne: apud haeredes Arnoldi Birckmanni, 1563.
Language(s): Latin. Appraised at 4d in 1589.

148.296 Stapletoni Speculum
Thomas Stapleton. *Speculum pravitatis haereticae.* Douai: ex officina Joannis Bogardi, 1580.
ARCR no. 1156. *Language(s)*: Latin. Appraised at 6d in 1589.

148.297 Actus consilii Tridentini
Acta Concilii Tridentini. (Councils–Trent). Continent: 1546–1569.
Language(s): Latin. Appraised at 6d in 1589.

148.298 censura Coloniensis
Censura et docta explicatio errorum catechismi J. Monhemii. (Cologne University). Cologne: apud Maternum Cholinum, 1560–1582.
Language(s): Latin. Appraised at 8d in 1589.

148.299 Choserii Enchiridion
Probably Franciscus Costerus. *Enchiridion controversiarum de religione.* Continent: 1585–1587.
Language(s): Latin. Appraised at 16d in 1589.

148.300 Catechismus Tridentinus
Catechismus ex decreto Concilii Tridentini. (Councils–Trent). Continent: date indeterminable.
Some editions are by Andreas Fabricius. *Language(s)*: Latin. Appraised at 16d in 1589.

148.301 Diacosiomartirion
John White, *Bishop. Diacosiomartyrion.* London: in aed. R. Cali, 1553.
STC 25388. *Language(s)*: Latin. Appraised at 7d in 1589.

148.302 his songe bookes
Manuscripts. Provenances unknown. Dates indeterminable.
Compilations of northern European sacred and secular music. *Language(s)*: English Latin. Appraised at 6s 8d in 1589. *Current location*: Christ Church Oxford, MSS. 984–988.

Edward Higgins. Scholar (M.A.): Probate Inventory. 1588

R. J. FEHRENBACH and RIVES NICHOLSON

Edward Higgins (Higgen) received a Bachelor of Arts degree from Queen's College on 17 March 1576 and a Master of Arts degree on 3 July 1581, and incorporated in 1583 at Cambridge (*Alumni Oxonienses*, 2:706) where his two brothers, Anthony and George, were educated (*Alumni Cantabrigienses*, 2:367). An inventory of his goods at Oxford compiled in February 1588, in which he is identified as a "late fellowe of Brasenose College deceased," includes a collection of over three hundred books. The book-list is arranged generally by size according to marginal notations, doubtless as the collection was found. Of the books listed, forty-four are unappraised but claimed by William Spire, bookseller, for the value of £4, 5*s* and 2*d*, the amount, according to a note preceding that group (149.256 through 149.299), Higgins owed Spire for the recently acquired books. Of the remaining books, well over half are in octavo, a smattering are in sextodecimo, with the remainder divided between folio and quarto editions. Another unlisted thirty-five books ("5. fol: 8. in 4°. 17. in 8°. and five in decimo sexto") are "claymed to be the colledges and therfore not prised."

Higgins's books indicate either a gentlemanly background or gentlemanly aspirations. In addition to the many works on theology and rhetoric that make up the heart of Higgins's library, there is also an intriguing gallimaufry of texts on subjects as diverse as viticulture (149.162), meteorology (149.109), and therapeutics (149.60), suggesting a mind that, if inclined to focus on matters doctrinal and oratorical, was a restlessly curious one, though one with practical rather than fanciful aims. True, the library's liberal scattering of works of both classical and contemporary literature, including a generous selection of verse, is evidence of a sensibility as capable of appreciating the purely aesthetic delights of poetry as it was the benefits of prudent husbandry. Yet what is most striking about the smaller constellations of books that encircle the library's theological core is their concern with the practical arts of day-to-day life. There is, for instance, a sizeable cluster of works on medicine, a smaller group dealing with herbs and agriculture, as well as assorted works on astrology and politics, hunting and courtly behavior, and shooting (149.144:2). They give the impression that for Higgins books were not so much a conduit into an abstract realm of scholarly cogitation as they were a means of better understanding the actual world in which he found himself and negotiating its many controversies, upheavals, and dangers.

The works of rhetoric and theology of which the library is predominantly made up strengthen this impression. The numerous works on logic and oratory by Ramus, Sturmius, Stöckel, and others, and the many grammars and dictionaries, which suggest sure-footedness in several different languages, particularly French, seem less scholarly implements for a formal academic study of rhetoric than oft-used tools of a man deeply acquainted with the practical art of disputation and the analysis of conflicting positions. The material on which these tools were chiefly applied appears to have been the controversial theological literature of the era in which his own library is so rich. Yet this is not the collection of a zealot seeking support for his own narrow doctrinal point of view; it is far too diverse, including not only the texts by Melanchthon and Bèze that were touchstones of the era but also a wide range of works featuring Calvinist, Anglican, and even Roman Catholic positions, though the latter tend to include Protestant rebuttals (149.49). These seem the books of a man of a careful, analytical, soberly religious turn of mind more interested in the careful exploration and understanding of the bewilderingly complex religious issues of his day than in the impassioned advocacy of any one doctrinal position—unless, of course, Higgins's wide reading in religious controversy was a way of arming himself with the enemy's ideas so as to better perform in the rhetorical jousting matches on religion.

Oxford University Archives, Bodleian Library: Hyp.B.13.

§

149.1	Biblia Roberti Stephani duobus voluminibus
149.2	Biblia interlineata
149.3	Byble, Englishe, Geneva, in folio
149.4	Biblia Tremellii, 4°
149.5	Biblia Tigurina, 4°
149.6	Rhemishe Testament, 4°
149.7	Bezae in novum testamentum annotationes
149.8	Erasmus in novum testamentum
149.9	Calvinus in Mosen
149.10:1	Zanchius de tribus elohim et divinis attributis, Zanchii Miscellanea
149.10:2	[See 149.10:1]
149.10:3	[See 149.10:1]
149.11	Peter Martirs common places in Englishe

149.12	Calvini Institutiones folio
149.13	Juels woorkes folio
149.14	Lexicon Scapulae
149.15	Ciceronis opera folio duobus voluminibus
149.16	Tindal, Frith, Barnes: woorkes
149.17	Defence of the aunswere to the admonition: whitgift
149.18	The woorkes of Sir Thomas more, folio, English
149.19	Some of Sir Thomas mores woorkes, Latine, folio
149.20	Dictionarye, frenche and latine
149.21	Froisardes chronicle
149.22	Tabulae in epistolas Pauli ad Romanos folio
149.23	Terentius Roberti Stephani folio
149.24	Erithraei tabulae
149.25	melanchthon de anima tabulae
149.26	Tragus, Herball
149.27	Destructorium viciorum
149.28	fabritii partitiones grammaticae
149.29	Lambertus de monte in Arist: natur: philosop: fol.
149.30	Albertus in Arist: de anima
149.31	Paulus venetus logike
149.32	Lesclarisment
149.33	Calvins Institutions, frenche
149.34	Gratulatio Buceri ad ecclesiam Anglicanam
149.35	Robortellus de arte dicendi
149.36	Nowel agaynst Dorman
149.37	Epistola Dalmad agaynst Haddon
149.38	Zanchius ad Ariani libellum
149.39	An aunswere to Nichols recantation
149.40	Junius ad testamenti veteris interpretationem
149.41	De politia et disciplina civili et ecclesiastica
149.42	Articuli de religione per Bucerum
149.43	Rodolphi Agricolae logi 4°
149.44	Clenardi grammatica graeca 4°
149.45	Bertrami hebraica grammatica
149.46	Foxe agaynst Osorius
149.47	Gascoigne woorkes
149.48	Apparatus latinae elocutionis per Riccium
149.49	Treatise of the crosse
149.50	Strebaei, latomi cum reliquis in Cicer: partitiones
149.51	Googes Husbandrye
149.52	Mirroure of magistrates
149.53	heresbachius de educandis principum liberis
149.54	Thomae Aquinatis secunda secundae
149.55	Ovides Metamorphosis, English
149.56:1	Grammatica hebraica: Tremellii et Isaaci

149.56:2	[See 149.56:1]
149.57	Aeneidos Virgilii in English
149.58:1	Olinthiacae demosthenis orats. 3es lat: english .2. vol.
149.58:2	[see149.58:1]
149.59	The woorkes of Sir Davye Lynsaye
149.60	The Haven of Health
149.61:A	Francisci philelphi de moribus disciplina
149.61:B	[See 149.61:A]
149.61:C	[See 149.61:A]
149.62:1	Altimari nonnulla opuscula: et ars medic: .2. volu
149.62:2	[See 149.62:1]
149.63	virgills Aeneides scottishe Dowglas
149.64	Zanchii fides
149.65	Scori Thesaurus Ciceron. 4°
149.66	versor in phis. Aris:
149.67	Strebaeus de electione et collocatione oratoria
149.68	Ramus in Ciceronis orat: consul:
149.69	Courtier, Englishe
149.70	Recordes Arithmetike
149.71	Besae epistolae
149.72	Thesaurus Pagnini hebr
149.73	Whitakerus in Duraeum
149.74	herbesi periodicae responsiones
149.75	Biblia Plantini
149.76	Manutius in epistolas Ciceronis ad Atticum
149.77	Bullingerus de persecutionibus
149.78	Sturmius in Partitiones Oratorias
149.79	Caelius secundus in Cicero. brut.
149.80	Bucchanani chronica
149.81	Gorshii dialectica
149.82	Chitrei rhetorica
149.83	Godescalci husdani de particulis linguae latinae
149.84	Erithraeus in orat: pro lege manil:
149.85	Sturmius de imitatione orat:
149.86	Epitome terrae partium
149.87	Caelius Secundus in top: Cic:
149.88	Image of both churches
149.89	Ramus de religione
149.90	Danaeus in Timotheum
149.91	Erithraeus de ratione scribendi epistolas
149.92	Hermogenes de arte oratoria
149.93	Erasmus de preparatione ad mortem
149.94	Melancthon in Romanos
149.95	Gerardus de inventione
149.96	Gorshius de figuris

149.97	Fortunatiani rhet libri 3es
149.98	Bosius in epistolas ad Atticum
149.99	Ciceronis officia
149.100	Augustini confessiones
149.101	Dodonaeus de spaera
149.102	Ethica Aristotelis Strigelii
149.103	Bodine de repub: french
149.104	Fritshius meteor:
149.105	Camerarii epistolae familiares
149.106	machiavelli princeps
149.107	matagonis de matagonibus
149.108	Fasciculus remediorum per mollerum
149.109	Meteorologica Garcaei
149.110	Dion Chrisostomus de regno
149.111	Commentarius de quotidiano sermone Corderii
149.112	Rondoletti methodus curandi morborum 2 voluminibus
149.113	Furchii institutiones medicae
149.114	Lodovicus vives de disciplinis
149.115	Rami grammatica
149.116	Schola Salernitana
149.117	Riccius in Hesiodum
149.118	Cureus de sensibus
149.119	Doctrina physica Melancthonis
149.120	Cheynei prima philosophia
149.121	Palingenius in English
149.122	Grammatica italica
149.123	Athanasius graece et lat:
149.124	Eitzen dialectica
149.125	bezae confessiones
149.126	prayse of follye
149.127	Analysis Cheynei in physiologiam Arist:
149.128	Neobarius de inveniendi argumenti disciplina
149.129	Franciscus de Port: de signis morborum
149.130	Cautii grammatica
149.131	Summa rhetoricarum preceptionum
149.132	Phrases hebraicae
149.133	Promptuarium linguae latinae
149.134	Elementa linguae hebreae Clavii
149.135	Valerii grammatica
149.136	D. Wilsons usurye
149.137:1	Phregii rhetorica, logica
149.137:2	[See 149.137:1]
149.138	Arithmetica Clavii
149.139	Arithmetica Tonstalli
149.140	Grammatica hebraica Junii

149.141 Grammatica hebraica Junii
149.142 Olevianus in evangelia
149.143 Crusii graeca grammatica
149.144:1 Aschames schoolemaster Toxophilus
149.144:2 [See 149.144:1]
149.145 Tussers Husbandrye
149.146 Execution of justice, with others
149.147 multiple [See 149.146]
149.148 Table Philosophye
149.149 Marnixi responsio
149.150 Bredenbachii epistolae 2ae
149.151 Sturmii nobilitas literata with others
149.152 multiple [See 149.151]
149.153 Polus de concilio etc.
149.154 Hexemeron Explicatum a Wolfango Epitome
149.155 Rhetorike logike inglish
149.156 Arithmetica Gemmae frisii
149.157 Erithraeus de figuris
149.158 Zenophontis Cyripaediae
149.159 Caelius Secundus pro ecclesiae autoritate
149.160 Ecclesiast Junii
149.161 Clerke De aulico
149.162 historia vitis et vini
149.163 Dion Cassius cum aliis
149.164 Sturmius de periodis
149.165 De sacramentis in genere Helliop
149.166 Poemata bezae
149.167 Hemmingii encheridion
149.168 Beza de repudiis et divortiis
149.169 Similitudines bibliae per Lemnium
149.170 Tremellius in Oseam
149.171 M*onophilo
149.172 Jo. Leonis de Africae descriptione lib.
149.173 bunelli epistolae
149.174 Sturmius de universa ratione elocutionis
149.175:1-3 Sturmius in hermogenem .3. volum.
149.176 Caelius secundus de artificio disserendi
149.177 Ludovici viv: retorica
149.178 Talaei Rhetorica
149.179 Medulla rhetoricae per Erithreum
149.180 Benefit of Xth [Christ's] Death with others
149.181 Confutatio cavillationum per Stephanum winton [Wintoniensem]
149.182 Pilkington on Aggeum
149.183 Comforte in affliction: kingsmil
149.184 Comforte agaynst calamityes

149.185	Garcaei collatio veteris et novi testamenti
149.186	formulae tractandarum concionum per Stockel
149.187	Junius in Judam
149.188	Baruch Canephius in French
149.189	hemmingius de lege naturae
149.190	Baii responsio ad quaestiones Marnixii
149.191	Ad censuras theologorum Parisiensium Ro. Stephani responsio
149.192	Smetoni responsio ad hammilt:
149.193	Albinus in Ecclesiasten
149.194	Prime of nature and grace
149.195	libellus de conjugio per hemmingium
149.196	The burning of paules churche
149.197	Sillogisticon Foxi
149.198	bullingerus of religion, frenche
149.199	Resolution
149.200	Bunnie one Calvins institutions
149.201	Tractatus Cuneri
149.202	Cassandri dialectica
149.203	Patricii commentarii linguae latinae
149.204	Goswinus wasserleider, logica
149.205	harmonye of the confessions
149.206:1	Logica et rhetorica Phregii
149.206:2	[See 149.206:1]
149.207	melancton logike
149.208	Witchcraft by Lever
149.209	Erotemata dialect: melancthon: per lossium
149.210	Prelectiones Talaei in Rami dialect:
149.211	Simon Paulus in epistolas
149.212	Danaei ethica 2 volum.
149.213	Danaei phisica 2 volum.
149.214	Javelli epitome in Arist: phisic:
149.215	britannia Camden
149.216	Hooper uppon Jonas
149.217	Collectanea Cognati
149.218	Rivius de stultitia mortalium
149.219	Courtier french italian
149.220	Kemperus in universam artem orat:
149.221	De vita Ciceronis
149.222	Sturmii classica epistolarum lib
149.223	Civile Conversation Guazzo
149.224	Piers Plowman
149.225	Drantes sermons
149.226	hemingius de methodis
149.227	Sturmii academicae epistolae
149.228	Beza de praedestinatione

149.229 Lensaeus de unica religione
149.230 Ludovici ab Avita [Avila] de bello germanico
149.231 Comminaeus de rebus gestis lodovici
149.232 Introductio Toleti
149.233 Censura Coloniensis
149.234 hooper one the commandementes
149.235 Ludovici vives introductio ad sapientiam
149.236 Allen of purgatorye
149.237 Biblia hebraica 7 voluminibus
149.238:1 Three Greeke testamentes
149.238:2 [See 149.238:1]
149.238:3 [See 149.238:1]
149.239 Fuchsius de historia stirpium
149.240 Pindarus 2 voluminibus
149.241 Practica Medicinalis
149.242 The Ould Fayth
149.243 Fuchsius de medendis morbis
149.244 Precationes bibliae
149.245 Testament Italian
149.246 Ephemeris historia
149.247 Apologia Juelli
149.248 methode to mortification
149.249 Bezaes psalmes english
149.250 Institutiones christianae lib. Othonis
149.251 Pharmacorum conficiendorum ratio
149.252 Exercyse of true fast
149.253 multiple   A cumpanye of ould bookes which could not be praysed severallye
149.254 multiple   Certayne note paper bookes
149.255 multiple   Certain bookes in velum sticcht in 4° with others
149.256 Bezaes testament in Englishe
149.257 Crusius in Rhetoricam melancthonis
149.258 methodica descriptio per Gellium Snecanum
149.259 Beza one the canticles frenche
149.260 Foxe de Christo gratis justificante
149.261 Jesuitismi pars secunda
149.262 Fulke agaynst Saunders
149.263 Caesars commentaryes
149.264 Alciati emblemata
149.265 Artis oratoriae precepta per wickerum
149.266 Terence
149.267 Linacres grammer
149.268 Logica Crellii
149.269 Strigellius in logicam melanct:
149.270 ursinus catechismus englishe

149.271	Lemnius de occultis miraculis
149.272	Vives de anima
149.273	Latimers sermons with others
149.274	Doctor Raynoldes conference
149.275	Bilsone in 4°
149.276	The nomenclator, Junius
149.277	De providentia, Gorrutius
149.278	De suba gratuiti foederis Olevian
149.279	Olevianus in Calvini Institutiones
149.280	Lascovius contra Claud. Jesuit.
149.281	Launeii epitome institutiones
149.282	Brumleri analisis de senectute
149.283	Partitiones Ciceronis Claudii mininois
149.284	Zenophontis Cyri paediae graece
149.285	Arist: rhet: Sigono interprete
149.286	Reformatio legum ecclesiasticarum
149.287	Concordance of the byble
149.288	Alarme to Englande
149.289	Quaestio theologica a Colero
149.290	Junii Academia
149.291	Granatensis quatuor volumina in 16° vel [vellum]
149.292	Index expurgatorius
149.293	Veronis Phisica
149.294	hotomanni francogalliae
149.295	Tomson in cantica
149.296	Brocardus in cantica
149.297	Chitraeus de affectibus
149.298	Catechismus hebr:
149.299	Philadelphi dialogi

§

149.1   Biblia Roberti Stephani duobus voluminibus

The Bible. Continent: Robertus Stephanus, *the Elder*, date indeterminable.

This is taken to be one or more of Stephanus's several folio editions, issued from either Paris or Geneva. The younger Robertus did not publish a folio Bible, which the appraisal and the priority of this entry certainly indicate is intended here. *Language(s)*: Latin (probable) Greek (perhaps) Hebrew (perhaps). Appraised at 16s in 1588.

149.2   Biblia interlineata

The Bible. Continent: date indeterminable.

Probably polyglot. *Language(s)*: Latin. Appraised at 26s 8d in 1588.

149.3 Byble, Englishe, Geneva, in folio
The Bible. Britain or Continent: 1560–1588.
STC 2093 *et seq. Language(s)*: English. Appraised at 9s in 1588.

149.4 Biblia Tremellii, 4°
The Bible. Translated by Joannes Immanuel Tremellius and François Du Jon, *the Elder.* London (probable): (different houses), 1579–1585.
STC 2056 *et seq.* Some editions are accompanied by Théodore de Bèze's version of the New Testament. *Language(s)*: Latin. Appraised at 6s 8d in 1588.

149.5 Biblia Tigurina, 4°
The Bible. Zürich: Probably Christoph Froschouer, date indeterminable.
The publication information assumes that a Bible printed in Zürich is intended and does not descriptively refer to the Biblical text usually called the "Zürich Bible" though printed in places other than Zürich. *Language(s)*: Latin. Appraised at 2s in 1588.

149.6 Rhemishe Testament, 4°
[*Bible–N.T.*]. Translated by Gregory Martin. Rheims: Jean de Foigny, 1582.
STC 2884. The *editio princeps* of the Roman Catholic English version. *Language(s)*: English. Appraised at 10s in 1588.

149.7 Bezae in novum testamentum annotationes
[*Bible–N.T.*]. Edited and translated, with commentary, by Théodore de Bèze. Geneva: Henricus Stephanus, 1565–1588.
The "major editions" of Bèze carried his *Annotationes*, which were not published separately until 1594. These editions are sometimes referred to as the compiler has done here; see especially BCI 2:117 (under Perne), where an extant 1565 edition of Bèze's New Testament is entered as "Annotationes" alone. The high valuation here gives additional evidence for its being one of these substantial folio editions. *Language(s)*: Greek Latin. Appraised at 16s in 1588.

149.8 Erasmus in novum testamentum
Desiderius Erasmus. [*New Testament: commentary*]. Continent: date indeterminable.
Language(s): Latin. Appraised at 5s in 1588.

149.9 Calvinus in Mosen
Jean Calvin. [*Genesis: commentary*]. Geneva: Robertus Stephanus, *the Elder*, 1554.
This record registers the presence of Calvin's commentary on Genesis, which is without doubt; the manuscript entry, however, particularly with its valuation, could very well represent Calvin's commentary on the Pentateuch, which was published in several editions from 1563 through 1583. *Language(s)*: Latin. Appraised at 9s in 1588.

149.10:1 Zanchius de tribus elohim et divinis attributis, Zanchii Miscellanea
Hieronymus Zanchius. *De tribus Elohim*. Frankfurt am Main: apud Georgium Corvinum, 1572–1573.
Language(s): Latin. Appraised with two others at 14s in 1588.

149.10:2 [See 149.10:1]
Hieronymus Zanchius. *De natura Dei, seu de divinis attributis, libri V*. Heidelberg: apud Jacobus Mylius, 1577.
Language(s): Latin. Appraised with two others at 14s in 1588.

149.10:3 [See 149.10:1]
Hieronymus Zanchius. *Miscellaneorum libri tres*. Neustadt an der Haardt: excud. Matthaeus Harnisch, 1582.
Language(s): Latin. Appraised with two others at 14s in 1588.

149.11 Peter Martirs common places in Englishe
Pietro Martire Vermigli (Peter Martyr). *The common places of . . . Peter Martyr*. Translated and partly gathered by Anthony Marten. London: [H. Denham and H. Middleton] (at the costs of H. Denham, T. Chard, W. Broome, and A. Maunsell), 1583.
STC 24669. This entry is marked with a marginal "x" and struck through. *Language(s)*: English. Appraised at 7s in 1588.

149.12 Calvini Institutiones folio
Jean Calvin. *Institutio Christianae religionis*. Continent: 1543–1572.
The date range of folio editions is from VHe; none was issued from English presses. *Language(s)*: Latin. Appraised at 6s in 1588.

149.13 Juels woorkes folio
John Jewel, *Bishop*. Unidentified. Place unknown: stationer unknown, date indeterminable.
STC/non-STC status unknown. No collected works and only a handful of folio editions of any of Jewel's works had been issued by the date of this inventory. The folio editions that had appeared are STC 14600 and 14606 (London) and Shaaber J168 (Geneva). This entry probably represents some or all of them. *Language(s)*: Latin (probable) English (perhaps). Appraised at 18s in 1588.

149.14 Lexicon Scapulae
Joannes Scapula. *Lexicon Graecolatinum novum*. Continent: date indeterminable.
Language(s): Greek Latin. Appraised at 15s in 1588.

149.15 Ciceronis opera folio duobus voluminibus
Marcus Tullius Cicero. [*Works*]. Continent: date indeterminable.
Language(s): Latin. Appraised at 20s in 1588.

149.16 Tindal, Frith, Barnes: woorkes
William Tyndale, John Frith, and Robert Barnes, *Doctor. The whole workes of W. Tyndall, John Frith, and Doct. Barnes*. Edited by John Foxe, *the Martyrologist*. London: J. Daye, 1573.

STC 24436. *Language(s)*: English. Appraised at 5s in 1588.

149.17 Defence of the aunswere to the admonition: whitgift
John Whitgift, *Archbishop. The defense of the aunswere to the Admonition, against the Replie*. London: H. Binneman for H. Toye, 1574.

STC 25430 *et seq*. Two editions in 1574. *Language(s)*: English. Appraised at 3s in 1588.

149.18 The woorkes of Sir Thomas more, folio, English
Sir Thomas More. *The workes of Sir T. More ... wrytten by him in the Englysh tonge*. Edited by William Rastell. London: at the costes of J. Cawod, J. Waly, and R. Tottell, 1557.

STC 18076. *Language(s)*: English. Appraised at 10s in 1588.

149.19 Some of Sir Thomas mores woorkes, Latine, folio
Sir Thomas More. [*Selected works*]. Louvain: (different houses), 1565–1566.

The only folio editions of More in Latin. See Shaaber M210–213. *Language(s)*: Latin. Appraised at 2s in 1588.

149.20 Dictionarye, frenche and latine
Unidentified [dictionary]. Continent: date indeterminable.

Language(s): French Latin. Appraised at 6s in 1588.

149.21 Froisardes chronicle
Jean Froissart. [*Chroniques*]. Britain or Continent: date indeterminable.

STC 11396 and non-STC. The manuscript entry suggests an English edition, but other languages are possible. The compiler placed an "x" in the margin next to this item. *Language(s)*: English (probable) French (perhaps) Latin (perhaps). Appraised at 4s in 1588.

149.22 Tabulae in epistolas Pauli ad Romanos folio
Probably *Tabulae locorum communium theologicorum: et epistolae D. Pauli ad Romanos*. Basle: per Sebastianum Henricpetri, 1575.

Language(s): Latin. Appraised at 4d in 1588.

149.23 Terentius Roberti Stephani folio
Publius Terentius, *Afer*. [*Works*]. Edited by Robert Estienne, *the Elder*. Continent: date indeterminable.

Numerous editions edited by Stephanus; some of them published by him as well. One assumes that the compiler intended him as editor. *Language(s)*: Latin. Appraised at 8d in 1588.

149.24 Erithraei tabulae
Valentinus Erythraeus. Unidentified. Continent: date indeterminable.
Whether his tabulation of Cicero and Sturmius (rhetoric) or his tabulation of Sturmius alone (logic) cannot be determined. *Language(s)*: Latin. Appraised at 18d in 1588.

149.25 melanchthon de anima tabulae
Philipp Melanchthon. *Liber de anima*. Edited by Joannes Grunius. Wittenberg: in officina typographica Simonis Gronenbergii, 1580.
A tabulation of the content of *De anima*. *Language(s)*: Latin. Appraised at 6d in 1588.

149.26 Tragus, Herball
Hieronymus Bock (Tragus). *Verae imagines omnium herbarum quarum descriptiones H. Bockius in suo herbario comprehendit*. Strassburg: bei Wendel Rihel, 1553.
Language(s): Latin. Appraised at 2s in 1588.

149.27 Destructorium viciorum
Alexander, *Anglus* (Alexander Carpenter). *Destructorium viciorum*. Continent: date indeterminable.
Not as likely the collection of fables, *Dialogus creaturarum*—an even older work—some editions of which carry the title, *Destructorium vitiorum*. *Language(s)*: Latin. Appraised at 6d in 1588.

149.28 fabritii partitiones grammaticae
Georgius Fabricius. *Partitionum grammaticarum, quae tabulis delineatae sunt, libri III*. Basle: per Joannem Oporinum, 1560.
Language(s): Greek Latin. Appraised at 12d in 1588.

149.29 Lambertus de monte in Arist: natur: philosop: fol.
Lambertus de Monte. [*Aristotle–Physica: commentary*]. Cologne: (different houses), 1489–1498.
Language(s): Latin. Appraised at 2s in 1588.

149.30 Albertus in Arist: de anima
Albertus Magnus. [*Aristotle–De anima: commentary*]. Continent: date indeterminable.
The commentary on *De anima* by Albertus, *de Saxonia* remained in manuscript. *Language(s)*: Latin. Appraised at 4d in 1588.

149.31 Paulus venetus logike
Paulus, *Venetus* (Paulus Nicolettus). *Logica*. Continent: date indeterminable.
Language(s): Latin. Appraised at 3s 4d in 1588.

149.32 Lesclarisment
Probably John Palsgrave. *Lesclarcissement de la langue francoyse*. London: [R. Pynson] (fynysshed by J. Haukyns), 1530.

STC 19166. An appropriate book for a collection with perhaps a dozen books in French. *Language(s)*: French. Appraised at 12d in 1588.

149.33 Calvins Institutions, frenche
Jean Calvin. [*Institutio Christianae religionis*]. Continent: date indeterminable. *Language(s)*: French. Appraised at 4s in 1588.

149.34 Gratulatio Buceri ad ecclesiam Anglicanam
Martin Bucer. *Gratulatio ad ecclesiam Anglicanam, de religionis Christi restitutione*. Strassburg (probable): [in officina Knoblochiana], 1548.

Language(s): Latin. Appraised at 8d in 1588.

149.35 Robortellus de arte dicendi
Franciscus Robortellus. *De artificio dicendi*. Bologna: typis Alexandri Benatii, 1567.

Language(s): Latin. Appraised at 16d in 1588.

149.36 Nowel agaynst Dorman
Alexander Nowell. Unidentified. London: (different houses), 1565–1567.

STC 18739 *et seq*. Several possibilities among Nowell's Protestant rejoinders to Roman Catholic Thomas Dorman, and with the unusually high valuation, perhaps all bound together. *Language(s)*: English. Appraised at 2s 6d in 1588.

149.37 Epistola Dalmad agaynst Haddon
Emanuel Dalmada, *Bishop of Angra*. *Epistola adversus epistolam Gualteri Haddoni contra Hieronymi Osorii Lusitani, episcopi Sylvensis epistolam*. Antwerp: ex officina Gulielmi Silvii, 1566.

Answers an epistle by Walter Haddon published in Paris in 1563, later (1565) translated into English. *Language(s)*: Latin. Appraised at 12d in 1588.

149.38 Zanchius ad Ariani libellum
Hieronymus Zanchius. *Ad cuiusdam Ariani libellum, Antithesis doctrinae Christi et Antichristi, de uno vero Deo, responsio*. Neustadt an der Haardt: typis Matthaei Harnisch, 1586.

Language(s): Latin. Appraised at 14d in 1588.

149.39 An aunswere to Nichols recantation
Dudley Fenner. *An answere unto the confutation of John Nichols his recantation*. London: J. wolfe for J. Harrison at T. Manne, 1583.

STC 10764. Actually supports STC 18533, *A declaration of the recantation of J.*

Nichols (for the space almost of two yeeres the popes scholer in the English seminarie at Rome) by John Nichols and answers STC 19402, which attacked Nichols. *Language(s)*: English. Appraised at 4d in 1588.

149.40 Junius ad testamenti veteris interpretationem

François Du Jon, *the Elder. Ad Testamenti Veteris interpretationem prokatablema.* Continent: date indeterminable.

Language(s): Latin Greek (perhaps). Appraised at 4d in 1588.

149.41 De politia et disciplina civili et ecclesiastica

I.B.A.C. *De politia et disciplina civili et ecclesiastica, tum Israeliticae, tum christianae, libri II.* Leyden: apud Leonardum Niestum, 1585.

Adams gives author as "T.C." and lists it under "De" (D176). *Language(s)*: Latin. Appraised at 14d in 1588.

149.42 Articuli de religione per Bucerum

Martin Bucer. *Acta colloquii in comitiis imperii Ratisponae habiti.* Continent: date indeterminable.

Language(s): Latin. Appraised at 8d in 1588.

149.43 Rodolphi Agricolae logi 4°

Rodolphus Agricola. *De inventione dialectica.* Continent: 1518–1558.

His epitome is possible, but less likely than the more widely published larger work, especially at this valuation. The date range of quarto editions is from *Aureliensis*. *Language(s)*: Latin. Appraised at 8d in 1588.

149.44 Clenardi grammatica graeca 4°

Nicolaus Clenardus. *[Institutiones linguae graecae].* Continent: 1530–1588.

Date range of quarto editions is from *Aureliensis*. *Language(s)*: Greek Latin. Appraised at 3s in 1588.

149.45 Bertrami hebraica grammatica

Bonaventure Corneille Bertram. *Comparitio grammaticae hebraicae et aramaicae.* Geneva: apud Eustathium Vignon, 1574.

Language(s): Aramaic Hebrew Latin. Appraised at 3s in 1588.

149.46 Foxe agaynst Osorius

Walter Haddon. *Contra Hieron. Osorium, . . . responsio apologetica.* Completed by John Foxe, *the Martyrologist.* London: ex off. J. Daii, 1577.

STC 12593. STC 11234, *De Christo gratis justificante,* though by Foxe and against Osorio, would probably not be entered as the compiler did here. *Language(s)*: Latin. Appraised at 3s in 1588.

149.47 Gascoigne woorkes
George Gascoigne. *The Whole woorkes of George Gascoigne esquyre*. London: A. Jeffes, 1587.

STC 11638 *et seq*. An enlarged edition (two appeared in 1587) of *A hundredth sundrie flowres bounde up in one small poesie*. *Language(s)*: English. Appraised at 3s in 1588.

149.48 Apparatus latinae elocutionis per Riccium
Bartholomaeus Riccius. *Apparatus latinae locutionis*. Strassburg: apud Mathiam Apiarium, 1535.

The only quarto edition. *Language(s)*: Latin. Appraised at 12d in 1588.

149.49 Treatise of the crosse
Perhaps James Calfhill. *An aunswer to the Treatise of the crosse*. London: H. Denham for L. Harryson, 1565.

STC 4368. This identification must remain tentative since several works carry the titular phrase, "Treatise of the cross." The original work with the phrase (STC 17496) is by John Martial, a Roman Catholic apologist, which Calfhill answers with the item cited here. Martial follows with a reply to Calfhill in a work again bearing the phrase (STC 17497). Martial's original is in octavo, but his reply is in quarto as is Calfhill's work. Calfhill's, however, is more likely to be in this library than a work by a "popish hereticke" as William Fulke describes Martial in his reply to STC 17497 (see STC 11456 for Fulke's work). Yet, conceivably Higgins is reading the opposition, and this is Martial's reply. *Language(s)*: English. Appraised at 16d in 1588.

149.50 Strebaei, latomi cum reliquis in Cicer: partitiones
Jacobus Lodovicus Strebaeus. [*Cicero–De partitione oratoria: commentary and text*]. Continent: date indeterminable.

Bartholomew Latomus is usually cited as editor. *Language(s)*: Latin. Appraised at 16d in 1588.

149.51 Googes Husbandrye
Conrad Heresbach. *Foure bookes of husbandry*. Translated by Barnaby Googe. London: (different houses), 1577–1586.

STC 13196 *et seq*. Enlarged by Googe as well. *Language(s)*: English. Appraised at 12d in 1588.

149.52 Mirroure of magistrates
Probably William Baldwin and others. *A myrroure for magistrates*. London: Thomas Marshe, 1559–1587.

STC 1247 *et seq*. Thomas Blenerhasset's *The seconde part of the Mirrour for magistrates* (STC 3131) is a less likely possibility, with George Whetstone's *A mirour for magestrates of cyties* (STC 25341) even less likely. But both must be considered. *Language(s)*: English. Appraised at 20d in 1588.

149.53 heresbachius de educandis principum liberis
Conrad Heresbach. *De educandis erudiendisque principum liberis, deque republica Christiana administranda* [and other works]. Frankfurt am Main: apud Johannem Feyerabend, impens. haeredum Sigismndi Feyerabend, 1570.
Language(s): Latin. Appraised at 14d in 1588.

149.54 Thomae Aquinatis secunda secundae
Thomas Aquinas, *Saint*. [*Summa theologica–Part II (2)*]. Continent: date indeterminable.
Language(s): Latin. Appraised at 2s in 1588.

149.55 Ovides Metamorphosis, English
Publius Ovidius Naso. [*Metamorphoses*]. Translated by Arthur Golding. London: (different houses), 1565–1587.
STC 18955 *et seq. Language(s)*: English. Appraised at 20d in 1588.

149.56:1 Grammatica hebraica: Tremellii et Isaaci
Joannes Immanuel Tremellius. Probably *Grammatica chaldaea et syra*. Geneva (probable): Henricus Stephanus, 1569.
Conceivably the Cevallarius *Rudimenta hebraicae linguae* to which Tremellius contributed, but it is more likely that the compiler thought Tremellius's Chaldaic-Syriac grammar was Hebrew. *Language(s)*: Chaldaic Latin Syriac. Appraised with one other at 3s 4d in 1588.

149.56:2 [See 149.56:1]
Joannes Isaac, *Levita*. *Grammatica hebraea*. Continent: 1564–1570.
A 1557 edition exists, but it is octavo; the item listed is quarto. *Language(s)*: Hebrew Latin. Appraised with one other at 3s 4d in 1588.

149.57 Aeneidos Virgilii in English
Publius Virgilius Maro. *Aeneid*. London: (different houses), 1557–1584.
STC 24798 *et seq*. Most of the editions did not contain the entire *Aeneid*. *Language(s)*: English. Appraised at 20d in 1588.

149.58:1 Olinthiacae demosthenis orats. 3es lat: english .2. vol.
Demosthenes. *Olynthiacae orationes tres*. Britain or Continent: date indeterminable.
STC 6577 and non-STC. Though STC 6577 is a collection with the *Olynthiacae orationes tres* leading, it may very well be represented here; published by Henry Denham, it would be a proper companion to the next. *Language(s)*: Latin. Appraised with one other at 12d in 1588.

149.58:2 [see 149.58:1]
Demosthenes. *The three orations of Demosthenes . . . in favour of the Olynthians, with fower orations against king Philip most nedefull to be redde in these daungerous dayes*. London: H. Denham, 1570.

STC 6578. See the annotations to the preceding. *Language(s)*: English. Appraised with one other at 12d in 1588.

149.59   The woorkes of Sir Davye Lynsaye
Sir David Lindsay. *The warkis of the famous and vorthie knicht Schir David Lyndesay.* Edinburgh: (different houses), 1568–1582.

STC 15658 *et seq. Language(s)*: English. Appraised at 12d in 1588.

149.60   The Haven of Health
Thomas Cogan. *The haven of health.* London: (different houses) for W. Norton, 1584–1588.

STC 5478 *et seq. Language(s)*: English. Appraised at 16d in 1588.

149.61:A   Francisci philelphi de moribus disciplina
Franciscus Philelphus. *De morali disciplina.* Venice: (different houses), 1552–1578 (composite publication).

Only published with the following two works. *Language(s)*: Latin. Appraised [a composite volume] at 20d in 1588.

149.61:B   [See 149.61:A]
Averroes. *Paraphrasis in libros de Republica Platonis.* [Composite publication].

See the annotations to 149.61:A. *Language(s)*: Latin. Appraised [a composite volume] at 20d in 1588.

149.61:C   [See 149.61:A]
Franciscus Robortellus. *In libros politicos Aristotelis disputatio.* [Composite publication].

See the annotations to 149.61:A. *Language(s)*: Latin. Appraised [a composite volume] at 20d in 1588.

149.62:1   Altimari nonnulla opuscula: et ars medic: .2. volu
Donatus Antonius Altimarus. *Nonnulla opuscula* [and other works]. Venice: (different houses), 1561–1570.

Language(s): Latin. Appraised with one other at 3s in 1588.

149.62:2   [See 149.62:1]
Donatus Antonius Altimarus. *De medendis humani corpus malis: ars medica.* Continent: 1558–1575.

Language(s): Latin. Appraised with one other at 3s in 1588.

149.63   virgills Aeneides scottishe Dowglas
Publius Virgilius Maro and Maphaeus Vegius. *The xiii bukes of Eneados.* Translated by Gawin Douglas, *Bishop*. London: W. Copland, 1553.

STC 24797. Book XIII is by Vegius. *Language(s)*: Scottish. Appraised at 6d in 1588.

149.64 Zanchii fides
Hieronymus Zanchius. *De religione christiana fides.* Neustadt an der Haardt: excud. Matthaeus Harnisch, 1586.
Only quarto edition available to Higgins. *Language(s)*: Latin. Appraised at 17d in 1588.

149.65 Scori Thesaurus Ciceron. 4°
Antonius Schorus. *Thesaurus verborum linguae latinae Ciceronianus.* Strassburg: (different houses), 1557–1570.
Language(s): Latin. Appraised at 14d in 1588.

149.66 versor in phis. Aris:
Joannes Versor. [*Aristotle–Physica: commentary*]. Continent: 1489–1497.
Language(s): Latin. Appraised at 8d in 1588.

149.67 Strebaeus de electione et collocatione oratoria
Jacobus Lodovicus Strebaeus. *De electione et oratoria collocatione verborum.* Paris: apud Michael Vasconsanum, 1538–1540.
Language(s): Latin. Appraised at 10d in 1588.

149.68 Ramus in Ciceronis orat: consul:
Pierre de La Ramée. [*Cicero–Selected works–Orations: commentary*]. Basle: Petrus Perna, 1575–1580.
Ong nos. 313–314. *Language(s)*: Latin. Appraised at 2s in 1588.

149.69 Courtier, Englishe
Baldassare Castiglione, *Count. The courtyer.* Translated by Sir Thomas Hoby. London: (different houses), 1561–1577.
STC 4778 *et seq.* Conceivably the 1588 multilingual edition (STC 4781), which carried the Hoby English translation as well as French and Italian versions, but this is probably English only. See 149.219 for a French-Italian edition and 149.161 for a Latin translation. *Language(s)*: English. Appraised at 16d in 1588.

149.70 Recordes Arithmetike
Robert Record. *The ground of artes teachyng the worke and practise of arithmetike.* London: (different houses), 1543–1586.
STC 20797.5 *et seq. Language(s)*: English. Appraised at 20d in 1588.

149.71 Besae epistolae
Théodore de Bèze. *Epistolarum theologicarum liber unus.* Geneva: Eustathius Vignon, 1573–1575.
Gardy nos. 296–297. *Language(s)*: Latin. Appraised at 18d in 1588.

149.72 Thesaurus Pagnini hebr
Sanctes Pagninus. *Thesauri linguae sanctae epitome.* Antwerp: Christopher Plan-

tin, 1570–1588.

The octavo size identifies this as the epitome, all editions of the complete thesaurus being in folio. The appraisal, however, seems high for that small format though that same valuation appears in a contemporary book-list from Cambridge (BCI 2:593). *Language(s)*: Hebrew Latin. Appraised at 2s in 1588.

149.73 Whitakerus in Duraeum

William Whitaker. *Responsionis ad decem illas rationes, quibus fretus E. Campianus, defensio contra confutationem J. Duraei Scoti*. London: H. Midletonus, imp. T. Chardi, 1583.

STC 25362. Argues against the Roman Catholic positions taken by Edmund Campian and John Durie, *Jesuit*. *Language(s)*: Latin. Appraised at 20d in 1588.

149.74 herbesi periodicae responsiones

Benedykt Herbest. *Periodicae responsionis libri V*. Leipzig: in officina M. Ernesti Voegelini, 1566.

Language(s): Latin. Appraised at 10d in 1588.

149.75 Biblia Plantini

The Bible. Antwerp: Christopher Plantin, date indeterminable.

Other languages are possible, and therefore the date range must be left indeterminable. *Language(s)*: Latin (probable). Appraised at 3s 4d in 1588.

149.76 Manutius in epistolas Ciceronis ad Atticum

Paolo Manuzio. [*Cicero–Epistolae ad Atticum: commentary*]. Continent: date indeterminable.

Probably the Frankfurt, 1580, edition published with a commentary by Bosius; see the annotations to 149.98. *Language(s)*: Latin. Appraised at 20d in 1588.

149.77 Bullingerus de persecutionibus

Heinrich Bullinger. *De persecutionibus ecclesiae christianae*. Zürich: apud Christophorum Froschouerum, 1573.

Staetdke no. 577. *Language(s)*: Latin. Appraised at 8d in 1588.

149.78 Sturmius in Partitiones Oratorias

Joannes Sturmius. *In partitiones oratorias Ciceronis dialogi*. Continent: date indeterminable.

Language(s): Latin. Appraised at 14d in 1588.

149.79 Caelius secundus in Cicero. brut.

Marcus Tullius Cicero. *De claris oratoribus, qui dicitur Brutus, et eum Coelii Secundi Curionis commentarii*. Basle: [Thomas Guarinus,] apud M. Isingrinium, 1564.

Commentary by Curio. Infrequently found in the standard sources; see CLC C1200 and VD16 C2947. *Language(s)*: Latin. Appraised at 8d in 1588.

149.80 Bucchanani chronica
George Buchanan. *Rerum Scoticarum historia*. Frankfurt am Main: excudebat Joan. Wechelus, impensis Sigismundi Feyerabendii, 1584.
The only octavo edition prior to the date of this inventory. *Language(s)*: Latin. Appraised at 3s in 1588.

149.81 Gorshii dialectica
Jacobus Gorscius. *Commentariorum artis dialecticae libri decem*. Leipzig: in officina Voegeliana, 1563 (probable).
Language(s): Latin. Appraised at 20d in 1588.

149.82 Chitrei rhetorica
David Chytraeus. *Praecepta rhetoricae inventionis*. Continent: 1556–1582.
The date range for octavo editions is drawn from *Aureliensis* and VD16. *Language(s)*: Latin. Appraised at 10d in 1588.

149.83 Godescalci husdani de particulis linguae latinae
Godeschalcus Stewechius. *De particulis linguae latinae*. Cologne: apud haeredes Arnoldi Birckmanni, 1580–1581.
Language(s): Latin. Appraised at 14d in 1588.

149.84 Erithraeus in orat: pro lege manil:
Valentinus Erythraeus. *In orationem M.T.C. pro lege Manilia de Pompeii laudibus annotationes*. Strassburg: excudebat Christianus Mylius, 1556.
Language(s): Latin. Appraised at 4d in 1588.

149.85 Sturmius de imitatione orat:
Joannes Sturmius. *De imitatione oratoria*. Edited by Valentinus Erythraeus. Strassburg: imprim. Berhardus Jobinus, 1574–1576.
Language(s): Latin. Appraised at 10d in 1588.

149.86 Epitome terrae partium
Joachim Vadianus. *Epitome trium terrae partium*. Zürich: Christoph Froschouer, 1534–1548.
Language(s): Latin. Appraised at 12d in 1588.

149.87 Caelius Secundus in top: Cic:
Caelius Secundus Curio. [*Cicero–Topica: commentary*]. Basle: [J. Oporinus], 1550–1556.
Language(s): Latin. Appraised at 14d in 1588.

149.88 Image of both churches
John Bale, *Bishop*. *The image of both churches, after the revelacion of saynt Johan the evangelyst*. Britain or Continent: 1548 (probable)–c.1570.

STC 1297 *et seq.* STC 1296.5, "16° in 8's," (1545) could perhaps be included among the possibilities as well. *Language(s)*: English. Appraised at 16d in 1588.

149.89 Ramus de religione
Pierre de La Ramée. *Commentariorum de religione christiana libri quatuor.* Frankfurt am Main: (different houses), 1576–1583.

All editions include a life of Ramus by Théophile de Banos. Ong is the source for the date range and stationer information, which provides that all editions are from the house of Andreas Wechsel with the 1583 edition published by his heirs. Ong nos. 637–639. *Language(s)*: Latin. Appraised at 16d in 1588.

149.90 Danaeus in Timotheum
Lambert Daneau. [*Timothy: commentary and text*]. (*Bible–N.T.*). Geneva: apud Eustathium Vignon, 1577–1578.

Language(s): Latin. Appraised at 16d in 1588.

149.91 Erithraeus de ratione scribendi epistolas
Valentinus Erythraeus. *De ratione legendi, explicandi et scribendi epistolas.* Strassburg: (different houses), 1573–1576.

Bernhard Jobin was involved in printing both editions. *Language(s)*: Latin. Appraised at 8d in 1588.

149.92 Hermogenes de arte oratoria
Hermogenes. *Ars rhetorica.* Continent: date indeterminable.

Perhaps "arte oratoria" is a verbal slip by the compiler, or, conceivably, a running title. *Language(s)*: Latin Greek (perhaps). Appraised at 6d in 1588.

149.93 Erasmus de preparatione ad mortem
Desiderius Erasmus. *De praeparatione ad mortem.* Continent: 1534–1555.

Date range from octavos listed in VHe, and includes editions that contain other works with this title leading. *Language(s)*: Latin. Appraised at 4d in 1588.

149.94 Melancthon in Romanos
Philipp Melanchthon. [*Romans: commentary*]. Continent: date indeterminable.

His commentary on Corinthians was often published with this work, but it is not indicated here. *Language(s)*: Latin. Appraised at 2d in 1588.

149.95 Gerardus de inventione
Gerardus Bucoldianus. *De inventione, et amplificatione oratoria.* Continent: 1534–1551.

Language(s): Latin. Appraised at 4d in 1588.

149.96 Gorshius de figuris
Joannes Garcaeus. *Tractatus brevis de erigendis figuris coeli.* Wittenberg: (different houses), 1556–1578.

Language(s): Latin. Appraised at 12d in 1588.

149.97 Fortunatiani rhet libri 3es
Chirius Fortunatianus. *Rhetoricorum libri III*. Continent: 1526–1568.
Also published with other works. *Language(s)*: Latin. Appraised at 8d in 1588.

149.98 Bosius in epistolas ad Atticum
Simeon Bosius. [*Cicero–Epistolae ad Atticum: commentary*]. Frankfurt am Main: apud Andream Wechelum, 1580.
Conceivably an edition by Bosius, but with the Manuzio commentary on Cicero in the collection elsewhere (149.76), a book with which the Bosius commentary was published with separate pagination (see Adams M464), this is taken to be Bosius's commentary separated. *Language(s)*: Latin. Appraised at 4d in 1588.

149.99 Ciceronis officia
Marcus Tullius Cicero. *De officiis*. Continent: date indeterminable.
Not an STC book unless it is a collection with *De officiis* leading. See STC 5265.7 *et seq*. *Language(s)*: Latin. Appraised at 12d in 1588.

149.100 Augustini confessiones
Augustine, *Saint. Confessiones*. Continent: date indeterminable.
Language(s): Latin. Appraised at 4d in 1588.

149.101 Dodonaeus de spaera
Rembert Dodoens. *Cosmographica in astronomiam et geographiam isagoge*. Continent: 1548–1584.
Language(s): Latin. Appraised at 4d in 1588.

149.102 Ethica Aristotelis Strigelii
Victorinus Strigelius. [*Aristotle–Ethica: commentary*]. Continent: 1572–1583.
Language(s): Latin. Appraised at 20d in 1588.

149.103 Bodine de repub: french
Jean Bodin, *Bishop*. *Les six livres de la république*. Continent: 1577–1583.
The 1576 *editio princeps*, also in French, was a folio edition, which would be appropriate for the valuation. This is, however, an octavo section of the list. *Language(s)*: French. Appraised at 4s in 1588.

149.104 Fritshius meteor:
Marcus Fritsche. [*De meteoris*]. Continent: 1555–1583.
Language(s): Latin. Appraised at 14d in 1588.

149.105 Camerarii epistolae familiares
Joachim Camerarius, *the Elder*. *Epistolarum familiarium libri VI*. Edited by Philippus and Joachim Camerarius, *the Younger*. Frankfurt am Main: apud haered. Andr. Wechell, 1583.
Language(s): Latin. Appraised at 16d in 1588.

149.106 machiavelli princeps
Niccoló Machiavelli. *De principe*. Continent: date indeterminable.
The manuscript entry favors the Latin version, but the entry could represent an Italian original. *Language(s)*: Latin. Appraised at 16d in 1588.

149.107 matagonis de matagonibus
François Hotman. *Matagonis de Matagonibus monitoriale adversus Italo-Galliam sive Antifranco-Galliam Antonii Matharelli Alvernogeni*. Place not given: stationer unknown, 1575–1578.
Language(s): Latin. Appraised at 4d in 1588.

149.108 Fasciculus remediorum per mollerum
Justus Moller. *Fasciculus remediorum ex Dioscoride et Mathiolo methodice accommodatorum*. Basle: ex officina Petri Pernae, 1579.
Language(s): Latin. Appraised at 10d in 1588.

149.109 Meteorologica Garcaei
Joannes Garcaeus. *Meteorologia*. Wittenberg: (different houses), 1568–1584.
Language(s): Latin. Appraised at 2s in 1588.

149.110 Dion Chrisostomus de regno
Dio, *Chrysostomus. De regno*. Venice: date indeterminable.
The sources complicate identifying the particular edition. General agreement exists that there is a 1470 or 1471 octavo edition and quarto editions from 1493 and 1578. The BL printed catalogue alone gives a 1570 octavo with no location provided, and that edition is absent from the BL online catalogue. One can assume that the 1570 edition is a ghost, perhaps a 1470/71 edition without a title page. That, however, leaves the only octavo edition to be in this library a book well over a century old valued at 2s, quite unlikely. Perhaps this is a 1578 quarto mistaken for an octavo, but a small quarto would probably not be valued at 2s either. *Language(s)*: Latin. Appraised at 2s in 1588.

149.111 Commentarius de quotidiano sermone Corderii
Mathurin Cordier. [*De corrupti sermonis emendatione*]. Continent: date indeterminable.
At least twenty octavo editions are extant, beginning with a 1530 printing; there may be more. A few editions, editions of 1541 and 1550 for two, bear a long title that begins as the manuscript entry does above. *Language(s)*: Latin. Appraised at 10d in 1588.

149.112 Rondoletti methodus curandi morborum 2 voluminibus
Guillaume Rondelet. *Methodus curandorum omnium morborum*. Continent: c.1570–1586.
The *editio princeps* is undated; Wellcome supplies c.1570, Adams c.1563, and NLM6 c.1567. *Language(s)*: Latin. Appraised at 2s in 1588.

149.113 Furchii institutiones medicae
Leonard Fuchs. *Institutiones medicinae*. Continent: 1555–1583.
Language(s): Latin. Appraised at 18d in 1588.

149.114 Lodovicus vives de disciplinis
Joannes Ludovicus Vives. *De disciplinis libri xx*. Continent: date indeterminable.
Language(s): Latin. Appraised at 16d in 1588.

149.115 Rami grammatica
Pierre de La Ramée. *[Grammatica]*. Britain or Continent: 1559–1585.
STC 15251.3 and non-STC. *Language(s)*: Latin. Appraised at 16d in 1588.

149.116 Schola Salernitana
[Regimen sanitatis Salernitatum]. (*Salerno*). Britain or Continent: date indeterminable.
STC 21600 *et seq.* and non-STC. *Language(s)*: Latin English (perhaps). Appraised at 16d in 1588.

149.117 Riccius in Hesiodum
Hesiod. *Opera et dies*. Edited, with a commentary, by Stephan Reich. Leipzig: imprimebat Georgius Defnerus, impensis Jacobi Apelii, 1580.
Language(s): Greek Latin. Appraised at 14d in 1588.

149.118 Cureus de sensibus
Joachim Cureus. *[Aristotle–De sensu et sensibilibus: commentary]*. Wittenberg: (different houses), 1567–1584.
Language(s): Latin. Appraised at 12d in 1588.

149.119 Doctrina physica Melancthonis
Philipp Melanchthon. *[Aristotle–Physica: commentary]*. Continent: 1549–1587.
Language(s): Latin. Appraised at 6d in 1588.

149.120 Cheynei prima philosophia
James Cheyne, *Canon of Tournai. Analysis in XIIII. libros Aristotelis de prima seu divina philosophia*. Douai: ex offina Joannis Bogardi, 1577–1578.
Shaaber C271–272. *Language(s)*: Latin. Appraised at 14d in 1588.

149.121 Palingenius in English
Marcellus Palingenius (Pietro Angelo Manzolli [Stellatus]). *The zodiake of life*. Translated by Barnaby Googe. London: (different houses) for R. Newbery, 1560–1565.
STC 19148 *et seq*. The 1560 edition contains the first three books only, the 1561 edition the first six books, and the 1565 edition all twelve. *Language(s)*: English. Appraised at 12d in 1588.

149.122   Grammatica italica
Unidentified [grammar]. Place unknown: stationer unknown, date indeterminable.
STC/non-STC status unknown. An Italian grammar by Scipio Lentulo was published in octavo in England by the date of this inventory. John Florio's grammar was issued in quarto, as was William Thomas's. *Language(s)*: Italian. Appraised at 6d in 1588.

149.123   Athanasius graece et lat:
Athanasius, *Saint*. Unidentified. Continent: date indeterminable.
Apparently only Athanasius's *Opera* (Cologne, 1532) and his *Dialogi V, de sancta Trinitate* (Geneva, 1570) were published in Greek and Latin in octavo format by the date of this inventory. *Language(s)*: Greek Latin. Appraised at 14d in 1588.

149.124   Eitzen dialectica
Paul von Eitzen. *Rudimenta artis dialecticae*. Wittenberg: in typis Joannes Schwertellii, 1574.
Language(s): Latin. Appraised at 14d in 1588.

149.125   bezae confessiones
Théodore de Bèze. *Confessio christianae fidei*. Continent: 1560–1588.
The English translation is unlikely. *Language(s)*: Latin. Appraised at 6d in 1588.

149.126   prayse of follye
Desiderius Erasmus. *The praise of folie*. Translated by Sir Thomas Chaloner, *the Elder*. London: T. Dawson and T. Gardiner, 1577.
STC 10502. The sole English translation in octavo. *Language(s)*: English. Appraised at 4d in 1588.

149.127   Analysis Cheynei in physiologiam Arist:
James Cheyne, *Canon of Tournai*. *Succincta in physiologiam Aristotelicam analysis*. Paris: apud Aegidium Gorbinum, 1580.
The analyses are of the *Physica, De coelo, De ortu et interitu, Meteorologica*, and *De anima*. *Language(s)*: Latin. Appraised at 4d in 1588.

149.128   Neobarius de inveniendi argumenti disciplina
Conrad Neobar. *De inveniendi argumenti disciplina libellus*. Continent: 1536–1537.
Language(s): Latin. Appraised at 3d in 1588.

149.129   Franciscus de Port: de signis morborum
François Du Port. *De signis morborum*. Paris: apud Dionysium Duvallium, 1584.
Language(s): Latin. Appraised at 3d in 1588.

149.130 Cautii grammatica
Antonius Caucius. *Grammatica gallica*. Continent: 1570–1586.
With the amount of French in Higgins's collection, this seems more likely, given the manuscript, than Caucius's works on Latin grammar, but they remain possibilities. *Language(s)*: French Latin. Appraised at 4d in 1588.

149.131 Summa rhetoricarum preceptionum
Probably Julius Severianus. [*Syntomata rhetorices*]. Continent: 1567–1584.
Long title sometimes reads: *Praecepta artis rhetoricae summatim de multis, ac syntomata* ... *Language(s)*: Latin. Appraised at 6d in 1588.

149.132 Phrases hebraicae
Robert Estienne, *the Elder*. *Phrases hebraicae*. Geneva: oliva (excud.) Roberti Stephanus, 1558.
Language(s): Hebrew Latin (probable). Appraised at 2s 6d in 1588.

149.133 Promptuarium linguae latinae
Promptuarium latinae linguae (Les mots français). Antwerp: in officina Christopheri Plantini, 1562–1576.
Based on the abridged dictionary of Robert Estienne, *the Elder*, with a preface by Plantin. *Language(s)*: French Latin. Appraised at 16d in 1588.

149.134 Elementa linguae hebreae Clavii
Joannes Clavius, *the Elder*. *Elementa linguae hebraeae*. Wittenberg: Joannes Crato, 1573–1577.
Language(s): Hebrew Latin. Appraised at 6d in 1588.

149.135 Valerii grammatica
Cornelius Valerius. *Grammaticarum institutionum libri IIII*. Continent: date indeterminable.
Language(s): Latin. Appraised at 8d in 1588.

149.136 D. Wilsons usurye
Thomas Wilson, *Secretary of State*. *A discourse uppon usurye, by waye of dialogue*. London: (different houses), 1572–1584.
STC 25807 *et seq. Language(s)*: English. Appraised at 8d in 1588.

149.137:1 Phregii rhetorica, logica
Joannes Thomas Freigius. *Ciceronianus*. Basle: per (ex off.) Sebastianum Henricpetri, 1575.
See 149.206:1 below for a nearly duplicate double entry by the compiler. *Language(s)*: Latin. Appraised with one other at 4d in 1588.

149.137:2 [See 149.137:1]
Joannes Thomas Freigius. Unidentified. Continent: date indeterminable.

Several of Freigius's works could be so identified. See, for example, Adams F1007 and F1019–1020, all of which were issued in octavo. See 149.206:1 for a nearly duplicate double entry by the compiler. *Language(s)*: Latin. Appraised with one other at 4d in 1588.

149.138   Arithmetica Clavii
Christoph Clavius. *Epitome arithmeticae practicae*. Continent: 1583–1585. *Language(s)*: Latin. Appraised at 6d in 1588.

149.139   Arithmetica Tonstalli
Cuthbert Tunstall, *Bishop*. *De arte supputandi libri quattuor*. Strassburg: ex officina Knoblociana per Georgium Machaeropeum, 1543–1551.
The London edition is quarto; the compiler lists this as octavo. *Language(s)*: Latin. Appraised at 10d in 1588.

149.140   Grammatica hebraica Junii
François Du Jon, *the Elder*. *Grammatica hebraeae linguae*. Frankfurt am Main: apud Andream Wechelum, 1580.
The only edition available to Higgins appears to be this quarto edition. In BCI, however, a 1588 entry (2:468 [Perne 2469]) is also given as octavo. The 1590 edition (octavo) is identified as the second edition, and the 1596 octavo edition as the third. *Language(s)*: Hebrew Latin. Appraised at 20d in 1588.

149.141   Grammatica hebraica Junii
François Du Jon, *the Elder*. *Grammatica hebraeae linguae*. Frankfurt am Main: apud Andream Wechelum, 1580.
For another, more valuable copy, see the preceding; see also the annotations to that entry. *Language(s)*: Hebrew Latin. Appraised at 14d in 1588.

149.142   Olevianus in evangelia
Caspar Olevian. *Notae in evangelia*. Herborn: [Christoph Corvinus], 1587. *Language(s)*: Latin. Appraised at 6d in 1588.

149.143   Crusii graeca grammatica
Martin Crusius. *Grammatica graeca, cum latina congruens*. Continent: 1552–1586. *Language(s)*: Greek Latin. Appraised at 2s in 1588.

149.144:1   Aschames schoolemaster Toxophilus
Roger Ascham. *The scholemaster or plaine and perfite way of teachyng children the Latin tong*. London: J. Daye, 1570–1584.
STC 832 *et seq*. None of the editions is octavo, however, according to STC. *Language(s)*: English Latin. Appraised with one other at 3s in 1588.

149.144:2   [See 149.144:1]
Roger Ascham. *Toxophilus, the schole of shootinge conteyned in two bookes*. London:

(different houses), 1545–1571.
STC 837 *et seq. Language(s)*: English. Appraised with one other at 3s in 1588.

149.145   Tussers Husbandrye
Thomas Tusser. *A hundreth good pointes of husbandrie*. London: (different houses), 1577–1586.
STC 24372 *et seq.* As with the Ascham works preceding, only quarto editions appear in STC. *Language(s)*: English. Appraised at 6d in 1588.

149.146   Execution of justice, with others
William Cecil, *Baron Burghley*. *The execution of justice in England for maintenaunce of publique and christian peace, without any persecution for questions of religion*. London: C. Barker, 1583.
STC 4902 *et seq.* Only quarto editions in STC. The phrase *with others* must mean other works since the long title of Cecil's work does not contain anything that could be so represented. *Language(s)*: English. Appraised, with a group of unidentified books, at 6d in 1588.

149.147 multiple   [See 149.146]
Unidentified. Place unknown: stationer unknown, date indeterminable.
STC/non-STC status unknown. See the annotations to the preceding. *Language(s)*: Unknown. Appraised, as a group with one other, at 6d in 1588.

149.148   Table Philosophye
Thomas Twyne. *The schoolemaster, or teacher of table philosophie*. London: R. Jones, 1576–1583.
STC 24411 *et seq.* Only quarto editions listed in STC. *Language(s)*: English. Appraised at 4d in 1588.

149.149   Marnixi responsio
Philips van Marnix van Sant Aldegonde. *Responsio ad M. Baii apologiam*. Antwerp: ex officina Aegidii Radaei, 1582.
See 149.187. *Language(s)*: Latin. Appraised at 4d in 1588.

149.150   Bredenbachii epistolae 2ae
Matthias Bredenbach. *Epistolae duae de negocio religionis* [and other works]. Cologne: ad intersignium Monocerotis, 1567.
Language(s): Latin. Appraised at 4d in 1588.

149.151   Sturmii nobilitas literata with others
Joannes Sturmius. *Ad Werteros fratres nobilitas literata*. Strassburg: (different houses), 1549–1557.
The English translation, *A ritch storehouse or treasurie ... called Nobilitas literata* must be considered a possibility given its title. One or more of the Rihelius brothers were involved with all the Strassburg Latin editions. As with 149.146, *with*

others must refer to additional works. *Language(s)*: Latin. Appraised with an unidentified group of books at 6d in 1588.

149.152 multiple [See 149.151]
Unidentified. Place unknown: stationer unknown, date indeterminable.

See the annotations to 149.151. *Language(s)*: Unknown. Appraised, as a group with one other, at 6d in 1588.

149.153 Polus de concilio etc.
Reginald Pole, *Cardinal*. *Liber de Concilio* [and other works]. Continent: 1562.

Three editions from different places in different sizes the same year. See Shaaber P181–182. Language(s): Latin. Appraised at 3d in 1588.

149.154 Hexemeron Explicatum a Wolfango Epitome
Wolfgang Fabricius Capito. *Hexameron Dei opus explicatum*. Strassburg: per Wendelinum Rihelium, 1539.

No epitome of this work appears to exist; doubtless an intended "Capito" in the manuscript entry was transformed into "Epitome" during dictation or copying. *Language(s)*: Latin. Appraised at 3d in 1588.

149.155 Rhetorike logike inglish
Dudley Fenner. *The artes of logike and rethorike. (The order of householde)*. Middleburg: R. Schilders, 1584.

STC 10765.5 *et seq*. Several editions in 1584, all quarto. There is an 1588 octavo edition, the size indicated in the list, but it is almost certainly too late for this collection, which was inventoried in February of that year. *Language(s)*: English. Appraised at 3d in 1588.

149.156 Arithmetica Gemmae frisii
Reiner Gemma, *Frisius*. *Arithmetica practicae methodus facilis*. Continent: 1540–1588.

Language(s): Latin. Appraised at 6d in 1588.

149.157 Erithraeus de figuris
Valentinus Erythraeus. *De grammaticorum figuris* [and other works]. Strassburg: (different houses), 1549–1561.

Language(s): Latin. Appraised at 6d in 1588.

149.158 Zenophontis Cyripaediae
Xenophon. *Cyropaedia*. Continent: date indeterminable.

Only English translations (1552 and 1567) were issued from England by the date of this inventory. *Language(s)*: Latin Greek (perhaps). Appraised at 6d in 1588.

149.159 Caelius Secundus pro ecclesiae autoritate
Caelius Secundus Curio. *Pro vera et antiquae ecclesiae Christi autoritate, in Anto-*

nium Florebellum Mutinensem, oratio. Basle: Joanncs Oporinus, c.1547.
Language(s): Latin. Appraised at 4d in 1588.

149.160   Ecclesiast Junii
François Du Jon, *the Elder. Ecclesiastici sive de natura et administrationibus ecclesiae Dei.* Frankfurt am Main: apud Andream Wechelum, 1581.

Two incomplete editions in early BL catalogues, one with a supplied place (Heidelberg) and no date and another with a supplied date (1585?) and no place, are assumed to be ghosts of this widely catalogued Frankfurt, 1581, edition. *Language(s)*: Latin. Appraised at 4d in 1588.

149.161   Clerke De aulico
Baldassare Castiglione, *Count. De curiali sive aulico libri quatuor.* Translated by Bartholomew Clerke. London: (different houses), 1571-1585.

STC 4782 *et seq.* Higgins's library also includes a French–Italian edition (149.219) and an English translation (149.69). *Language(s)*: Latin. Appraised at 12d in 1588.

149.162   historia vitis et vini
Rembert Dodoens. *Historia vitis vinique* [and other works]. Cologne: apud Maternum Cholinum, 1580.
Language(s): Latin. Appraised at 6d in 1588.

149.163   Dion Cassius cum aliis
Dion Cassius. *Historia Romana.* Continent: date indeterminable.

A widely published work; therefore, whether what is intended here is an edition with other works included (see Adams D507 for such an octavo edition) or whether the compiler's *cum aliis* refers to additional books evaluated as a group with the Dion Cassius (at 2s that could be likely) cannot be determined. *Language(s)*: Latin. Appraised at 2s in 1588.

149.164   Sturmius de periodis
Joannes Sturmius. *De periodis.* Strassburg: (different houses), 1550-1567.
Language(s): Latin Greek (perhaps). Appraised at 8d in 1588.

149.165   De sacramentis in genere Helliop
Valentinus Hellopaeus Zickzai. *De sacramentis in genere.* Geneva: sumptibus Eustathii Vignon et Jacobi Stoer, 1585.
Language(s): Latin. Appraised at 20d in 1588.

149.166   Poemata bezae
Théodore de Bèze. *Poemata.* Continent: 1548-1576.

Many editions are undated, with Gardy and Adams supplying several. *Language(s)*: Latin. Appraised at 12d in 1588.

149.167   Hemmingii encheridion
Niels Hemmingsen. *Enchiridion theologicum*. Britain or Continent: 1557–1581. STC 13056.5 *et seq.* and non-STC. *Language(s)*: Latin. Appraised at 12d in 1588.

149.168   Beza de repudiis et divortiis
Théodore de Bèze. *Tractatio de repudiis et divortiis*. Geneva: (different houses), 1569–1587.
Gardy nos. 248–250. *Language(s)*: Latin. Appraised at 24d in 1588.

149.169   Similitudines bibliae per Lemnium
Levinus Lemnius. *Similitudinum ac parabolarum quae in Bibliis ex herbis atque arboribus desumuntur explicatio*. Continent: 1566–1584.
Language(s): Latin. Appraised at 12d in 1588.

149.170   Tremellius in Oseam
Joannes Immanuel Tremellius. *In Hoseam prophetam interpretatio et enarratio*. [Bible–O.T.]. Geneva: excudebat [sic] Nicolaus Barbirius et Thomas Courteau, 1563.
Language(s): Latin. Appraised at 12d in 1588.

149.171   M*onophilo
Probably Étienne Pasquier. *Le monophile*. Paris: (different houses), 1554–1567.
Language(s): French. Appraised at 4d in 1588.

149.172   Jo. Leonis de Africae descriptione lib.
Joannes Leo Africanus. *De totius Africae descriptione libri IX*. Continent: 1556–1559.
Language(s): Latin. Appraised at 14d in 1588.

149.173   bunelli epistolae
Pierre Bunel. [*Epistolae*]. Continent: 1551–1581.
Some editions also include letters by Paolo Manuzio. *Language(s)*: Latin. Appraised at 6d in 1588.

149.174   Sturmius de universa ratione elocutionis
Joannes Sturmius. *De universa ratione elocutionis rhetoricae*. Strassburg: per Bernhardum Jobinum, 1576 (probable).
Language(s): Latin. Appraised at 16d in 1588.

149.175:1–3   Sturmius in hermogenem .3. volum.
Hermogenes. Unidentified. Strassburg (probable): date indeterminable.
Joannes Sturmius translated and edited several works by Hermogenes prior to the date of this inventory, all of which seem to have been published in Strassburg in octavo. See, for example, Adams H356, H362–364. A collection of these are perhaps represented by the manuscript entry. Another possibility for one of the

three volumes is Sturmius's *De statibus causarum civilium universa doctrina Hermogenis*, Adams S1992. See BCI 2:419 for a nearly duplicate manuscript entry in a 1609 inventory. *Language(s)*: Latin. Appraised at 3s in 1588.

149.176 Caelius secundus de artificio disserendi
Caelius Secundus Curio. *De omni artificio disserendi atque tractandi, summa*. Basle: ex officina Joannis Oporini, 1547.
Language(s): Latin. Appraised at 4d in 1588.

149.177 Ludovici viv: retorica
Joannes Ludovicus Vives. *De ratione dicendi. De consultatione praeceptiones*. Continent: 1533–1537.
Language(s): Latin. Appraised at 6d in 1588.

149.178 Talaei Rhetorica
Aldomarus Talaeus (Omer Talon). *Rhetorica*. Continent: 1548–1588.
Ramus had a major role in the composition of this work. *Language(s)*: Latin. Appraised at 6d in 1588.

149.179 Medulla rhetoricae per Erithreum
Valentinus Erythraeus. *Microtechne, seu Medulla rhetoricae Tullianae*. Nuremberg: in officina Theodorici Gerlachii, 1575.
Language(s): Latin. Appraised at 4d in 1588.

149.180 Benefit of Xth [Christ's] Death with others
Antonio dalla Paglia (Aonio Paleario). *The benefite that christians receive by Jesus Christ crucifyed*. Translated by Arthur Golding. London: (different houses), 1573–1580.

STC 19114 *et seq*. STC says that the original was actually authored by Benedetto da Mantova, not Paleario, and revised by M.A. Flaminio. The stationer George Bishop had a role in all editions. The odd manuscript entry *Xth* is a scribal error, though doubtless it was intended as an abbreviation for the possessive of "Christ." *Language(s)*: Latin. Appraised at 10d in 1588.

149.181 Confutatio cavillationum per Stephanum winton [Wintoniensem]
Stephen Gardiner, *Bishop* (Marcus Antonius Constantius, *pseudonym*). *Confutatio cavillationum quibus eucharistiae sacramentum ab impiis Capernaitis impeti solet*. Continent: 1552–1554.

Gardiner was Bishop of Winchester. *Language(s)*: Latin. Appraised at 6d in 1588.

149.182 Pilkington on Aggeum
James Pilkington, *Bishop*. Probably *Aggeus the prophete declared by a large commentarye*. London: W. Seres, 1560.

STC 19926 *et seq*. Pilkington's joint edition of his commentaries on Haggai and

Abdias (STC 19927), with the first leading, cannot be ruled out. *Language(s)*: English. Appraised at 3d in 1588.

149.183 Comforte in affliction: kingsmil
Andrew Kingsmill. *A most excellent and comfortable treatise, for all such as are troubled in minde.* Edited by Francis Mills. London: (different houses), 1577–1585.
STC 15000 *et seq. Language(s)*: English. Appraised at 8d in 1588.

149.184 Comforte agaynst calamityes
Juan Perez de Pineda. *An excelent comfort to all christians, against all kinde of calamities.* Translated by John Danyel. London: T. East for (different houses), 1576.
STC 19626 *et seq.* One edition, with a variant; two imprints: the first, East for William Norton; the second, East for Abraham Veale. *Language(s)*: English. Appraised at 6d in 1588.

149.185 Garcaei collatio veteris et novi testamenti
Joannes Garcaeus. *Summi pontificis Veteris et Novi Testamentum collatio.* Leipzig: (different houses), 1574–1585.
Language(s): Latin. Appraised at 4d in 1588.

149.186 formulae tractandarum concionum per Stockel
Leonhard Stöckel. *Formulae tractandarum sacrarum concionum.* Bardejov: Guttgesel, 1578.
Language(s): Latin. Appraised at 6d in 1588.

149.187 Junius in Judam
François Du Jon, *the Elder. In epistolam S. Judae apostoli.* Antwerp: in aedibus Aegidius Radaeus, 1584.
Language(s): Latin. Appraised at 6d in 1588.

149.188 Baruch Canephius in French
Baruch Canephius, *pseudonym* (Philippe de Mornay). *Atheomachie ou, Refutation des erreurs et detestables impietez des atheistes.* Continent: 1582.
Two editions in the same year from different printing houses. *Language(s)*: French. Appraised at 2d in 1588.

149.189 hemmingius de lege naturae
Niels Hemmingsen. *De lege naturae apodictica methodus.* Wittenberg: (different houses), 1562–1577.
Language(s): Latin. Appraised at 6d in 1588.

149.190 Baii responsio ad quaestiones Marnixii
Michael Baius. *Pro responsione ad quaestiones P. Marnixii apologia.* Continent: 1581–1583.
See 149.147. *Language(s)*: Latin. Appraised at 2d in 1588.

149.191 Ad censuras theologorum Parisiensium Ro. Stephani responsio
Robert Estienne, *the Elder. Ad censuras theologorum Parisiensium responsio*. Geneva: oliva Roberti Stephani, 1552.
Language(s): Latin. Appraised at 2d in 1588.

149.192 Smetoni responsio ad hammilt:
Thomas Smeton. *Ad virulentum Archibaldi Hamiltonii apostatae dialogum*. Edinburgh: ap. J. Rosseum, pro H. Charteris, 1579.
STC 22651. The only extant edition is quarto. *Language(s)*: Latin. Appraised at 2d in 1588.

149.193 Albinus in Ecclesiasten
Alcuin. *In Ecclesiasten*. Basle: ex officina Bebelian, 1531.
Language(s): Latin. Appraised at 2d in 1588.

149.194 Prime of nature and grace
John Prime. *The fruitefull and briefe discourse in two bookes: the one of nature, the other of grace*. London: T. Vautrollier for G. Bishop, 1583.
STC 20370. *Language(s)*: English. Appraised at 4d in 1588.

149.195 libellus de conjugio per hemmingium
Niels Hemmingsen. *Libellus de conjugio, repudio, et divortio*. Leipzig: imprim. Joannes Steinman, 1578–1581.
Language(s): Latin. Appraised at 6d in 1588.

149.196 The burning of paules churche
James Pilkington, *Bishop. The burnynge of Paules church in London in 1561*. London: William Seres, 1563.
STC 19931. Reprints and answers John Morwen's *An addicion*, which seems not to be otherwise extant. *Language(s)*: English. Appraised at 4d in 1588.

149.197 Sillogisticon Foxi
John Foxe, *the Martyrologist. Syllogisticon hoc est: argumenta, . . . de re et materia sacramenti eucharistici*. London: J. Daius, 1563?
STC 11249. *Language(s)*: Latin. Appraised at 3d in 1588.

149.198 bullingerus of religion, frenche
Heinrich Bullinger. *Resolution de tous les poincts de la religion chrestienne*. Geneva: (different houses), 1557–1565.
A 1556 French edition is in sextodecimo. All of the octavo editions were published in Geneva with the exception of a 1563 edition which was published in Caen. *Language(s)*: French. Appraised at 4d in 1588.

149.199 Resolution
Probably Robert Parsons and Edmund Bunny. *The first booke of the christian*

exercise, pertaining to resolution. Britain: 1584–1586.

STC 19355 *et seq.* This Protestant adaptation of Parsons's work was issued numerous times, and often referred to as "Bunny's Resolution." See the next item. *Language(s)*: English. Appraised at 14d in 1588.

149.200   Bunnie one Calvins institutions
Jean Calvin. *Institutio Christianae religionis.* Edited by Edmund Bunny. London: (different houses), 1576–1580.

STC 4414 *et seq.* The possibilities, besides STC 4414, include STC 4426.4, 4426.6, and 4426.8, all abridgements, with the last an English translation. *Language(s)*: Latin (perhaps) English (perhaps). Appraised at 4d in 1588.

149.201   Tractatus Cuneri
Petrus Petri, *Bishop of Leeuwarden, called Cunerus. Tractatus aliquot insigniores de gravissimis theologiae christianae controversiis.* Cologne: apud Petrum Haach, 1583. *Language(s)*: Latin. Appraised at 8d in 1588.

149.202   Cassandri dialectica
Georgius Cassander. Probably *Tabulae praeceptionum dialecticarum quae artis methodum complectuntur.* Continent: 1545–1561.

His less often published *Tabulae locorum dialecticorum* is possible. *Language(s)*: Latin. Appraised at 4d in 1588.

149.203   Patricii commentarii linguae latinae
Perhaps Nicolaus Perottus. *Cornucopia.* Continent: date indeterminable.

Neither of the Patrizis (Francesco, *Bishop* and Francesco, *Philosophical writer*) can be associated with anything with such a title, and the manuscript entry almost duplicates the subtitle of Perottus's work. "Patricii" is taken to be a scribal error, perhaps aural, perhaps a misreading of an original draft list. See a misreading of a "Capito" as "Epitome" at 149.154. *Language(s)*: Latin. Appraised at 6d in 1588.

149.204   Goswinus wasserleider, logica
Goswin Wasserleider. *Logica ad P. Rami dialecticam conformata.* Frankfurt am Main: haeredes A. Wecheli, 1584–1587.

Ong nos. 288 and 303. *Language(s)*: Latin. Appraised at 10d in 1588.

149.205   harmonye of the confessions
An harmony of the confessions of the faith of the christian and reformed churches. (*Christian and Reformed Churches*). Compiled by J. F. Salvart. Cambridge: T. Thomas, pr. to the Univ. of Cambridge, 1586.

STC 5155. The identification relies on the assumption that the manuscript entry represents an English work; Adams C2511, among others, is a possibility if the compiler entered a Latin work in English. *Language(s)*: English. Appraised at 16d in 1588.

149.206:1 Logica et rhetorica Phregii

Joannes Thomas Freigius. Unidentified. Continent: date indeterminable.

Several of Freigius's works could be so identified. See, for example, Adams F1007 and F1019–1020, all of which were issued in octavo. See 149.137:1 above for a nearly duplicate double entry by the compiler. *Language(s)*: Latin. Appraised with one other at 8d in 1588.

149.206:2 [See 149.206:1]

Joannes Thomas Freigius. *Ciceronianus*. Basle: per (ex off.) Sebastianum Henricpetri, 1575.

See 149.137:1 above for a nearly duplicate double entry by the compiler. *Language(s)*: Latin. Appraised with one other at 8d in 1588.

149.207 melancton logike

Philipp Melanchthon. [*Dialectica*]. Continent: date indeterminable. *Language(s)*: Latin. Appraised at 4d in 1588.

149.208 Witchcraft by Lever

Ralph Lever. *The arte of reason, rightly termed, witcraft*. London: H. Bynneman, 1573.

STC 15541. *Language(s)*: English. Appraised at 3d in 1588.

149.209 Erotemata dialect: melancthon: per lossium

Lucas Lossius. *Erotemata dialecticae et rhetoricae Philippi Melancthonis, et praeceptionum Erasmi Roterodami*. Continent: date indeterminable.

Commentary on Melanchthon's *Dialectica* and Erasmus's *De copia verborum*. *Language(s)*: Latin. Appraised at 4d in 1588.

149.210 Prelectiones Talaei in Rami dialect:

Pierre de La Ramée. [*Dialectica*]. Commentary by Aldomarus Talaeus (Omer Talon). Continent: date indeterminable.

Talaeus's commentary was not printed alone. *Language(s)*: Latin. Appraised at 4d in 1588.

149.211 Simon Paulus in epistolas

Simon Paulli, *the Elder*. [*Postilla–Epistolae*]. Continent: date indeterminable. *Language(s)*: Latin. Appraised at 20d in 1588.

149.212 Danaei ethica 2 volum.

Lambert Daneau. *Ethices christiana libri tres*. Geneva: apud Eustathium Vignon, 1577–1583.

There is a 1588 octavo edition, but it would not be in this collection inventoried in February 1588 (1587 old style). *Language(s)*: Latin. Appraised at 2s 4d in 1588.

149.213 Danaei phisica 2 volum.
Lambert Daneau. *Physices christiana pars altera*. Geneva: (different houses), 1576–1582.

There is a 1588 octavo edition, but it would not be in this collection inventoried in February 1588 (1587 old style). *Language(s)*: Latin. Appraised at 2s 4d in 1588.

149.214 Javelli epitome in Arist: phisic:
Chrysostomus Javellus. [*Aristotle–Selected works–Philosophia naturalis–Epitome*]. Continent: date indeterminable.

Language(s): Latin. Appraised at 12d in 1588.

149.215 britannia Camden
William Camden. *Britannia sive florentissimorum regnorum Angliae, Scotiae, Hiberniae chorographica descriptio*. London: [Eliot's Court Press,] per R. Newbery, 1586–1587.

STC 4503 *et seq*. *Language(s)*: Latin. Appraised at 16d in 1588.

149.216 Hooper uppon Jonas
John Hooper, *Bishop*. *An oversight, and deliberacion upon the prophete Jonas*. London: (different houses), 1550–1560?

STC 13763 *et seq*. *Language(s)*: English. Appraised at 8d in 1588.

149.217 Collectanea Cognati
Gilbert Cousin (Gilbertus Cognatus). Unidentified. Continent: date indeterminable.

Several of Cousin's collections could be represented. *Language(s)*: Latin. Appraised at 6d in 1588.

149.218 Rivius de stultitia mortalium
Joannes Rivius. *De stultitia mortalium, in procrastinanda correctione vitae, liber*. Basle: Joannes Oporinus, 1547.

Language(s): Latin. Appraised at 4d in 1588.

149.219 Courtier french italian
Baldassare Castiglione, *Count*. *Il cortegiano*. Continent: 1585–1587.

This is taken to be a diglot, though at the valuation, which is considerably higher than those in this section of the inventory, the manuscript entry may represent two books, one Italian, one French. See 149.69 for an English version and 149.161 for a Latin translation. *Language(s)*: French Italian. Appraised at 2s in 1588.

149.220 Kemperus in universam artem orat:
Otho Kemper. *In universam oratoriae facultatis artem methodica institutio*. Basle: per Sixtum Henricpetri, 1568 (probable).

Language(s): Latin. Appraised at 4d in 1588.

149.221 De vita Ciceronis
Unidentified. Continent: date indeterminable.
Of the many possibilities, consider Maffeius, Vallambert, Preuss, and d'Angelo.
Language(s): Latin. Appraised at 4d in 1588.

149.222 Sturmii classica epistolarum lib
Joannes Sturmius. *Classicarum epistolarum, libri III*. Strassburg: excudebat Josias Rihelius, 1565–1573.
Language(s): Latin. Appraised at 2d in 1588.

149.223 Civile Conversation Guazzo
Stefano Guazzo. *The civile conversation of M. Steeven Guazzo written first in Italian*. London: (different houses), 1581–1586.
STC 12422 *et seq*. Both editions are quartos in eights, and the English versions are by different translators. *Language(s)*: English. Appraised at 14d in 1588.

149.224 Piers Plowman
[Piers, *Ploughman*]. London: (different houses), 1550–1553.
STC 19903 *et seq*. It is impossible to tell which of the flytings is intended here; its octavo size does not suggest Langland's *Vision of Pierce Plowman*, which was published only in quarto. The Langland must remain a possibility, however, given that the compiler is not reliable regarding size. *Language(s)*: English. Appraised at 4d in 1588.

149.225 Drantes sermons
Thomas Drant, *Poet and Divine*. Unidentified [sermons]. London: (different houses), 1570?–1584.
Unidentifiable in the STC. STC 7170 and STC 7171 are both possibilities, perhaps the later collection more likely. *Language(s)*: English. Appraised at 4d in 1588.

149.226 hemingius de methodis
Niels Hemmingsen. *De lege naturae apodictica methodus*. Wittenberg: (different houses), 1562–1577.
Language(s): Latin. Appraised at 4d in 1588.

149.227 Sturmii academicae epistolae
Joannes Sturmius. *Academicae epistolae urbanae*. Strassburg: excudebat Josias Rihelius, 1569 (probable).
Language(s): Latin. Appraised at 2d in 1588.

149.228 Beza de praedestinatione
Théodore de Béze. *De praedestinationis doctrina*. Geneva: Eustathius Vignon, 1532–1533.
Language(s): Latin. Appraised at 6d in 1588.

149.229 Lensaeus de unica religione
Joannes Lensaeus. *De unica religione studio catholicorum principum in republica conservanda.* Cologne: apud Godefridum Kempensem, 1579.
Language(s): Latin. Appraised at 6d in 1588.

149.230 Ludovici ab Avita [Avila] de bello germanico
Luis de Avila. *Commentariorum de bello Germanico libri duo.* Translated by Gulielmus Malinaeus. Antwerp: in aedibus Joan. Steelsii, 1550.
Language(s): Latin. Appraised at 3d in 1588.

149.231 Comminaeus de rebus gestis lodovici
Philippe de Comines. [*Memoires*]. Translated by Joannes Philippson, *Sleidanus.* Continent: date indeterminable.
Language(s): Latin. Appraised at 4d in 1588.

149.232 Introductio Toleti
Franciscus Toletus, *Cardinal.* Probably [*Aristotle–Selected works–Logica: commentary*]. Continent: date indeterminable.
A number of editions with the title *Introductio in dialecticam Aristotelis. Language(s)*: Latin. Appraised at 3d in 1588.

149.233 Censura Coloniensis
Censura et docta explicatio errorum catechismi J. Monhemii. (Cologne University). Basle: apud Maternum Cholinum, 1560–1582.
Language(s): Latin. Appraised at 10d in 1588.

149.234 hooper one the commandementes
John Hooper, *Bishop. A declaration of the ten holy commaundementes.* Zürich: [A. Fries], 1549 (probable).
STC 13746. *Language(s)*: English. Appraised at 3d in 1588.

149.235 Ludovici vives introductio ad sapientiam
Joannes Lodovicus Vives. *Introductio ad sapientiam* [and other works]. Continent: date indeterminable.
Language(s): Latin (probable). Appraised at 3d in 1588.

149.236 Allen of purgatorye
William Allen, *Cardinal. A defense and declaration of the catholike churchies* [sic] *doctrine, touching purgatory.* Antwerp: J. Latius, 1565.
STC 371. *Language(s)*: English. Appraised at 3d in 1588.

149.237 Biblia hebraica 7 voluminibus
[*Bible–O.T.*]. Continent:
Plantin issued the Bible in Hebrew in a number of sextodecimo volumes be-

tween 1566 and 1580. This may represent a collection from his press. *Language(s)*: Hebrew. Appraised at 10s in 1588.

149.238:1 Three Greeke testamentes
[*Bible–N.T.*]. Britain or Continent: date indeterminable.
STC 2793 and non-STC. The 1587 sextodecimo published in London, the first Greek New Testament printed in England, would make a good candidate for one of these editions. *Language(s)*: Greek. Appraised with two others at 4s in 1588.

149.238:2 [See 149.238:1]
[*Bible–N.T.*]. Britain or Continent: date indeterminable.
STC 2793 and non-STC. See the notes to 149.238:1. *Language(s)*: Greek. Appraised with two others at 4s in 1588.

149.238:3 [See 149.238:1]
[*Bible–N.T.*]. Britain or Continent: date indeterminable.
STC 2793 and non-STC. See the notes to 149.238:1. *Language(s)*: Greek. Appraised with two others at 4s in 1588.

149.239 Fuchsius de historia stirpium
Leonard Fuchs. *De historia stirpium*. Continent: 1542–1555.
BL and Wellcome list a 1547 edition as sextodecimo; however, Stübler lists no sextodecimo among the Latin editions, though the Paris, 1546, edition is duodecimo. The others are octavo and folio. *Language(s)*: Latin. Appraised at 10d in 1588.

149.240 Pindarus 2 voluminibus
Pindar. Probably [*Works*]. Continent: date indeterminable.
Language(s): Latin (probable) Greek (perhaps). Appraised at 20d in 1588.

149.241 Practica Medicinalis
Leonellus de Victoriis *(Faventinus)*. *Practica medicinalis*. Continent: date indeterminable.
Language(s): Latin. Appraised at 10d in 1588.

149.242 The Ould Fayth
Probably Heinrich Bullinger. *The olde fayth, an evydent probacion out of the holy scripture*. Translated by Myles Coverdale, *Bishop*. Britain or Continent: 1541–1581.
STC 4070.5 *et seq*. In the absence of an English sextodecimo, the 1581 duodecimo edition is more likely than the 1541 and 1547 octavos. There may, however, have been a sextodecimo, now lost. STC 4070.5 was printed in Antwerp. *Language(s)*: English. Appraised at 8d in 1588.

149.243 Fuchsius de medendis morbis
Leonard Fuchs. Perhaps [*De medendi methodo*]. Continent: date indeterminable.
This work appeared under several titles, but none of which contain the word *morbis* found in the manuscript entry. Perhaps another misreading or mishearing by the compiler, in this case for the word "corporis" which does appear in some titles. *Language(s)*: Latin. Appraised at 10d in 1588.

149.244 Precationes bibliae
Unidentified. Continent: date indeterminable.
Perhaps the collection compiled by Otto Brunfels, but there were other collections. See Adams P2069 ff. *Language(s)*: Latin. Appraised at 8d in 1588.

149.245 Testament Italian
[*Bible–N.T.*]. Continent: date indeterminable.
Language(s): Italian. Appraised at 12d in 1588.

149.246 Ephemeris historia
Probably Michael Beuther. *Ephemerides historica*. Paris: Michaelis Fezandat et Roberti Granjon, in taberna Gryphiana, 1551.
Language(s): Latin. Appraised at 6d in 1588.

149.247 Apologia Juelli
John Jewel, *Bishop*. *Apologia ecclesiae anglicanae*. Britain or Continent: 1581–1586.
STC 14582 and non-STC. No sextodecimo edition appeared by the date of this inventory; dating above assumes that the compiler mistook a duodecimo for the slightly smaller format. See Shaaber J172 for Continental edition, also duodecimo. *Language(s)*: Latin. Appraised at 6d in 1588.

149.248 methode to mortification
Diego de Estella. *A methode unto mortification: called heretofore, The contempt of the world*. London: J. Windet, 1586.
STC 10542. A Protestant version. Surely this title is intended even though the sole edition appears in duodecimo rather than the sextodecimo indicated. *Language(s)*: English. Appraised at 10d in 1588.

149.249 Bezaes psalmes english
Théodore de Bèze. *The psalmes of David, truely opened and explaned*. (*Bible–O.T.*). Translated by Anthony Gilby. London: J. Harrison a. H. Middleton, 1580.
STC 2033. STC 2034, also in English, is in duodecimo, which conceivably may be represented here; see the annotations on size in the two preceding items. *Language(s)*: English. Appraised at 6d in 1588.

149.250 Institutiones christianae lib. Othonis
Pedro de Soto. *Institutionis christianae libri tres priores: jussu D. Othonis Cardinalis*

et episcopi Augustani a doctis. Continent: 1548–1553.

Othonis is a reference to the name of Otto von Waldburg, *Truchsess, Archbishop of Augsburg* found in the long title. The editions in the date range include both octavo and sextodecimo sizes. *Language(s)*: Latin. Appraised at 2d in 1588.

149.251 Pharmacorum conficiendorum ratio
Valerius Cordus. [*Dispensatorium*]. Continent: date indeterminable.
Language(s): Latin. Appraised at 2d in 1588.

149.252 Exercyse of true fast
The holie exercise of a true fast. Edited by Thomas Cartwright. London: [H. Middleton?] for J. Harison and T. Man, 1580.

STC 24251.5. William Wilkinson is sometimes cited as the editor. This is another edition of STC 24251.3, which has a different title. *Language(s)*: English. Appraised at 4d in 1588.

149.253 multiple A cumpanye of ould bookes which could not be praysed severallye
Unidentified. Places unknown: stationers unknown, dates indeterminable.
STC/non-STC status unknown. *Language(s)*: Unknown. Appraised as a group at 5s in 1588.

149.254 multiple Certayne note paper bookes
Unidentified. Provenances unknown: dates indeterminable.
Manuscripts. Likely personal notebooks. *Language(s)*: Unknown. Appraised as a group at 18d in 1588.

149.255 multiple Certain bookes in velum sticcht in 4° with others
Unidentified. Places unknown: stationers unknown, dates indeterminable.
STC/non-STC status unknown. *Language(s)*: Unknown. Appraised as a group at 12s in 1588.

149.256 Bezaes testament in Englishe
[*Bible–N.T.*]. Translated from Greek by Théodore de Bèze; translated into English by Laurence Tomson. London: C. Barkar, 1576–1577.

STC 2878 *et seq*. *Language(s)*: English. Appraised with a group at 4£ 5s 2d in 1588.

149.257 Crusius in Rhetoricam melancthonis
Philipp Melanchthon. [*Rhetorica*]. Edited by Martin Crusius. Continent: date indeterminable.
Language(s): Latin. Appraised with a group at 4£ 5s 2d in 1588.

149.258 methodica descriptio per Gellium Snecanum
Gellius Snecanus (Jelle Hotzes). *Methodica descriptio, et fundamentum trium lo-*

corum scripturae [and other works]. Continent: date indeterminable.
Language(s): Latin. Appraised with a group at 4£ 5s 2d in 1588.

149.259 Beza one the canticles frenche
Théodore de Bèze. *Sermons sur les trois premiers chapitres du Cantique des Cantiques de Salomon*. Geneva: par Jehan le Preux, 1586.
Gardy no. 359. *Language(s)*: French. Appraised with a group at 4£ 5s 2d in 1588.

149.260 Foxe de Christo gratis justificante
John Foxe, *the Martyrologist*. *De Christo gratis justificante*. London: T. Purfutius, imp. G. Byshop, 1583.
STC 11234. The book includes a sermon by William Fulke. *Language(s)*: Latin. Appraised with a group at 4£ 5s 2d in 1588.

149.261 Jesuitismi pars secunda
Laurence Humphrey. *Jesuitismi pars secunda: Puritanopapismi, seu doctrinae jesuiticae confutatio*. London: H. Middletonus, imp. G. B[ishop], 1584.
STC 13962. *Language(s)*: Latin. Appraised with a group at 4£ 5s 2d in 1588.

149.262 Fulke agaynst Saunders
William Fulke. *D. Heskins, D. Sanders, and M. Rastel, overthrowne*. London: H. Middleton f. G. Bishop, 1579.
STC 11433. A response to STC 13250, STC 21696, and STC 20726. *Language(s)*: English. Appraised with a group at 4£ 5s 2d in 1588.

149.263 Caesars commentaryes
Caius Julius Caesar. [*Commentarii*]. London: (different houses), 1530 (probable)–1564.
STC 4335 *et seq*. The manuscript entry suggests an English version, and if so, the 1564 Golding translation is more likely to be in this 1588 inventory, especially as an octavo, than the Rastell folio diglot of c. 1530, which would probably have accounted for most of the valuation of this separately listed group of more than forty books. *Language(s)*: English Latin (perhaps). Appraised with a group at 4£ 5s 2d in 1588.

149.264 Alciati emblemata
Andrea Alciati. *Emblemata*. Continent: date indeterminable.
Language(s): Latin. Appraised with a group at 4£ 5s 2d in 1588.

149.265 Artis oratoriae precepta per wickerum
Hanss Jacob Wecker. *Artis oratoriae praecepta in tabularum formam redactum*. Basle: per Eusebium Episcopium et Nicol. frat. haeredes, 1582.
Language(s): Latin. Appraised with a group at 4£ 5s 2d in 1588.

149.266 Terence
Publius Terentius, *Afer*. Probably [*Works*]. Britain or Continent: date indeterminable.
STC 23885 *et seq.* and non-STC. *Language(s)*: Latin English (perhaps). Appraised with a group at 4£ 5s 2d in 1588.

149.267 Linacres grammer
Thomas Linacre. *Rudimenta grammatices*. Translated by George Buchanan. Britain or Continent: 1525?–1566.
STC 15636 *et seq.* and non-STC. Linacre's *Progymnasmata grammatices vulgaria* published in a single edition in 1512 is, at this date, only a very remote possibility. *Language(s)*: Latin . Appraised with a group at 4£ 5s 2d in 1588.

149.268 Logica Crellii
Fortunatus Crellius. [*Aristotle–Selected works–Logica: commentary*]. Continent: 1581–1585.
Language(s): Latin. Appraised with a group at 4£ 5s 2d in 1588.

149.269 Strigellius in logicam melanct:
Victorinus Strigelius. *In erotemata dialecticae P. Melanchthonis hypomnemata*. Continent: 1566?–1586.
Language(s): Latin. Appraised with a group at 4£ 5s 2d in 1588.

149.270 ursinus catechismus englishe
The catechisme, or maner to teach children and others the christian fayth. (*Heidelberg catechism*). Britain: 1572?–1588.
STC 13028 *et seq.* Zacharias Ursinus had a hand in the original, as did Caspar Olevian. Translators vary with the editions. *Language(s)*: English. Appraised with a group at 4£ 5s 2d in 1588.

149.271 Lemnius de occultis miraculis
Levinus Lemnius. *De miraculis occultis naturae libri IIII*. Continent: date indeterminable.
Language(s): Latin. Appraised with a group at 4£ 5s 2d in 1588.

149.272 Vives de anima
Joannes Lodovicus Vives. *De anima et vita libri tres* [and other works]. Continent: 1534–1563.
Language(s): Latin. Appraised with a group at 4£ 5s 2d in 1588.

149.273 Latimers sermons with others
Hugh Latimer, *Bishop*. [*Sermons*]. London: 1562–1584.
STC 15276 *et seq.* STC 15274–1524.7 remain possibilities, but the *with others* in the manuscript entry suggests a larger collection, as the 1562 *27 sermons* . . . is, and the phrase may even be an approximation of the long title that reads, in part:

"as certayne other commyng to our handes of late." *Language(s)*: English. Appraised with a group at 4£ 5s 2d in 1588.

149.274 Doctor Raynoldes conference
John Rainolds and John Hart, *Jesuit*. *The summe of the conference betwene J. Rainoldes and J. Hart [Jesuit]*. London: (different houses), 1584–1588.

STC 20626 *et seq*. A report of a conference, in support of the Protestant cause, that Rainolds had with Hart, an imprisoned Roman Catholic priest. It was published with Hart's approval and, to that degree, Hart should be considered a collaborator. An English translation of STC 20264 (*Sex theses de sacra scriptura, et ecclesia*) is included. George Bishop had a stationer's role in both editions. *Language(s)*: English. Appraised with a group at 4£ 5s 2d in 1588.

149.275 Bilsone in 4°
Thomas Bilson, *Bishop*. *The true difference betweene christian subjection and unchristian rebellion*. Oxford: J. Barnes, 1585.

STC 3071. The only work of Bilson's published before the date of this inventory; the second edition (STC 3072; 1586) is in octavo. *Language(s)*: English. Appraised with a group at 4£ 5s 2d in 1588.

149.276 The nomenclator, Junius
Adrian Junius. *The nomenclator*. Britain or Continent: date indeterminable.

STC 14860 and non-STC. Various vernaculars in addition to German are possible. *Language(s)*: German Greek Latin. Appraised with a group at 4£ 5s 2d in 1588.

149.277 De providentia, Gorrutius
Andreas Gorrutius. *De providentia divina*. Geneva: sumptibus Eustathii Vignon et Jacobi Stoer, 1585.

Language(s): Latin. Appraised with a group at 4£ 5s 2d in 1588.

149.278 De suba gratuiti foederis Olevian
Caspar Olevian. *De substantia foederis gratuiti inter Deum et electos*. Geneva: apud Eustathium Vignon, 1585.

Language(s): Latin. Appraised with a group at 4£ 5s 2d in 1588.

149.279 Olevianus in Calvini Institutiones
Jean Calvin. [*Institutio christianae religionis–Epitome*]. Edited by Caspar Olevian. Herborn: Christoph Corvinus, 1586.

Apparently the only edition by Olevian. See Erichson. *Language(s)*: Latin. Appraised with a group at 4£ 5s 2d in 1588.

149.280 Lascovius contra Claud. Jesuit.
Petrus Monedulatus Lascovius. *Theorematum de puro et expresso Dei verbo nuper propositorum, examen et refutatio*. Geneva: apud Jacobum Chouët, 1584.

Language(s): Latin. Appraised with a group at 4£ 5s 2d in 1588.

149.281   Launeii epitome institutiones
Jean Calvin. [*Institutio christianae religionis–Epitome*]. Edited by William Lawne. London: T. Vautrollerius, 1583–1584.

STC 4427 *et seq*. *Language(s)*: Latin. Appraised with a group at 4£ 5s 2d in 1588.

149.282   Brumleri analisis de senectute
Marcus Beumler. *Analysis dialectica M.T. Ciceronis Catonis Majoris, sive dialogi de Senectute: ad methodum Petri Rami accommodata*. Speyer: Bernardus Albinus, 1583.

Language(s): Latin. Appraised with a group at 4£ 5s 2d in 1588.

149.283   Partitiones Ciceronis Claudii mininois
Marcus Tullius Cicero. *De partitione oratoria*. Edited by Claude Mignault. Continent: date indeterminable.

Language(s): Latin. Appraised with a group at 4£ 5s 2d in 1588.

149.284   Zenophontis Cyri paediae graece
Xenophon. *Cyropaedia*. Continent: date indeterminable.

Language(s): Greek. Appraised with a group at 4£ 5s 2d in 1588.

149.285   Arist: rhet: Sigono interprete
Aristotle. *Rhetorica*. Translated by Carlo Sigonio. Continent: 1565–1584.

Language(s): Latin. Appraised with a group at 4£ 5s 2d in 1588.

149.286   Reformatio legum ecclesiasticarum
Thomas Cranmer, *Archbishop* (with Walter Haddon, Richard Cox, and others). *Reformatio legum ecclesiasticarum*. Edited by John Foxe, *the Martyrologist*. London: ex off. J. Daii, 1571.

STC 6006. May actually have appeared in 1572 according to STC. *Language(s)*: Latin. Appraised with a group at 4£ 5s 2d in 1588.

149.287   Concordance of the byble
Unidentified [Biblical concordance]. Britain or Continent: date indeterminable.

STC/non-STC status unknown. The manuscript entry seems more likely to represent an English version; see, for example, STC 3015 and STC 17300. *Language(s)*: English (probable) Latin (perhaps). Appraised with a group at 4£ 5s 2d in 1588.

149.288   Alarme to Englande
Barnaby Rich. *Allarme to England, foreshewing what perilles are procured, where the people live without regarde of martiall lawe*. London: (different houses), 1578.

STC 20978 *et seq*. Christopher Barker had a hand in both 1578 editions.

Language(s): English. Appraised with a group at 4£ 5s 2d in 1588.

149.289 Quaestio theologica a Colero
Joannes Jacobus Colerus. *Quaestio theologica num anima sit ex traduce, an vero à Deo quotidie inspiretur.* Zürich: ex officina Froschouiana, 1586.
Language(s): Latin. Appraised with a group at 4£ 5s 2d in 1588.

149.290 Junii Academia
François Du Jon, *the Elder. Academia.* Heidelberg: [Hieronymus Commelinus], 1587.
Stationer's name supplied by VD16. *Language(s)*: Latin. Appraised with a group at 4£ 5s 2d in 1588.

149.291 Granatensis quatuor volumina in 16° vel [vellum]
Luis, *de Granada.* Unidentified. Place unknown: stationer unknown, date indeterminable.
STC/non-STC status unknown. *Language(s)*: Latin (probable). Appraised with a group at 4£ 5s 2d in 1588.

149.292 Index expurgatorius
Index librorum prohibitorum. Continent: date indeterminable.
Language(s): Latin. Appraised with a group at 4£ 5s 2d in 1588.

149.293 Veronis Phisica
Sebastian Verro. *Physicorum libri X.* London: ex off. H. Bynneman, 1581.
STC 24688. *Language(s)*: Latin. Appraised with a group at 4£ 5s 2d in 1588.

149.294 hotomanni francogalliae
François Hotman. *Francogallia.* Continent: 1573–1586.
Language(s): Latin. Appraised with a group at 4£ 5s 2d in 1588.

149.295 Tomson in cantica
William Tomson. *In canticum canticorum quod scripsit Schelomo explanatio.* London: ex off. R. Waldegrave, 1583.
STC 24114 . *Language(s)*: Latin. Appraised with a group at 4£ 5s 2d in 1588.

149.296 Brocardus in cantica
Giacopo Brocardo. *In Canticum Canticorum Salomonis expositio mystica.* Bremen: excudebat Theodorus Gluichstein, 1585.
Language(s): Latin. Appraised with a group at 4£ 5s 2d in 1588.

149.297 Chitraeus de affectibus
Nathan Chytraeus. *Ethe kai pathe, seu de affectibus movendis Aristotelis ex II. rhetoricorum doctrina explicata.* Herborn: excudebat Christophorus Corvinus, 1586.
Language(s): Latin. Appraised with a group at 4£ 5s 2d in 1588.

149.298 Catechismus hebr:
Unidentified [catechism]. Continent: date indeterminable.
Language(s): Hebrew. Appraised with a group at 4£ 5s 2d in 1588.

149.299 Philadelphi dialogi
Nicolas Barnaud (Eusebius Philadelphus, *pseudonym*). *Dialogi ab Eusebio Philadelpho cosmopolita in Gallorum et caeterarum rationum gratiam compositi*. Edinburgh: ex typ. J. Jamaei, 1574.
STC 1463. The Edinburgh location is fictitious, as is the printer. The work was printed abroad, perhaps in Strassburg, with a few editions of a French translation issued in 1574 as well. The work is sometimes attributed to Théodore de Bèze and François Hotman. *Language(s)*: Latin French (perhaps). Appraised with a group at 4£ 5s 2d in 1588.

Matthew Parkin. Scholar (B.A.): Probate Inventory. 1589

R. J. FEHRENBACH

Matthew Parkin, of London, matriculated from Christ Church on 31 May 1583, aged fourteen, and was granted the Bachelor of Arts degree on 13 June 1588 (*Alumni Oxonienses*, 3:1117). Parkin died a little over a year later since the administration of his estate, granted to a pewterer named Blythe, occurred in late 1589. Though undated, the document for the administration of his estate is listed in a sequence of admons in the Oxford University Archives that would place it sometime between September and December of 1589, with late November being the most likely date.

Parkin's collection of books is made up primarily of philosophy, history, theology, and literature, including the standard works associated with an Oxford scholar taking the Master's course, as well as a handful of works not typically found in a scholar's library. The inventory of his books is arranged in sizes by the compiler, probably because the collection was also so arranged. There are more books in English (about 15%) than are usually found in a scholar's library at this date, but, as expected, the dominant language of the works is Latin. Two Greek-Latin dictionaries appear, as do several works in Greek. There is a clear reformist stripe to the theological books, with Luther, Beza, and Zwingli appearing along with the contemporary polemics of the Italian reformer Caelius Secundus Curio, and the English writers, John Foxe and Philip Stubbes. The fervently reformist Edwin Sandys, Bishop of York under Elizabeth, is represented with his sermons. Among the several Bibles are at least three in Latin, including the Vulgate, which are accompanied by Beza's Latin New Testament as well as an English Bible. Homer and Ovid appear only in English, though a Latin Virgil and Sallust, both with commentary, are listed, along with multi-volumed editions of Plutarch, Cicero, and Livy, among the Latin classical works.

Aside from Stubbes's *The Anatomie of Abuses*, among the less academic works listed is the sole work of Elizabeth's long-time Master of the Revels, Edmund

Tilney: *The Flower of Friendshippe*, a fictive treatment of courtesy and marriage. By far, however, the most interesting, and doubtless the most historically important item to appear in Parkin's collection is a copy of the English Faustbook ("Doctor faustus" at 150.36) that pre-dates the 1592 edition (STC 10711). The appearance of an English Faustbook in a 1589 inventory offers the possibility that Marlowe could have read this source for his play, *Doctor Faustus*, at least three years earlier than has been thought to be the case, allowing the play to be among his earlier works, as some have posited, rather than his last. For details laying out the connection between the "Doctor faustus" entry and Marlowe's play, as well as the matters of dating Parkin's inventory discussed above, see Fehrenbach 2001.

Oxford University Archives, Bodleian Library: Hyp.B.17.

§

Fehrenbach, R.J. 2001. "A Pre-1592 English Faust Book and the Date of Marlowe's *Doctor Faustus*." *The Library*, 7th series, 2:327–335.

§

150.1	An English Bible
150.2	Luther in genesin
150.3	Bezae testamentum lat. annotationibus
150.4	Concordantia Bibliae
150.5	Plinii Nat. Historia
150.6	Xenophon graec Lat.
150.7	Cooperi dictionarium
150.8	Aristotelis opera uno volumine
150.9	Virgilius cum commentar:
150.10	Lexicon graecum
150.11	Nizolius
150.12	Zuingeri tabulae in Ethica
150.13	Plutarchi vitae
150.14:1–3	Tres libri chartacei
150.15	Buridan in Ethica
150.16	Biblia lat:
150.17	Textoris Officina
150.18:1	Tollet in Physica et De Anima
150.18:2	[See 150.18:1]
150.19	Aristotelis Ethica
150.20	Salustius cum commentar:
150.21	Clenardi grammatica graeca
150.22	Byshopp of Yorkes sermons

150.23	Dictionarium latino graecum
150.24:1	Casi Logica et Ethica
150.24:2	[See 150.24:1]
150.25	Biblia Tremelii
150.26	Poeticum dictionarium
150.27	Mathisius in Topica
150.28	Pasquin in traunce
150.29	A cleane paper booke
150.30	Stultifera Navis
150.31	Aristotelis Physica cum commentar:
150.32	Aristotelis Metaphysica
150.33	Johannis de Garlandia Synomyna [Synonyma]
150.34	The Pope Confuted
150.35	Secrettes of Alexis
150.36	Doctor faustus
150.37	Homeri Illiades, English
150.38	Plutarchi Moralia 3bus voluminibus
150.39	Livii opera 4or voluminibus
150.40	Resolutio Christiana
150.41	The Flower of Frendshipp
150.42	Recordes Arithmetique
150.43	Javelli Logica
150.44	Lilii grammatica
150.45	Postillae Arsatii
150.46	Osorius de gloria
150.47	Titelman in psalmos
150.48	Sleidan de quatuor imperiis
150.49	Syntaxis Posselii
150.50	Hadamarius de institutione principum
150.51:1	Valerii Ethica et Physica
150.51:2	[See 150.51:1]
150.52	Bezae Confessiones
150.53	Mureti Orationes
150.54	Anatomie of Abuses, 2 part
150.55:1	Valerii Grammatica, Rhetorica, Dialectica
150.55:2	[See 150.55:1]
150.55:3	[See 150.55:1]
150.54	Johannes de Sacra Bosco
150.55	Rami Logica
150.56	The Prayse of Musique
150.57	Scorus de ratione discendi
150.58	Lippus Brandolinus
150.59	Freigii Paedagogus
150.60	Herodotus
150.61	Tullii opera .8. vol

150.62	Rulandi Synonyma
150.63	Caesaris Commentari
150.64	Nowell's Catechisme
150.65	Lemnius de complexionibus
150.66:A	De antiquitate universitatum Angliae
150.66:B	[See 150.66:A]
150.67:1	Osorius de vera sapientia, cum Chitraeo
150.67:2	[See 150.67:1]
150.68	Sophoclis tragaediae latine
150.69	Terentius
150.70	Lemnius de naturae miraculis
150.71	Biblia Jeronimi latin
150.72	Bezae Testamentum latin
150.73	Natalis Comes
150.74	Justinus
150.75	Aphthonius
150.76	Quintus Curtius
150.77	Herodian
150.78	Flores Aristotelis
150.79	Psalmorum libri latin
150.80	Ovides epistles

§

150.1   An English Bible
The Bible. Britain or Continent: 1535–1588.
STC 2063 et seq . *Language(s)*: English. Appraised at 6s 8d in 1589.

150.2   Luther in genesin
Martin Luther. [*Genesis: commentary*]. Continent: date indeterminable.
Language(s). Latin. Appraised at 7s in 1589.

150.3   Bezae testamentum lat. annotationibus
[*Bible–N.T.*]. Translated and edited by Théodore de Bèze. Continent: date indeterminable.
No folio edition of Bèze's New Testament, indicated here, was published in England until after the date of this inventory, and none with his Annotations, which were printed only in his "major editions." See 150.72 below. *Language(s)* : Latin Greek (perhaps). Appraised at 6s in 1589.

150.4   Concordantia Bibliae
Unidentified [Biblical concordance]. Continent: date indeterminable.
Language(s): Latin. Appraised at 3s in 1589.

150.5 Plinii Nat. Historia
Pliny, *the Elder*. *Historia naturalis*. Continent: date indeterminable.
Language(s): Latin. Appraised at 8s in 1589.

150.6 Xenophon graec Lat.
Xenophon. Probably [*Works*]. Continent: date indeterminable.
Language(s): Greek Latin. Appraised at 6s 8d in 1589.

150.7 Cooperi dictionarium
Thomas Cooper, *Bishop*. *Thesaurus linguae Romanae et Britannicae*. London: (different houses), 1565–1587.
STC 5686 *et seq*. *Language(s)*: English Latin. Appraised at 14s in 1589.

150.8 Aristotelis opera uno volumine
Aristotle. [*Works*]. Continent: date indeterminable.
Language(s): Latin (probable) Greek (perhaps). Appraised at 6s 8d in 1589.

150.9 Virgilius cum commentar:
Publius Virgilius Maro. [*Works*]. Britain or Continent: date indeterminable.
STC 24788 and non-STC. *Language(s)*: Latin. Appraised at 8s in 1589.

150.10 Lexicon graecum
Unidentified [dictionary]. Continent: date indeterminable.
Language(s): Greek Latin. Appraised at 9s in 1589.

150.11 Nizolius
Marius Nizolius. Probably [*Observationes*]. Continent: date indeterminable.
Language(s): Latin. Appraised at 5s in 1589.

150.12 Zuingeri tabulae in Ethica
Theodor Zwinger. [*Aristotle–Ethica: commentary*]. Basle: (different houses), 1566–1582.
Eusebius Episcopus was involved in the printing of both editions. *Language(s)*: Latin. Appraised at 4s in 1589.

150.13 Plutarchi vitae
Plutarch. *Vitae parallelae*. Continent: date indeterminable.
The 1579 folio edition in English (STC 20065) would probably not be entered as above. *Language(s)*: Latin. Appraised at 6s in 1589.

150.14:1–3 Tres libri chartacei
Unidentified. Provenances unknown: dates indeterminable.
Manuscripts. *Language(s)*: Unknown. Appraised as a group at 3s in 1589.

150.15 Buridan in Ethica
Joannes Buridanus. [*Aristotle–Ethica: commentary*]. Paris: (different houses), 1489–1518.
Three folio editions, as indicated here, in the date range. *Language(s)*: Latin. Appraised at 6d in 1589.

150.16 Biblia lat:
The Bible. Britain or Continent: date indeterminable.
STC 2055 *et seq*. and non-STC. *Language(s)*: Latin. Appraised at 4s in 1589.

150.17 Textoris Officina
Joannes Ravisius, (Textor). [*Officina*]. Continent: date indeterminable .
Language(s): Latin. Appraised at 3s in 1589.

150.18:1 Tollet in Physica et De Anima
Franciscus Toletus, *Cardinal*. [*Aristotle–Physica: commentary*]. Continent: date indeterminable.
Toletus's commentary on the *Physica* was published in composite volumes with his commentary on Aristotle's *De generatione et corruptione*, but not with his commentary on *De anima*. This entry, then, represents two discrete volumes, perhaps bound together. *Language(s)*: Latin. Appraised with one other at 4s 6d in 1589.

150.18:2 [See 150.18:1]
Franciscus Toletus, *Cardinal*. [*Aristotle–De anima: commentary*]. Continent: date indeterminable.
See the annotations to 150.18:1. *Language(s)*: Latin. Appraised with one other at 4s 6d in 1589.

150.19 Aristotelis Ethica
Aristotle. *Ethica*. Britain or Continent: date indeterminable.
STC 752 and non-STC. STC 752 (1479) is the only quarto edition, indicated here, issued in England by the date of this inventory. *Language(s)*: Latin Greek (perhaps). Appraised at 18d in 1589.

150.20 Salustius cum commentar:
Caius Sallustius Crispus. Probably [*Works*]. Continent: date indeterminable.
No STC edition was issued in quarto by the date of this inventory. *Language(s)*: Latin. Appraised at 16d in 1589.

150.21 Clenardi grammatica graeca
Nicolaus Clenardus. [*Institutiones linguae graecae*]. Continent: date indeterminable.
All STC editions are octavo; the compiler lists this item as quarto. *Language(s)*: Greek Latin. Appraised at 4s in 1589.

150.22 Byshopp of Yorkes sermons

Edwin Sandys, *Archbishop. Sermons made by the most reverende Edwin, archbishop of Yorke*. London: H. Midleton for T. Charde, 1585.

STC 21713. *Language(s)*: English. Appraised at 18d in 1589.

150.23 Dictionarium latino graecum

Unidentified [dictionary]. Continent: date indeterminable.

It is tempting to identify this as a copy of Budaeus's popular dictionary, but of the ten editions published before the date of this inventory, only one is in quarto (Paris, 1554). Jean Crespin's dictionary was published, apparently, only in quarto editions, so it might be intended here. Other possibilities exist also; see, for example, Adams D421 and D423. *Language(s)*: Greek Latin. Appraised at 3s in 1589.

150.24:1 Casi Logica et Ethica

John Case. *Summa veterum interpretum in universam dialecticam Aristotelis*. London: T. Vautrollierus, 1584.

STC 4762. The Continental editions did not appear until after Parkin's death. *Language(s)*: Latin. Appraised with one other at 4s in 1589.

150.24:2 [See 150.24:1]

John Case. *Speculum moralium quaestionum in universam ethicen Aristotelis*. Oxford: ex off. typ. Jos. Barnesii, 1585.

STC 4759. Only octavo editions had been issued from Continental printers by the date of this inventory. *Language(s)*: Latin. Appraised with one other at 4s in 1589.

150.25 Biblia Tremelii

The Bible. Translated by Joannes Immanuel Tremellius and François Du Jon, *the Elder*. London: Henry Middleton (and other houses), 1580.

STC 2056 *et seq*. This is taken to be an edition entirely by Tremellius (and Du Jon), without the Bèze version of the New Testament. The Tremellius Latin and polyglot versions published on the Continent from 1569 were all folio editions; the compiler identifies this copy as quarto. Several variants appeared in 1580. *Language(s)*: Latin. Appraised at 7s in 1589.

150.26 Poeticum dictionarium

Probably Charles Estienne. [*Dictionarium historicum ac poeticum*]. Continent: date indeterminable.

Hermann Torrentinus's encyclopedia, sometimes referred to in a similar way, was not as widely published in quarto form as was Estienne's. *Language(s)*: Latin. Appraised at 4s in 1589.

150.27 Mathisius in Topica

Aristotle. *Topica*. Translated by Joachim Perion, with commentary by Gerardus Matthisius, *Geldrensis*. Cologne: excudebat Petrus Horst, 1561–1566.

Matthisius's commentary on Aristotle's *Topica* was not published separately. *Language(s)*: Latin. Appraised at 8d in 1589.

150.28 Pasquin in traunce
Caelius Secundus Curio. *Pasquine in a traunce a christian and learned dialogue*. Translated by William Page. London: (different houses), 1566?–1584.
STC 6130 *et seq*. *Language(s)*: English. Appraised at 2d in 1589.

150.29 A cleane paper booke
A blank book. Appraised at 4d in 1589.

150.30 Stultifera Navis
Sebastian Brant. *Stultifera navis*. Continent: date indeterminable.
There is no reason to think this is one of the early sixteenth-century English translations issued in quarto. The Latin-English editions published by the date of this inventory were both folio editions. Most of the Latin editions in quarto are incunables, making a reasonable date range difficult to determine. *Language(s)*: Latin. Appraised at 6d in 1589.

150.31 Aristotelis Physica cum commentar:
Aristotle. *Physica*. Continent: date indeterminable.
There is no way to identify the commentator. *Language(s)*: Latin. Appraised at 3s 4d in 1589.

150.32 Aristotelis Metaphysica
Aristotle. *Metaphysica*. Continent: date indeterminable.
Language(s): Latin. Appraised at 12d in 1589.

150.33 Johannis de Garlandia Synomyna [Synonyma]
Joannes de Garlandia. *Synonyma*. Britain or Continent: 1487–1518.
STC 11608a.1 *et seq*. and non-STC. The first definitely dated edition is 1487 (Reutlingen); early, undated Cologne editions are variously supplied with dates ranging from c. 1485 to c. 1495. Whichever edition Parkin owned, however, it was over seventy years old. *Language(s)*: Latin. Appraised at 6d in 1589.

150.34 The Pope Confuted
John Foxe, *the Martyrologist*. *The pope confuted*. Translated by James Bell, *Bishop*. London: T. Dawson for R. Sergier, 1580.
STC 11241. *Language(s)*: English. Appraised at 3d in 1589.

150.35 Secrettes of Alexis
Alessio, *Piemontese, pseudonym* (Girolamo Ruscelli). *The secretes of the reverende maister Alexis of Piemount*. London: (different houses), 1558–1578.
STC 293 *et seq*. The date range includes the editions of various parts. The first three parts were translated from the French by William Warde, and the fourth

part was translated from the Italian by Richard Androse. *Language(s)*: English. Appraised at 8d in 1589.

150.36 Doctor faustus

Johann Faustus, *Doctor*. [*The historie of the damnable life, and deserved death of doctor John Faustus*]. Assumed to have been translated by P.F. London (probable): stationer unknown, date indeterminable.

Not in the STC, but see STC 10711 and 10715. Conventionally the "author" is cited as above. The *editio princeps* of the work is in German (Frankfurt, 1587), and the first extant English translation, 1592 (STC 10711), is announced by its printer, Thomas Orwin, as being: "Newly imprinted, and amended: according to the true copie at Franckfort, and translated by P.F. gent." No quarto edition, the format of this item, appeared in German, which language, in addition, Parkin gives no evidence elsewhere of reading. This entry, then, gives evidence of the English Faustbook having been available at least by 1589, which in turn provides evidence that Christopher Marlowe's play, *Doctor Faustus*, could have been written earlier than is frequently argued (post 1592); the English translation, as it appears in the 1592 edition, is definitely Marlowe's source. The title supplied above is the title of the 1592 extant Orwin edition. For additional material on Parkin's copy representing an early English Faustbook, see Fehrenbach 2001. *Language(s)*: English. Appraised at 2d in 1589.

150.37 Homeri Illiades, English

Homer. *Ten books of Homers Iliades*. Translated by Arthur Hall. London: [H. Bynneman?] for R. Newberie, 1581.

STC 13630 *et seq*. Two issues in 1581. *Language(s)*: English. Appraised at 4d in 1589.

150.38 Plutarchi Moralia 3bus voluminibus

Plutarch. *Moralia*. Continent: date indeterminable.

The only octavo edition published in England by the date of this inventory is in one volume and in English. *Language(s)*: Latin (probable) Greek (perhaps). Appraised at 5s 6d in 1589.

150.39 Livii opera 4or voluminibus

Titus Livius. [*Historiae Romanae decades*]. Continent: date indeterminable.

See Adams L1322 for a four-volume octavo edition of Livy (Venice, 1518–1521); there may be others. The 1589 octavo edition published in London was not in four volumes. *Language(s)*: Latin. Appraised at 6s 8d in 1589.

150.40 Resolutio Christiana

Unidentified. Place unknown: stationer unknown, date indeterminable.

STC/non-STC status unknown. If misheard or garbled in entering, perhaps Edmund Bunny's Protestant version of Robert Parsons's *The book of Christian Exercise* (see STC 19355), or perhaps either Selneccer's *Institutio christiana* or his

Responsio vera et Christiana ad Theo. Bezae.... Selneccer's position seems, however, slightly out of place in this generally Calvinist library. *Language(s)*: Latin (probable). Appraised at 14s in 1589.

150.41 The Flower of Frendshipp

Edmund Tilney. *A brief and pleasant discourse of duties in mariage, called the Flower of friendshippe*. London: (different houses), 1568–1587.

STC 24076 *et seq*. Seven editions, all but the last of which were printed by Henry Denham. Tilney was Elizabeth's Master of the Revels during most of her reign. *Language(s)*: English. Appraised at 6d in 1589.

150.42 Recordes Arithmetique

Robert Record. *The ground of artes teachyng the worke and practise of arithmetike*. London: (different houses), 1543–1586.

STC 20797.5 *et seq*. Editions after 1561 carried additions by John Dee. *Language(s)*: English. Appraised at 12d in 1589.

150.43 Javelli Logica

[*Aristotle–Selected works–Logic: commentary*]. Continent: date indeterminable.

This could just as well be Javellus's epitome form since both were published in octavo size. *Language(s)*: Latin. Appraised at 10d in 1589.

150.44 Lilii grammatica

William Lily. *Institutio compendiaria totius grammaticae*. Britain or Continent: 1544–1585.

STC 15610.8 *et seq*. The earlier editions were issued in quarto, and a few STC editions were printed in Geneva. *Language(s)*: Latin English (perhaps). Appraised at 8d in 1589.

150.45 Postillae Arsatii

Arsatius Schofer. *Enarrationes Evangeliorum dominicalium, ad dialecticam methodum accommodatae*. Augsburg: excud. Henricus Steyner, 1538.

Language(s): Latin. Appraised at 8d in 1589.

150.46 Osorius de gloria

Jeronimo Osorio da Fonseca, *Bishop*. [*Selected works*]. Continent: date indeterminable.

De gloria is the leading title in many editions of Osorio's *Selected works*. The sole single edition of *De gloria* (1552) is in quarto. *Language(s)*: Latin. Appraised at 12d in 1589.

150.47 Titelman in psalmos

Franz Titelmann. [*Psalms: commentary and text*]. (*Bible–O.T.*). Continent: date indeterminable.

Language(s): Latin. Appraised at 12d in 1589.

150.48 Sleidan de quatuor imperiis

Joannes Philippson, *Sleidanus. De quatuor summis imperiis.* Britain or Continent: date indeterminable.

STC 19847 and non-STC. *Language(s)*: Latin. Appraised at 4d in 1589.

150.49 Syntaxis Posselii

Joannes Posselius. *Syntaxis linguae graecae.* Continent: 1565–1589.
Language(s): Greek Latin. Appraised at 3d in 1589.

150.50 Hadamarius de institutione principum

Reinhard Lorich (Hadamarius). *De institutione principum loci communes.* Frankfurt am Main: (different houses), 1538–1563.

The 1538 edition was published by Christian Egenolph, the 1541 and 1563 editions by his heirs. *Language(s)*: Latin. Appraised at 8d in 1589.

150.51:1 Valerii Ethica et Physica

Cornelius Valerius. *Ethicae, seu De moribus philosophiae brevis et perspicua descriptio.* Continent: 1566–1582.

Language(s): Latin. Appraised with one other at 6d in 1589.

150.51:2 [See 150.51:1]

Cornelius Valerius. *Physicae, seu de naturae philosophia institutio.* Continent: 1567–1584.

Language(s): Latin. Appraised with one other at 6d in 1589.

150.52 Bezae Confessiones

Théodore de Bèze. *Confessio christianae fidei.* Britain or Continent: 1560–1589.
STC 2006 and non-STC. *Language(s)*: Latin. Appraised at 8d in 1589.

150.53 Mureti Orationes

Marcus Antonius Muretus. [*Selected works–Orations*]. Continent: date indeterminable.

Language(s): Latin. Appraised at 6d in 1589.

150.54 Anatomie of Abuses, 2 part

Philip Stubbes. *The second part of the Anatomie of abuses, conteining the display of corruptions.* London: R. W(ard) for W. Wright, 1583.

STC 23380 *et seq. Language(s)*: English. Appraised at 4d in 1589.

150.55:1 Valerii Grammatica, Rhetorica, Dialectica

Cornelius Valerius. *Grammaticarum institutionum libri IIII.* Continent: date indeterminable.

Language(s): Latin. Appraised with two others at 20d in 1589.

150.55:2 [See 150.55:1]
Cornelius Valerius. *In universam bene dicendi rationem tabula*. Continent: date indeterminable.
Language(s): Latin. Appraised with two others at 20d in 1589.

150.55:3 [See 150.55:1]
Cornelius Valerius. *Tabulae totius dialectices*. Continent: date indeterminable.
Language(s): Latin. Appraised with two others at 20d in 1589.

150.54 Johannes de Sacra Bosco
John Holywood (Joannes Sacrobosco). Probably *Sphaera mundi*. Continent: date indeterminable.
Language(s): Latin. Appraised at 4d in 1589.

150.55 Rami Logica
Pierre de La Ramée. [*Dialectica*]. Britain or Continent: date indeterminable. STC 15241.7 *et seq.* and non-STC. *Language(s)*: Latin. Appraised at 8d in 1589.

150.56 The Prayse of Musique
The praise of musicke. Oxford: J. Barnes, 1586.
STC 20184. Attributed to John Case in STC 4246, but, according to Madan (1:279), probably by someone else. *Language(s)*: English. Appraised at 2d in 1589.

150.57 Scorus de ratione discendi
Antonius Schorus. *De ratione discendae docendaeque linguae latinae et graecae*. Strassburg: (different houses), 1549–1575.
Language(s): Greek Latin. Appraised at 3d in 1589.

150.58 Lippus Brandolinus
Aurelius Brandolinus (Lippus). Probably *De ratione scribendi*. Britain or Continent: date indeterminable. 1549–1573.
STC 3542 and non-STC. The context suggests his work on rhetoric. His *De humanae vitae conditione*, also published in octavo, is a less likely possibility. *Language(s)*: Latin. Appraised at 6d in 1589.

150.59 Freigii Paedagogus
Joannes Thomas Freigius. *Pedagogus*. Basle: per Sebastianm Henricpetri, 1582.
Language(s): Latin. Appraised at 8d in 1589.

150.60 Herodotus
Herodotus. [*Historiae*]. Continent (probable): date indeterminable.
Probably not an STC book, but see STC 13224. Conceivably this could be the English version published in 1584 in octavo. *Language(s)*: Greek (probable) Latin (probable). Appraised at 18d in 1589.

150.61 Tullii opera .8. vol
Marcus Tullius Cicero. [*Works*]. Continent. date indeterminable.
Language(s): Latin. Appraised at 16s in 1589.

150.62 Rulandi Synonyma
Martin Ruland, *the Elder*. *Synonyma*. Augsburg: (different houses), 1563–1585.
Language(s): Greek Latin. Appraised at 12d in 1589.

150.63 Caesaris Commentari
Caius Julius Caesar. *Commentarii*. Continent (probable): date indeterminable.
Language(s): Latin. Appraised at 2s in 1589.

150.64 Nowell's Catechisme
Alexander Nowell. *Catechismus*. London: (different houses), 1573–1584.
STC 18707. Nowell's Larger Catechism appeared only once in octavo (STC 18707, in 1573). All of the seventeen editions of the Shorter Catechism (STC 18711–18711b) and the Middle Catechism (STC 18712–18715; STC 18726–18728; STC 18730–18733.3) that Parkin could have owned were published in octavo, making one of them more likely. *Language(s)*: Latin English (perhaps) Greek (perhaps). Appraised at 4d in 1589.

150.65 Lemnius de complexionibus
Levinus Lemnius. *De habitu et constitucione corporis*. Continent: 1561–1587.
Language(s): Latin. Appraised at 12d in 1589.

150.66:A De antiquitate universitatum Angliae
Joannes Caius. *De antiquitate Cantabrigiensis academiae libri duo*. London: per H. Bynneman, 1568 [composite publication].
STC 4344. *Language(s)*: Latin. Appraised [a composite volume] at 12d in 1589.

150.66:B [See 150.66:A]
Thomas Caius. *Assertio antiquitatis Oxoniensis academiae*. [Composite publication].
STC 4344. *Language(s)*: Latin. Appraised [a composite volume] at 12d in 1589.

150.67:1 Osorius de vera sapientia, cum Chitraeo
Jeronimo Osorio da Fonseca, *Bishop*. *De vera sapientia*. Continent: date indeterminable.
Language(s): Latin. Appraised with one other at 16d in 1589.

150.67:2 [See 150.67:1]
Probably David Chytraeus. Unidentified. Continent (probable): date indeterminable.
Almost certainly not an STC book. Something by Nathan Chytraeus must be considered, but he is only a remote possibility. The only STC book of David

Chytraeus's available to Parkin is a translation of a work on liturgy, *Dispositiones epistolarum* (STC 5263-5264). A more likely companion to the Osorius, if bound with it, would be Chytraeus's *Regulae vitae*, which was published only on the Continent. *Language(s)*: Latin. Appraised with one other at 16d in 1589.

150.68 Sophoclis tragaediae latine
Sophocles. [*Works*]. Continent: date indeterminable.
Language(s): Latin. Appraised at 6d in 1589.

150.69 Terentius
Publius Terentius, *Afer*. [*Works*]. Britain or Continent: date indeterminable.
STC 23885.7 *et seq.* and non-STC. The first octavo edition published in England appeared in 1575. *Language(s)*: Latin. Appraised at 20d in 1589.

150.70 Lemnius de naturae miraculis
Levinus Lemnius. *De miraculis occultis naturae libri IIII*. Continent: date indeterminable.
Language(s): Latin. Appraised at 18d in 1589.

150.71 Biblia Jeronimi latin
The Bible. Continent: date indeterminable.
The only Vulgate published in England (STC 2055) was in quarto; the compiler identifies this copy as octavo. *Language(s)*: Latin. Appraised at 18d in 1589.

150.72 Bezae Testamentum latin
[*Bible–N.T.*]. Edited by Théodore de Bèze. Britain or Continent: date indeterminable.
STC 2802 *et seq.* and non-STC. One of Bèze's "small editions," it could have been one published in England. See 150.3. *Language(s)*: Latin. Appraised at 18d in 1589.

150.73 Natalis Comes
Natalis Comes. Unidentified. Continent: date indeterminable.
Language(s): Latin. Appraised at 2s in 1589.

150.74 Justinus
Trogus Pompeius and Justinus, *the Historian*. [*Epitomae in Trogi Pompeii historias*]. Britain or Continent: date indeterminable.
STC 24287 *et seq.* and non-STC. *Language(s)*: Latin. Appraised at 6d in 1589.

150.75 Aphthonius
Aphthonius, *Sophista*. *Progymnasmata*. Britain or Continent: date indeterminable.
STC 699 *et seq.* and non-STC. *Language(s)*: Latin. Appraised at 6d in 1589.

150.76 Quintus Curtius
Quintus Curtius Rufus. *De rebus gestis Alexandri Magni*. Continent: date indeterminable.
No possible STC editions in sextodecimo. *Language(s)*: Latin. Appraised at 4d in 1589.

150.77 Herodian
Herodian. [*Historiae*]. Continent: date indeterminable.
Language(s): Latin Greek (perhaps). Appraised at 4d in 1589.

150.78 Flores Aristotelis
Probably Jacques Bouchereau, compiler. *Flores illustriores Aristotelis*. Continent: date indeterminable.
Language(s): Latin. Appraised at 8d in 1589.

150.79 Psalmorum libri latin
[*Bible–O.T.–Psalms*]. Britain or Continent: date indeterminable.
STC 2356 *et seq.* and non-STC. The first sextodecimo edition from England appeared in 1575 (STC 2356). *Language(s)*: Latin. Appraised at 5d in 1589.

150.80 Ovides epistles
Publius Ovidius Naso. *Heroides*. Continent: date indeterminable.
No solo edition of the *Heroides* was published in England prior to the date of this inventory. *Language(s)*: Latin. Appraised at 6d in 1589.

PLRE Cumulative Catalogue

In the following lists, *entry* refers to a single entry made by a compiler of a manuscript book-list; *record* refers to a single record created from an *entry* by an editor. An *entry* may contain more than one *record*; conversely, a *record* may constitute only part of an *entry*. A *record* always represents at least one book but may represent more, including a volume set.

I. PLRE Database Totals
Book-lists: 180; Entries: 9,449; Records: 9,915
Number of Books Represented: More than 11,051
 (Of the 9,915 records, 113 records specify two or more unidentified books for a determinable total of 1,249 books, adding a net 1,136 books to the record total. In addition, fifty-five records contain an indeterminable number of books, identified in the database as *multiple*. At least 90 manuscript entries may represent the same book [as in the books conveyed from one owner to another, both of whom are listed in the PLRE catalogue, or books that appear in an owner's purchasing list and later are listed in his probate inventory].)

II. Book-list Indices
A. Arrangement and Size of Each PLRE Unit
Volume 1: PLRE 1–4   1,394 records (seven records in Volume 5)
Volume 2: PLRE 5–66   1,151 records
Volume 3: PLRE 67–86   1,365 records
Volume 4: PLRE 87–112   1,673 records
Volume 5: PLRE 113–137   1,815 records
Volume 6: PLRE 138–150   1,632 records
APND Lists: PLRE Ad1–Ad30   885 records

B. Owners of Book-lists Arranged by Owners' Names

Owner and book-list information below is ordered in the following manner:

> **Name, degree(s). (Born–died) PLRE number.** Profession. Social status. *Date* [of book-list, actual or *terminus ad quem*]: 1631. *Type* [of book-list]: inventory (probate). *Entries*: 25; *Records*: 29.

Allen, Richard, B.A. (c.1547–1569) PLRE 79. Scholar. Professional. *Date:* 1569. *Type:* inventory (probate). *Entries:* 97; *Records:* 98.

Allen, Thomas, B.A. (?–1561) PLRE 69. Scholar. Professional. *Date:* 1561. *Type:* inventory (probate). *Entries:* 34; *Records:* 35.

Anlaby (Aulaby), Edmund, M.A., B.Th. (?–1559) PLRE Ad5. Scholar. Professional. *Date:* 1533, 1559. *Type:* bookseller's accounts, inventory (probate). *Entries:* 28; *Records:* 33.

Atkins, Henry, M.A. (?–1560) PLRE 113. Scholar. Professional. *Date:* 1560. *Type:* inventory (probate). *Entries:* 16; *Records:* 16.

Atkinson, John, M.A. (?–1570) PLRE 83. Scholar. Professional. *Date:* 1570. *Type:* inventory (probate). *Entries:* 25; *Records:* 25.

Austin (given name unknown). (?–?) PLRE 98. Scholar (probable). Professional (probable). *Date:* 1572. *Type:* inventory. *Entries:* 20; *Records:* 20.

Badger, John, M.A. (?–1577) PLRE 115. Scholar. Professional. *Date:* 1577. *Type:* inventory (probate). *Entries:* 78; *Records:* 79.

Balborough, William, D.U.L. (?–1514) PLRE 29. Scholar. Professional. *Date:* 1514. *Type:* inventory (probate). *Entries:* 25; *Records:* 29.

Balyn, John, B.A. (?–1513) PLRE 25. Scholar. Professional. *Date:* 1513. *Type:* inventory (probate). *Entries:* 18; *Records:* 18.

Barwyck, Stephen. (?–1547) PLRE Ad29. Butler, Scholar (probable) (student, probable). Retainer, Professional (probable). *Date:* 1547. *Type:* inventory (probate). *Entries:* 35; *Records:* 36.

Batchelor, Robert. (1506–?) PLRE Ad6. Cleric (chaplain), Scholar. Professional. *Date:* 1533. *Type:* bookseller's accounts. *Entries:* 8; *Records:* 10.

Battbrantes, William. (?–1572) PLRE 99. Scholar (student, probable). Professional. *Date:* 1572. *Type:* inventory (probate). *Entries:* 35; *Records:* 35.

Beaumont, Edward, B.A. (1531–1552) PLRE 64. Scholar. Professional. *Date:* 1552. *Type:* inventory (probate). *Entries:* 117; *Records:* 118.

Beddow, John, M.A. (?–c.1577) PLRE 91. Scholar (schoolmaster). Professional. *Dates:* 1571 and 1577. *Type:* inventories. *Entries:* 40; *Records:* 41.

Bidnell, William, M.A. (?–1512) PLRE 23. Scholar. Professional. *Date:* 1512. *Type:* inventory (probate). *Entries:* 9; *Records:* 9.

Bill, Thomas, M.A. (?–1552) PLRE Ad7. Physician, Scholar. Professional. *Date:* 1532. *Type:* bookseller's accounts. *Entries:* 4; *Records:* 4.

Bisley (given name unknown), M.A. (perhaps), B.Th. (perhaps). (?–1543?) PLRE 60. Scholar. Professional. *Date:* 1543. *Type:* inventory (probate). *Entries:* 122; *Records:* 134.

Blomefield, Miles. (1525–1603) PLRE Ad2. Physician, Alchemist. Professional. *Date:* reconstruction. *Type:* reconstruction. *Entries:* 24; *Records:* 25.

Bolt, Thomas. (1557–?) PLRE 132. Scholar (student). Professional. *Date:* 1578. *Type:* inventory. *Entries:* 86; *Records:* 87.

Bonenfant, Thomas, M.A. (?–?) PLRE Ad8. Scholar. Professional. *Date:* 1533. *Type:* bookseller's accounts. *Entries:* 17; *Records:* 18.

Bowerman, John, M.A., B.C.L. (?–1507) PLRE 5. Scholar. Professional. *Date:* 1507. *Type:* will. *Entries:* 3; *Records:* 4.

Bradford, Ralph, M.A. (c.1502?) PLRE Ad9. Scholar. Professional. *Date:* c.1527. *Type:* bookseller's accounts. *Entries:* 13; *Records:* 14.

Brewer, John, M.A. (?–1535) PLRE Ad10. Scholar. Professional. *Date:* 1533. *Type:* bookseller's accounts. *Entries:* 4; *Records:* 4.

Bromsby, John, B.Th. (?–?) PLRE Ad11. Scholar. Professional. *Date:* 1531. *Type:* bookseller's accounts. *Entries:* 4; *Records:* 5.

Brown, William, M.A. (?–1558) PLRE 67. Scholar. Professional. *Date:* 1558. *Type:* inventory (probate). *Entries:* 223; *Records:* 242.

Bryan, Robert, D.Cn.L. (?–1508) PLRE 11. Scholar. Professional. *Date:* 1508. *Type:* inventory (probate). *Entries:* 19; *Records:* 19.

Buckingham, Edward, B.Cn.L. (?–1568) PLRE Ad12. Scholar. Professional. *Date:* 1533. *Type:* bookseller's accounts. *Entries:* 3; *Records:* 3.

Burton, Edmund, M.A. (?–1529) PLRE 43. Scholar. Professional. *Date:* 1529. *Type:* inventory (probate). *Entries:* 42; *Records:* 46.

Bury, John, B.A. (probable). (?–1567) PLRE 74. Scholar. Professional. *Date:* 1567. *Type:* inventory (probate). *Entries:* 19; *Records:* 19.

Carpenter, Thomas, M.A. (?–1577) PLRE 116. Scholar. Professional. *Date:* 1577. *Type:* inventory (probate). *Entries:* 83; *Records:* 84.

Carter, John, B.C.L. (?–1509) PLRE 17. Scholar. Professional. *Date:* 1509. *Type:* inventory (probate). *Entries:* 3; *Records:* 5.

Cartwright, Thomas, M.A. (?–1532) PLRE 50. Scholar. Professional. *Date:* 1532. *Type:* inventory (probate) and will. *Entries:* 8; *Records:* 11.

Cauthorn, John, B.A. (?–?) PLRE Ad13. Scholar. Professional. *Date:* 1531. *Type:* bookseller's accounts. *Entries:* 12; *Records:* 12.

Chantry, William, B.A. (?–1507) PLRE 6. Scholar. Professional. *Date:* 1507. *Type:* will. *Entries:* 2; *Records:* 3.

Charnock, Roger, M.A. (1549–?) PLRE 117. Scholar. Professional. *Date:* 1577. *Type:* inventory. *Entries:* 80; *Records:* 83.

Chastelain, George. (?–1513) PLRE 26. Stationer. Middle class. *Date:* 1513. *Type:* inventory (probate). *Entries:* 1; *Records:* 1.

Cheke, Agnes. (?–1549) PLRE Ad30. Merchant (vintner). Middle class, Privileged person. *Date:* 1549. *Type:* inventory (probate) *Entries:* 3; *Records:* 4.

Cheyne, Henry, M.A. (?–?) PLRE 138. Scholar. Professional. *Date:* 1581. *Type:* inventory (against debt). *Entries:* 39; *Records:* 43.

Chogan, William. (?–1537) PLRE 56. Scholar (student). Professional. *Date:* 1537. *Type:* will. *Entries:* 1; *Records:* 1.

Cliff, Richard, M.A. (?–1566) PLRE 73. Cleric (chaplain), Scholar. Professional. *Date:* 1566. *Type:* inventory (probate) and will. *Entries:* 261; *Records:* 261.

Cliffley (given name unknown). (?–?) PLRE 118. Cleric (probable). Professional (probable). *Date:* 1577. *Type:* inventory. *Entries:* 22; *Records:* 22.

Coles, John, B.Th. (?–1529) PLRE 44. Scholar. Professional. *Date:* 1529. *Type:* inventory (probate). *Entries:* 5; *Records:* 5.

Collins, Robert. (?–?) PLRE 24. Scholar (student). Professional. *Date:* 1512. *Type:* receipt. *Entries:* 8; *Records:* 8.

Conner, John, B.Th. (c.1490–1569) PLRE 80. Cleric, Scholar. Professional. *Date:* 1569. *Type:* inventory (probate). *Entries:* 46; *Records:* 48.

Cox, Richard, D.Th. (1500–1581) PLRE 1. Cleric (bishop). Gentry. *Date:* 1581. *Type:* inventory. *Entries:* 196; *Records:* 208.

Dalaber, Anthony. (?–1562) PLRE 45. Scholar (student). Professional. *Date:* 1529. *Type:* inventory. *Entries:* 8; *Records:* 8.

Davy, William (perhaps), B.Cn.L. (?–1546) PLRE Ad14. Scholar. Professional. *Date:* 1533. *Type:* bookseller's accounts. *Entries:* 9; *Records:* 9.

Dawson, William, M.A. (?–1577) PLRE 119. Scholar. Professional. *Date:* 1577. *Type:* inventory (probate). *Entries:* 37; *Records:* 37.

Day, Thomas, B.C.L. (?–1570) PLRE 84. Cleric, Scholar. Professional. *Date:* 1570. *Type:* inventory (probate). *Entries:* 137; *Records:* 149.

Dayrell, William, B.A. (?–1577) PLRE 120. Scholar. Professional. *Date:* 1577. *Type:* inventory (probate). *Entries:* 30; *Records:* 30.

Deegen, Peter. (?–1527) PLRE 37. Scholar (student). Professional. *Date:* 1527. *Type:* will. *Entries:* 5; *Records:* 5.

Derbyshire, William. (?–1551) PLRE 61. Scholar (student). Professional. *Date:* 1551. *Type:* inventory (probate). *Entries:* 11; *Records:* 23.

Dering, Sir Edward. (1598–1644) PLRE 4. Member of Parliament. Gentry. *Date:* 1628 and c.1642. *Type:* account book, catalogue, and reconstruction. *Entries:* 638; *Records:* 683. (See Volume 1 and Volume 5.)

Dewer, William, M.A. (probable). (?–1514) PLRE 30. Scholar. Professional. *Date:* 1514. *Type:* inventory (probate). *Entries:* 6; *Records:* 10.

Dewhurst, Giles, M.A. (?–1577) PLRE 121. Scholar. Professional. *Date:* 1577. *Type:* inventory (probate). *Entries:* 45; *Records:* 45.

Dickinson, Thomas (probable), B.A. (?–1558) PLRE Ad15. Scholar. Professional. *Date:* 1533. Type: bookseller's accounts. *Entries:* 7; *Records:* 9.

Digby, George and Simon. (?–?) PLRE 81. Scholars (students). Professional. *Date:* 1569. *Type:* inventory. *Entries:* 47; *Records:* 48.

Digby, Simon. (see George Digby).

Dowe, Robert, B.C.L. (1553–1588) PLRE 148. Scholar. Professional. *Date:* 1589. *Type:* inventory (probate). *Entries:* 302; *Records:* 305.

Dunnet, John. (?–1570) PLRE 85. Scholar (student). Professional. *Date:* 1570. *Type:* inventory (probate). *Entries:* 37; *Records:* 37.

Dyllam, Walter. (?–?) PLRE 106. Scholar (student). Professional. *Date:* 1575. *Type:* inventory. *Entries:* 1; *Records:* 3.

Faringdon, Tristram. (?–1577) PLRE 122. Scholar (student). Professional. *Date:* 1577. *Type:* inventory (probate). *Entries:* 17; *Records:* 18.

Ferne, Richard, M.A. (?–1577) PLRE 123. Scholar. Professional. *Date:* 1577. *Type:* inventory (probate). *Entries:* 51; *Records:* 51.

Forster, John, B.C.L. (?–1584) PLRE 141. Scholar. Professional. *Date:* 1584. *Type:* inventory (probate). *Entries:* 21; *Records:* 21.

Foster, Thomas. (?–1577) PLRE 124. Unknown. Privileged person (probable). *Date:* 1577. *Type:* inventory (probate). *Entries:* 9; *Records:* 9.

Froster, Roger. (?–1514) PLRE 31. Scholar (student). Professional. *Date:* 1514. *Type:* inventory (probate). *Entries:* 1; *Records:* 1.

Gilbert, John. (?–?) PLRE Ad16. Scholar (student). Professional. *Date:* 1528. *Type:* bookseller's accounts. *Entries:* 2; *Records:* 2.

Gilbert, Nicholas. (see Hilbert, Nicholas).

Glover, John, M.A. (?–1578) PLRE 133. Scholar. Professional. *Date:* 1578. *Type:* inventory (probate). *Entries:* 279; *Records:* 280.

Gofton, William, B.C.L. (?–1507) PLRE 7. Scholar. Professional. *Date:* 1507. *Type:* inventory (probate). *Entries:* 11; *Records:* 12.

Goldsmith, Francis. (?–?) PLRE Ad17. Scholar (student) (probable). Professional (probable). *Date:* 1533. *Type:* bookseller's accounts. *Entries:* 1; *Records:* 1.

Grant, Philip. (?–1560) PLRE 114. Scholar (student). Professional. *Date:* 1560. *Type:* inventory (probate). *Entries:* 26; *Records:* 26.

Gray, John. (?–1577) PLRE 125. Scholar (student). Professional. *Date:* 1577. *Type:* inventory (probate). *Entries:* 18; *Records:* 18.

Griffin, Roger, B.A. (?–1510) PLRE 19. Scholar. Professional. *Date:* 1510. *Type:* inventory (probate). *Entries:* 2; *Records:* 2.

Griffith, Thomas, M.A., B.M. (perhaps). (?–1562) PLRE 70. Scholar, Physician (perhaps). Professional. *Date:* 1562. *Type:* inventory (probate). *Entries:* 92; *Records:* 97.

Gryce, William, D.Th. (?–1528) PLRE 41. Scholar. Professional. *Date:* 1528. *Type:* inventory (probate). *Entries:* 15; *Records:* 15.

Hamlyn, William, M.A. (?–1534) PLRE 51. Scholar. Professional. *Date:* 1534. *Type:* inventory (probate). *Entries:* 10; *Records:* 15.

Hart, Robert, M.A. (?–1571) PLRE 92. Scholar. Professional. *Date:* 1571. *Type:* inventory (probate). *Entries:* 135; *Records:* 137.

Hartburn, John, M.A. (?–1513) PLRE 27. Scholar. Professional. *Date:* 1513. *Type:* inventory (probate). *Entries:* 2; *Records:* 4.

Harwood, Thomas, B.A., D.M. (?–?) PLRE Ad18. Scholar. Professional. *Date:* 1530. *Type:* bookseller's accounts. *Entries:* 14; *Records:* 14.

Hawarden, Robert, M.A. (?–1527) PLRE 38. Scholar. Professional. *Date:* 1527. *Type:* inventory (probate). *Entries:* 6; *Records:* 6.

Haynes, John, M.A. (1562–1585) PLRE 144. Scholar. Professional. *Date:* 1585. *Type:* inventory (probate). *Entries:* 71; *Records:* 72.

Heath, John, M.A. (?–?) PLRE 140. Scholar. Professional. *Date:* 1582. *Type:* inventory (against debt). *Entries:* 5; *Records:* 5.

Heywood, John, B.A. (?–1514) PLRE 32. Scholar. Professional. *Date:* 1514. *Type:* inventory (probate). *Entries:* 13; *Records:* 14.

Higgins, Edward, M.A. (?–1588) PLRE 149. Scholar. Professional. *Date:* 1588. *Type:* inventory (probate). *Entries:* 299; *Records:* 311.

Hilbert, John. (see Gilbert, John).

Hilbert, Nicholas. (c.1509–1561) PLRE Ad19. Scholar (student). Professional. *Date:* 1528. *Type:* bookseller's accounts. *Entries:* 1; *Records:* 1.

Hill, Thomas. (?–1585) PLRE 145. Scholar (probable). Professional (probable). *Date:* 1585. *Type:* inventory (probate). *Entries:* 55; *Records:* 55.

Hodges, Thomas, B.A. (?–1539) PLRE 58. Scholar. Professional. *Date:* 1539. *Type:* inventory (probate). *Entries:* 28; *Records:* 33.

Hogan, Matthias. (?–1508) PLRE 12. Scholar (student). Professional. *Date:* 1508. *Type:* inventory (probate). *Entries:* 2; *Records:* 2.

Hooper, Robert, M.A. (?–c.1571) PLRE 93. Scholar. Professional. *Date:* 1571. *Type:* inventory (probate). *Entries:* 77; *Records:* 77.

Hoppe, Edward, M.A. (?–1538) PLRE 57. Scholar. Professional. *Date:* 1538. *Type:* will. *Entries:* 17; *Records:* 19.

Hornby, Nicholas, B.A., M.A. (perhaps). (?–?) PLRE Ad20. Scholar. Professional. *Date:* c.1532. *Type:* bookseller's accounts. *Entries:* 4; *Records:* 4.

Hornsley, John. (?–1578) PLRE 134. Scholar. Professional. *Date:* 1578. *Type:* inventory (probate). *Entries:* 89; *Records:* 91.

Horsley, Thomas. (?–?) PLRE Ad21. Scholar. Professional. *Date:* 1533. *Type:* bookseller's accounts. *Entries:* 4; *Records:* 4.

Horsman, Leonard, M.A. (?–1551) PLRE Ad22. Scholar. Professional. *Date:* 1531. *Type:* bookseller's account. *Entries:* 24; *Records:* 25.

Horsman, Ralph. (?–?) PLRE Ad23. Scholar (student). Professional. *Date:* 1531. *Type:* bookseller's accounts. *Entries:* 2; *Records:* 2.

Hunt, Robert, D.C.L., D.Th. (c.1499–1536) PLRE 53. Scholar. Professional. *Date:* 1536. *Type:* inventory (probate). *Entries:* 2; *Records:* 5.

Hurde, William. (?–1551) PLRE 62. Scholar (student). Professional. *Date:* 1551. *Type:* inventory (probate). *Entries:* 20; *Records:* 21.

Hutchinson, Henry, B.A. (1550–1573) PLRE 103. Scholar. Professional. *Date:* 1573. *Type:* inventory (probate). *Entries:* 99; *Records:* 99.

Jackson, Lionel, M.A. (?–1514) PLRE 33. Scholar. Professional. *Date:* 1514. *Type:* inventory (probate) and will. *Entries:* 32; *Records:* 33.

Jewel, John, D.Th. (1522–1571) PLRE Ad1. Cleric (bishop). Professional. *Date:* reconstruction. *Type:* reconstruction. *Entries:* 74; *Records:* 74.

Johnson, James. (?–1568) PLRE 77. Cleric (chaplain). Professional. *Date:* 1568. *Type:* inventory (probate). *Entries:* 4; *Records:* 4.

Johnson, Philip, B.Th. (?–1576) PLRE 110. Scholar. Professional. *Date:* 1576. *Type:* inventory (probate). *Entries:* 270; *Records:* 274.

Jones, Lewis, B.A. (?–1571) PLRE 94. Scholar. Professional. *Date:* 1571. *Type:* inventory (probate). *Entries:* 41; *Records:* 41.

Jones, Robert. (?–1567) PLRE 75. Sexton. Professional. *Date:* 1567. *Type:* inventory (probate). *Entries:* 23; *Records:* 27.

Kettelby, William, M.A. (?–c.1572) PLRE 104. Scholar. Professional. *Date:* 1573. *Type:* inventory (probate). *Entries:* 93; *Records:* 96.

Kitley, John, M.A. (?–1531) PLRE 49. Scholar. Professional. *Date:* 1531. *Type:* inventory (probate). *Entries:* 1; *Records:* 2.

Kitson, John, M.A. (?–1536) PLRE 54. Scholar. Professional. *Date:* 1536. *Type:* will. *Entries:* 1; *Records:* 1.

Kyffen, John, B.Cn.L. (?–1514) PLRE 34. Scholar. Professional. *Date:* 1514. *Type:* inventory (probate). *Entries:* 22; *Records:* 24.

Lacy, Dunstan, M.A. (?–1534) PLRE 52. Scholar. Professional. *Date:* 1534. *Type:* will. *Entries:* 27; *Records:* 29.

Lanham, Richard, B.A. (?–?) PLRE 105. Scholar. Professional. *Date:* 1573. *Type:* inventory. *Entries:* 4; *Records:* 4.

Lewis, John. (?–1579) PLRE 137. Manciple, Merchant (white-baker). Middle class, Privileged person. *Date:* 1579. *Type:* inventory (probate). *Entries:* 78; *Records:* 78.

Lilbourn, William, M.A. (?–1514) PLRE 35. Scholar. Professional. *Date:* 1514. *Type:* inventory (probate). *Entries:* 9; *Records:* 10.

Lisle (given name unknown). (?–?) PLRE 86. Scholar (student). Professional. *Date:* 1570. *Type:* inventory. *Entries:* 11; *Records:* 11.

Llewellyn, David ap. (?–?) PLRE Ad24. Cleric (friar). Professional. *Date:* 1533. *Type:* bookseller's accounts. *Entries:* 7; *Records:* 7.

Lombard, Nicholas, M.A. (?–1575) PLRE 107. Scholar. Professional. *Date:* 1575. *Type:* inventory (probate) and will. *Entries:* 131; *Records:* 132.

Ludby, Richard. (?–1567) PLRE 76. Cleric. Professional. *Date:* 1567. *Type:* inventory (probate). *Entries:* 25; *Records:* 25.

Lye, Richard. (?–1575) PLRE 108. Manciple. Professional, Privileged person. *Date:* 1575. *Type:* inventory (probate). *Entries:* 94; *Records:* 95.

Marshall, John, M.A. (?–1577) PLRE 126. Scholar. Professional. *Date:* 1577. *Type:* inventory (probate). *Entries:* 30; *Records:* 30.

Mason, Roger, B.Cn.L. (?–1513) PLRE 28. Scholar. Professional. *Date:* 1513. *Type:* inventory (probate). *Entries:* 1; *Records:* 1.

Maudesley, Thomas, B.A. (?–1571) PLRE 95. Scholar (student). Professional. *Date:* 1571. *Type:* inventory (probate). *Entries:* 17; *Records:* 17.

Merven, George, B.A. (?–1529) PLRE 46. Scholar. Professional. *Date:* 1529. *Type:* inventory (probate). *Entries:* 5; *Records:* 5.

Mitchell, John. (?–1572) PLRE 100. Servant. Retainer, Privileged person. *Date:* 1572. *Type:* inventory (probate). *Entries:* 11; *Records:* 11.

Morcote, John, M.A. (?–1508) PLRE 13. Scholar. Professional. *Date:* 1508. *Type:* inventory (probate). *Entries:* 75; *Records:* 80.

Morrey, Thomas, M.A. (?–1584) PLRE 142. Scholar. Professional. *Date:* 1584. *Type:* inventory (probate) and will. *Entries:* 158; *Records:* 161.

Morgan, Thomas. (?–?) PLRE 87. Scholar (student). Professional. *Date:* 1570. *Type:* inventory. *Entries:* 4; *Records:* 4.

Mychegood, Robert. (?–1508) PLRE 14. Cleric (probable). Professional (probable). *Date:* 1509. *Type:* inventory (probate). *Entries:* 8; *Records:* 8.

Napper, William, B.A. (c.1544–1569) PLRE 82. Scholar. Professional. *Date:* 1569. *Type:* inventory (probate). *Entries:* 118; *Records:* 118.

Neale, Thomas. (1553–1572) PLRE 101. Scholar (student). Professional. *Date:* 1572. *Type:* inventory (probate). *Entries:* 6; *Records:* 6.

Newby, Thomas, M.A. (1561–1587) PLRE 147. Scholar. Professional. *Date:* 1588. *Type:* inventory (probate). *Entries:* 45; *Records:* 45.

Pannell, William, M.A. (?–1537) PLRE Ad25. Scholar. Professional. *Date:* 1533. *Type:* bookseller's accounts. *Entries:* 14; *Records:* 15.

Pantry, John, M.A., D.Th. (?–1541) PLRE 59. Scholar. Professional. *Date:* 1541. *Type:* will and reconstruction. *Entries:* 3; *Records:* 3.

Parkin, Matthew, B.A. (1569–1589) PLRE 150. Scholar. Professional. *Date:* 1589. *Type:* inventory (probate). *Entries:* 80; *Records:* 89.

Peerpoynt, William. (?–?) PLRE Ad26. Scholar (student). Professional. *Date:* 1531. *Type:* bookseller's accounts. *Entries:* 6; *Records:* 6.

Petcher, Robert, M.A. (?–1507) PLRE 8. Scholar. Professional. *Date:* 1507. *Type:* will. *Entries:* 1; *Records:* 2.

Pope, Thomas, B.A. (?–1578) PLRE 135. Scholar. Professional. *Date:* 1578. *Type:* inventory (probate). *Entries:* 40; *Records:* 41.

Powell, James, M.A. (?–1575) PLRE 109. Scholar. Professional. *Date:* 1575. *Type:* inventory (probate). *Entries:* 42; *Records:* 42.

Price, John, B.Cn.L., B.C.L. (?–1554) PLRE 66. Scholar. Professional. *Date:* 1554. *Type:* inventory (probate). *Entries:* 17; *Records:* 25.

Purfrey, Anthony, B.C.L. (?–1527) PLRE 39. Scholar. Professional. *Date:* 1527. *Type:* inventory (probate). *Entries:* 7; *Records:* 7.

Purviar, Robert, M.A. (?–1536) PLRE 55. Scholar. Professional. *Date:* 1536. *Type:* will and reconstruction. *Entries:* 7; *Records:* 7.

Quarrendon, Thomas, B.C.L. (?–c.1507) PLRE 9. Scholar. Professional. *Date:* 1507. *Type:* inventory (probate). *Entries:* 14; *Records:* 15.

Rawson, Nicholas, B.Th. (?–1511) PLRE 20. Scholar. Professional. *Date:* 1511. *Type:* inventory (probate). *Entries:* 6; *Records:* 6.

Reynolds, James, M.A. (?–1577) PLRE 127. Scholar. Professional. *Date:* 1577. *Type:* inventory (probate). *Entries:* 229; *Records:* 231.

Reynolds, Jerome, M.A., B.M. (perhaps). (?–1571) PLRE 96. Scholar, Physician. Professional. *Date:* 1571. *Type:* inventory (probate). *Entries:* 108; *Records:* 108.

Reynolds, John, M.A. (?–1571) PLRE 97. Scholar. Professional. *Date:* 1571. *Type:* inventory (probate). *Entries:* 59; *Records:* 59.

Ringstead, Henry. (?–1561) PLRE Ad27. Appraiser. Privileged person. *Date:* 1533. *Type:* bookseller's acounts. *Entries:* 1; *Records:* 1.

Robinson, John. (?–1508) PLRE 15. Manciple. Professional, Privileged person. *Date:* 1508. *Type:* inventory (probate). *Entries:* 2; *Records:* 2.

Robinson, John, M.A. (?–1511) PLRE 21. Scholar. Professional. *Date:* 1511. *Type:* inventory (probate). *Entries:* 6; *Records:* 6.

Rothley, John, B.Cn.L., B.C.L. (?–1511) PLRE 22. Scholar. Professional. *Date:* 1507. *Type:* inventory. *Entries:* 23; *Records:* 24.

Roxburgh, John, M.A. (?–1509) PLRE 18. Scholar. Professional. *Date:* 1509. *Type:* inventory (probate). *Entries:* 1; *Records:* 1.

Ruckwood, Thomas. (?–1581) PLRE 139. Cleric, Scholar. Professional. *Date:* 1581. *Type:* inventory (probate). *Entries:* 43; *Records:* 43.

Scott, Alan, M.A. (?–1578) PLRE 136. Cleric, Scholar. Professional. *Date:* 1578. *Type:* inventory (probate). *Entries:* 44; *Records:* 44.

Seacole, Richard, B.A. (1550–1577) PLRE 128. Scholar. Professional. *Date:* 1577. *Type:* inventory (probate). *Entries:* 123; *Records:* 125.

Shoesmith, John. (?–1568) PLRE 78. Profession unknown. Privileged person (probable). *Date:* 1568. *Type:* inventory (probate). *Entries:* 11; *Records:* 11.

Sibthorpe, Henry. (?–c.1664) (and Lady Anne Southwell) PLRE Ad3. Soldier, Statesman. Gentry. *Date:* c.1640, c.1650. *Type:* inventory. *Entries:* 110; *Records:* 110.

Simons, Thomas, M.A., B.M. (?–1553) PLRE 65. Scholar. Professional. *Date:* 1553. *Type:* inventory (probate). *Entries:* 131; *Records:* 143.

Simpson, John, M.A. (?–1577) PLRE 129. Scholar. Professional. *Date:* 1577. *Type:* inventory (probate). *Entries:* 130; *Records:* 130.

Singleton, Robert, M.A. (?–1577) PLRE 130. Scholar. Professional. *Date:* 1577. *Type:* inventory (probate). *Entries:* 119; *Records:* 120.

Slatter, Richard, M.A. (?–?) PLRE 111. Scholar. Professional. *Date:* 1576. *Type:* inventory. *Entries:* 12; *Records:* 12.

Smallwood, William, M.A. (?–?) PLRE 102. Scholar. Professional. *Date:* 1572. *Type:* inventory. *Entries:* 17; *Records:* 17.

Southwell, Lady Anne. (?–1636) (see Henry Sibthorpe).

Stanhope, Sir Edward, D.U.L. (c.1546–1608) PLRE 2. Lawyer. Nobility. *Date:* c.1612. *Type:* will and reconstruction. *Entries:* 161; *Records:* 207.

Stanley, Thomas, B.A. (?–1577) PLRE 131. Scholar. Professional. *Date:* 1577. *Type:* inventory (probate). *Entries:* 40; *Records:* 40.

Stocker, William, M.A. (?–?) PLRE 88. Scholar. Professional. *Date:* c.1570. *Type:* inventory. *Entries:* 23; *Records:* 23.

Stonely, Richard. (c.1520–1600) PLRE Ad4. Court official (Teller of the Exchequer). Gentry. *Date:* 1597. *Type:* inventory against debt. *Entries:* 412; *Records:* 418.

Sykes, Nicholas. (?–1562) PLRE 71. Butler. Retainer, Privileged person. *Date:* 1562. *Type:* inventory (probate). *Entries:* 42; *Records:* 42.

Talley, Abbot of. (?–?) PLRE 42. Cleric (monk). Professional. *Date:* 1528. *Type:* inventory. *Entries:* 2; *Records:* 3.

Tatham, John, M.A. (?–1576) PLRE 112. Scholar. Professional. *Date:* 1576. *Type:* inventory (probate). *Entries:* 222; *Records:* 222.

Tatham, Thomas, M.A. (?–1586) PLRE 146. Scholar. Professional. *Date:* 1586. *Type:* inventory (probate). *Entries:* 360; *Records:* 373.

Thixtell, John, B.Th. (?–1541) PLRE Ad28. Scholar. Professional. *Date:* 1528. *Type:* bookseller's accounts. *Entries:* 14; *Records:* 15.

Thomson, Thomas, M.A. (?–1514) PLRE 36. Scholar. Professional. *Date:* 1514. *Type:* will. *Entries:* 14; *Records:* 17.

Thomson, William, M.A. (?–1507) PLRE 10. Scholar. Professional. *Date:* 1507. *Type:* inventory (probate). *Entries:* 30; *Records:* 30.

Thornbury, Thomas. (?–1570) PLRE 89. Scholar (student, perhaps). Professional. *Date:* 1570. *Type:* inventory (probate). *Entries:* 5; *Records:* 5.

Tichborne (given name unknown), B.C.L. (probable). (?–?) PLRE 90. Scholar. Professional. *Date:* 1570. *Type:* inventory. *Entries:* 93; *Records:* 93.

Tolley, David, M.A., B.M. (c.1506–1558) PLRE 68. Physician. Professional. *Date:* 1558. *Type:* inventory (probate). *Entries:* 50; *Records:* 50.

Townrow, Henry, B.A. (?–1565) PLRE 72. Scholar. Professional. *Date:* 1565. *Type:* inventory (probate). *Entries:* 18; *Records:* 18.

Townshend, Sir Roger. (1596–1636) PLRE 3. Member of Parliament. Gentry. *Date:* c.1625. *Type:* inventory. *Entries:* 286; *Records:* 296.

Tye, Anthony, M.A. (?–1584) PLRE 143. Scholar. Professional. *Date:* 1584. *Type:* inventory (probate). *Entries:* 106; *Records:* 109.

Upton, William, M.A., B.Th. (perhaps). (?–1527) PLRE 40. Scholar. Professional. *Date:* 1527. *Type:* will. *Entries:* 1; *Records:* 1.

Wicking, John. (?–1551) PLRE 63. Almsman. Retainer. *Date:* 1551. *Type:* inventory (probate) and will. *Entries:* 1; *Records:* 1.

Wood, Richard, M.A. (?–1508) PLRE 16. Scholar. Professional. *Date:* 1508. *Type:* inventory (probate). *Entries:* 13; *Records:* 13.

Woodruff, William, M.A. (?–?) PLRE 47. Scholar. Professional. *Date:* 1529. *Type:* inventory. *Entries:* 35; *Records:* 35.

Yardley, William, B.Cn.L., B.C.L. (?–1530) PLRE 48. Scholar. Professional. *Date:* 1530. *Type:* inventory (probate). *Entries:* 11; *Records:* 11.

C. Owners of Book-lists According to PLRE Number

1. LISTS IN PLRE VOLUMES

PLRE 1: Cox, Richard, D.Th.
PLRE 2: Stanhope, Sir Edward, D.U.L.
PLRE 3: Townshend, Sir Roger
PLRE 4: Dering, Sir Edward
PLRE 5: Bowerman, John, M.A., B.C.L.
PLRE 6: Chantry, William, B.A.

PLRE 7: Gofton, William, B.C.L.
PLRE 8: Petcher, Robert, M.A.
PLRE 9: Quarrendon, Thomas, B.C.L.
PLRE 10: Thomson, William, M.A.
PLRE 11: Bryan, Robert, D.Cn.L.
PLRE 12: Hogan, Matthias
PLRE 13: Morcote, John, M.A.
PLRE 14: Mychegood, Robert
PLRE 15: Robinson, John
PLRE 16: Wood, Richard, M.A.
PLRE 17: Carter, John, B.C.L.
PLRE 18: Roxburgh, John, M.A.
PLRE 19: Griffin, Roger, B.A.
PLRE 20: Rawson, Nicholas, B.Th.
PLRE 21: Robinson, John, M.A.
PLRE 22: Rothley, John, B.Cn.L., B.C.L.
PLRE 23: Bidnell, William, M.A.
PLRE 24: Collins, Robert
PLRE 25: Balyn, John, B.A.
PLRE 26: Chastelain, George
PLRE 27: Hartburn, John, M.A.
PLRE 28: Mason, Roger, B.Cn.L.
PLRE 29: Balborough, William, D.U.L.
PLRE 30: Dewer, William, M.A. (probable)
PLRE 31: Froster, Roger
PLRE 32: Heywood, John, B.A.
PLRE 33: Jackson, Lionel, M.A.
PLRE 34: Kyffen, John, B.Cn.L.
PLRE 35: Lilbourn, William, M.A.
PLRE 36: Thomson, Thomas, M.A.
PLRE 37: Deegen, Peter
PLRE 38: Hawarden, Robert, M.A.
PLRE 39: Purfrey, Anthony, B.C.L.
PLRE 40: Upton, William, M.A., B.Th. (perhaps)
PLRE 41: Gryce, William, D.Th.
PLRE 42: Talley, Abbot of
PLRE 43: Burton, Edmund, M.A.
PLRE 44: Coles, John, B.Th.
PLRE 45: Dalaber, Anthony
PLRE 46: Merven, George, B.A.
PLRE 47: Woodruff, William, M.A.
PLRE 48: Yardley, William, B.Cn.L., B.C.L.
PLRE 49: Kitley, John, M.A.
PLRE 50: Cartwright, Thomas, M.A.
PLRE 51: Hamlyn, William, M.A.
PLRE 52: Lacy, Dunstan, M.A.
PLRE 53: Hunt, Robert, D.C.L., D.Th.
PLRE 54: Kitson, John, M.A.

PLRE 55: Purviar, Robert, M.A.
PLRE 56: Chogan, William
PLRE 57: Hoppe, Edward, M.A.
PLRE 58: Hodges, Thomas, B.A.
PLRE 59: Pantry, John, M.A., D.Th.
PLRE 60: Bisley, M.A. (perhaps), B.Th. (perhaps)
PLRE 61: Derbyshire, William
PLRE 62: Hurde, William
PLRE 63: Wicking, John
PLRE 64: Beaumont, Edward, B.A.
PLRE 65: Simons, Thomas, M.A., B.M.
PLRE 66: Price, John, B.Cn.L., B.C.L.
PLRE 67: Brown, William, M.A.
PLRE 68: Tolley, David, M.A., B.M.
PLRE 69: Allen, Thomas, B.A.
PLRE 70: Griffith, Thomas, M.A., B.M. (perhaps)
PLRE 71: Sykes, Nicholas
PLRE 72: Townrow, Henry, B.A.
PLRE 73: Cliff, Richard, M.A.
PLRE 74: Bury, John, B.A. (probable)
PLRE 75: Jones, Robert
PLRE 76: Ludby, Richard
PLRE 77: Johnson, James
PLRE 78: Shoesmith, John
PLRE 79: Allen, Richard, B.A.
PLRE 80: Conner, John, B.Th.
PLRE 81: Digby, George and Simon
PLRE 82: Napper, William, B.A.
PLRE 83: Atkinson, John, M.A.
PLRE 84: Day, Thomas, B.C.L.
PLRE 85: Dunnet, John
PLRE 86: Lisle
PLRE 87: Morgan, Thomas
PLRE 88: Stocker, William, M.A.
PLRE 89: Thornbury, Thomas
PLRE 90: Tichborne, B.C.L. (probable)
PLRE 91: Beddow, John, M.A.
PLRE 92: Hart, Robert, M.A.
PLRE 93: Hooper, Robert, M.A.
PLRE 94: Jones, Lewis, B.A.
PLRE 95: Maudesley, Thomas, B.A.
PLRE 96: Reynolds, Jerome, B.A., B.M. (perhaps)
PLRE 97: Reynolds, John, M.A.
PLRE 98: Austin
PLRE 99: Battbrantes, William
PLRE 100: Mitchell, John
PLRE 101: Neale, Thomas
PLRE 102: Smallwood, Thomas, M.A.

CUMULATIVE CATALOGUE 269

PLRE 103: Hutchinson, Henry, B.A.
PLRE 104: Kettelby, William, M.A.
PLRE 105: Lanham, Richard, B.A.
PLRE 106: Dyllam, Walter
PLRE 107: Lombard, Nicholas, M.A.
PLRE 108: Lye, Richard
PLRE 109: Powell, James, M.A.
PLRE 110: Johnson, Philip, B.Th.
PLRE 111: Slatter, Richard, M.A.
PLRE 112: Tatham, John, M.A.
PLRE 113: Atkins, Henry, M.A.
PLRE 114: Grant, Philip
PLRE 115: Badger, John, M.A.
PLRE 116: Carpenter, Thomas, M.A.
PLRE 117: Charnock, Roger, M.A.
PLRE 118: Cliffley
PLRE 119: Dawson, William, M.A.
PLRE 120: Dayrell, William, B.A.
PLRE 121: Dewhurst, Giles, M.A.
PLRE 122: Faringdon, Tristram
PLRE 123: Ferne, Richard, M.A.
PLRE 124: Foster, Thomas
PLRE 125: Gray, John
PLRE 126: Marshall, John, M.A.
PLRE 127: Reynolds, James, M.A.
PLRE 128: Seacole, Richard, B.A.
PLRE 129: Simpson, John, M.A.
PLRE 130: Singleton, Robert, M.A.
PLRE 131: Stanley, Thomas, B.A.
PLRE 132: Bolt, Thomas
PLRE 133: Glover, John, M.A.
PLRE 134: Hornsley, John, M.A.
PLRE 135: Pope, Thomas, M.A.
PLRE 136: Scott, Alan, M.A.
PLRE 137: Lewis, John
PLRE 138: Cheyne, Henry
PLRE 139: Ruckwood, Thomas
PLRE 140: Heath, John
PLRE 141: Forster, John
PLRE 142: Morrey, Thomas
PLRE 143: Tye, Anthony
PLRE 144: Haynes, John
PLRE 145: Hill, Thomas
PLRE 146: Tatham, Thomas
PLRE 147: Newby, Thomas
PLRE 148: Dowe, Robert
PLRE 149: Higgins, Edward
PLRE 150: Parkin, Matthew

2. APND LISTS

[The source of each book-list follows the name of the owner. In the case of groups of lists from one source, the reference may precede the group.]

PLRE Ad1: Jewel, John, Bishop, D.Th.
  (Neil Ker, "The Library of John Jewel." *Bodleian Library Record* [1977] 9:256–65.)
PLRE Ad2: Blomefield, Miles.
  (Donald Baker and J. L. Murphy, "The Books of Myles Blomefylde." *The Library*, 5th ser. [1976] 31:374–85; John C. Coldewey, "Myles Blomefylde's Library: Another Book." *English Language Notes* [1977] 14:249–50.)
PLRE Ad3: Sibthorpe, Captain Henry (and Lady Anne Southwell).
  (Sister Jean Carmel Cavanaugh, S. L., "The Library of Lady Southwell and Captain Sibthorpe." *Studies in Bibliography* [1967] 20:243–54).
PLRE Ad4: Stonely, Richard.
  (Leslie Hotson, "The Library of Elizabeth's Embezzling Teller." *Studies in Bibliography* [1949] 2:49–61).

APND lists PLRE Ad5–Ad28 are taken from: Elisabeth Leedham-Green, D. E. Rhodes, and F. H. Stubbings. *Garrett Godfrey's Accounts c. 1527–1533*. Cambridge Bibliographical Society, Monograph no. 12. Cambridge: Cambridge University Library, 1992. [*Note:* Degrees assigned are senior degrees that had been earned when books were purchased.]

PLRE Ad5: Anlaby (Aulaby), Edmund (some entries drawn from BCI 1:244–45), M.A. (1533), B.Th. (1559)
PLRE Ad6: Batchelor, Robert
PLRE Ad7: Bill, Thomas, M.A.
PLRE Ad8: Bonenfant, Thomas, M.A.
PLRE Ad9: Bradford, Ralph, M.A.
PLRE Ad10: Brewer, John, M.A.
PLRE Ad11: Bromsby, John, B.Th.
PLRE Ad12: Buckingham, Edward, B.Cn.L.
PLRE Ad13: Cauthorn, John, B.A.
PLRE Ad14: Davy, William (perhaps), B.A.
PLRE Ad15: Dickinson, Thomas (probable), B.A.
PLRE Ad16: Gilbert, John
PLRE Ad17: Goldsmith, Francis
PLRE Ad18: Harwood, Thomas, B.A., D.M.
PLRE Ad19: Hilbert, Nicholas
PLRE Ad20: Hornby, Nicholas, M.A.
PLRE Ad21: Horsley, Thomas
PLRE Ad22: Horsman, Leonard, M.A.
PLRE Ad23: Horsman, Ralph
PLRE Ad24: Llewellyn, David ap
PLRE Ad25: Pannell, William, M.A.
PLRE Ad26: Peerpoynt, William
PLRE Ad27: Ringstead, Henry

PLRE Ad28: Thixtell, John, B.Th.
PLRE Ad29: Barwyck, Stephen (BCI 1:93–94)
PLRE Ad30: Cheke, Agnes (BCI 1:101–2)

D. Dates of Book-lists (actual or *terminus ad quem*), with PLRE Number

1507:	PLRE 5, 6, 7, 8, 9, 10, 22
1508:	PLRE 11, 12, 13, 15, 16
1509:	PLRE 14, 17, 18
1510:	PLRE 19
1511:	PLRE 20, 21
1512:	PLRE 23, 24
1513:	PLRE 25, 26, 27, 28
1514:	PLRE 29, 30, 31, 32, 33, 34, 35, 36
1527:	PLRE 37, 38, 39
c.1527:	PLRE Ad9
1528:	PLRE 40, 41, 42, Ad19, Ad28
1529:	PLRE 43, 44, 45, 46, 47
1530:	PLRE 48, Ad18
1531:	PLRE 49, Ad11, Ad13, Ad22, Ad23, Ad26
1532:	PLRE 50, Ad7
c.1532:	PLRE Ad20
1533:	PLRE Ad5 (part), Ad6, Ad8, Ad10, Ad12, Ad14, Ad15, Ad16, Ad17, Ad21, Ad24, Ad25, Ad27
1534:	PLRE 51, 52
1536:	PLRE 53, 54, 55
1537:	PLRE 56
1538:	PLRE 57
1539:	PLRE 58
1541:	PLRE 59
1543:	PLRE 60
1547:	PLRE Ad29
1549:	PLRE Ad30
1551:	PLRE 61, 62, 63
1552:	PLRE 64
1553:	PLRE 65
1554:	PLRE 66
1558:	PLRE 67, 68
1559:	PLRE Ad5 (part)
1560:	PLRE 113, 114
1561:	PLRE 69
1562:	PLRE 70, 71
1565:	PLRE 72
1566:	PLRE 73
1567:	PLRE 74, 75, 76
1568:	PLRE 77, 78
1569:	PLRE 79, 80, 81, 82, 90 (part)

1570:	PLRE 83, 84, 85, 86, 87, 88, 89, 90
1571:	PLRE 91, 92, 93, 94, 95, 96, 97
1572:	PLRE 98, 99, 100, 101, 102
1573:	PLRE 103, 104, 105
1575:	PLRE 106, 107, 108, 109
1576:	PLRE 110, 111, 112
1577:	PLRE 91 (part), 115, 116, 117, 118, 119, 120, 121, 122, 123, 124, 125, 126, 127, 128, 129, 130, 131
1578:	PLRE 132, 133, 134, 135, 136
1579:	PLRE 137
1581:	PLRE 1, 138, 139
1582:	PLRE 140
1584:	PLRE 141, 142, 143
1585:	PLRE 144, 145
1586:	PLRE 146
1587:	PLRE 147
1588:	PLRE 148, 149
1589:	PLRE 150
1597:	PLRE Ad4
c.1612:	PLRE 2
c.1625:	PLRE 3
1628:	PLRE 4 (part)
c.1640:	PLRE Ad3 (part)
c.1642:	PLRE 4 (part)
c.1650:	PLRE Ad3 (part)
No date (reconstruction):	
	PLRE 2 (part), 4 (part), 55 (part), 59 (part), Ad1, Ad2

III. Summaries and Concordances

A. Manuscript Types

1. RECORD TOTALS FROM EACH MANUSCRIPT TYPE

Account book:	177
Bookseller's accounts:	188
Catalogue:	503
Inventory:	1,157
Inventory (against debt):	461
Inventory (probate):	6,961
Inventory (probate) and Will:	86
Memorial book (benefaction):	200
Receipt:	8
Will:	58
No manuscript (reconstruction):	112

CUMULATIVE CATALOGUE 273

2. NUMBER OF MANUSCRIPT TYPES PROVIDING BOOK-LISTS
(*Some lists derive from more than one manuscript type.*)

Account book:	1
Bookseller's accounts:	23
Catalogue:	1
Inventory:	21
Inventory (against debt):	2
Inventory (probate):	111
Inventory (probate) and Will:	7
Memorial book (benefaction):	1
Receipt:	1
Will:	16
No manuscript (reconstruction):	4

3. MANUSCRIPT TYPES ACCORDING TO PLRE NUMBERS
(*Some lists derive from more than one manuscript type.*)

Account book: PLRE 4 (part)
Bookseller's accounts: PLRE Ad5 (part), Ad6, Ad7, Ad8, Ad9, Ad10, Ad11, Ad12, Ad13, Ad14, Ad15, Ad16, Ad17, Ad18, Ad19, Ad20, Ad21, Ad22, Ad23, Ad24, Ad25, Ad26, Ad27, Ad28
Catalogue: PLRE 4 (part)
Inventory: PLRE 1, 3, 22, 42, 45, 47, 81, 86, 87, 88, 90, 91, 98, 102, 105, 106, 111, 117, 118, 132, 140, Ad3
Inventory (against debt): PLRE 138, Ad4
Inventory (probate): PLRE 7, 9, 10, 11, 12, 13 (part), 14, 15, 16, 17, 18, 19, 20, 21, 23, 25, 26, 27, 28, 29, 30 (part), 31, 32, 34, 35, 36 (part), 38, 39, 41, 43, 44, 46, 48, 49, 51, 53, 57 (part), 58, 60, 61, 62, 64 (part), 65, 66, 67, 68, 69, 70, 71, 72, 73 (part), 74, 75, 76, 77, 78, 79, 80, 82, 83, 84, 85, 89, 92, 93, 94, 95, 96, 97, 99, 100, 101, 103, 104, 107 (part), 108, 109, 110, 112, 113, 114, 115, 116, 119, 120, 121, 122, 123, 124, 125, 126, 127, 128, 129, 130, 131, 133, 134, 135, 136, 137, 139, 141, 142, 143, 144, 145, 146, 147, 148, 149, 150, Ad5 (part), Ad30
Inventory (probate) and Will: PLRE 33 (part), 50, 52 (part), 57, 63, 64 (part), 107 (part)
Memorial book (benefaction): PLRE 2 (part)
Receipt: PLRE 24
Will: PLRE 5, 6, 8, 13 (part), 30 (part), 33 (part), 36 (part), 37, 40, 52 (part), 54, 55 (part), 56, 57 (part), 59 (part), 73 (part)
No manuscript (reconstruction): (See also Account book, Catalogue, Memorial book, and Will) PLRE 2 (part), 4 (part), 55 (part), 59 (part), Ad1, Ad2

B. Renaissance Locations of Book-lists

1. RECORD TOTALS FOR EACH LOCATION

Cambridgeshire, Cambridge:	464
Cambridgeshire, Downham:	187
Cambridgeshire, Fenstanton:	21
Kent, Surrenden:	680
London:	418
Middlesex, Acton:	110
Norfolk:	296
Northamptonshire, Brackley:	2
Oxfordshire, Oxford:	7,631
No Renaissance location (reconstruction):	112

2. PLRE NUMBERS OF LISTS IN EACH LOCATION

Cambridgeshire, Cambridge: PLRE 2, Ad5, Ad6, Ad7, Ad8, Ad9, Ad10, Ad11, Ad12, Ad13, Ad14, Ad15, Ad16, Ad17, Ad18, Ad19, Ad20, Ad21, Ad22, Ad23, Ad24, Ad25, Ad26, Ad27, Ad28, Ad29, Ad30

Cambridgeshire, Downham: PLRE 1 (part)

Cambridgeshire, Fenstanton: PLRE 1 (part)

Kent, Surrenden: PLRE 4

London: PLRE Ad4

Middlesex, Acton: PLRE Ad3

Norfolk: PLRE 3

Northamptonshire, Brackley: PLRE 91 (part)

Oxfordshire, Oxford: PLRE 5, 6, 7, 8, 9, 10, 11, 12, 13, 14, 15, 16, 17, 18, 19, 20, 21, 22, 23, 24, 25, 26, 27, 28, 29, 30, 31, 32, 33, 34, 35, 36, 37, 38, 39, 40, 41, 42, 43, 44, 45, 46, 47, 48, 49, 50, 51, 52, 53, 54, 55, 56, 57, 58, 59, 60, 61, 62, 63, 64, 65, 66, 67, 68, 69, 70, 71, 72, 73, 74, 75, 76, 77, 78, 79, 80, 81, 82, 83, 84, 85, 86, 87, 88, 89, 90, 91 (part), 92, 93, 94, 95, 96, 97, 98, 99, 100, 101, 102, 103, 104, 105, 106, 107, 108, 109, 110, 111, 112, 113, 114, 115, 116, 117, 118, 119, 120, 121, 122, 123, 124, 125, 126, 127, 128, 129, 130, 131, 132, 133, 134, 135, 136, 137, 138, 139, 140, 141, 142, 143, 144, 145, 146, 147, 148, 149, 150

No Renaissance location (reconstruction): PLRE 2 (part), 4 (part), 55 (part), 59 (part), Ad1, Ad2

C. Professions of Owners

1. TOTALS OF PROFESSIONS REPRESENTED

Alchemist (see Physician)	
Almsman:	1
Appraiser:	1
Butler:	2
Cleric:	1

CUMULATIVE CATALOGUE 275

Cleric (probable):	2
Cleric (bishop):	1
Cleric (chaplain):	3
Cleric (friar):	1
Cleric (monk):	1
Cleric, Scholar:	3
Court Official:	1
Lawyer:	1
Manciple:	3
Merchant (vintner):	1
Merchant (white-baker)	1
Member of Parliament:	2
Physician:	1
Physician, Alchemist:	1
Physician, Scholar:	2
Physician (perhaps), Scholar:	1
Scholar:	100
(see also Cleric, Physician, Schoolmaster)	
Scholar (student):	22
Schoolmaster, Scholar:	1
Servant:	1
Sexton:	1
Soldier, Statesman:	1
Statesman (see Soldier)	
Stationer:	1
Unknown:	2

2. NUMBER OF RECORDS LISTED FOR EACH PROFESSION

Alchemist (see Physician)	
Almsman:	1
Appraiser:	1
Butler:	78
Cleric:	25
Cleric (probable):	30
Cleric (bishop):	282
Cleric (chaplain):	275
Cleric (friar):	7
Cleric (monk):	3
Cleric, Scholar:	241
Court Official:	418
Lawyer:	207
Manciple:	175
Merchant (vintner):	4
Merchant (white-baker):	78
Member of Parliament:	979
Physician:	50
Physician, Alchemist:	25

Physician, Scholar:	112
Physician (perhaps), Scholar:	97
Scholar:	6,234
(see also Cleric, Physician, Schoolmaster)	
Scholar (student):	459
Schoolmaster, Scholar:	41
Servant:	11
Sexton:	27
Soldier, Statesman:	110
Statesman (see Soldier)	
Stationer:	1
Unknown:	11

3. BOOK-LISTS BY PROFESSIONS, WITH PLRE NUMBERS

Alchemist (see Physician)
Almsman: PLRE 63
Appraiser: PLRE Ad27
Butler: PLRE 71, Ad29
Cleric: PLRE 76
Cleric (probable): PLRE 14
Cleric (bishop): PLRE 1, Ad1
Cleric (chaplain): PLRE 73, 77, Ad6
Cleric (friar): PLRE Ad24
Cleric (monk): PLRE 42
Cleric, Scholar: PLRE 80, 84, 136
Court Official: PLRE Ad4
Lawyer: PLRE 2
Manciple: PLRE 15, 108, 137
Member of Parliament: PLRE 3, 4
Merchant (vintner): PLRE Ad30
Merchant (white-baker): PLRE 137
Physician: PLRE 50
Physician, Alchemist: PLRE Ad2
Physician, Scholar: PLRE 96, Ad7
Physician (perhaps), Scholar: PLRE 70
Scholar (see also Cleric, Physician, Schoolmaster): PLRE 5, 6, 7, 8, 9, 10, 11, 13, 16, 17, 18, 19, 20, 21, 22, 23, 25, 27, 28, 29, 30, 32, 33, 34, 35, 36, 38, 39, 40, 41, 43, 44, 46, 47, 48, 49, 50, 51, 52, 53, 54, 55, 57, 58, 59, 60, 64, 65, 66, 67, 69, 72, 74, 79, 82, 83, 88, 90, 92, 93, 94, 97, 102, 103, 104, 105, 107, 109, 110, 111, 112, 113, 115, 116, 117, 118, 119, 120, 121, 122, 123, 125, 126, 127, 128, 129, 130, 131, 132, 133, 134, 135, 138, 140, 141, 142, 143, 144, 145, 146, 147, 148, 149, 150, Ad5, Ad8, Ad9, Ad10, Ad11, Ad12, Ad13, Ad14, Ad15, Ad18, Ad20, Ad21, Ad22, Ad23, Ad25, Ad28
Scholar (student): PLRE 12, 24, 31, 37, 45, 56, 61, 62, 83, 85, 86, 87, 89, 95, 98, 99, 101, 106, 114, 139, Ad16, Ad17, Ad19, Ad26
Schoolmaster, Scholar: PLRE 91
Servant: PLRE 100

Sexton: PLRE 75
Soldier, Statesman: PLRE Ad3
Statesman (see Soldier)
Stationer: PLRE 26
Unknown: PLRE 78, 124

D. Social Status of Owners

1. TOTAL OF RECORDS IN PLRE DATABASE

Gentry:	1,715
Middle class:	83
Nobility:	207
Privileged person (with others):	200
Privileged person (probable):	20
Professional:	7,749
Professional (probable):	85
Retainer:	90

2. BOOK-LISTS BY SOCIAL STATUS, WITH PLRE NUMBERS

Gentry: PLRE 1, 3, 4, Ad3, Ad4
Middle class: PLRE 26, 137, Ad30
Nobility: PLRE 2
Privileged person (sometimes with others): PLRE 71, 100, 108, Ad27, Ad30
Privileged person (probable): PLRE 78, 124
Professional: PLRE 5, 6, 7, 8, 9, 10, 11, 12, 13, 15, 16, 17, 18, 19, 20, 21, 22, 23, 24, 25, 27, 28, 29, 30, 31, 32, 33, 34, 35, 36, 37, 38, 39, 40, 41, 42, 43, 44, 45, 46, 47, 48, 49, 50, 51, 52, 53, 54, 55, 56, 57, 58, 59, 60, 61, 62, 67, 68, 69, 70, 72, 73, 74, 75, 76, 77, 79, 80, 81, 82, 83, 84, 85, 86, 87, 88, 89, 90, 91, 92, 93, 94, 95, 96, 97, 98, 99, 101, 102, 103, 104, 105, 106, 107, 109, 110, 111, 112, 113, 114, 115, 116, 117, 118, 119, 120, 121, 122, 123, 125, 126, 127, 128, 129, 130, 131, 132, 133, 134, 135, 136, 138, 139, 140, 141, 142, 143, 144, 146, 147, 148, 149, 150, Ad1, Ad2, Ad5, Ad6, Ad7, Ad8, Ad9, Ad10, Ad11, Ad12, Ad13, Ad14, Ad15, Ad16, Ad17, Ad18, Ad19, Ad20, Ad21, Ad22, Ad23, Ad24, Ad25, Ad26, Ad28
Professional (probable): PLRE 14, 118, 145
Retainer: PLRE 63, 71, 100, Ad29

Additions and Corrections

The following entries in Volumes 1–5 have been revised to include additions and corrections, both substantive and accidental, that have been made to the PLRE database since the publication of Volume 5. A correction to a Volume 5 index follows the revised entries.

3.1   The praise of Follye in 4°.
Desiderius Erasmus. *The praise of folie. Moriae encomium.* Translated by Sir Thomas Chaloner, *the Elder*. London: (different houses), 1549–1577.
STC 10500 et seq. *Language(s)*: English.

92.70   Arithmetica Tonstalli
Cuthbert Tunstall, *Bishop*. *De arte supputandi libri quattuor*. Britain or Continent: 1522–1551.
STC 24319 and non-STC. See notes to 92.41. *Language(s)*: Latin. Appraised at 12d in 1571.

92.135   Serebeus orator
Jacobus Lodovicus Strebaeus. Unidentified. Continent: date indeterminable.
Possibilities include *De partibus oratoriae M.T. Ciceronis, De electione et oratoria collocatione verborum*, and *In dialogos Ciceronis de oratore commentaria*. *Language(s)*: Latin. Appraised at 2s in 1571.

97.45   Curio in Topica
Caelius Secundus Curio. [*Cicero—Topica: commentary*]. Basle: [J. Oporinus], 1550–1556.
Language(s): Latin. Appraised at 6d in 1571.

103.25   Nowell against dorman
Alexander Nowell. Unidentified. London: (different houses), 1565–1567.
STC 18739 et seq. Several possibilities among Nowell's Protestant rejoinders to Roman Catholic Thomas Dorman. *Language(s)*: English. Appraised at 2d in 1573.

103.60 Talaei rhetorica
Audomarus Talaeus (Omer Talon). *Rhetorica*. Continent: date indeterminable. Generally agreed that Ramus had a major role in the composition of this work. *Language(s)*: Latin. Appraised at 2d in 1573.

110.66 ozorius de justicia
Jeronimo Osorio da Fonseca, *Bishop*. *De justitia*. Continent: 1564–1574. *Language(s)*: Latin. Appraised at 8d in 1576.

110.240 de furoribus galliae
François Hotman. *De furoribus Gallicis*. Britain or Continent: 1573.
STC 13844 et seq. At least two editions, one from Basle, the other from London, with Edinburgh falsely given in imprint. *Language(s)*: Latin. Appraised at 2d in 1576.

116.40 Osorius contra Haddonum
Jeronimo Osorio da Fonseca, *Bishop*. *In Gualterum Haddonum magistrum libellorum supplicum libri tres*. Continent: 1567–1576.
Probably not an STC book, but see STC 18889. An English version of Osorio's reply was published in Louvain. *Language(s)*: Latin (probable). Appraised at 8d in 1577.

123.23 Cathekismus Calvini
Jean Calvin. *[Catechism]*. Britain or Continent: 1538–1575.
STC 4375 and non-STC. *Language(s)*: Latin. Appraised at 12d in 1577.

130.4 Foxii Martires latine
John Foxe, *the Martyrologist*. *Rerum in ecclesia gestarum commentarii*. Continent: 1554–1563.
Shaaber F183–186. *Language(s)*: Latin. Appraised at 2s in 1577.

132.74 cathechismus Calvini
Jean Calvin. *[Catechism]*. Britain or Continent: date indeterminable.
STC 4375 *et seq.* and non-STC. *Language(s)*: Latin (probable). Appraised at 1d in 1578.

112.119 gortius de figuris
Jacobus Gorscius. *De figuris, tum grammaticis, tum rhetoricis, libri V*. Cracow: in officina typographica Matthaei Siebeneycher, 1560.
Language(s): Latin. Appraised at 6d in 1576.

Volume 5 *Index I* (Authors and Works)
For: Erasmus, Desiderius ... *Enchiridion militis Christiani*: 114.15; 120.106; 123.37
Read: Erasmus, Desiderius ... *Enchiridion militis Christiani*: 114.15; 130.106; 123.37

ADDITIONS AND CORRECTIONS

ADDRESSES FOR REQUESTING DATA
OR FOR SENDING CORRECTIONS

R. J. Fehrenbach
Department of English
College of William and Mary
Williamsburg, VA 23187–8795 USA

E. S. Leedham-Green
Darwin College
Silver Street
Cambridge CB3 9EU UK

Index I
Authors and Works

The words *perhaps* and *probable* indicate degrees of doubt about an identification. Names and titles appear in accordance with the methodology described in the introduction to this volume. A search of the database, available upon request, will provide more detailed information, including cross-referencing, than can be offered here.

Abbreviamentum statutorum: 148.132
abstract of all the penall statutes, An: 146.237
Acciaiolus, Donatus. *Aristotle–Ethica: commentary*: 145.13
Achillinus, Alexander. *Works*: 138.39
Acta Concilii Tridentini: 148.297; (probable) 147.18
Actuarius, Joannes. *De urinis*: 143.100
Aegidius Columna, Romanus. *Aristotle–Physica: commentary*: 146.12
Aelianus, Claudius. *Varia historia*: 146.89; 148.243
Aeschines. *Selected works–Orations*: 145.31; 146.183:1; 146.183:2
Aeschylus. *Works*: 143.57; 144.56
Aesop. *Fabulae*: 143.36; 144.67; 148.32

Agricola, Georgius. *Unidentified*: 138.28
Agricola, Rodolphus. *De inventione dialectica*: 149.43; *De inventione dialectica* (probable): 145.40
Agrippa, Henricus Cornelius. *De incertitudine et vanitate scientiarum*: 146.57; *De occulta philosophia*: 146.114; 146.220
Albertus Magnus. *Aristotle–De anima: commentary*: 149.30; *De secretis mulierum et virorum*: 148.290; *Unidentified*: 145.05
Alciati, Andrea. *Emblemata*: 147.33; 149.264
Alcionio, Pietro. *De exilio*: 143.92; 146.48
Alcuin. *In Ecclesiasten*: 149.193

Alessio, *Piemontese* (pseudonym). *De secretis*: 143.99; *secretes of the reverende maister Alexis of Piemount, The*: 150.35

Alexander, *Anglus*. *Destructorium viciorum*: 149.27

Alexandrinus, Julius. *Salubrium sive de sanitate tuenda*: 146.213

Allen, William, *Cardinal. defense and declaration of the catholike churchies* [sic] *doctrine, touching purgatory, A*: 149.236

Altimarus, Donatus Antonius. *De medendis humani corporis malis: ars medica*: 149.62:2

Altimarus, Donatus Antonius. *Nonnulla opuscula* [and other works]: 149.62:1

Ambrose, *Saint*. *Epistles–Paul: commentary and text*: 144.22

Ammianus, Marcellinus. *Res gestae* (probable): 144.15

Ammonius, *Hermeae*. *Aristotle–Categoriae: commentary*: 143.61

Anonymous. *praise of musicke, The*: 150.56; *Preces privatae*: 146.264; *Vocabularius juris utriusque*: 139.5; 146.41; 148.138

Anselm, *Saint, Archbishop of Canterbury*. *Selected works–Opuscula*: 144.39

Anthologia graeca: 143.62; (probable): 144.5; 144.50

Antoninus Liberalis. *Transformationum congeries* [and other works]: 143.41

Aphthonius, *Sophista*. *Progymnasmata*: 143.56; 146.119; 146.202; 147.26; 150.75

Apian, Peter. *Cosmographia*: 138.17

Apollinarius, *Bishop*. *Psalms: commentary and text*: 143.39

Appian, *of Alexandria*. *Historia Romana*: 143.16

Apuleius, Lucius. *Metamorphoses*: 148.42

Aquaevilla, Nicolaus de. *Sermones dominicales*: 142.114

Aquinas, Thomas, *Saint*. *Epistles–Paul: commentary*: 141.4; *Gospels: commentary* (part): 141.21; *Quaestiones*: 144.49; 146.298; *Summa theologica–Part II* (2): 149.54

Ardoynis, Santes de. *Opus de venenis*: 138.23

Aretaeus, *Cappadox*. *Unidentified*: 143.102

Aretius, Benedictus. *Acts: commentary*: 146.356; *Commentarii in Evangelium secundum Joannem*: 146.352; *Commentarii in Evangelium secundum Lucam*: 146.353:2; *Commentarii in Evangelium secundum Marcum*: 146.353:1; *Commentarii in Evangelium secundum Matthaeum*: 146.354 *Commentarii in omnes epistolas Pauli, et Canonicas, itemque in Apocalypsin*: 146.321; *De coena Domini*: 142.74; *Examen theologicum*: 142.75; 146.283; *Problemata theologica*: 146.355; *Valentini Gentilis justo capitis supplicio Bernae affecti brevis historia*: 146.308

Aristotle. *De anima*: 143.48; *Ethica*: 143.47; 144.4; 145.6; 146.68; 146.73; 147.12; 148.183; 148.262; 150.19; *Flores illustriores Aristotelis*: 146.65; *Flores illustriores Aristotelis* (probable): 150.78; *Historia animalium*: 146.266; *Metaphysica*: 147.11; 150.32; *Organon*: 139.9; 139.22; 147.6; 148.52; 148.140; 148.275; 148.286; *Physica*: 145.32; 146.9; 148.285; 150.31; *Politica*: 143.29; 146.127; 148.54; *Rhetorica*: 146.193; 148.73; 149.285; *Selected works–Logica*: 139.3; *Selections*: 146.62; *Topica*: 144.25; 150.27; *Works*: 150.8;

Aristotle (spurious). *Problemata*: 145.03; 146.252

Arnobius, *the Younger*. *Psalms: commentary*: 142.53

Ars notariatus: 148.135

Arsenios, *Archbishop of Monemvasia*. *Scholia in septem Euripidis tragoedias*: 144.9

INDEX I: AUTHORS AND WORKS

Ascham, Roger. *Familiarium epistolarum libri tres*: 146.175; 148.116; *scholemaster or plaine and perfite way of teachyng children the Latin tong, The*: 149.144:1; *Toxophilus, the schole of shootinge conteyned in two bookes*: 149.144:2

Athanasius, *Saint. Dialogi V, de sancta Trinitate*: 144.14; *Unidentified*: 149.123

Athenagoras. *Unidentified*: 148.43

Augustine, *Saint. Confessiones*: 148.152; 149.100; *De consensu evangelistarum*: 142.71; *De doctrina Christiana*: 142.70; *De haeresibus*: 146.274; *De praedestinatione sanctorum*: 142.72; *Works*: 144.47

Augustine, *Saint* (spurious). *Meditationes*: 139.25

Averroes. *Paraphrasis in libros de Republica Platonis*: 149.61:B

Avila, Luis de. *Commentariorum de bello Germanico libri duo*: 149.230

Avitus, Alcimus Ecdicius. *De origine mundi* [and other works]: 143.67

Baccanelli, Giovanni Battista. *De consensu medicorum in curandis morbis. De consensu medicorum in cognoscendis simplicibus liber* (probable): 138.14

Bacon, Roger. *De l'admirable pouvoir et puissance de l'art et nature, ou est traicté de la pierre philosophale*: 138.37

Badius, Jodocus, *Ascensius* (perhaps). *Unidentified*: 143.51

Baeza, Gaspar de. *In Caroli quinti Augusti hispaniae regis illustrem constitutionem*: 148.1

Bairo, Pietro. *Unidentified*: 138.15

Baius, Michael. *Pro responsione ad quaestiones P. Marnixii apologia*: 149.190

Baker, John, *Minister* (perhaps). *Lectures of J. B[aker] upon the xii. articles of our christian faith. Also a briefe confession* (perhaps): 147.43

Balduinus, Franciscus. *Ad edicta veterum principum Rom. de christianis*: 146.32

Baldus de Ubaldis (probable). *Unidentified*: 146.359

Baldwin, William (probable). *myrroure for magistrates, A* (probable): 149.52

Bale, John, *Bishop. image of both churches, after the revelacion of saynt Johan the evangelyst, The*: 149.88

Baret, John. *alvearie or triple [quadruple] dictionarie, An*: 148.201

Barletta, Gabriel. *Sermones*: 139.37

Barlezio, Marino. *Historia de vita et gestis Scanderbegi*: 148.27

Barnaud, Nicolas. *Dialogi ab Eusebio Philadelpho cosmopolita in Gallorum et caeterarum rationum gratiam compositi*: 149.299

Basil, *Saint, the Great. Unidentified*: 146.303

Bebel, Heinrich. *Facetiae*: 146.52

Beda, *the Venerable. Unidentified*: 144.32:1; 144.32:2

Bembo, Pietro. *Epistolae*: 148.115; *Historiae Venetae libri XII*: 148.3

Bernard, *Saint. Opuscula*: 144.40

Bertram, Bonaventure Corneille. *Comparitio grammaticae hebraicae et aramaicae*: 149.45; *De politia judaica*: 142.60; 146.281

Beumler, Marcus. *Analysis dialectica M.T. Ciceronis Catonis Majoris, sive dialogi de Senectute: ad methodum Petri Rami accommodata*: 149.282

Beuther, Michael (probable). *Ephemerides historica* (probable): 149.246

Beverus, Joannes. *Aristotle–Physica: commentary*: 146.234

Bèze, Théodore de. *Adversus sacramentariorum errorem pro vera Christi praesentia in coena Domini*: 146.284; *Confessio christianae fidei*: 142.20; 146.300; 149.125; 150.52; *De haereticis a civili magistratu puniendis*: 142.17; *De jure magistratuum in subditos*:

142.153; *De praedestinationis doctrina*: 149.228; *De veris et visibilibus ecclesiae catholicae notis*: 142.21; *Epistolarum theologicarum liber unus*: 149.71; *Poemata*: 148.254; 149.166; *psalmes of David, truely opened and explaned, The*: 149.249; *Quaestionum et responsionum christianarum libellus*: 142.19; *Sermons sur les trois premiers chapitres du Cantique des Cantiques de Salomon*: 149.259; *Tractatio de repudiis et divortiis*: 149.168; *Unidentified*: 142.18; 146.295

Bible, The: 139.26; 142.45; 142.46; 142.158; 143.27; 145.12; 146.310; 146.314; 146.329; 147.1; 147.2; 148.48; 148.105; 149.1; 149.2; 149.3; 149.4; 149.5; 149.75; 150.1; 150.16; 150.25; 150.71; *Selections*: 148.102
  Old Testament: 149.237; (part) (probable): 147.3
  Apocrypha (perhaps): 143.71
  Daniel: 142.3:2
  Ecclesiastes: 142.63 (see 142.28)
  Genesis: 142.39; 143.26; 146.270:1; 146.270:2
  Hosea: 147.40; 149.170
  Isaiah: 148.155
  Job (perhaps): 142.27
  Minor prophets: 142.26
  Pentateuch (perhaps): 142.1
  Proverbs: 147.29 (see 142.28)
  Proverbs, Ecclesiastes, Song of Solomon: 142.28
  Psalms: 141.20; 142.66; 142.95; 142.117; 142.122; 143.39; 143.72; 143.75; 144.69; 146.32; 146.319:2; 148.68; 148.100; 149.249; 150.47; 150.79; (perhaps): 142.10; 142.53
  Song of Solomon: 146.322 (see 142.28)
  New Testament: 139.14; 141.10; 142.16; 142.49:1; 142.49:2; 142.50; 142.51; 144.64; 145.21; 145.53; 146.320; 146.328; 147.7; 148.76; 148.92; 148.95; 148.101; 148.103; 149.6; 149.7; 149.238:1; 149.238:2; 149.238:3; 149.245; 149.256; 150.3; 150.72
  Acts: 143.8:2
  Ephesians: 142.9
  Epistles–Paul: 142.113; 144.10; 144.22
  Epistles–Thessalonians: 142.89
  Epistles–Timothy: 149.90
  Gospels: 139.11; 141.6; 143.8:1
  Gospels–John: 141.13
  Gospels–Mark: 142.48
  Revelation: 142.47
Biblical concordance (unidentified): 147.25; 149.287; 150.4
Bilson, Thomas, *Bishop*. *true difference betweene christian subjection and unchristian rebellion, The*: 147.10; 148.93; 149.275
Biondo, Flavio. *Roma triumphans*: 148.143
Blank book: 150.29
Bock, Hieronymus. *Verae imagines omnium herbarum quarum descriptiones H. Bockius in suo herbario comprehendit*: 149.26
Bodin, Jean, *Bishop*. *De republica*: 148.18; *Les six livres de la république*: 149.103; *Methodus ad facilem historiarum cognitionem*: 146.80; 148.230
Boemus, Joannes. *Omnium gentium mores, leges et ritus*: 146.81
Boethius, Anicius M.T.S. *Arithmetica*: 146.260
Boethius, Hector (perhaps). *Scotorum historiae* (perhaps): 142.127
Bonaventura, *Saint*. *Sermones de morte*: 142.104
Bonfinius, Antonius. *Symposion trimeron*: 146.60
book of precedents, A: 143.81; 147.32; 148.196
Bosius, Simeon. *Cicero–Epistolae ad Atticum: commentary*: 149.98

Brandolinus, Aurelius. *De ratione scribendi* (probable): 148.117; 150.58; *De ratione scribendi*: 146.174

Brant, Sebastian. *Expositiones omnium titulorum juris tam civilis quam canonici*: 146.43; *Stultifera navis*: 148.193; 150.30; *Unidentified*: 146.24

Brant, Sebastian (probable). *Titulorum omnium juris tam civilis quam canonici expositiones*: 148.195

Brasavola, Antonio Musa. *Unidentified*: 138.24

Brassicanus, Joannes Alexandrus. *Unidentified*: 143.22

Bredenbach, Matthias. *Epistolae duae de negocio religionis* [and other works]: 149.150

Brentz, Johann, the Elder. *De administranda pie republica*: 146.134

Brinkelow, Henry. *complaynt of Roderyck Mors, for the redresse of certen wicked lawes, The*: 142.102

Brisson, Barnabé. *De ritu nuptiarum liber singularis*: 146.28

Brocardo, Giacopo. *In Canticum Canticorum Salomonis expositio mystica*: 149.296

Brulefer, Stephanus. *Reportata in quattuor sancti Bonaventurae sententiarum libros Scoti subtilis secundi*: 142.103

Brunfels, Otto. *Iatrion medicamentorum simplicium*: 143.98

Brunfels, Otto (probable). *Pandectae scripturarum* (probable): 142.54

Bucer, Martin. *Acta colloquii in comitiis imperii Ratisponae habiti*: 142.41; 149.42; *De vera et falsa Caenae Dominicae administratione* (probable): 142.42; *Gratulatio ad ecclesiam Anglicanam, de religionis Christi restitutione*: 149.34; *Scripta anglicana fere omnia*: 142.40

Buchanan, George. *Rerum Scoticarum historia*: 148.30; 149.80

Bucoldianus, Gerardus. *De inventione, et amplificatione oratoria* (probable): 149.95

Budaeus, Gulielmus. *Commentarii linguae graecae*: 138.11; *De asse et partibus eius*: 138.29; 143.7; *Forensia*: 148.207

Bullinger, Heinrich. *Compendium christianae religionis*: 142.30; *De fine seculi et juditio venturo Domini nostri Jesu Christi*: 146.273; *De persecutionibus ecclesiae christianae*: 149.77; *Resolution de tous les poincts de la religion chrestienne*: 149.198; *Sermonum decades*: 142.29; 146.311; 146.340:1; 146.340:2

Bullinger, Heinrich (probable). *olde fayth, an evydent probacion out of the holy scripture, The* (probable): 149.242

Bunel, Pierre. *Epistolae*: 146.176; 149.173

Burgo, Joannes de. *Pupilla oculi*: 144.33

Buridanus, Joannes. *Aristotle–Ethica: commentary*: 150.15

C, I.B.A. *De politia et disciplina civili et ecclesiastica, tum Israeliticae, tum christianae, libri II*: 149.41

Caesar, Caius Julius. *Commentarii*: 144.11; 145.27; 146.78; 148.229; 149.263; 150.63

Caius, Joannes. *De antiquitate Cantabrigiensis academiae libri duo*: 150.66:A

Caius, Thomas. *Assertio antiquitatis Oxoniensis academiae*: 150.66:B

Calepino, Ambrogio. *Dictionarium*: 139.6; 140.2; 144.43; 148.5

Calfhill, James. *aunswere to the Treatise of the crosse, An*: 142.108

Calfhill, James (perhaps). *aunswer to the Treatise of the crosse, An* (perhaps): 149.49

Callimachus. *Hymni*: 143.23

Calvin, Jean. *Acta synodi Tridentinae cum antidoto*: 142.14; *Catechism*: 142.118; 144.66; 148.104; *Daniel: commentary and text*: 142.3:2; *Defensio orthodoxae fidei de sacra Trinitate*: 144.13; *Epistles–Paul: commentary*: 142.7; *Epistolae*: 142.12; *Ezekiel: commentary*: 142.4; *Genesis: commentary*: 146.319:1; 149.9; *Harmonia*: 142.6; *Institutio christianae religionis*: 142.11; 144.7; 145.01; 147.14; 148.45; 148.91; 149.12; 149.33; 149.200; *Institutio christianae religionis–Epitome*: 149.279; 149.281; *Isaiah: commentary*: 142.3:1; 146.351; *Jeremiah and Lamentations: commentary*: 142.2; *Joshua: commentary* (probable): 142.8; *Minor prophets: commentary*: 142.5; *Pentateuch: commentary*: 142.1; *Psalms: commentary and text*: 142.10; 146.319:2; *Responsio ad Balduini convicia*: 142.13; *sermons of M. John Calvin, upon the epistle too the Ephesians, The*: 142.9

Camden, William. *Britannia sive florentissimorum regnorum Angliae, Scotiae, Hiberniae chorographica descriptio*: 148.161; 149.215

Camerarius, Joachim, *the Elder*. *Epistolarum familiarium libri VI*: 149.105

Campanus, Joannes Antonius (perhaps). *Unidentified*: 146.51

Campensis, Joannes. *Grammatica hebraica*: 143.77

Canephius, Baruch (pseudonym). *Atheomachie ou, Refutation des erreurs et detestables impietez des atheistes*: 149.188

Canisius, Petrus, *Saint*. *Summa doctrinae christianae*: 145.46

Cano, Francisco Melchor, *Bishop*. *De locis theologicis*: 146.263; 148.294; *Unidentified*: 142.52

Capito, Wolfgang Fabricius. *Hexameron Dei opus explicatum*: 144.27; 149.154

Cardano, Girolamo. *De rerum varietate*: 138.30; 146.214; *De subtilitate*: 146.215; *In Cl. Ptolemaei de astrorum judiciis*: 138.10; 143.89; *Libellus de restitutione temporum et motum coelestium*: 143.95

Carion, Johann. *Chronica*: 146.77; 148.223; 148.232; 148.235

Case, John. *Speculum moralium quaestionum in universam ethicen Aristotelis*: 150.24:2; *Summa veterum interpretum in universam dialecticam Aristotelis*: 150.24:1

Case, John (perhaps). *Aristotle–Selected works–Logica: commentary* (perhaps): 145.33

Cassander, Georgius. *Tabulae praeceptionum dialecticarum quae artis methodum complectuntur* (probable): 149.202

Castalio, Sebastian. *Dialogorum sacrorum libri quatuor*: 142.61; 146.338

Castiglione, Baldassare, *Count. courtyer, The*: 149.69; *De curiali sive aulico libri quatuor ex Italico sermone in Latinum conversi*: 146.129; 149.161; *Il cortegiano*: 149.219

Catechesis religionis christianae: quae in ecclesiis et scholis Palatinatus traditur: 146.292

Catechisms (unidentified): 145.34; 149.298

Catechismus ex decreto Concilii Tridentini: 141.9; 148.300

Cato, Dionysius. *Disticha*: 148.24

Catullus, Caius Valerius. *Works* (probable): 144.60

Caucius, Antonius. *Grammatica gallica*: 149.130

Cecil, William, *Baron Burghley*. *execution of justice in England for maintenaunce of publique and christian peace, without any persecution for questions of religion, The*: 142.101; 149.146

Celsus, Aulus Cornelius. *De re medica*: 143.90

Censura et docta explicatio errorum catechismi J. Monhemii: 148.298; 149.233

Ceporinus, Jacobus. *Compendium grammaticae graecae*: 145.30

Charisius, Flavius Sosipater. *Artis grammaticae libri quinque*: 139.18

# INDEX I: AUTHORS AND WORKS

Charpentier, Pierre. *Epistola ad Franciscum Portum*: 146.47
Chemnitius, Martinus. *Examen concilii Tridentini*: 142.15; *Unidentified*: 146.315
Cheyne, James, *Canon of Tournai. Analysis in XIIII. libros Aristotelis de prima seu divina philosophia*: 149.120; *Succincta in physiologiam Aristotelicam analysis*: 149.127
Chronologia hebraeorum major: 148.150
Chytraeus, David. *Chronologia historiae Herodoti et Thucydidis*: 146.90; *De lectione historiarum*: 146.91; *De ratione discendi*: 148.178; *De scribenda historia*: 146.103; *De studio theologiae recte inchoando*: 146.285; 146.290; *Praecepta rhetoricae inventionis*: 149.82; *Regulae vitae*: 146.54
Chytraeus, David (probable). *Unidentified*: 150.67:2
Chytraeus, Nathan. *Ethe kai pathe, seu de affectibus movendis Aristotelis ex II. rhetoricorum doctrina explicata*: 149.297
Cicero, Marcus Tullius. *De claris oratoribus, qui dicitur Brutus, et eum Coelii Secundi Curionis commentarii*: 149.79; *De officiis*: 146.67; 146.87; 148.23; 149.99; *De partitione oratoria*: 149.283; *Epistolae ad Atticum*: 146.168; *Epistolae ad familiares*: 139.39; 145.37; 148.118; *Philippicae*: 148.62; *Quaestiones Tusculanae*: 142.143; 145.49; *Selected works–Epistolae*: 143.46; 144.6; 146.113; 146.167; (probable): 148.56; *Selected works–Orations*: 141.11; 145.45; 146.69; *Selected works–Philosophica*: 146.70; 148.177; 148.180; *Selected works–Rhetorica*: 146.212; *Selections*: 145.42; 146.64; *Topica*: 144.16; 148.84; *Works*: 143.14; 144.1; 146.172; 148.36; 149.15; 150.61
Cicero, Marcus Tullius (spurious). *Rhetorica ad Herennium*: 141.12

Claius, Joannes, *the Elder*. *Elementa linguae hebraeae*: 149.134
Claudianus, Claudius. *Works*: 143.73; (probable): 148.241
Clavasio, Angelus de. *Summa Angelica*: 148.133
Clavius, Christoph. *Epitome arithmeticae practicae*: 149.138
Clenardus, Nicolaus. *Institutiones linguae graecae*: 144.61; 145.43; 146.144; 146.148; 148.122; 149.44; 150.21; (probable): 143.55; *Tabula in grammaticen hebraeam*: 146.150; 147.35
Clenardus, Nicolaus (probable). *Institutiones linguae graecae* (probable): 148.124
Clichtoveus, Jodocus. *Homiliae*: 146.261
Cogan, Thomas. *haven of health, The*: 149.60
Colerus, Joannes Jacobus. *Quaestio theologica num anima sit ex traduce, an vero à Deo quotidie inspiretur*: 149.289
Comes, Natalis. *Unidentified*: 150.73
Comines, Philippe de. *Memoires*: 146.106; 148.41; 149.231
Consilia matrimonialia: 146.14
Constantinus, Africanus. *Works* (probable): 138.22
Cooper, Thomas, *Bishop*. *Thesaurus linguae Romanae et Britannicae*: 143.2; 150.7
Cooper, Thomas, *Bishop* (probable). *Thesaurus linguae Romanae et Britannicae* (probable): 148.192
Cordier, Mathurin. *De corrupti sermonis emendatione*: 149.111
Cordus, Valerius. *Annotationes in Pedacii Dioscoridis Anazarbei De medica materia libros V* [and other works]: 138.3
Cordus, Valerius. *Dispensatorium*: 149.251
Corner, Christoph. *Psalms: commentary and text*: 142.66
Corpus juris canonici: 146.2; 146.30 *Liber Extra*: 146.3

Corpus juris civilis: 139.16; 140.1; 141.1; 141.17; 146.1; 146.5; 146.15; 146.18; 146.35; 146.42; 146.111; 148.6; 148.125; 148.198; 148.205 *Index*: 146.40

Corradus, Sebastian. *Quaestura*: 143.64

Corro, Antonio de. *Sapientissimi regis Salomonis . . . in Latinam linguam ab A. Corrano versa*: 142.63

Corsettus, Antonius. *Repertorium in opera Nicolae de Tudeschis*: 146.4

Cosmographica in astronomiam et geographiam isagoge: 149.101

Costerus, Franciscus (probable). *Enchiridion controversiarum de religione* (probable): 148.299

Councils–Trent: 141.9; 142.14; 142.15; 146.262; 147.18; 148.297; 148.300

Cousin, Gilbert. *Unidentified*: 149.217

Covarruvias a Leyva, Diego, *Bishop of Segovia*. *Unidentified*: 146.21

Cranmer, Thomas, *Archbishop. Reformatio legum ecclesiasticarum*: 146.44; 149.286

Crellius, Fortunatus. *Aristotle–Selected works–Logica: commentary*: 149.268

Crescentiis, Petrus de. *Unidentified*: 138.5:2

Crespin, Jean (perhaps). *Lexicon graecolatinum* (perhaps): 148.197

Crinitus, Petrus. *De honesta disciplina* [and other works]: 148.220

Cromer, Martin, *Bishop. Unidentified*: 148.160

Crusius, Martin. *Grammatica graeca, cum latina congruens*: 143.35; 149.143

Cureus, Joachim. *Aristotle–De sensu et sensibilibus: commentary*: 146.241; *Aristotle–De sensu et sensibilibus: commentary*: 149.118; *Unidentified*: 142.138

Cureus, Joachim (probable). *Aristotle–De sensu et sensibilibus: commentary* (probable): 148.287

Curio, Caelius Secundus. *Cicero–Topica: commentary*: 149.87; *De omni artificio disserendi atque tractandi, summa*: 149.176; *Francisci Spierae historia, a quatuor summis viris*: 146.105; *Pasquine in a traunce a christian and learned dialogue*: 150.28; *Pro vera et antiquae ecclesiae Christi autoritate, in Antonium Florebellum Mutinensem, oratio*: 149.159

Curtius Rufus, Quintus. *De rebus gestis Alexandri Magni*: 150.76; *historie of Quintus Curcius, contayning the actes of the greate Alexander, The*: 141.15

Cyprian, Saint. *Epistolae*: 143.76; *Works*: 142.69

Dalmada, Emanuel, *Bishop of Angra*. *Epistola adversus epistolam Gualteri Haddoni contra Hieronymi Osorii Lusitani, episcopi Sylvensis epistolam*: 149.37

Dance of Death: 146.277

Daneau, Lambert. *Ad novas Gulielmi Genebrardi calumnias*: 148.87; *De veneficis quas sortiarios vocant*: 146.236:1; 146.236:2; *Elenchi haereticorum*: 142.77; 146.268; *Ethices christiana libri tres*: 148.272; 149.212; *Physices christiana pars altera*: 149.213; *Timothy: commentary and text*: 149.90; *Unidentified*: 142.76

Dasypodius, Petrus. *Dictionarum Latin-germanicum*: 146.142

Decio, Felippo. *De regulis juris*: 143.42

Demosthenes. *Adversus Leptinem*: 146.189; 148.170; *De falsa legatione*: 146.182; *Olynthiacae orationes tres*: 144.70; 146.180; 148.20; 149.58:1; *three orations of Demosthenes . . . in favour of the Olynthians, with fower orations against king Philip most nedefull to be redde in these daungerous dayes, The*: 149.58:2; *Works*: 143.60; (perhaps): 144.29

Dering, Edward. *sparing restraint, of many lavishe untruthes, which M. doctor Harding dothe challenge, A*: 142.86;

INDEX I: AUTHORS AND WORKS

XXVII. lectures, or readings, upon part of the epistle to the Hebrues: 142.120
De ritibus et institutis ecclesiae tigurinae opusculum: 146.294
Desainliens, Claude. *French schoolemaister, The*: 143.63
Despautère, Jean. *Unidentified*: 148.261
Dessenius, Bernardus. *De compositione medicamentorum*: 138.6:2
Dictionaries (unidentified): 149.20; 145.15; 147.28; 148.119; 150.10; 150.23
Dictys, Cretensis. *De bello Troiano*: 145.35; 146.82
Dinus de Mugello. *De regulis juris*: 146.253
Dio, Chrysostomus. *De regno*: 149.110
Diodorus, Siculus. *Bibliotheca historica*: 144.68
Diogenes Laertius. *De vita et moribus philosophorum*: 148.233
Dion Cassius. *Historia Romana*: 149.163; *Scriptores historiae Augustae* (probable): 148.210
Dionysius Areopagita. *Works*: 146.318
Dioscorides. *De medica materia*: 138.4:2
Dodoens, Rembert. *Cosmographica in astronomiam et geographiam isagoge*: 149.101; *Historia vitis vinique* [and other works]: 149.162
Donzellini, Girolamo. *Epistolae principum rerum publicarum ac sapientum virorum*: 148.114
Drant, Thomas, *Poet and Divine*. *Unidentified [sermons]*: 149.225
Driedo, Joannes. *Unidentified*: 140.4
Duarenus, Franciscus. *De sacris ecclesiae ministeriis ac beneficiis libri VIII*: 148.136
Du Bellay, Martin. *Commentariorum de rebus Gallicis libri decem*: 148.9
Du Corroy, Simon. *Pandecta legis evangelicae*: 143.68; 143.69
Du Jon, François, *the Elder*. *Academia*: 149.290; *Ad Testamenti Veteris interpretationem prokatablema*: 149.40; *Ecclesiastici sive de natura et administrationibus ecclesiae Dei*: 149.160; *Grammatica hebraeae linguae*: 149.140; 149.141; *In epistolam S. Judae apostoli*: 149.187
Duns, John, Scotus. *Aristotle–Metaphysica: commentary*: 143.15; *Aristotle–Unidentified: commentary* (probable): 144.45; *Sentences II: commentary*: 144.38; *Unidentified*: 141.3
Du Port, François. *De signis morborum*: 149.129
Du Preau, Gabriel. *De vitis, sectis, et dogmatibus omnium haereticorum, elenchus alphabeticus*: 146.349
Durandus, Gulielmus I, *Bishop of Mende*. *Speculum juris*: 146.348
Durans, Johann Dilectus. *De arte testandi, et cautelis ultimarum voluntatum*: 146.110
Durie, John, *Jesuit*. *Confutatio responsionis Gulielmus Whitaker*: 148.47

Eber, Paul. *Calendarium historicum*: 138.38
Eckius, Joannes. *Enchiridion locorum communium adversus Lutheranos*: 142.62
Ehem, Christoph. *De principiis juris libri septem*: 139.17
Eitzen, Paul von. *Rudimenta artis dialecticae*: 149.124
Elyot, Sir Thomas. *Bibliotheca Eliotae*: 141.2
Eobanus, Helius, *Hessus*. *De tuenda bona valetudine*: 142.155
England–Statutes
 Abridgements and Extracts: 146.237; 148.132
 Institutes: 146.39
Epiphanius, *Bishop of Constantia*. *Unidentified*: 146.358
Epistolae japanicae, de multorum gentilium in variis insulis ad Christi fidem per Societatis Jesu theologos conversione: 146.102

Erasmus, Desiderius. *Adagia*: 140.3; 141.5; 142.124; 146.159; 148.246; *De conscribendis epistolis*: 146.204; *De duplici copia verborum ac rerum*: 139.27; 147.31; *De octo partium orationis constructione*: 148.63; *De praeparatione ad mortem*: 149.93; *De ratione studii*: 146.287:1; *De recta pronuntiatione* [and other works]: 146.181; 148.65; *Ecclesiastes, sive de ratione concionandi*: 146.323; *Epistolae*: 148.200; *Lingua*: 146.59; 148.245; *Moriae encomium*: 146.178; *New Testament: commentary*: 143.3; 149.8; *New Testament: paraphrase* (part): 146.320; 148.76; *Parabolae sive similia*: 146.55; *praise of folie, The*: 148.171; 149.126

Erasmus, Desiderius (probable). *Colloquia* (probable): 146.162; *De duplici copia verborum ac rerum* (probable): 146.163

Erythraeus, Valentinus. *De elocutione*: 146.209; *De grammaticorum figuris* [and other works]: 149.157; *De ratione legendi, explicandi et scribendi epistolas libri tres*: 149.91; *In orationem M.T.C. pro lege Manilia de Pompeii laudibus annotationes*: 149.84; *Microtechne, seu Medulla rhetoricae Tullianae*: 149.179; *Unidentified*: 149.24

Estella, Diego de. *methode unto mortification: called heretofore, The contempt of the world, A*: 149.248

Estienne, Charles (probable). *Dictionarium historicum ac poeticum* (probable): 150.26

Estienne, Henri. *De abusu linguae graecae*: 148.126; *Dictionarium medicum*: 138.36; *Parodiae morales*: 143.74

Estienne, Henri (probable). *Thesaurus graecae linguae* (probable): 143.1

Estienne, Robert, the Elder. *Ad censuras theologorum Parisiensium responsio*: 142.80; 149.191; *Concordantiae Bibliorum utriusque Testamenti*: 142.43; *Phrases hebraicae*: 149.132; *Promptuarium latinae linguae (Les mots français)*: 149.133

Euclid. *Elementa*: 146.243

Euclid. *Elementa* (probable): 148.61; 148.67

Euripides. *Hecuba*: 148.83; *Works*: 143.31; 144.18; (probable): 148.185

Euripides (attributed). *Rhesus*: 143.43

Eusebius, Pamphili, Bishop. *Historia ecclesiastica*: 146.357; *Unidentified*: 143.80; *De evangelica praeparatione*: 146.341

Eutropius, Flavius. *Historia Romana*: 144.65

Faber, Jacobus, Stapulensis. *Aristotle–Physica: commentary and paraphrase*: 139.8; *Aristotle–Selected works–Logica: commentary*: 139.2; *Unidentified*: 144.46

Fabricius, Franciscus, Marcoduranus. *M. Tullii Ciceronis historia*: 148.222

Fabricius, Franciscus, Marcoduranus (probable). *M. Tullii Ciceronis historia* (probable): 146.86

Fabricius, Georgius. *Partitionum grammaticarum, quae tabulis delineatae sunt, libri III*: 149.28

Falletti, Girolamo. *Orationes XII*: 146.184

Fallopius, Gabriel. *De morbo gallico*: 138.35

Faustus, Johann, Doctor. *historie of the damnable life, and deserved death of doctor John Faustus, The*: 150.36

Fenner, Dudley. *answere unto the confutation of John Nichols his recantation, An*: 149.39; *artes of logike and rethorike, The. (The order of householde)*: 149.155

Fernelius, Joannes. *Febrium curandarum methodus generalis*: 146.208; *Medicina*: 143.88; *Therapeutices universalis seu medendi rationis libri septem*: 143.101

Ferrarius, Joannes Matthaeus, *de Gradi. Practica*: 146.238

Ficino, Marsilio. *Unidentified*: 146.217

Field, John. *admonition to the parliament. (A view of popishe abuses yet remaining in the Englishe church), An*: 142.100

Fisher, John, *Saint and Cardinal. De veritate corporis et sanguinis Christi in eucharistia*: 143.20

Flacius, Matthias, *Illyricus. Catalogus testium veritatis*: 146.289

Flaminio, Marco Antonio. *Psalms: commentary and text*: 146.342

Floccus, Andreas Dominicus. *De magistratibus sacerdotiisque Romanorum*: 148.7; (probable): 145.55; 146.104

Flores poetarum: 146.56

Florus, Lucius Annaeus. *Epitomae de Tito Livio bellorum omnium annorum*: 148.226

Fortescue, Sir John. *Prenobilis militis, cognomento Forescu, . . . de politica administratione, et legibus civilibus Anglie, commentarius*: 148.130

Fortunatianus, Chirius. *Rhetoricorum libri III*: 149.97

Fox Morzillo, Sebastiano. *De naturae philosophia, seu de Platonis et Aristotelis consensione*: 146.218; 148.55; *De regni regisque institutione*: 146.133; *Ethices philosophiae compendium*: 145.23; 148.271

Fox Morzillo, Sebastiano (probable). *De naturae philosophia, seu de Platonis et Aristotelis consensione* (probable): 148.280

Foxe, John, *the Martyrologist. De Christo crucifixo concio*: 143.25; *De Christo gratis justificante*: 142.83; 149.260; *pope confuted, The*: 150.34; *Rerum in ecclesia gestarum commentarii*: 142.82; *Syllogisticon hoc est: argumenta, . . . de re et materia sacramenti eucharistici*: 149.197; *Unidentified*: 144.37

Franchini, Francesco, *Bishop* (probable). *Poemata* (probable): 148.252

Freigius, Joannes Thomas. *Ciceronianus*: 149.137:1; 149.206:2; *Pedagogus*: 150.59; *Unidentified*: 149.137:2; 149.206:1

Fritsche, Marcus. *De meteoris*: 149.104

Froissart, Jean. *Chroniques*: 149.21

Fuchs, Leonard. *De componendorum medicamentorum ratione*: 138.6:1; *De historia stirpium*: 149.239; *De medendi methodo* (perhaps): 149.243; *Institutiones medicinae*: 149.113; *Methodus seu ratio compendiaria perveniendi ad medicinam*: 146.210; *Unidentified*: 138.13

Fulke, William. *D. Heskins, D. Sanders, and M. Rastel, overthrowne*: 149.262; *In sacram divi Joannis Apocalypsim praelectiones*: 142.47

Fumanelli, Antonio (probable). *Unidentified*: 138.18:2

Funck, Johann. *Chronologia*: 148.16

Galen. *De simplicium medicamentorum facultatibus*: 138.25; 146.206; *Works–Epitome*: 143.86

Gameren, Hannardus de, *Mosaeus. Vera et simplex narratio eorum quae ab adventu D. Joannis Austriaci supremi in Belgio gesta sunt*: 148.168

Garcaeus, Joannes. *Meteorologia*: 149.109; *Summi pontificis Veteris et Novi Testamentum collatio*: 149.185; *Tractatus brevis de erigendis figuris coeli*: 149.96

Gardiner, Stephen, *Bishop. Confutatio cavillationum quibus eucharistiae sacramentum ab impiis Capernaitis impeti solet*: 149.181

Garlandia, Joannes de. *Synonyma*: 150.33

Gascoigne, George. *whole woorkes of George Gascoigne esquyre, The*: 149.47

Gellius, Aulus. *Noctes Atticae*: 144.28

Gemma, Reiner, *Frisius. Arithmetica practicae methodus facilis*: 146.250; 149.156; *De principis astronomiae et cosmographiae, deque usu globi*: 146.247; *De principiis astronomiae et*

cosmographiae, deque usu globi. De orbis divisione et insulis: 138.7
Gentilis, Albericus. *Unidentified*: 148.186
Gentillet, Innocent. *Commentariorum de regno aut quovis principatu recte administrando libri tres. Adversus N. Machiavellum*: 142.59; 148.164
Georgievits, Bartholomaeus. *De Turcarum moribus epitome*: 146.101
Genealogy (unidentified): 143.84:2
Gerardus, Andreas, *Hyperius. Aristotle–Physica: paraphrase*: 147.24; *De theologo, sive De ratione studii theologici*: 146.332; *Elementa christianae religionis*: 146.288; *Methodus theologiae sive loci communes*: 146.325; *Opuscula theologica*: 146.324; 146.330; *Unidentified*: 148.98
Gesner, Conrad. *Appendix bibliothecae*: 148.181
Giovio, Paolo, *Bishop. Unidentified*: 146.76; *Works*: 148.148
Giraldus, Lilius Gregorius. *Suarum quorundam annotationum dialogismi XXX*: 148.79
Goeden, Henning. *Ordinis judiciarii processus*: 146.34:A
Gordonio, Bernardus de. *Practica, seu Lilium medicinae*: 146.207
Gorrutius, Andreas. *De providentia divina*: 149.277
Gorschius, Jacobus. *Commentariorum artis dialecticae libri decem*: 149.81; *De figuris, tum grammaticis, tum rhetoricis, libri V*: 146.198
Grammar (unidentified): 147.34; 148.34; 149.122
Gregorius, Petrus, *Tholosanus. Syntagma juris universi atque legum*: 148.259
Gregory I, *Saint, Pope. Song of Solomon: commentary and text*: 146.322
Greiser, Daniel. *Enarratio brevis et orthodoxa evangeliorum dominicalium et festorum aliquot*: 146.335

Grynaeus, Johann Jacob. *Chronologia brevis evangelicae historiae logicique artificii in epistola Pauli ad Romanos declaratio*: 142.64
Grynaeus, Simon. *Aristotle (spurious)–De mundo: commentary*: 148.265
Guazzo, Stefano. *Civile conversation*: 148.236; *civile conversation of M. Steeven Guazzo written first in Italian, The*: 149.223
Guicciardini, Francesco (probable). *Unidentified*: 148.2
Guido, *de Cauliaco. Chirurgia*: 138.27
Guido, *de Cauliaco* (probable). *Unidentified*: 138.32
Guilliaudus, Claudius. *John: commentary and text*: 141.13
Guinterius, Joannes. *Commentarius de balneis, et aquis medicatis*: 146.228
Gulielmus, *Parisiensis, Professor. Gospels and Epistles (liturgical): commentary and text*: 146.312

Habermann, Johann. *enemy of security, The*: 145.52
Haddon, Walter. *Contra Hieron. Osorium, ... responsio apologetica*: 149.46
Haddon, Walter (perhaps). *Dialogus contra papistarum tyrannidem*: 142.105
Hamelmann, Hermann (perhaps). *Unanimis omnium patrum consensus de vera justificatione hominis coram Deo* (perhaps): 142.112
Harchius, Jodocus. *De eucharistiae mysterio*: 146.272
Harding, Thomas. *Unidentified*: 148.40
harmony of the confessions of the faith of the christian and reformed churches, An: 147.20; 149.205
Harvey, Gabriel. *Ode natalitia, vel opus eius feriae quae S. Stephani protomartyris nomine celebrata est. In memoriam P. Rami*: 146.143; *Smithus; vel musarum lachrymae*: 148.184
Harvey, Richard. *astrological discourse*

upon the conjunction of Saturne and Jupiter, An: 147.37
Hasfurtus, Joannes, *Virdungus*. *Unidentified*: 146.258
Haymo, *Bishop of Halberstadt. Homiliae*: 139.23; 139.42; *Unidentified*: 144.35
Heerbrand, Jacob. *Disputatio theologica contra abominandum Missae pontificiae sacrificium*: 142.94
Hegendorff, Christoph (perhaps). *Dialecticae legalis libri quinque* (perhaps): 148.173
Heidelberg catechism: 146.292; 149.270
Heliodorus. *Historia Aethiopica*: 143.19
Hemmingsen, Niels. *De lege naturae apodictica methodus*: 149.189; 149.226; *Enchiridion theologicum*: 149.167; *Gospels (liturgical): commentary*: 145.11; 147.15; *Libellus de conjugio, repudio, et divortio*: 146.27; 149.195; *Pastor, sive pastoris optimus vivendi agendique modus*: 146.271; *Unidentified*: 142.78; 146.20; *way of lyfe, The*: 142.156
Herbest, Benedykt. *Periodicae responsionis libri V*: 149.74
Herborn, Nikolaus. *In psalmum septuagesimum octavum enarratio lamentoria, pro miseranda populi Christiani de populatione*: 146.286
Heresbach, Conrad. *De educandis erudiendisque principum liberis, deque republica Christiana administranda* [and other works]: 149.53; *Foure bookes of husbandry*: 149.51
Hermogenes. *Ars rhetorica*: 149.92; *Rhetorica*: 146.205; *Unidentified*: 149.175:1–3
Herodian. *Historiae*: 150.77
Herodotus. *Historiae*: 148.227; 150.60
Heshusius, Tilemannus, *Bishop* (perhaps). *Unidentified*: 144.17
Hesiod. *Opera et dies*: 149.117; *Works*: 143.78
Heywood, John. *Unidentified*: 148.206
Hierocles, *of Alexandria. Pythagoras–*

Carmina aurea: commentary and text: 148.191
Hippocrates. *De capitis vulneribus liber*: 138.34; *De flatibus*: 143.97; *Works*: 138.26
holie exercise of a true fast, The: 149.252
Holywood, John. *Sphaera mundi*: 145.16; (probable): 150.54
Homer. *Iliad*: 143.6; 143.34; 143.44; 146.117; 146.118; *Odyssey*: 148.175; *Ten books of Homers Iliades*: 150.37; *Works* (probable): 145.22; 146.336
Hondorff, Andreas. *Theatrum historicum, sive Promptuarium exemplorum*: 142.37
Honterus, Joannes. *Rudimenta cosmographica*: 146.249:1; 146.249:2
Hooper, John, *Bishop. declaration of the ten holy commaundementes, A*: 149.234; *oversight, and deliberacion upon the prophete Jonas, An*: 149.216
Hopper, Joachim. *Institutiones imperiales*: 146.35
Horatius Flaccus, Quintus. *Works* (probable): 147.27; 148.240
Hotman, François. *De furoribus Gallicis*: 142.147; *Francogallia*: 149.294; *Matagonis de Matagonibus monitoriale adversus Italo-Galliam sive Antifranco–Galliam Antonii Matharelli Alvernogeni*: 149.107
Humphrey, Laurence. *Jesuitismi pars secunda: Puritanopapismi, seu doctrinae jesuiticae confutatio*: 149.261; *Joannis Juelli Angli, episcopi Sarisburiensis vita et mors, eiusque verae doctrinae defensio*: 146.94; 148.51; 148.144; *Unidentified*: 146.192
Hunnaeus, Augustinus. *Aristotle–Organon: commentary*: 139.21

Ibn Butlan. *Tacuini sanitatis*: 138.5:1
Illustrium aliquot Germanorum carminum liber: 146.126
Imagines mortis: 146.277

Indagine, Joannes ab. *Chiromantia*: 146.248
Index librorum prohibitorum: 149.292
Institutiones linguae graecae: 145.43
Institutions, or principall groundes of the lawes and statutes of England: 146.39
Isaac, Joannes, *Levita. Grammatica hebraea*: 149.56:2
Isocrates. *Ad Demonicum*: 146.190; *Archidamus*: 146.187; *Evagoras*: 146.191; *Selected works–Orations*: 146.171; (probable): 145.39; *Unidentified*: 148.129; *Works*: 142.125
Isselt, Michael ab. *De bello Coloniensi*: 148.4

Javellus, Chrysostomus. *Aristotle–Selected works–Logic: commentary*: 150.43; *Aristotle–Selected works–Philosophia naturalis–Epitome*: 149.214
Jerome, *Saint. Unidentified*: 148.257
Jewel, John, *Bishop. Apologia ecclesiae anglicanae*: 142.115; 143.40; 149.247; 146.291; *Certaine sermons preached before the Queenes majestie, and at Paules crosse*: 142.88; *Thessalonians: commentary and text*: 142.89; *Unidentified*: 14; *apologie, or aunswer in defence of the Church of England, An*: 144.58
Joannes, *Arundinensis* (perhaps). *De religione sacrosancta dialogus* (perhaps): 148.295
Joannes, *Canonicus. Aristotle–Physica: commentary*: 146.11
Joannes, *de Altavilla. Archithrenius*: 148.260
John XXI, *Pope. Unidentified*: 147.17
John, *Chrysostom, Saint. Epistles–Paul: commentary and text*: 144.10; *In epistolam ad Romanos homiliae octo priores*: 147.13
Josephus, Flavius. *Antiquitates Judaicae*: 145.07; *De bello judaico*: 140.5
Junius, Adrian. *nomenclator, The*: 149.276

Justices of Peace (perhaps): 139.41
Justinian I. *Institutiones*: 139.16; 141.17; 143.65; 146.18; 146.42; 146.111; 148.125; 148.198
Justinus, *Martyr. Works*: 143.12
Justus, *Pascasius. Alea, sive de curanda ludendi in pecuniam cupiditate*: 146.74
Juvenalis, Decimus Junius. *Works* (probable): 144.8; 148.242

Katzschius, Joannes. *De gubernanda sanitate*: 146.225
Kemper, Otho. *In universam oratoriae facultatis artem methodica institutio*: 149.220;
Kingsmill, Andrew. *most excellent and comfortable treatise, for all such as are troubled in minde, A*: 149.183
Kis, Stephanus. *Theologiae sincerae loci communes*: 147.8
Kis, Stephanus (probable). *Speculum romanorum pontificum* (probable): 147.41
Knox, John. *answer to a great number of blasphemous cavillations written by an anabaptist and adversarie to Gods eternal predestination, An*: 142.154
Krantz, Albert. *Ecclesiastica historia sive Metropolis*: 148.163:1; *Saxonia*: 148.163:2

L'Espine, Jean de (probable). *excellent treatise of christian righteousnes, An* (probable): 142.97
La Place, Pierre de. *De statu religionis et reipublicae in regno Galliae*: 146.93; *treatise of the excellencie of a christian man, A*: 142.98
La Ramée, Pierre de. *Aristotelicae animadversiones*: 148.283; *Aristotle–Metaphysics: commentary*: 148.188; *Aristotle–Physica: commentary*: 148.187; *Cicero–De fato: commentary*: 146.255; *Cicero–Selected works–Orations: commentary*: 148.284; 149.68; *Commentariorum de religione christiana libri*

INDEX I: AUTHORS AND WORKS 297

quatuor: 149.89; *Dialectica*: 146.135; 148.33; 148.278; 148.282; 149.210; 150.55; *Grammatica*: 149.115; *Unidentified*: 145.20; 146.196; *Virgilius–Bucolics: commentary and text*: 148.281; *Virgilius–Georgics: commentary*: 146.122

La Roche de Chandieu, Antoine de. *Unidentified*: 142.79

Lactantius, Lucius Coelius. *Works*: 147.22; (probable): 142.67; 146.326

Lagus, Conradus. *Methodicus juris utriusque traditio*: 146.19; 148.139

Lambinus, Dionysius. *Horace–Unidentified: commentary* (probable): 148.50

Lancelotto, Giovanni Paolo. *Institutiones juris canonici*: 146.22

Languet, Hubert. *Vindiciae contra tyrannos*: 148.174

Lascovius, Petrus Monedulatus. *Theorematum de puro et expresso Dei verbo nuper propositorum, examen et refutatio*: 149.280

Latimer, Hugh, Bishop. *Sermons*: 149.273

Latomus, Jacobus, the Elder. *Unidentified*: 146.296

Lavater, Ludwig. *Historia de origine et progressu controversiae sacramentariae, de coena Domini*: 146.269; *De spectris*: 146.231

Lax, Gaspar. *Arithmetica speculativa*: 148.85

Leland, John. *Assertio inclytissimi Arturii regis Britanniae*: 148.71

Lemnius, Levinus. *De habitu et constitucione corporis*: 144.23; 148.269; 150.65; (probable): 146.224 *De miraculis occultis naturae libri IIII*: 149.271; 150.70; *Libelli tres (De astrologia, De praefixo cuique vitae termino, De honesto animi et corporis oblectamento)*: 146.226; *Similitudinum ac parabolarum quae in Bibliis ex herbis atque arboribus desumuntur explicatio*: 149.169

Lensaeus, Joannes. *De unica religione studio catholicorum principum in republica conservanda*: 149.229

Leo Africanus, Joannes. *De totius Africae descriptione libri IX*: 149.172

Lever, Ralph. *arte of reason, rightly termed, witcraft, The*: 149.208

Lily, William. *Institutio compendiaria totius grammaticae*: 150.44

Linacre, Thomas. *Rudimenta grammatices*: 149.267; (probable): 139.4; 148.108

Lindanus, Willelmus, Bishop. *Tabulae vigentium nunc atque grassantium passim haereseon*: 148.82

Lindsay, Sir David. *warkis of the famous and vorthie knicht Schir David Lyndesay, The*: 149.59

Lipsius, Justus. *Unidentified*: 148.141

Littleton, Sir Thomas. *Tenures*: 145.48; 146.95

Liturgies–Church of England
  Book of Common Prayer: 139.31; (probable) 142.116

Livius, Titus. *Historiae Romanae decades*: 148.17; 150.39; *Historiae Romanae decades–Selected works*: 143.9

Longolius, Christophorus. *Epistolae*: 148.22; *Orationes duae pro defensione sua*: 146.169

Lorich, Reinhard. *De institutione principum loci communes*: 146.132; 50.50

Lossius, Lucas. *Erotemata dialecticae et rhetoricae Philippi Melancthonis, et praeceptionum Erasmi Roterodami*: 149.209

Louis I, *Prince de Condé. Literae*: 148.11; *Literae . . . Testificatio causarum quae eum arma sumere coegerunt* [and other works]: 142.148

Lucanus, Marcus Annaeus. *Pharsalia*: 141.18; 143.10; 146.124; 148.19

Lucian, of Samosata. *Unidentified*: 145.41; 146.128; 148.225; *Works*: 143.52; 148.224

Lucian, *of Samosata* (perhaps). *Unidentified*: 144.19

Lucretius Carus, Titus. *De rerum natura*: 144.57

Luis, *de Granada*. *Unidentified*: 149.291

Luther, Martin. *Allegoriarum, typorum et exemplorum veteris et novi testamenti libri duo*: 142.58; *commentarie upon the fiftene psalmes, called psalmi graduum, A*: 142.95; *Confutatio determinationis Doctorum Parrhisiensium, contra M.L., ex Ecclesiasticis doctoribus denuo recognita et locupleta*: 142.109; *Genesis: commentary*: 150.2; *Romans: commentary*: 142.107; *Unidentified*: 146.305

Lycosthenes, Conrad. *Apophthegmata*: 145.14; 146.71

Lyndewode, William, *Bishop*. *Constitutiones provinciales*: 146.26; 146.31

Macchiavelli, Niccolò. *De principe*: 146.131; 148.165; 149.106

Macrobius, Ambrosius Aurelius Theodosius. *In somnium Scipionis* (probable): 148.221

Mantica, Francesco, *Cardinal* (probable). *Tractatus de conjecturis ultimarum voluntatum* (probable): 146.16

Manuscripts, including (probable) and (perhaps): 143.82; 143.84:1:1-14; 144.52:1-3; 146.254:1-2; 146.280; 147.4; 147.45; 148.302; 149.254; 150.14:1-3; 143.84:2; 139.29

Manuzio, Aldo, *the Elder* (perhaps). *Orthographia et flexus dictionum graecarum omnium apud Statium* (perhaps): 146.152

Manuzio, Aldo, *the Younger*. *Purae, elegantes et copiosae latinae linguae phrases*: 145.47; 146.160;

Manuzio, Paolo. *Antiquitatum Romanarum liber de legibus*: 146.29; *Cicero–Epistolae ad Atticum: commentary*: 148.59; 149.76; *Epistolae* (probable): 146.165

Marlorat, Augustine. *Thesaurus sacrae scripturae*: 146.313

Marnix van Sant Aldegonde, Philips van. *Responsio ad M. Baii apologiam*: 149.149

Martialis, Marcus Valerius. *Epigrammata*: 146.123; *Unidentified*: 148.39

Martinius, Petrus. *Grammatica hebraica*: 147.30

Martinus Polonus. *Margarita decreti, seu Tabula Martiniana*: 139.38

Matthisius, Gerardus. *Epitoma Aristoteleae logicae graecolatina* (perhaps): 145.36; *Unidentified*: 146.242

Maximus, *of Tyre*. *Sermones*: 143.53

Medici antiqui omnes, qui latinis literis diversorum morborum genera et remedia persecuti sunt: 138.18:1

Meier, Georg, *Professor at Wittenberg*. *Sententiae veterum poetarum*: 146.53

Mela, Pomponius. *De orbis situ*: 148.179

Melanchthon, Philipp. *Aristotle–Ethica: commentary*: 146.61; *Aristotle–Physica: commentary*; 149.119; (probable): 146.227; *Dialectica*: 139.20; 146.137; 149.207; *Liber de anima*: 146.229; 149.25; *Loci communes theologici*: 146.293; *Rhetorica*: 149.257; *Romans: commentary*: 142.81; 149.94; *Unidentified*: 146.146

Melanchthon, Philipp (probable). *Rhetorica* (probable): 146.179

Menzel, Hieronymus. *Responsio ad calumnias Osii*: 142.93

Mercerus, Joannes, *Professor of Hebrew*. *Commentarii in librum Job*: 142.27; *Commentarii in Salomonis Proverbia, Ecclesiasten, et Canticum canticorum*: 142.28; *Minor prophets: commentary and text*: 142.26

Mercurialis, Hieronymus. *Unidentified*: 146.350

Mesue, Joannes. *Mesuae qui Graecorum ac Arabum postremus medicinam practicam illustravit*: 138.2

Middendorp, Jacob. *De celebrioribus universi terrarum orbis academiis*: 148.113
Mizauld, Antoine. *Unidentified*: 146.232
Moller, Justus. *Fasciculus remediorum ex Dioscoride et Mathiolo methodice accommodatorum*: 149.108
Monte, Lambertus de. *Aristotle–Physica: commentary*: 149.29
More, Sir Thomas. *Selected works*: 149.19; *Unidentified*: 148.120; *Utopia*: 148.162; *workes of Sir T. More ... wrytten by him in the Englysh tonge, The*: 149.18
Morelius, Gulielmus. *De verbis anomalis*: 146.154
Morellus, Theodoricus. *Enchiridion ad verborum copiam*: 146.157
Mornay, Philippe de. *Tractatus de ecclesia*: 144.30
Mouchy, Antoine de. *In octo libros Topicorum Aristotelis hypomnema*: 145.17
Muenster, Sebastian. *Grammatica hebraica*: 143.38
Muretus, Marcus Antonius. *Selected works–Orations*: 146.177; 150.53; 148.21; (probable): 148.218
Musculus, Wolfgang. *Genesis: commentary and text*: 142.39; *Loci communes*: 142.38
Musculus, Wolfgang (probable). *Loci communes*: 146.316; (probable): 148.90
Mynsinger, Joachim. *Apotelesma*: 146.6:1

Natura brevium: 146.38
necessary doctrine and erudition for any christen man, sette furthe by the kynges majestie, A (perhaps): 139.30
Nemius, Joannes. *Orthographiae ratio*: 146.153
Neobar, Conrad. *De inveniendi argumenti disciplina libellus*: 149.128
Nicephorus Callistus (perhaps). *Ecclesiastica historia* (perhaps): 141.16
Niger, Franciscus, *Venetus. Grammatica*: 139.32
Nizolius, Marius. *Observationes*: 146.7; 148.208; (probable): 150.11
Nonnus, Panopolitanus. *Unidentified*: 143.24
Nowell, Alexander. *Catechismus*: 146.276; 148.94; 150.64; *Unidentified*: 149.36
Nunius Velius, Petrus. *Dialecta libri tres*: 146.141

Ockland, Christopher. *Anglorum praelia, ab anno domini 1327 usque ad annum 1558*: 142.146
Oderborn, Paul. *Joannis Basilidis magni Muscoviae ducis vita*: 148.99
Odofredus, Denari. *Summa de libellis formandis*: 146.34:B
Oecolampadius, Joannes. *Graecae literaturae dragmata*: 146.149
Oldendorp, Johann. *Unidentified*: 146.33
Olevian, Caspar. *De substantia foederis gratuiti inter Deum et electos*: 149.278; *Notae in evangelia*: 149.142
Oratorum veterum orationes: 143.11
Oriano, Lanfrancus de. *Practica Lanfranci*: 146.25
Origen. *Works* (probable): 144.42
Ortelius, Abraham. *Theatrum orbis terrarum*: 148.13
Osorio da Fonseca, Jeronimo, *Bishop. De regis institutione et disciplina*: 146.345; *De gloria*: 146.344; *De justitia*: 146.346; 148.159; *De nobilitate civili libri II. De nobilitate christiana libri III*: 141.8; *De rebus Emmanuelis regis Lusitaniae*: 148.156; *De regis institutione et disciplina*: 148.154; *De vera sapientia*: 148.157; 150.67:1; *In Gualterum Haddonum magistrum libellorum supplicum libri tres*: 146.347; 147.21; 148.153; *Isaiah: commentary and paraphrase*: 148.155; *Selected works*: 147.19; 150.46; (probable): 148.158

Overton, John. *Jacobs troublesome journey to Bethel*: 147.38
Ovidius Naso, Publius. *Fasti*: 145.29; *Heroides*: 148.250; 150.80; *Metamorphoses*: 143.17; 144.34; 144.59. 148.251:1; 148.251:2; 149.55; *Selected works*: 139.13; *Tristia*: 144.63; 148.72; 148.176; 148.248
Ovidius Naso, Publius (probable). *Metamorphoses*: 142.141

Paglia, Antonio dalla. *benefite that christians receive by Jesus Christ crucifyed, The*: 149.180;
Pagninus, Sanctes. *Thesauri linguae sanctae epitome*: 146.147; 149.72
Paiva de Andrade, Diogo de, *the Elder*. *Defensio Tridentiae fidei*: 146.262; *Orthodoxarum explicationum libri decem*: 148.86
Palingenius, Marcellus. *Zodiacus vitae*: 146.121; 148.255; *zodiake of life, The*: 149.121
Palmyraenus, Aulus Antonius. *In academicas quaestiones Ciceronis scholion*: 143.28
Palsgrave, John (probable). *Lesclarcissement de la langue francoyse* (probable): 149.32
Pantaleon, Heinrich. *Chronographia ecclesiae christianae*: 146.107
Paracelsus. *De tartaro libri septem perquam utiles*: 146.211
Paradin, Claude. *Symbola*: 146.88; 148.219
Parsons, Robert (probable). *first booke of the christian exercise, pertaining to resolution, The* (probable): 149.199
Pasquier, Étienne (probable). *monophile, Le* (probable): 149.171
Paulli, Simon, *the Elder*. *Postilla–Epistolae*: 149.211
Paulus, *Venetus*. *Logica*: 149.31
Pausanias. *Graeciae descriptio*: 148.25
Pelegromius, Simon. *Synonymorum sylva olim a Simone Pelegromio collecta, nunc è Belgarum sermone in Anglicanum transfusa, et redacta per H. F. Accesserunt huic editioni synonyma quaedam poetica*: 147.23
Perez de Pineda, Juan. *excelent comfort to all christians, against all kinde of calamities, An*: 149.184
Perion, Joachim. *De dialectica*: 146.136; 148.273; *De rebus gestis vitisque Apostolorum*: 146.96; *Unidentified*: 146.186
Perottus, Nicolaus (perhaps). *Cornucopia*: 141.7; (perhaps): 149.203
Perpinianus, Petrus Joannes. *Orationes*: 146.185
Persius Flaccus, Aulus. *Works*: 146.125
Peter Lombard. *Sententiarum libri IIII*: 144.26; 144.51; (probable): 146.327
Petrarca, Francesco. *De remediis*: 148.244; *Unidentified*: 138.8
Petri, Petrus, *Bishop of Leeuwarden, called Cunerus*. *Tractatus aliquot insigniores de gravissimis theologiae christianae controversiis*: 149.201
Peucer, Kaspar. *Commentarius de praecipuis divinationum generibus* 146.219; 148.288
Pezel, Christoph. *Unidentified*: 142.90
Pflacher, Moses (probable). *Analysis typica omnium cum veteris tum novi Testamenti librorum historicorum* (probable): 147.9
Philelphus, Franciscus. *De morali disciplina*: 149.61:A
Philippson, Joannes, *Sleidanus*. *De quatuor summis imperiis*: 142.133; 146.99; 150.48
Philo, *Judaeus*. *Libri Quatuor. Primus de mundi fabricatione, secundus de decem praeceptis, tertius de magistratu seu principe deligendo, quartus de officio judices*: 146.299; *Selected works*: 146.343
Philostratus. *De vita Apollonii Tyanei* (perhaps): 146.83
Phraseologia Isocratis graecolatina: 143.30

INDEX I: AUTHORS AND WORKS 301

Pico della Mirandola, Giovanni, *Count*. *Unidentified*: 144.48
Pictorius, Georg. *Pantapolion, continens omnium ferme quadrupedum*: 146.230
Piers, Ploughman. *Piers, Ploughman*: 149.224
Pilkington, James, *Bishop. Aggeus the prophete declared by a large commentarye* (probable): 149.182; *burnynge of Paules church in London in 1561, The*: 149.196
Pindar. *Works* (probable): 149.240
Pinder, Ulrich. *Compendium breve de bone valetudinis cura*: 146.339
Pius II, *Pope. Unidentified*: 143.58
Placitus, Sextus. *Unidentified*: 138.21
Plato. *Selections*: 146.63; *Works*: 138.20
Plautus, Titus Maccius. *Comoediae*: 142.131; 148.215; 146.120
Pliny, *the Elder. Historia naturalis*: 138.1; 143.104; 150.5
Pliny, *the Elder* (perhaps). *Historia naturalis* (perhaps): 142.123
Pliny, *the Younger. Epistolae*: 142.149; 146.166; 148.112; *Panegyricus*: 139.12
Plutarch. *Moralia*: 143.4; 145.18; 148.239; 150.38; *Vitae parallelae*: 150.13; 143.5; *Vitae parallelae–Epitome*: 146.79; 148.268; (probable): 142.145; *Works*: 148.237; 148.238
Pole, Reginald, *Cardinal. Liber de Concilio* [and other works]: 149.153
Politianus, Angelus. *Works*: 148.203
Porphyrius, *of Tyre. Unidentified*: 144.36
Porta, Giovanni Battista della. *Magia naturalis*: 146.257
Posselius, Joannes. *Syntaxis linguae graecae*: 145.10; 148.88; 148.128; 150.49
Possevino, Antonio (probable). *Unidentified*: 148.213
praise of musicke, The: 150.56
Practica cancellariae apostolicae cum stylo et formis in romana curia usitatis (perhaps): 142.85

Prime, John. *fruitefull and briefe discourse in two bookes: the one of nature, the other of grace, The*: 149.194
Psalmi seu precationes ex variis scripturae locis collectae: 148.102
Ptolemy, Claudius. *Unidentified*: 148.8
Purbach, Georg. *Novae theoricae planetarum*: 146.245
Puteo, Franciscus de, *Carthusian. Cathena aurea super psalmos*: 145.08
Pythagoras. *Carmina aurea*: 146.49

Quintilianus, Marcus Fabius. *Institutiones oratoriae*: 139.24; *Unidentified*: 148.58; 148.64

Rainolds, John. *Joannis Rainoldi orationes duae: ex iis quas habuit in collegio Corporis Christi, anno 1576*: 147.39; *Sex theses de sacra scriptura, et ecclesia*: 142.111; *summe of the conference betwene J. Rainoldes and J. Hart [Jesuit], The*: 149.274
Rainolds, William. *refutation of sundry reprehensions, cavils, and false sleightes, by which M. Whitaker laboureth to deface the late English translation, and catholike annotations of the new Testament, A*: 148.60
Ratramnus, *Monachus. De corpore et sanguine Domini*: 142.91
Ravennas, Petrus. *Alphabetum aureum utriusque juris*: 146.17
Ravisius, Joannes (Textor). *Epistolae*: 148.264; *Epitheta*: 145.38; *Officina*: 146.10; 148.234; 150.17
Rebuffus, Petrus. *Tractatus de decimis tam feudalibus, quam aliis*: 146.23
Record, Robert. *ground of artes teachyng the worke and practise of arithmetike, The*: 149.70; 150.42;
Regimen sanitatis Salernitatum: 148.267; 148.270; 149.116
Reisch, Gregor. *Margarita philosophica*: 147.5

Resendius, Lucius Andreas. *Sententia et exempla ex probatissimis quibusque scriptoris collecta*: 148.57

Rhodolphus, Caspar (probable). *Dialectica* (probable): 146.138; 148.277;

Riccius, Bartholomaeus. *Apparatus latinae locutionis*: 149.48; *De imitatione libri tres*: 146.195

Rich, Barnaby. *Allarme to England, foreshewing what perilles are procured, where the people live without regarde of martiall lawe*: 149.288

Ridley, Nicholas. *De coena Dominica assertio*: 146.304

Rivius, Joannes. *De consolandis aegrotantibus*: 146.302; *De stultitia mortalium, in procrastinanda correctione vitae, liber*: 149.218

Robortellus, Franciscus. *De artificio dicendi*: 149.35; *In libros politicos Aristotelis disputatio*: 149.61:C

Rondelet, Guillaume. *Methodus curandorum omnium morborum*: 149.112

Ruellius, Joannes. *De natura stirpium*: 138.33

Rufus, *of Ephesus*. *De medicamentis purgantibus*: 143.103

Ruland, Martin, *the Elder*. *Synonyma*: 144.24; 150.62

Ruland, Martin, *the Elder* (probable). *Synonyma*: 142.130

Sadoletus, Jacobus. *Epistolae*: 146.161

Saint German, Christopher. *Doctor and student*: 148.131

Sallustius Crispus, Caius. *Unidentified*: 146.85; 146.112; 148.75; 148.228:2; *Works* (probable): 150.20

Sambucus, Joannes. *Tres dialogi de imitatione Ciceroniana*: 146.188

Sandeo, Felino Maria (probable). *Decretales: commentary* (probable): 146.3

Sanders, Nicholas. *De typica et honoraria sacrarum imaginum adoratione libri duo*: 146.279

Sandys, Edwin, *Archbishop*. *Sermons made by the most reverende Edwin, archbishop of Yorke*: 150.22

Sanson, Franciscus, *de Senis* (perhaps). *Quaestiones super Physicam Aristotelis* (perhaps): 143.59

Sarcerius, Erasmus. *Methodus in praecipuos scripturae divinae locos*: 142.65

Scaliger, Julius Caesar. *Poetices libri septem*: 143.21

Scapula, Joannes. *Lexicon graecolatinum novum*: 144.2; 149.14

Schade, Petrus, *Mosellanus* (perhaps). *Unidentified*: 148.12

Schegk, Jacob, *the Elder*. *Commentarius in III libros De anima*: 143.85:B; *In octo Physicorum, sive de auditione physica libros Aristotelis, commentaria*: 143.85:A

Schofer, Arsatius. *Enarrationes Evangeliorum dominicalium, ad dialecticam methodum accommodatae*: 150.45

Schorus, Antonius. *De ratione discendae docendaeque linguae latinae et grecae*: 150.57; *Phrases linguae latinae*: 143.33; 146.158; 148.106; *Thesaurus verborum linguae latinae Ciceronianus*: 149.65

Scriptores historiae Augustae (part) (probable): 148.10

Seneca, Lucius Annaeus. *Naturales quaestiones*: 138.9; *Selected Works*: 142.126; *Selections–Flores selecti*: 146.45; *Tragoediae*: 142.132; *Works*: 148.14; (perhaps): 148.256

Serapion, *the Elder*. *De simplicium medicamentorum historia libri septem*: 138.19

Serenus Sammonicus, Quintus. *De re medica*: 143.93

Sermons (undidentified): 139.36; 146.265; 146.306; 147.36:1–2; 149.225

Serres, Jean de. *Gasparis Colinii Castilloni, magni quondam Franciae Amerallii, vita*: 148.147

Severianus, Julius (probable). *Syntomata rhetorices* (probable): 149.131

Seyssel, Claude de, *Bishop of Marseilles*. *De republica Galliae*: 148.167
Shepery, John. *Hyppolitus Ovidianae Phaedrae respondens*: 147.44; 148.145
Sigonio, Carlo. *De antiquo jure italiae libri tres*: 148.142; *Unidentified*: 148.292
Silvagius, Matthaeus. *Selected works*: 148.137
Simler, Josias. *De principiis astronomiae libri duo*: 143.54; *De vera Jesu Christi secundum humanam naturam in his terris praesentia*: 146.282
Simonius, Simon. *Aristotle–De sensuum instrumentis: commentary*. *Aristotle–De memoria et reminiscentia: commentary*: 148.81; *De vera nobilitate*: 146.46; 148.291; *Unidentified*: 148.266
Simplicius, *of Cilicia*. *Aristotle–Physica: commentary*: 143.105
Smeton, Thomas. *Ad virulentum Archibaldi Hamiltonii apostatae dialogum*: 149.192
Smith, Sir Thomas, *Doctor of Civil Laws*. *De recta et emendata linguae Anglicae scriptione, dialogus*: 148.80; *De recta et emendata linguae graecae pronuntiatione epistola*: 148.121
Snecanus, Gellius. *Methodica descriptio, et fundamentum trium locorum scripturae* [and other works]: 149.258
Song books (unidentified): 148.302
Sophocles. *Works*: 143.66; 144.20; 150.68; (probable): 145.24
Soto, Pedro de. *Institutionis christianae libri tres priores: jussu D. Othonis Cardinalis et episcopi Augustani a doctis theologis lecti et probati*: 149.250
Spagnuoli, Baptista. *Unidentified*: 145.50
Spangenberg, Johann. *Gospels and Epistles (liturgical): commentary and text*: 146.333; *Margarita theologica*: 145.51
Sprenger, Jacob. *Malleus maleficarum*: 144.31
Stöckel, Leonhard. *Formulae tractandarum sacrarum concionum*: 149.186

Stanyhurst, Richard. *De rebus in Hibernia gestis libri quattuor*: 148.212; *Unidentified*: 145.25
Stapleton, Thomas. *Speculum pravitatis haereticae*: 148.296
Stephanus, *Atheniensis*. *Galen–De methodo medendi ad Glauconem: commentary*: 138.31
Stewechius, Godeschalcus. *De particulis linguae latinae*: 149.83
Strabo. *Geographia*: 148.77
Strebaeus, Jacobus Lodovicus. *Cicero–De partitione oratoria: commentary and text*: 149.50; *De electione et oratoria collocatione verborum*: 149.67; *Unidentified*: 146.200:2; 148.29
Strigelius, Victorinus. *Aristotle–Ethica: commentary*: 146.58; 149.102; *In erotemata dialecticae P. Melanchthonis hypomnemata*: 149.269
Strozzi, Ercole. (See Tito Vespasiano Strozzi)
Strozzi, Tito Vespasiano. *Strozzi poetae pater et filius*: 143.37
Stubbes, Philip. *second part of the Anatomie of abuses, conteining the display of corruptions, The*: 150.54
Sturmius, Joannes. *Academicae epistolae urbanae*: 149.227; *Ad Werteros fratres nobilitas literata*: 149.151; *Classicarum epistolarum, libri III*: 149.222; *De imitatione oratoria*: 149.85; *De periodis*: 146.201; 149.164; *De universa ratione elocutionis rhetoricae*: 149.174; *In partitiones oratorias Ciceronis dialogi*: 146.203; 149.78; *Luctus ad Joachimum Camerarium* [and other works]: 143.45
Surius, Laurentius. *Commentaria brevis rerum in orbe gestarum*: 148.149
Susenbrotus, Joannes. *Epitome troporum ac schematum*: 139.7; 146.200:1; (probable): 148.70; *Unidentified*: 148.189
Symmachus, Quintus Aurelius. *Epistolae*: 146.173

Tabulae locorum communium theologicorum: et epistolae D. Pauli ad Romanos (probable): 149.22
Tacitus, Publius Cornelius. *Works*: 148.15
Talaeus, Aldomarus. *Rhetorica*: 148.107; 149.178; 146.194
Terentius, Publius, *Afer. Works*: 139.1; 144.21; 147.42; 148.44; 148.74; 148.214; 149.23; 150.69; (probable): 149.266
Themistius. *Unidentified*: 143.70; 146.216
Theodoret, *Bishop. De providentia*: 142.68
Theodorus, *Gaza. Institutiones grammaticae*: 146.155
Theophylact, *Archbishop of Achrida. Acts: commentary and text*: 143.8:2; *Gospels: commentary and text*: 139.11; 141.6; 143.8:1
Thomas, à Kempis. *De imitatione Christi*: 146.278; 146.301
Thomas, *Hibernicus. Flores omnium fere doctorum*: 144.55; 145.04; 146.331
Thucydides. *De bello peloponnesiaco*: 143.13; 148.23
Tilney, Edmund. *brief and pleasant discourse of duties in mariage, called the Flower of friendshippe, A*: 150.41
Titelmann, Franz. *Aristotle–Selected works–Philosophia naturalis: commentary*: 145.54; 148.276; *Dialectica*: 141.14; 145.26; 146.139; 148.279; *Psalms: commentary and text*: 141.20; 150.47
Toletus, Franciscus, *Cardinal. Aristotle–De anima: commentary*: 150.18:2; *Aristotle–Physica: commentary*: 143.106; 145.09; 150.18:1; *Aristotle–Selected works–Logica: commentary*: 145.02; (probable): 149.232
Tomson, William. *In canticum canticorum quod scripsit Schelomo explanatio*: 149.295

Torrentinus, Hermann. *Elucidarius carminum*: 148.247
Torrentinus, Hermann (probable). *Elucidarius carminum* (probable): 146.151
Toxites, Michael. *Cicero (spurious)–Rhetorica ad Herennium: commentary and text*: 146.199
Trapezuntius, Georgius. *Rhetorica*: 146.197
Travers, Robert. *learned and a very profitable exposition made upon the CXI. psalme, A*: 142.99
Travers, Walter. *Ecclesiastica disciplina*: 142.151; 146.267
Trebellius Pollio. *Scriptores historiae Augustae* (part) (probable): 148.211
Tremellius, Joannes Immanuel. *Grammatica chaldaea et syra*: 146.145; (probable): 149.56:1; *In Hoseam prophetam interpretatio et enarratio*: 149.170
Tritheim, Johann von. *De septem secundeis*: 146.233
Triverius, Hieremias. *Commentarii in VII libros Aphorismorum Hippocratis*: 143.94
Trogus Pompeius. *Epitomae in Trogi Pompeii historias*: 145.28; 146.84; 148.228:1; (probable): 150.74
Trovamala, Baptista. *Summa roselle de casibus conscientie*: 148.134
Tudeschis, Nicolaus. *Decretales: commentary*: 146.2
Tunstall, Cuthbert, *Bishop. Compendium et synopsis in decem libros ethicorum Aristotelis*: 148.274; *De arte supputandi libri quattuor*: 146.109; 146.246; 149.139
Turnebus, Adrianus. *Adversariorum*: 148.37
Tusser, Thomas. *hundreth good pointes of husbandrie, A*: 149.145
Twyne, Thomas. *schoolemaster, or teacher of table philosophie, The*: 149.148
Tyndale, William. *whole workes of W.*

INDEX I: AUTHORS AND WORKS 305

Tyndall, John Frith, and Doct. Barnes, The: 149.16

Unidentified author: *Aristotle–Metaphysica and Physica: commentary*: 139.40; *Aristotle–Physica: commentary* (probable): 148.78; *Aristotle–Politica: commentary*: 143.32; *Cicero–Epistolae ad Atticum: commentary*: 148.46

Unidentified author and work: 138.12; 139.19; 139.28; 139.29; 139.33; 139.34; 139.36; 139.43:1–16; 142.55; 142.56; 142.57; 142.73; 142.84; 142.92; 142.96; 142.106; 142.110; 142.119; 142.128; 142.129; 142.134; 142.135; 142.136; 142.139:1; 142.139:2; 142.140; 142.142; 142.144; 142.150; 142.152; 142.157:1–5; 143.49; 143.82; 143.83:1-22; 143.84:1:1–14; 143.96; 144.3; 144.12; 144.41; 144.52:1-3; 144.53; 144.62; 144.71:1–20; 145.15; 145.34; 146.8; 146.13; 146.36; 146.50; 146.72; 146.98; 146.156:1; 146.156:2; 146.221; 146.223; 146.239; 146.244; 146.254:1–2; 146.256; 146.259; 146.265; 146.280; 146.287:2; 146.306; 146.309; 146.360; 146.360; 147.4; 147.25; 147.28; 147.34; 147.36:1–2; 147.45; 148.10; 148.34; 148.35; 148.38; 148.66; 148.97; 148.119; 148.123; 148.146; 148.151; 148.166; 148.169; 148.172; 148.182; 148.190; 148.194; 148.199; 148.209; 148.217; 148.253; 148.258; 148.263; 148.289; 148.293; 149.20; 149.122; 149.147; 149.152; 149.221; 149.244; 149.253; 149.254; 149.255; 149.287; 149.298; 150.4; 150.10; 150.14:1–3; 150.23; 150.40

Urbach, Joannes de. *Processus judiciarius*: 146.97

Ursinus, Zacharias. *catechisme, or maner to teach children and others the christian fayth, The*: 149.270

Vadianus, Joachim. *Epitome trium terrae partium*: 149.86

Valerius Maximus. *Facta et dicta memorabilia*: 139.15; 146.92; 148.249

Valerius, Cornelius. *De sphaera*: 146.235; 146.251; *Ethicae, seu De moribus philosophiae brevis et perspicua descriptio*: 146.240; 150.51:1; *Grammaticarum institutionum libri IIII*: 150.55:1; 149.135; *In universam bene dicendi rationem tabula*: 145.44; 150.55:2; *Physicae, seu de naturae philosophia institutio*: 150.51:2; *Tabulae totius dialectices*: 143.50; 148.69; 150.55:3

Valla, Laurentius. *Elegantiae*: 146.170; *Unidentified*: 144.44

Valverde de Amusco, Juan. *Vivae imagines partium corporis humani*: 138.4:1

Varennius, Joannes. *Syntaxis linguae graecae*: 148.127

Vasseus, Joannes. *Here beginnith a litel treatise conteyninge the jugement of urynes*: 143.91

Vatablus, Franciscus. *Unidentified*: 148.96

Vegetius Renatus, Flavius. *De re militari libri quatuor* (probable): 138.16

Velcurio, Joannes. *Aristotle–Physica: commentary*: 148.31; *Unidentified*: 142.137

Vermigli, Pietro Martire. *common places of ... Peter Martyr, The*: 149.11; *Corinthians: commentary*: 142.32; *Defensio ad Riccardi Smythaei Angli duos libellos de caelibatu sacerdotum, et votis monasticis*: 142.35; 146.297; 142.34; *Loci communes*: 146.337; *Preces sacrae ex Psalmis Davidis desumptae*: 142.36; *Romans: commentary*: 142.31; *Tractatio de sacramento eucharistiae, habita in universitate Oxoniensi* (probable): 142.33

Verro, Sebastian. *Physicorum libri X*: 149.293

Versor, Joannes. *Aristotle–Physica: commentary*: 149.66
Victoriis, Leonellus de. *Practica medicinalis*: 149.241
Vigelius, Nicolaus. *Institutionum juris publici libri III*: 146.37; *Unidentified*: 148.204
Viperano, Giovanni Antonio. *De historia scribenda liber*: 146.100; *De rege et regno liber*: 146.130
Virgilius Maro, Publius. *Aeneid*: 149.57; *Works*: 143.18; 150.9; (probable): 141.19; 146.115; 146.116; 148.216; *xiii bukes of Eneados, The*: 149.63
Vitruvius Pollio, Marcus. *De architectura*: 139.35
Vivaldus, Joannes Ludovicus. *Aureum opus de veritate contritionis*: 146.307
Vives, Joannes Lodovicus. *De anima et vita libri tres* [and other works]: 148.111; 149.272; *De disciplinis libri xx*: 139.10; 148.110; 149.114; *De officio mariti*: 146.66; *De ratione dicendi. De consultatione praeceptiones*: 149.177; (probable): 146.222; *De veritate fidei christianae*: 146.275; *Familiarium colloquiorum formulae, sive linguae latinae exercitatio*: 148.109; 146.164; *Introductio ad sapientiam* [and other works]: 149.235
Vocabularius juris utriusque: 139.5; 146.41; 148.138
volume of the bokes called Apocripha, The (perhaps): 143.71

Walther, Rudolph. *Mark: commentary and text*: 142.48
Wasserleider, Goswin. *Logica ad P. Rami dialecticam conformata*: 149.204
Wecker, Hanss Jacob. *Artis oratoriae praecepta in tabularum formam redactum*: 149.265; *Medicinae utriusque syntaxes*: 143.87
Wesenbecius, Matthaeus. *Digesta: commentary*: 146.6:2; *Unidentified*: 148.202

Whitaker, William. *Ad rationes decem Edmundi Campiani jesuitae, responsio*: 148.89; (perhaps): 142.87; *aunswere to a certaine booke, written by M. W. Rainoldes, An*: 147.16; *Responsionis ad decem illas rationes, quibus fretus E. Campianus, defensio contra confutationem J. Duraei Scoti*: 149.73
White, John, Bishop. *Diacosiomartyrion*: 148.301
Whitgift, John, Archbishop. *defense of the aunswere to the Admonition, against the Replie, The*: 149.17
Wigand, Johann. *Postilla*: 146.334; *Syntagma, seu corpus doctrinae veri et omnipotentis Dei, ex veteri Testamento tantum*: 142.44; 146.317
Wildenbergius, Hieronymus. *Aristotle–Unidentified: commentary* (probable): 145.19
Wilkinson, William. *confutation of certaine articles delivered unto the Familye of Love, A*: 144.54
Willich, Jodocus. *De pronuntiatione rhetorica*: 146.108; *Erotemata dialectices*: 146.140; (probable): 142.121
Wilson, Thomas, Secretary of State. *discourse uppon usurye, by waye of dialogue, A*: 149.136
Withals, John (perhaps). *shorte dictionarie for yonge begynners, A* (perhaps): 148.53
Wolfius, Hieronymus. *In Officia Catonem Laelium Paradoxa et Scipionis Somnium commentarii*: 146.75

Xenophon. *Cyropaedia*: 149.158; 149.284; *Works*: 148.26; (probable): 150.6

Zanchius, Hieronymus. *Ad cuiusdam Ariani libellum, Antithesis doctrinae Christi et Antichristi, de uno vero Deo, responsio*: 149.38; *De aperiendis in ecclesia scholis oratio* (perhaps): 142.25;

De natura Dei, seu de divinis attributis, libri V: 142.23; 149.10:2; *De religione christiana fides*: 149.64; *De tribus Elohim*: 142.22; 149.10:1; *Miscellaneorum libri tres*: 142.24; 149.10:3

Zenobius. *Compendium veterum proverbiorum*: 143.79

Zickzai, Valentinus Hellopaeus. *De sacramentis in genere*: 149.165

Zwinger, Theodor. *Aristotle–Ethica: commentary*: 148.28; 148.49; 150.12

Index II
Editors and Compilers

Arsenios, *Archbishop of Monemvasia*: 144.9

Bèze, Théodore de: 139.14; 142.16; 145.53; 146.328; 147.7; 148.92; 149.7; 150.3; 150.72
Badius, Jodocus, *Ascensius*: 148.260
Bonacci, Giovanni: 138.35
Bouchereau, Jacques (probable): 146.65; 150.78
Budé, Jean: 142.3:2; 142.4
Bunny, Edmund: 149.200

Camerarius, Joachim, *the Younger*: 149.105
Camerarius, Philippus: 149.105
Cartwright, Thomas: 149.252
Casa, Giovanni della: 148.3
Christopherson, John, *Bishop*: 146.357
Clichtoveus, Jodocus: 139.8
Crusius, Martin: 149.257
Crusius, Martin (probable): 146.179

Daneau, Lambert: 146.274

Ducherius, Gilbertus (probable): 143.9
Du Jon, François, *the Elder*: 148.105

Edrichus, George: 147.44; 148.145
Egnatius, Joannes Baptista (probable): 148.210; 148.211
Erasmus, Desiderius: 142.53; 144.22; 148.95
Erythraeus, Valentinus: 149.85
Estienne, Henri: 142.148; 143.11
Estienne, Robert, *the Elder*: 143.12; 146.69; 149.23

Field, John (probable): 142.120
Fisher, John, *Saint and Cardinal*: 148.102
Foxe, John, *the Martyrologist*: 142.95; 146.44; 149.16; 149.46; 149.286

Garbrand, John: 142.88; 142.89
Grant, Edward: 146.175
Grunius, Joannes: 149.25

Hegendorff, Christoph: 148.84

INDEX II: EDITORS AND COMPILERS

Hertelius, Jacobus: 142.58
Hopkins, John: 142.122

Jonviller, Charles de: 142.3:2; 142.4

Latomeus, Bartholomew: 149.50
Lavinius, Petrus: 143.17
Lawne, William: 149.281
Leunclavius, Joannes: 146.60
Lipsius, Justus: 148.15

Marten, Anthony: 149.11
Matthisius, Gerardus, *Geldrensis*: 150.27
Melanchthon, Philipp: 144.16
Mignault, Claude: 147.33; 149.283
Mills, Francis: 149.183

Neander, Michael, *of Sorau*: 143.30

O'Fihely, Maurice: 143.15
Olevian, Caspar: 149.279

Peletier, Jacques: 146.250
Philippson, Joannes, *Sleidanus*: 148.167
Pulton, Ferdinand: 146.237

Quentin, Jean: 142.114

Rastell, William: 149.18
Reich, Stephan: 149.117

Salvart, J. F.: 147.20; 149.205
Sichardus, Joannes: 146.343
Sternhold, Thomas: 142.122

Tremellius, Joannes Immanuel: 148.105

Wigand, Johann: 142.112
Wolfius, Hieronymus: 142.125

Xylander, Gulielmus: 143.41

Ziletti, Giovanni Battista: 146.14

Index III
Translators

Aemilius, Georg: 146.277
Androse, Richard: 150.35

Bèze, Théodore de: 139.14; 142.16; 145.53; 146.328; 147.7; 148.92; 149.7; 149.256; 150.3
Bell, James, *Bishop*: 150.34
Brende, John: 141.15
Brixius, Germanus: 147.13
Buchanan, George (probable): 139.4; 148.108; 149.267
Budaeus, Gulielmus: 148.265
Bull, Henry: 142.95

Castalio, Sebastian: 146.314
Chaloner, Sir Thomas, *the Elder*: 148.171; 149.126
Christopherson, John, *Bishop*: 146.299; 146.357
Clerke, Bartholomew: 146.129; 149.161
Coverdale, Miles, *Bishop* (probable): 149.242

Danyel, John: 149.184
Douglas, Gawin, *Bishop*: 149.63
Du Jon, François, *the Elder*: 142.45; 149.4; 150.25

Eobanus, Helius, *Hessus*: 148.68
Estienne, Henri: 143.11

F., P. (probable): 150.36
Field, John, *Minister*: 142.97
Foxe, John, *the Martyrologist*: 143.25

Gadaldini, Agostino: 138.31
Genebrardus, Gilbertus, *Archbishop*: 148.150
Gilby, Anthony: 149.249
Girard de Tournus, Jacques: 138.37
Golding, Arthur: 142.9; 149.55; 149.180
Googe, Barnaby: 149.51; 149.121
Gubernator, Joannes: 148.219

Hall, Arthur: 150.37
Hoby, Sir Thomas: 149.69
Hopkins, John: 142.122

Jerome, *Saint*: 150.71
Jonas, Justus: 142.107

Lambinus, Dionysius: 143.11; 145.06; 148.28; 148.49
Llwyd, Humphrey: 143.91
Lonicer, Philipp: 142.37

Malinaeus, Gulielmus: 149.230
Marten, Anthony: 149.11
Martin, Gregory: 149.6
Mutoni, Niccolo: 138.19

Neander, Michael, *of Sorau*: 143.30

Page, William: 150.28
Perion, Joachim: 150.27
Philippson, Joannes, *Sleidanus*: 146.106; 148.167; 149.231

Rogers, Thomas, *M.A.*: 145.52

Sigonio, Carlo: 149.285
Sternhold, Thomas: 142.122
Strigelius, Victorinus: 146.187
Sturmius, Joannes (probable): 149.175:1–3
Sureau, Hugues: 148.9

Taverner, Richard (perhaps): 143.71
Telius, Sylvester: 146.131; 148.165
Tomson, Laurence: 142.98; 149.256
Tremellius, Joannes Immanuel: 142.45; 149.4; 150.25

Warde, William: 150.35
Wecker, Hanss Jacob: 143.99

Xylander, Gulielmus: 143.41

Index IV
Stationers
(Publishers, Printers, Booksellers)

The stationers' names in the annotated book-lists are drawn either from imprints and colophons, which offer the names in a variety of forms, or from bibliographical sources, none of which consistently agree with another on those forms. For indexing purposes and for searching the database, PLRE has, therefore, constructed a uniform stationers' name list. English stationers' names, with a few exceptions, are derived from the STC, Volume 3; the forms of Continental names derive from a number of sources, including the STC, but most especially Adams. Accordingly, the names below do not always duplicate forms that appear in the annotated book-lists.

Albinus, Bernardus: 149.282
Aldine Press: 146.184
Apel, Jacob: 149.117
Apiarius, Matthias: 149.48
Arrivabenus, Andreas: 138.19

Badius, Jodocus, *Ascensius*: 148.260
Barbirius, Nicolaus: 149.170
Barker, Christopher: 142.88; 142.98; 149.146; 149.256; 149.288
Barker, Christopher (perhaps): 147.43
Barker, Christopher (probable): 142.101; 147.10; 147.38; 147.39; 147.44; 148.145; 149.275; 150.24:2; 150.56
Bebel, Joannes: 149.193
Benacius, Alexander: 149.35
Berthelet, Thomas: 141.2
Bindoni, Francesco di Alessandro: 148.137
Birckman, Arnold, Heirs of: 148.295; 149.83
Bishop, George: 142.9; 142.83; 142.111; 149.180; 149.194; 149.260; 149.261; 149.262; 149.274

INDEX IV: STATIONERS

Bogard, Jean: 148.296; 149.120
Bonhomme, Mathias: 138.37
Brubach, Petrus: 142.93; 146.335
Bynneman, Henry: 147.37; 148.184; 149.17; 149.208; 149.293; 150.66:A; 150.66:B
Bynneman, Henry (probable): 150.37

Calenius, Gervinus: 146.213
Caly, Robert: 148.301
Cawood, John: 149.18
Charlewood, John (probable): 142.63
Chard, Thomas: 142.87; 149.73; 150.22
Charteris, Henry: 149.192
Cholinus, Maternus: 148.222; 148.298; 149.162; 149.233
Chouët, Jacques: 149.280
Coldock, Francis: 146.175; 148.116
Colinaeus, Simon: 145.17
Commelinus, Hieronymus (probable): 149.290
Copland, William: 149.63
Corvinus, Christoph: 149.279; 149.297
Corvinus, Christoph (probable): 149.142
Corvinus, Georg: 142.37; 149.10:1; 142.22
Courteau, Thomas: 149.170
Crato, Johann: 149.134
Crato, Johann, Heirs of: 148.99
Crespin, Jean: 142.154; 146.304; 148.81
Crespin, Jean (probable): 142.13

Dawson, Thomas: 149.126; 150.34
Dawson, Thomas (probable): 142.9
Day, John 1: 143.25; 144.54; 146.44; 146.94; 148.51; 148.144; 149.16; 149.46; 149.144:1; 149.197; 149.286
Day, John 1 (perhaps): 143.71
Defner, Georg: 149.117
Denham, Henry: 142.86; 142.108; 145.52; 148.201; 149.11; 149.58:2
Denham, Henry (perhaps): 149.49

Duval, Denys: 149.129
Dupuys, Jacques: 148.14; 148.18

East, Thomas: 149.184
Egenolph, Christian, Heirs of: 146.225
Eliot's Court Press: 148.161; 149.215
Episcopius, Eusebius: 144.2; 146.75; 149.265; 150.12
Episcopius, Nicolaus 1: 147.13
Episcopius, Nicolaus, Heirs of: 149.265
Estienne, Henri 2: 148.126

Feyerabend, Johann: 149.53
Feyerabend, Sigismund: 142.37; 149.80
Feyerabend, Sigismund, Heirs of: 149.53
Fezandat, Michael (probable): 149.246
Foigny, Jean de: 149.6
Fouler, Joannes: 146.279
Fries, Augustin (probable): 149.234
Froben, House of: 147.13
Froschouer, Christoph: 142.29; 142.32; 142.34; 142.36; 142.48; 146.269; 146.282; 148.181; 149.77; 149.86
Froschouer, Christoph (probable): 149.5
Froschouer, Christoph, *the Younger*: 143.54
Froschouer, House of: 149.289

Gardiner, Thomas: 149.126
Gerardus, Joannes (probable): 142.14
Gerlach, Dietrich: 149.179
Giunta, Jacobus, Heirs of: 143.94
Giunta, Luc'Antonio, Heirs of: 138.2
Gluichstein, Theodorus: 149.296
Gorbin, Gilles: 149.127
Granjon, Robert (probable): 149.246
Gravius, Bartholomeus: 146.234
Gronenberg, Simon: 149.25
Guarinus, Thomas: 143.41; 146.288
Guttgesel: 149.186
Gymnicus, Arnold (probable): 142.58

Haach, Petrus: 149.201
Harnisch, Matthaeus: 142.24; 149.10:3; 149.38; 149.64
Harrison, John 1: 149.249
Harrison, John 2: 149.39; 149.252
Harrison, Luke: 142.9; 142.98
Harrison, Luke (perhaps): 149.49
Henricpetri, Sebastian: 142.64; 149.22; 149.137:1; 149.206:2; 150.59
Henricus, Nicolaus 1: 142.112; 146.334
Henripetri, Sixtus: 149.220
Hervagius, House of: 144.2; 146.75
Hervagius, Joannes: 142.38; 143.85:A; 143.85:B
Hock, Alexander: 142.94
Horst, Petrus: 150.27
How, William: 142.156

Isingrinius, House of (probable): 139.17
Isingrinius, Michael: 149.79

James, Jacob, *pseudonym*: 149.299
Jeffes, Abel: 149.47
Jobin, Bernhard: 149.85; 149.91; 149.174
Jones, Richard: 149.148

Kempensis, Godefridus: 148.4; 149.229
Kilianus, Johann: 142.42
Knobloch, House of: 149.139
Knobloch, House of (perhaps): 149.34

La Barre, Nicolaus de: 148.85
Latius, Joannes: 149.236
Le Preux, Franciscus: 146.352; 146.353:1; 146.353:2
Le Preux, Joannes: 146.321; 149.259
Locatellus, Bonetus: 143.15

Manutius, Aldus, Sons of: 138.18:1
Manutius, Aldus, *the Elder*: 148.42
Marchant, Martin: 148.168
Mareschall, Joannes: 142.153

Marsh, Thomas (probable): 149.52
Mena, Hugo: 148.1
Meyer, Joannes, Heirs of (perhaps): 142.25
Middleton, Henry: 142.111; 149.73; 149.261; 149.262; 150.22; 150.25
Middleton, Henry (perhaps): 149.252
Monocerotis, ad intersignium: 149.150
Mylius, Christian 1: 149.84
Mylius, Jacob: 142.23; 149.10:2

Newbery, Ralph: 142.89; 149.121; 150.37
Niest, Leonard: 149.41
Norton, William: 149.60
Nutium, Martin: 146.226

Oporinus: 146.325
Oporinus, House of: 143.30; 146.37; 146.60; 146.324; 146.330
Oporinus, Joannes: 146.32; 146.74; 146.199; 146.273; 146.302; 149.28; 149.176; 149.218
Oporinus, Joannes (probable): 146.105; 149.87; 149.159

Perna, House of: 147.8
Perna, Petrus: 142.35; 142.40; 146.272; 146.297; 148.148; 148.284; 149.68; 149.108
Perna, Petrus (probable): 146.211
Perrin, François: 146.308
Petri, Adam: 142.109; 146.343
Petri, Henricus: 138.22; 146.230
Pfortzheim, Jacobus Wolff de: 142.103
Plantin, Christopher: 138.4:1; 146.100; 146.130; 146.147; 146.153; 148.15; 148.212; 149.72; 149.75; 149.133
Purfoot, Thomas 1: 142.47; 142.83; 149.260
Pynson, Richard (probable): 149.32

Quentel, Joannes, Heirs of: 146.35
Quentel, Peter: 146.286

Rade, Gilles van den: 149.149; 149.187
Rhamba, Joannes: 146.46; 148.291
Rihelius, Josias: 138.3; 146.209; 149.222; 149.227
Rihelius, Theodosius: 146.228
Rihelius, Wendelin: 143.45; 144.27; 149.26; 149.154
Roigny, Jean: 138.25
Ross, John: 149.192

Schilders, Richard: 149.155
Schirat, Michael: 146.267
Schirat, Michael (probable): 142.151
Schneider, Andreas: 144.14
Schott, Johann: 138.5:1
Schwertel, Johann: 149.124
Scotus, Gualterius: 148.79
Seres, William 1: 142.105; 146.264; 149.182; 149.196
Siebeneicher, Matthias: 146.198
Silvius, Gulielmus: 149.37
Steelsius, Joannes: 149.230
Steiner, Heinrich: 150.45
Steinman, Johann: 146.27; 149.195
Stephanus, Henricus 2: 138.36; 142.26; 142.148; 143.11; 143.74; 146.145; 147.7; 148.11; 149.7; 149.56:1
Stephanus, Henricus 2 (probable): 143.1
Stephanus, Robertus 1: 142.17; 142.80; 143.12; 144.13; 146.69; 146.319:1; 148.84; 149.1; 149.9; 149.132; 149.191
Stephanus, Robertus 1 (probable): 148.210; 148.211
Stephanus, Robertus 2: 148.80; 148.121
Stephanus, Robertus 1 or 2: 146.310
Stoer, Jacobus: 146.284
Stroud, John (probable): 142.100

Thomas, Thomas 1: 147.20; 149.205
Torrentinus, Laurentius: 146.344
Tottel, Richard: 143.91

Ulricher, Georg (probable): 143.98

Vascosanus, Michael: 148.274
Vascosanus, Michael (probable): 149.67
Vautrollier, Thomas 1: 146.143; 142.87; 142.95; 142.97; 142.99; 147.23; 149.194; 149.281; 150.24:1
Veale, Abraham: 143.63
Velpius, Rutgerus: 146.102
Verstegen (Rowlands), Richard: 148.60
Vignon, Eustathius: 142.21; 142.27; 142.28; 142.60; 146.268; 146.274; 146.281; 148.87; 148.272; 149.45; 149.71; 149.90; 149.165; 149.212; 149.228; 149.277; 149.278
Vignon, Eustathius (probable): 142.77
Voegelin, Ernest: 149.74
Voegelin, House of: 149.81; 146.187

Waldegrave, Robert: 149.295
Waldkirch, Konrad von: 147.41
Ward, Roger: 150.54
Wechel, Andreas: 148.9; 149.89; 149.98; 149.140; 149.141; 149,160
Wechel, Andreas, Heirs of: 149.105; 149.204
Wechel, Johann: 149.80
Whitchurch, Edward: 148.130
Windet, John: 149.248
Withagius, Joannes: 146.299
Wolfe, John: 149.39
Wolfe, Reyner: 144.58
Wolfe, Reyner (probable): 148.71

Ziletti, Giordano: 148.114; 148.142

Index V
Places of Publication

Antwerp: 138.4:1; 146.100; 146.130; 146.133; 146.147; 146.153; 146.226; 146.235; 146.251; 146.299; 148.15; 149.37; 149.72; 149.75; 149.133; 149.149; 149.187; 149.230; 149.236
Augsburg: 142.130; 150.45; 150.62

Bardejov: 149.186
Basle: 138.22; 139.17; 142.35; 142.38; 142.39; 142.40; 142.58; 142.64; 142.103; 142.109; 143.28; 143.30; 143.41; 143.85:A; 144.2; 146.32; 146.37; 146.60; 146.74; 146.75; 146.105; 146.199; 146.211; 146.230; 146.272; 146.273; 146.288; 146.297; 146.302; 146.314; 146.324; 146.325; 146.330; 146.343; 147.8; 147.13; 148.28; 148.49; 148.148; 148.284; 149.22; 149.28; 149.68; 149.79; 149.87; 149.108; 149.137:1; 149.159; 149.176; 149.193; 149.206:2; 149.218; 149.220; 149.233; 149.265; 150.12; 150.59
Basle (probable): 146.126; 147.41

Bologna: 149.35
Bremen: 149.296
Britain: 139.31; 142.116; 142.119; 142.144; 143.25; 146.360; 147.16; 148.93; 149.199; 149.270
Britain (probable): 142.57; 142.84; 142.96; 142.110; 142.152; 147.36:1–2
Britain or Continent: 139.1; 139.4; 139.7; 139.14; 139.26; 139.27; 139.39; 141.10; 141.11; 141.12; 141.19; 142.11; 142.19; 142.20; 142.33; 142.45; 142.46; 142.49:1; 142.49:2; 142.51; 142.61; 142.62; 142.72; 142.102; 142.117; 142.118; 142.122; 142.133; 142 141; 142.143; 142.147; 142.158; 143.18; 143.47; 143.55; 143.56; 143.72; 144.7; 144.11; 144.19; 14⌊.21; 144.33; 144.34; 144.59; 144.63; 144.66; 144.67; 144.69; 145.01; 145.03; 145.12; 145.14; 145.27; 145.28; 145.29; 145.30; 145.32; 145.33; 145.37; 145.42; 145.43; 145.44;

INDEX V: PLACES OF PUBLICATION 317

145.45; 145.47; 145.48; 145.49; 145.51; 145.53; 146.11; 146.26; 146.64; 146.71; 146.73; 146.78; 146.84; 146.95; 146.99; 146.109; 146.115; 146.116; 146.119; 146.121; 146.135; 146.148; 146.162; 146.163; 146.165; 146.172; 146.174; 146.200:1; 146.202; 146.204; 146.246; 146.252; 146.291; 146.300; 146.313; 146.328; 146.329; 146.337; 146.338; 147.2; 147.9; 147.12; 147.14; 147.19; 147.24; 147.26; 147.27; 147.31; 147.34; 147.42; 148.17; 148.19; 148.20; 148.24; 148.30; 148.31; 148.32; 148.33; 148.44; 148.45; 148.48; 148.62; 148.68; 148.70; 148.72; 148.74; 148.91; 148.92; 148.95; 148.100; 148.101; 148.102; 148.105; 148.108; 148.117; 148.118; 148.122; 148.136; 148.158; 148.176; 148.183; 148.193; 148.197; 148.214; 148.216; 148.228:1; 148.229; 148.240; 148.248; 148.250; 148.251:1; 148.251:2; 148.255; 148.264; 148.267; 148.278; 148.282; 148.290; 149.3; 149.21; 149.58:1; 149.88; 149.115; 149.116; 149.167; 149.238:1; 149.238:2; 149.238:3; 149.242; 149.247; 149.266; 149.267; 149.276; 149.287; 150.1; 150.9; 150.16; 150.19; 150.33; 150.44; 150.48; 150.52; 150.55; 150.58; 150.69; 150.72; 150.74; 150.75; 150.79;

Cambridge: 147.20; 149.205
Cologne: 143.20; 145.36; 146.35; 146.213; 146.286; 148.4; 148.113; 148.222; 148.295; 148.298; 149.29; 149.83; 149.150; 149.162; 149.201; 149.229; 150.27
Continent: 138.1; 138.4:2; 138.5:2; 138.6:1; 138.6:2; 138.7; 138.8; 138.9; 138.10; 138.11; 138.13; 138.14; 138.15; 138.16; 138.17; 138.18:2; 138.20; 138.21; 138.23; 138.24; 138.26; 138.27; 138.28; 138.29; 138.30; 138.31; 138.32; 138.33; 138.34; 138.35; 138.38; 139.2; 139.3; 139.5; 139.6; 139.8; 139.9; 139.10; 139.11; 139.12; 139.13; 139.15; 139.16; 139.18; 139.20; 139.21; 139.22; 139.23; 139.24; 139.25; 139.28; 139.32; 139.35; 139.37; 139.38; 139.40; 139.42; 140.1; 140.2; 140.3; 140.4; 140.5; 141.1; 141.3; 141.4; 141.5; 141.6; 141.7; 141.8; 141.9; 141.13; 141.14; 141.16; 141.17; 141.18; 141.20; 141.21; 142.3:2; 142.12; 142.16; 142.30; 142.31; 142.41; 142.43; 142.44; 142.50; 142.52; 142.53; 142.54; 142.59; 142.65; 142.66; 142.67; 142.68; 142.69; 142.70; 142.71; 142.74; 142.75; 142.81; 142.82; 142.85; 142.90; 142.91; 142.107; 142.113; 142.121; 142.123; 142.124; 142.125; 142.127; 142.128; 142.129; 142.131; 142.132; 142.134; 142.135; 142.136; 142.138; 142.145; 142.149; 142.150; 142.155; 143.3; 143.4; 143.5; 143.6; 143.7; 143.8:1; 143.8:2; 143.10; 143.13; 143.14; 143.16; 143.17; 143.19; 143.22; 143.23; 143.24; 143.26; 143.27; 143.29; 143.31; 143.33; 143.34; 143.35; 143.36; 143.37; 143.38; 143.42; 143.43; 143.44; 143.46; 143.48; 143.50; 143.51; 143.52; 143.53; 143.57; 143.59; 143.60; 143.62; 143.64; 143.65; 143.66; 143.67; 143.68; 143.69; 143.70; 143.73; 143.75; 143.76; 143.77; 143.78; 143.79; 143.80; 143.86; 143.87; 143.88; 143.89; 143.90; 143.92; 143.93; 143.95; 143.99; 143.100; 143.101; 143.102; 143.103; 143.104; 143.105; 143.106; 144.1; 144.4; 144.5; 144.8; 144.9; 144.10; 144.15;

144.16; 144.17; 144.18; 144.20; 144.22; 144.23; 144.24; 144.25; 144.26; 144.28; 144.29; 144.30; 144.31; 144.32:1; 144.32:2; 144.35; 144.36; 144.38; 144.39; 144.40; 144.42; 144.43; 144.44; 144.45; 144.46; 144.47; 144.49; 144.50; 144.51; 144.55; 144.56; 144.57; 144.60; 144.61; 144.64; 144.65; 144.68; 144.70; 145.02; 145.04; 145.06; 145.07; 145.08; 145.09; 145.10; 145.11; 145.13; 145.15; 145.16; 145.18; 145.19; 145.21; 145.22; 145.23; 145.24; 145.26; 145.31; 145.35; 145.38; 145.39; 145.40; 145.46; 145.54; 145.55; 146.1; 146.2; 146.3; 146.4; 146.5; 146.6:1; 146.6:2; 146.7; 146.8; 146.10; 146.12; 146.14; 146.15; 146.16; 146.17; 146.18; 146.19; 146.21; 146.22; 146.23; 146.25; 146.28; 146.29; 146.30; 146.33; 146.34:A; 146.40; 146.41; 146.42; 146.43; 146.45; 146.47; 146.48; 146.49; 146.51; 146.52; 146.53; 146.54; 146.55; 146.56; 146.57; 146.58; 146.59; 146.61; 146.62; 146.63; 146.65; 146.66; 146.67; 146.68; 146.70; 146.76; 146.77; 146.79; 146.80; 146.81; 146.82; 146.83; 146.86; 146.87; 146.88; 146.89; 146.90; 146.91; 146.92; 146.93; 146.96; 146.97; 146.101; 146.103; 146.104; 146.106; 146.107; 146.108; 146.110; 146.111; 146.113; 146.114; 146.117; 146.118; 146.120; 146.122; 146.123; 146.124; 146.125; 146.127; 146.131; 146.134; 146.136; 146.137; 146.138; 146.139; 146.140; 146.141; 146.142; 146.144; 146.146; 146.149; 146.150; 146.151; 146.152; 146.154; 146.155; 146.156:2; 146.157; 146.158; 146.159; 146.160; 146.161; 146.164; 146.166; 146.167; 146.168; 146.169; 146.170; 146.171; 146.173; 146.176; 146.177; 146.178; 146.179; 146.180; 146.181; 146.182; 146.183:1; 146.183:2; 146.185; 146.186; 146.188; 146.189; 146.190; 146.191; 146.193; 146.194; 146.195; 146.196; 146.197; 146.200:2; 146.203; 146.205; 146.206; 146.207; 146.208; 146.210; 146.212; 146.214; 146.215; 146.216; 146.217; 146.218; 146.220; 146.222; 146.224; 146.227; 146.229; 146.232; 146.233; 146.236:1; 146.236:2; 146.238; 146.240; 146.242; 146.243; 146.245; 146.247; 146.248; 146.249:1; 146.249:2; 146.250; 146.253; 146.255; 146.257; 146.258; 146.259; 146.260; 146.261; 146.262; 146.263; 146.266; 146.270:1; 146.270:2; 146.271; 146.275; 146.277; 146.278; 146.283; 146.285; 146.287:1; 146.287:2; 146.289; 146.290; 146.292; 146.293; 146.296; 146.298; 146.301; 146.303; 146.305; 146.306; 146.307; 146.309; 146.310; 146.311; 146.312; 146.316; 146.317; 146.318; 146.320; 146.322; 146.323; 146.326; 146.327; 146.331; 146.332; 146.333; 146.336; 146.340:1; 146.340:2; 146.341; 146.342; 146.345; 146.346; 146.347; 146.348; 146.349; 146.350; 146.354; 146.355; 146.356; 146.357; 146.358; 146.359; 147.1; 147.3; 147.5; 147.6; 147.11; 147.15; 147.17; 147.18; 147.21; 147.22; 147.28; 147.29; 147.30; 147.33; 147.35; 147.40; 148.2; 148.3; 148.5; 148.6; 148.7; 148.13; 148.16; 148.18; 148.21; 148.22; 148.23; 148.25; 148.26; 148.27; 148.29; 148.36; 148.37; 148.38; 148.39; 148.40; 148.41; 148.46; 148.47; 148.50; 148.52; 148.54; 148.55; 148.56; 148.57; 148.58; 148.59; 148.61; 148.63; 148.64; 148.65; 148.67; 148.69; 148.73; 148.76; 148.77;

INDEX V: PLACES OF PUBLICATION 319

148.82; 148.83; 148.86; 148.88; 148.90; 148.96; 148.98; 148.103; 148.104; 148.106; 148.107; 148.109; 148.110; 148.111; 148.112; 148.115; 148.123; 148.124; 148.125; 148.127; 148.128; 148.129; 148.133; 148.134; 148.135; 148.138; 148.139; 148.140; 148.143; 148.149; 148.150; 148.152; 148.153; 148.154; 148.155; 148.156; 148.157; 148.159; 148.160; 148.163:1; 148.163:2; 148.164; 148.165; 148.170; 148.173; 148.174; 148.175; 148.177; 148.180; 148.185; 148.187; 148.188; 148.191; 148.195; 148.198; 148.200; 148.202; 148.203; 148.204; 148.205; 148.207; 148.208; 148.212; 148.215; 148.218; 148.219; 148.220; 148.221; 148.223; 148.224; 148.226; 148.227; 148.230; 148.231; 148.232; 148.233; 148.234; 148.235; 148.237; 148.238; 148.239; 148.241; 148.242; 148.243; 148.244; 148.245; 148.246; 148.247; 148.249; 148.252; 148.254; 148.256; 148.257; 148.258; 148.262; 148.265; 148.266; 148.268; 148.269; 148.270; 148.271; 148.273; 148.275; 148.276; 148.277; 148.279; 148.280; 148.281; 148.283; 148.285; 148.286; 148.287; 148.292; 148.294; 148.297; 148.299; 148.300; 149.1; 149.2; 149.8; 149.12; 149.14; 149.15; 149.20; 149.23; 149.24; 149.27; 149.30; 149.31; 149.33; 149.40; 149.42; 149.43; 149.44; 149.50; 149.54; 149.56:2; 149.62:2; 149.66; 149.76; 149.78; 149.82; 149.92; 149.93; 149.94; 149.95; 149.97; 149.99; 149.100; 149.101; 149.102; 149.103; 149.104; 149.106; 149.111; 149.112; 149.113; 149.114; 149.119; 149.123; 149.125; 149.128; 149.130; 149.131; 149.135; 149.137:2; 149.138; 149.143; 149.153; 149.156; 149.158; 149.163; 149.166; 149.169; 149.172; 149.173; 149.177; 149.178; 149.181; 149.188; 149.190; 149.202; 149.203; 149.206:1; 149.207; 149.209; 149.210; 149.211; 149.214; 149.217; 149.219; 149.221; 149.231; 149.232; 149.235; 149.237; 149.239; 149.240; 149.241; 149.243; 149.244; 149.245; 149.250; 149.251; 149.257; 149.258; 149.264; 149.268; 149.269; 149.271; 149.272; 149.283; 149.284; 149.285; 149.292; 149.294; 149.298; 150.2; 150.3; 150.4; 150.5; 150.6; 150.8; 150.10; 150.11; 150.13; 150.17; 150.18:1; 150.18:2; 150.20; 150.21; 150.23; 150.26; 150.30; 150.31; 150.32; 150.38; 150.39; 150.43; 150.46; 150.47; 150.49; 150.51:1; 150.51:2; 150.53; 150.55:1; 150.55:2; 150.55:3; 150.54; 150.61; 150.65; 150.67:1; 150.68; 150.70; 150.71; 150.73; 150.76; 150.77; 150.78; 150.80

Continent (probable): 138.12; 142.56; 142.92; 142.126; 142.140; 143.9; 143.32; 143.49; 144.6; 144.48; 144.62; 146.9; 146.36; 146.223; 146.239; 146.244; 146.256; 146.315; 148.8; 148.35; 148.43; 148.66; 148.97; 148.119; 148.162; 148.169; 148.172; 148.179; 148.182; 148.190; 148.199; 148.213; 148.217; 148.253; 148.263; 148.289; 150.60; 150.63; 150.67:2

Cracow: 146.198

Douai: 148.296; 149.120

Edinburgh: 149.59; 149.192; 149.299

Florence: 146.344

Frankfurt am Main: 142.22; 142.37; 142.93; 146.132; 146.225; 146.335; 148.9; 149.10:1; 149.53; 149.80; 149.89; 149.98; 149.105; 149.140; 149.141; 149.160; 149.204; 150.50;

Frankfurt am Main (probable): 142.15

Geneva: 138.36; 142.1; 142.2; 142.3:1; 142.4; 142.5; 142.6; 142.7; 142.8; 142.10; 142.13; 142.14; 142.17; 142.21; 142.26; 142.27; 142.28; 142.60; 142.77; 142.80; 142.154; 143.1; 143.11; 144.13; 146.231; 146.268; 146.274; 146.281; 146.284; 146.295; 146.304; 146.308; 146.319:1; 146.319:2; 146.351; 147.7; 148.81; 148.87; 148.272; 149.7; 149.9; 149.45; 149.71; 149.90; 149.132; 149.165; 149.168; 149.170; 149.191; 149.198; 149.212; 149.213; 149.228; 149.259; 149.277; 149.278; 149.280

Geneva (probable): 142.148; 143.74; 146.145; 148.11; 148.126; 149.56:1

Granada: 148.1

Heidelberg: 142.23; 142.151; 146.267; 149.10:2; 149.290

Hemel Hempstead (probable): 142.100

Herborn: 149.142; 149.279; 149.297

Lausanne: 146.352; 146.353:1; 146.353:2

Leiden: 149.41

Leipzig: 144.14; 146.27; 146.46; 146.187; 148.291; 149.74; 149.81; 149.117; 149.185; 149.195

London: 139.30; 139.41; 141.2; 141.15; 142.9; 142.47; 142.63; 142.83; 142.86; 142.87; 142.88; 142.89; 142.95; 142.97; 142.98; 142.99; 142.101; 142.105; 142.108; 142.111; 142.115; 142.120; 142.146; 142.156; 143.2; 143.40; 143.63; 143.71; 143.81; 143.91; 144.37; 144.54; 144.58; 145.52; 146.31; 146.38; 146.39; 146.44; 146.94; 146.129; 146.143; 146.175; 146.192; 146.237; 146.264; 146.276; 147.23; 147.32; 147.37; 147.43; 148.51; 148.53; 148.71; 148.89; 148.94; 148.116; 148.130; 148.131; 148.132; 148.144; 148.161; 148.171; 148.184; 148.192; 148.196; 148.201; 148.206; 148.236; 148.301; 149.11; 149.16; 149.17; 149.18; 149.32; 149.36; 149.39; 149.46; 149.47; 149.49; 149.51; 149.52; 149.55; 149.57; 149.58:2; 149.60; 149.63; 149.69; 149.70; 149.73; 149.121; 149.126; 149.136; 149.144:1; 149.144:2; 149.145; 149.146; 149.148; 149.161; 149.180; 149.182; 149.183; 149.184; 149.194; 149.196; 149.197; 149.200; 149.208; 149.215; 149.216; 149.223; 149.224; 149.225; 149.248; 149.249; 149.252; 149.256; 149.260; 149.261; 149.262; 149.263; 149.273; 149.274; 149.281; 149.286; 149.288; 149.293; 149.295; 150.7; 150.22; 150.24:1; 150.25; 150.28; 150.34; 150.35; 150.37; 150.41; 150.42; 150.54; 150.64; 150.66:A

London (probable): 149.4; 150.36

Louvain: 146.102; 146.234; 146.279; 149.19

Luxembourg: 148.168

Lyon: 138.37; 142.153; 143.21; 143.94; 148.259

Middleburg: 149.155

Morges: 146.321

Neuburg ad Danubium: 142.42

Neustadt an der Haardt: 142.24; 142.25; 149.10:3; 149.38; 149.64

Nuremberg: 149.179

Oxford: 147.10; 147.38; 147.39; 147.44; 148.145; 149.275; 150.24:2; 150.56

Paris: 138.25; 142.104; 142.114; 143.12; 143.39; 143.97; 145.17; 146.69; 148.14; 148.60; 148.80; 148.84; 148.85; 148.121; 148.210; 148.211; 148.260; 148.274; 149.67; 149.127;

INDEX V: PLACES OF PUBLICATION

149.129; 149.171; 149.246; 150.15
Place not given: 146.339; 149.107
Place unknown: 139.19; 139.33; 139.34; 139.36; 142.18; 142.55; 142.73; 142.76; 142.78; 142.79; 142.106; 142.137; 142.139:1; 142.139:2; 142.142; 142.157:1-5; 143.58; 143.83:1-22; 143.96; 144.3; 144.12; 144.41; 144.53; 145.05; 145.20; 145.25; 145.34; 145.41; 145.50; 146.13; 146.20; 146.24; 146.50; 146.72; 146.85; 146.98; 146.112; 146.128; 146.156:1; 146.221; 146.265; 146.360; 147.25; 148.10; 148.12; 148.34; 148.75; 148.78; 148.120; 148.141; 148.146; 148.147; 148.151; 148.166; 148.186; 148.189; 148.194; 148.209; 148.225; 148.228:2; 148.261; 148.293; 149.13; 149.122; 149.147; 149.152; 149.253; 149.255; 149.291; 150.40
Places unknown: 139.43:1-16; Places unknown: 144.71:1-20
Provenance unknown (manuscripts): 139.29; 143.82; 143.84:1:1-14; 143.84:2; 144.52:1-3; 146.254:1-2; 146.280; 147.4; 147.45; 148.302; 149.254; 150.14:1-3

Rheims: 149.6

Speyer: 149.282
Strassburg: 138.3; 138.5:1; 143.45; 144.27; 146.201; 146.209; 146.228; 148.167; 149.26; 149.48; 149.65; 149.84; 149.85; 149.91; 149.139; 149.151; 149.154; 149.157; 149.164; 149.174; 149.222; 149.227; 150.57
Strassburg (probable): 143.98; 149.34; 149.175:1-3

Tübingen: 142.94

Ursell: 142.112; 146.334

Venice: 138.2; 138.18:1; 138.19; 138.39; 143.15; 143.61; 146.184; 148.42; 148.79; 148.114; 148.137; 148.142; 149.61:A; 149.62:1; 149.110

Wittenberg: 146.219; 146.241; 148.99; 148.178; 148.288; 149.25; 149.96; 149.109; 149.118; 149.124; 149.134; 149.189; 149.226

Zürich: 142.29; 142.32; 142.34; 142.36; 142.48; 143.54; 146.269; 146.282; 148.181; 149.5; 149.77; 149.86; 149.234; 149.289
Zürich (probable): 146.294

Index VI
Dates of Publication

Date ranges are not included. The abbreviation *c.* derives from the bibliographical source consulted. The word *probable* is a PLRE qualification.

1510: 146.339
1515: 148.85
1517: 148.260
1521: 148.42
1523: 142.109
1527: 143.20; 146.343
1528: 148.84
1529: 146.286
1530: 149.32
1531: 149.193
1533: 147.13
1533?: 143.98
1535: 145.17; 149.48
1538: 150.45
1539: 144.27; 149.154
1542: 143.45; 148.137
1543: 138.25; 146.69
1543?: 148.130
1544: 143.28; 148.71; 148.210; 148.211
1546: 142.42; 143.85:A
1547: 138.18:1; 142.14; 149.176; 149.218
c.1547: 149.159
1548: 149.34
1549: 143.71
1549 (probable): 149.234
1550: 146.105; 149.230
1551: 143.12; 143.94; 148.3; 149.246
1552: 138.19; 142.80; 146.344; 149.191
1553: 143.91; 146.299; 148.301; 149.26; 149.63
1554: 142.17; 144.13; 146.226; 146.319:1; 148.274; 149.9
1555: 148.181
1556: 139.17; 146.304; 149.84
1557: 138.37; 146.32; 146.273; 149.18
1558: 138.2; 142.93; 146.184; 149.132
1558 (probable): 143.30
1559: 143.54; 146.294
1560: 142.154; 146.198; 148.142; 149.28; 149.182

INDEX VI: DATES OF PUBLICATION

1561: 138.3; 142.58; 146.74
1562: 142.13; 142.105; 142.112; 149.153
1563: 146.230; 146.269; 146.288; 148.295; 149.170; 149.196;
1563 (probable): 149.81;
1563?: 149.197
1564: 138.36; 146.187; 148.86; 149.79
1565: 142.108; 146.228; 149.49; 149.236
1566: 148.1; 148.81; 149.37; 149.74
1567: 146.209; 146.308; 146.335; 149.35; 149.150
1568: 142.86; 143.41; 148.80; 148.121; 150.66:A
1568 (probable): 149.220
1569: 145.36; 146.10080; 146.130; 146.145; 146.279; 149.56:1
1569 (probable): 149.227
c.1569: 148.11; 142.148;
1570: 146.324; 149.53; 149.58:2
1571: 146.44; 146.330; 149.286
1572: 142.100; 146.37; 146.46; 146.60; 146.153; 148.291
1573: 142.27; 142.28; 142.47; 142.147; 144.14; 146.94; 146.126; 146.272; 148.51; 148.144; 149.16; 149.77; 149.208
1574: 142.151; 146.267; 146.284; 148.114; 149.17; 149.45; 149.124; 149.299
1575: 142.37; 143.11; 143.25; 143.74; 146.143; 146.213; 148.147; 149.22; 149.137:1; 149.179; 149.206:2
1576: 142.153; 149.184
1576 (probable): 149.174
1577: 142.9; 142.23; 142.40; 142.95; 149.10:2; 149.46; 149.126
1578: 148.87; 148.148; 148.168; 148.184; 149.186; 149.288
1578 (probable): 142.156
1579: 142.21; 142.25; 142.63; 142.94; 144.54; 149.108; 149.192; 149.229; 149.262
1580: 142.64; 142.111; 144.2; 148.296; 149.25; 149.98; 149.117; 149.127; 149.140; 149.141; 149.162; 149.249; 149.252; 150.25; 150.34
1581: 142.87; 149.160; 149.293; 150.37
1582: 142.24; 149.6; 149.10:3; 149.149; 149.188; 149.265; 150.59
1583: 142.83; 142.88; 142.101; 146.321; 147.37; 148.60; 149.11; 149.39; 149.73; 149.105; 149.146; 149.194; 149.201; 149.260; 149.282; 149.295; 150.54
1584: 148.212; 149.80; 149.129; 149.155; 149.187; 149.261; 149.280; 150.24:1
1585: 147.8; 147.10; 147.16; 148.15; 148.99; 149.41; 149.165; 149.275; 149.277; 149.278; 149.296; 150.22; 150.24:2
1586: 147.20; 147.38; 148.18; 149.64; 149.205; 149.248; 149.259; 149.279; 149.289; 149.297; 150.56
1586 (probable): 147.44; 148.145
1587: 147.9; 147.39; 148.14; 149.47; 149.142; 149.290

R. J. Fehrenbach is Professor of English, Emeritus, at the College of William and Mary.

E. S. Leedham-Green is retired Deputy Keeper of the Archives and Fellow of Darwin College, Cambridge, and Vice-President of the Bibliographical Society. She is General Editor of *Libri Pertinentes*, a bibliographical series relating to sixteenth- and seventeenth-century libraries.